TANGO

AND

RELATED

DANCES

TANGO & Related DANCES

A Reference for Coupledancers

A Couple's Guide to Tango Dancing

First Edition - 1 January 2010

COMPILED By *CoupleDanceWorld* Under the Direction of THOMAS L. NELSON

AuthorHouse™
1663 Liberty Drive
Bloomington, IN 47403
www.authorhouse.com
Phone: 1-800-839-8640

International Standard Book Number: 978-1-4490-0601-3 (sc)
Library of Congress Control Number: 2009907030

Thomas L. Nelson,
CoupleDanceWorld,
8581 Owensmouth Ave., Canoga Park, CA 91304

First Edition

First published by AuthorHouse on 8/26/2009
Printed in the United States of America
Bloomington, Indiana
on acid-free paper.

With the hope that this book provides the world with something useful:

CONTENTS

1. PREFACE and OVERVIEW

2. ABOUT THE AUTHOR

3. KEY COUPLEDANCE DEFINITIONS and TERMINOLOGY

4. CLASSIFICATION of COUPLEDANCE WORDS

5. TANGO SUMMARY

6. COUPLEDANCER'S REFERENCE DATA for TANGO

7. GLOSSARY for TANGO

8. BIBLIOGRAPHY

·

1.   PREFACE and OVERVIEW

A conglomeration of Coupledance terms in alphabetical order, this book is for use by couples who dance together in any mode, fashion or style of *Tango* and its related dances. In *Tango* dancing, much that had been only verbal in the past is hereby passed on to you in written form.

As to the **source** of these contents, all of the included material tailored only for *Tango* in this *TANGO and Related DANCES* Book, has been derived mainly from our massive *Dancing and Related Skills* Encyclopedia, and also a bit from our *Roundancer's Glossary*, both of which cover all types of Coupledancing. All three books have been written by Tom Nelson and published in the name of *CoupleDanceWorld*. If within, one cannot find that particular reference to a certain item one may be seeking, be sure to peruse the *Glossary* section that is also contained in this book. In addition, one might consult our separate, voluminous *Dancing and Related Skills* Encyclopedia.

Always accessible for reference, this *TANGO and Related DANCES* Book contains much data and suggestions for all who want to excel, to perfect their *Tango* dancing styles, making *Tango* dancing easier and more fun. Even though most useful to the dedicated *Tango* dancer, what follows may also be of interest to casual enthusiasts. If you are a beginner, spice up your life! Take this frolicking dimension. *Tango* dance!

Like language, more or less, each *Tango* dance is continually in process of change. Nothing endures but change, (*Heraclitus*,) (but) the more things change, the more they remain the same, (*Alphonse Karr*). *Tango* dancing follows trends. Certain *Tango* dances that were dead and gone are hereby resurrected somewhat herein. Still, while many are fads that eventually wane away, certain *Tango* dances become phenomena for generations. More than an alphabetical catalog of *Tango* dance steps, these Classics are explored and explained extensively in this book.

Some people demand that there be a right way or otherwise it's WRONG. Some people have this NEED for being dictated THE "correct way". Sorry, there is no such thing in real life with *Tango* dancing. There are Doctor's Opinions instead. This book is a compilation of the opinions of many "Doctors of *Tango* Dancing." Ingenuity can become lost under a blanket of rules. Don't say, "One must **always**, or **never**, dance this way or that," because **always** and **never** are rarely true. This book reports how various steps are (or were) actually danced, and NOT how these steps should be danced. Always question the definite, set in concrete, "correct" ways of dancing certain Steps. Their answers are always open to question.

The word **Coupledancing**, in general, is defined as dancing in conjunction with a partner, or men and women dancing together in rhythmical movement to music. In bodily communication of feelings, encompassing more than Ballroom and Swingclub Dancing, Coupledancing is dancing in unison, moving as one, attuned in harmonious accord. You will find that all *Tango* dances herein are variable, adaptive, creative and immensely satisfying.

In Coupledancing, whenever we humans hit upon some bodily Movement, Figure or Pattern that strikes our fancy, we tend to **give it a name**, perhaps out of necessity, for our conversing on the subject. This book has the terminology of these names in alphabetical order, thereby becoming a collection of narrative descriptions on *Tango* dancing.

This book is specialized and technical, with explanatory definitions, interpretations and notes. Get involved in these "together" activities with your partner!

2.   ABOUT THE AUTHOR

To begin with, about the Dance Specialist and compiler in charge of this book, Tom Nelson wishes to thank his contributors and helpers. He wishes to thank his many teachers, both for private and for group Coupledance lessons, he has had through the years. These include: Phil Adams, Neale Allen, Lee Atkinson, Art Balloy, Skippy Blair, George and Sharri Blume, Ron and Lois Cassard, Felix Chavez, Opal and Joe Cohen, Dean and Mary Collins, Steve and Elizabeth Cullip, Lisa Fay, Alice Ferris, Ray Fox, Ed and Diane Gaines, Hi and Cookie Gibson, Silky Griffith and Betty, Laure Haile, Ray and Kitty Harrison, Frank Hermann, Finn and Berthe Hoffler, Tom Hyatt, Jonathan and Sylvia, Michael and Mari Kiehm, Lori Llamas, John March, Mickey and Clara Marshall, Bill Martin, Roger and Shirley McAndrews, Margaret Michael, John Michaelson, Fred and Keiko Migliorini, Carol Montez, John Morton, Sherry Novak, Eddie and Audrey Palmquist, Dan Rand and Kendy, Ricky and Kay Sexton, Ken and Shiela Sloan, Sonny Watson, Jill Weston, Ron and Nancy Yanke, Glenn and Lezlie Yata, and numerous others.

Tom says,"About me? I'm a `Dance Specialist'. My trade is Coupledancing." The Author, with more than seventy-five years of constant, multiple and diverse kinds of Coupledancing under his belt, is a learned authority about the contents of this text. He is uniquely qualified with more than 26 years of teaching Coupledancing, mostly in his own `CoupleDanceWorld* studio. Much herein was learned through his own practice and discipline.

At the age of six, in 1931, Tom was formally taught Coupledance routines with his sister in a dance school run by his aunt. By the age of 14, Tom was already proficient and experienced on the dancefloor at many dances. He had been formally taught more than just the fundamentals of the Shag, Twostep, Foxtrot, Rumba and the Waltz. He was an accomplished Coupledancer when he went in the service at age 17 for World War II. He was fortunate to dance to many of the "big bands". Tom swore to himself "to become the best dancer in the world." He became a Cadet then a Pilot in the Army Air Force. While in the service, he Coupledanced at every chance, at USO's, hotels, dance halls, even in a Navy-only wharf dive and at the Hollywood Paladium. He loved to dance the Lindy. He was sometimes able to accurately guess from where a lady was from in the U.S. by her mode of dancing. Tom could perceive different dance trends in various parts of the country, especially of how different Swings were danced. On occupation duty, Tom danced much with Tokyo ladies, Seoul ladies and with Manila ladies.

Back to college in 1947, Tom picked up the Tango, Balboa and the Samba. Later, Tom learned the Mambo, ChaCha, the Twist, the Pony, Watusi, Mashed Potato, and many other dances. By 1970, Tom had become the proverbial "Studio-Hopper," with formal lessons in West-Coast-Swing, different Hustles, International and Latin, and in most all Coupledances. Tom has logged many thousands of hours on the dancefloor. Tom began teaching Coupledancing in 1977, and began Roundancing in 1980, which he has continued to Coupledance with a relish to date.

3.   KEY COUPLEDANCE DEFINITIONS and TERMINOLOGY

Being a conglomeration of **TANGO** Coupledance terms in alphabetical order, this **TANGO and Related DANCES** Book is for use by couples who dance together in any mode, fashion or style of **TANGO**.

In General: This **TANGO and Related DANCES** Book defines and enumerates names, words and terms with their relation to **TANGO** Coupledancing.

Thesaurus: This **TANGO and Related DANCES** is also a Dance Thesaurus, guiding one to related **TANGO** Coupledance subjects.

Description of Dances: Those **TANGO** Dances currently Coupledanced by many are in sufficient detail herein to completely describe the subject term, position, action, movement, figure, or pattern.

Actions and Movements Common to Various Dances: Many of the same particular actions or movements that one's body is capable of executing, are common to different Coupledances. It is possible to address most all bodily actions and movements, since such activities are not infinite. Therefore, this **TANGO and Related DANCES** Book lumps together the major Coupledances subject to such actions or movements, figures or patterns. All overall Coupledance styles influence and feed upon each other.

Defining Elsewhere: Capitalized words or terms are further defined elsewhere within this book.

Footwork: Unless otherwise noted, partners always Coupledance the Pattern, Figure or subject-item on opposing feet, mirror-image, rather than on their same identical feet.

Defining Left and Right Footwork: Always in *Italics*, **Right Feet** words begin Capitalized while left feet words begin in lower-case letters, throughout this **TANGO and Related DANCES** Book.

Turning Right and Left: "Clockwise" and "Counter-Clockwise" are viewed as if the clock face is upon the Dancefloor, and not on the ceiling.

Defining Rotations: With noted exceptions, the amounts of rotation notated herein, for turns, swivels, spirals, etc., refer to foot-rotation, and not necessarily to the amount of body-rotation.

Omitted Data: With noted exceptions; (1) Level of difficulty or level of skill required, (2) Orientation of steps or figures with hall, (3) Preceding or following figures to the subject figure, and (4) Heel-toe footwork. All of these have usually been omitted from each subject figure or pattern for the sake of simplification.

(Continued)

3.   KEY COUPLEDANCE DEFINITIONS and TERMINOLOGY (Continued)

Items with Multiple Names: All the various item names known at the time of printing are listed accordingly. The name selected for listing first in the writeup herein is not necessarily the name preferred by some, but is the name the writer considers the most commonly used.

Item Names with Multiple Meanings: Certain names have multiple listings or definitions, and are numbered herein for clarity.

Marks that Precede Item Names: Perhaps there are no such marks contained herein, but if an item is preceded by an "X", it has yet to be completely defined. An item preceded by "TRY" has a portion with its correctness in doubt.

Disclaimer: This book on **TANGO and Related DANCES** is **not a "bible"**, and does not specify REQUIRED methods or modes. This book only **reports** how certain Coupledances were danced at the time of writing, or before, as seen through experience by the author, authortative writeups, and through skilled, consulting associates.

Accreditation: This **TANGO and Related DANCES** book is without accreditation by teaching organizations such as the Imperial Society of Teachers of Dancing. *CoupleDanceWorld* makes no attempt to meet or duplicate certain prescribed standards, such as those of the ISTD, by which various competitions are judged.

Evolution: Just as this **TANGO and Related DANCES** is bound to develop and change, so do the **TANGO** Coupledances contained herein. Coupledances develop and change like a living thing, due to various inputs by different parties evolving their dancing through the years.

4.1 CLASSIFICATION of COUPLEDANCE WORDS

Classifying the Definitive Coupledance Terms Used in This Book, from the Minute to the Overall:

Term = Common, generalized or Basic, pertaining to Coupledancing

Position or **Stance** or **Hold** = Couples' Body Positions

Action = Motion without Change-of-Weight; a non-Step Movement

Movement, Move, Motion, Step or **Break** = Change-of-Weight with at least one Step taken

Figure = Coupledance Step combinations spanning at least one Measure

Pattern or **Sequence** or **Compound-Step** or **Routine-Section** = multi-Figures with a name, beginning and ending

Coupledance = The complete dance or Routine

Genre or **Amalgamation** = Family of Coupledances, Routines or Patterns

Routine = Several different Amalgamations joined together.

5.   TANGO SUMMARY

GlobeTrotting-Coupledances:

There was a unique period in history in which Coupledances having ties with more than one nation, both emigrated and converged within a very short period of time, involving the entire world. Time was the early twentieth century. Coupledancing spread world-wide with its newborn Musical Rhythms during the early twentieth century. New happenings were brewing concurrently with popular Music, originating mostly from the United States. This Coupledancing developed to become exceptionately popular within the Global spread of peoples from just before World-War I until just after World-War II.

Sheet-Music had become cheap and easy to print up. The American "Tin-Pan-Alley" is the Coupledance Term for the Genre of popular Sheet-Music publishing businesses, and "Tunesmiths" is the Coupledance Term for the myriads of Pop-Song Composers and Lyricists of Tin-Pan-Alley. All had produced the Music to which we have Coupledanced.

The popularity of piano playing played a great part in this spread of Coupledancing. So much so that by 1909, Skilled pianists plus the old-fashioned Pianola (Player-Piano) with its 88-note scale range Music-Rolls, was primary of the major Musical instruments to which Coupledancers danced. From 1921 until the practical end of Music-Rolls in 1931, excellent piano performances were fashioned. These Music-Rolls in the Pianola were played extensively during this short period as a major instrument to which Coupledancers danced. The Love-Song-Era, the era in which over half the Music Coupledanced was Love-Songs, lasted mainly between 1918 and 1960. The American Coupledancing culture had come to consist mainly of Jazz that became Swing, and these Love-Songs.

The 1930s was the real start of the Big-Band-Era. Dancing to Live-Big-Bands and its singers was a great pleasure! Beginning about the late 1930s, Ballroom Dancing took off from a new drive in Music, which was the Big-Band-Sound. These new bandleaders were director/composers, as they had been since John Philip Sousa and his Dance-Band of 1892. Coupledancing in this period was mostly limited to American Foxtrot and Waltz, Eastern and West-Coast-Swing, and American Latins.

Pop-Song Tunesmith Composers and their Lyricists reigned supreme until the late 1950s, when the TV Performances by Musicians began to be valued more, mostly by teenagers the world over, more than by their written Sheet-Music and its words. There were other causes for this demise. Big-Bands lasted till about the late 1950s, when imposed floor taxes on large Dancefloors, coupled with increased union rates for Musician pay, killed the Big-Bands. Coupledancing eventually suffered the world over.

Among many others, there were five major different GlobeTrotting Amalgamations of Coupledances. These were (and are): (1) the **International Dance**; (2) the **Swing Dance**; (3) the Caribbean **Latin Dance**; (4) the Brazilian **Latin Dance**; and (5) the **Tango Dance**. Each of these Amalgamations is represented by its own characteristic flavor.

Beginning in England about 1924, with Coupledancers from all over the world Competing world-wide to Canned-Music, **International Dance** is a Competitive Amalgamation, consisting of the International Standard and Modern Smooth Coupledancing, and the International Latin and Rhythm Coupledancing Genres. Of these, the Modern Smooth and Rhythm Coupledancing Genres are the American versions of International Dance relating to Competitions. International Competitions still culminate at a place called Blackpool in England. This has influenced the Social-Dancing of American Foxtrot and Waltz Genres world-wide. All this is actively still current, mostly danced to the Big-Bands.

(Continued)

5.   TANGO SUMMARY   (Continued)

GlobeTrotting-Coupledances: (Continued)

Regarding the American **Swing Dance** Amalgamation, it included the Eastern Swing Genre, the West-Coast-Swing Genre, Hustle Genre, Jive, and the Balboa. This entire Swing Family was **born in the United States**, and was driven by its Coupledancing to the Big-Bands.

Regarding the Caribbean **Latin Dance** Amalgamation, it included the Rumba Genre, Mambo and Salsa Genres, ChaCha Genre, Bolero, Slow-Twostep, and the DiscoCha. Early twentieth century Latin-Music of the Caribbean Islands was syncretic and Musically featured mainly the Clave and Guitar. There, there happened to be a tendency to combine and/or reconcile the diverse Musical and Dance Traditions from its many geographic sources. These included certain European sources such as England and Gypsy Spain that **contributed to their Cuban birth**. Moorish and central Africa also played a Rhythmic part.

Regarding the Brazilian **Latin Dance** Amalgamation, it included the Samba Genre, the Merengue, Cumbia, and the Disco Twostep. This early twentieth century Latin-Music was **born in South-America**. There, there happened to be a tendency to combine and/or reconcile the diverse Musical and Dance Traditions from its many geographic sources that included Portugal and the Moorish and central Africa.

Regarding the Argentine **Tango Dance** Amalgamation, it included the original Argentine Tango and its Genre which Musically featured its Bandoneon sound, the American Tango, Continental Tango, and the International Tango, among others. This book is the story of **Tango**.

5.   TANGO SUMMARY   (Continued)

Introduction to TANGO:

During the very early 1900s, and along with their *"heart-and-soul"* **Bandoneon** music, well-to-do Argentineans visiting Paris found that they had become professional **Canyengue-Tango** demonstrators. Young well-to-do Parisians were excited and intrigued by **Tango's** sensuality. During the same years, these same Parisians were concurrently intrigued by Paris's own violent Apache Dance. The woman completely gives herself up to the Man in both dances. This was unacceptable by French elders in power who banned both, in conflict with the same young rebel Parisians who were enticed by such erotic dancing.

Besides, this Rotary **Canyengue-Tango** from Buenos Aires had no rules. It was even totally extemporaneous. Attempting to analyze and teach **Tango** during those very early 1900s, the French, English, Americans, etc., critiqued for Basic-Steps. There were none. The British wanted linear movement and preciseness, perhaps for adjudication in competitions. Americans wanted it simplified. This all was antithemeatic to the Argentine dancers literally living **Tango** daily and never dancing it entirely in the same fashion. And so the helpful Argentinean professionals acquiesced. Complying, these Milongueros invented Basic-Steps but only for export.

After some stylistic changes and European agreement on rules, the **Continental Tango** developed in France from 1912 and into the early 1920s. The **International Tango** was standardized in London in 1921. Derived from the French version, the **American Tango** came home about 1926, where it was further simplified for easy dance lessons.

The **Petroleo-Tango** evolved in Argentina in the 1940s. It tended to its own rules, not Europe's. But with Hollywood's influence, the very showy **Show-Tango** had been developed by the Argentineans in the 1950s. By the 1980s in Buenos Aires, their **Petroleo-Tango** had blossomed into the **Solon-Tango** Genre with its numerous sub-types and Styles: The Rotary-Tango, Linear-Tango, the Tango-Orillero, Tango-Apilado, Milonguero-Tango, Club-Style Tango, Tango-Nuevo, and the Liquid-Tango.

The all-important **Tango** music varies considerably. With some six or eight different **Tango** sub-rhythms and with different cadences, this all makes **Tango** music versatile, with the **Bandoneon** being the one constant. On top of this, **Tango** music differs extremely between the British and Argentine Style of **Tango**s.

Although several of their Buenos Aires **Tango**s are now designed to travel, nearly each one of the numerous Genre of **Argentine Tango** dances is a series of short spot-dances with important interruptions. The couple stops dancing whereupon the man proceeds to caress the lady, but only with his legs and feet. They both playfully make movements then they embrace and slowly start their shortened dance again. Suddenly there are, in turn, swiveling feet flashing and intertwining. With upper-bodies relaxed, their lower-bodies perform swiftly with accurate movement. Both partners abandon themselves to inventing the most audacious improvisations before again soon halting.

In comparison, Argentineans picture the brittle and jerky **International Tango** as ruined **Tango**. **Tango** in name only, that one is more similar to British Slow-Foxtrot and Slow-Waltz. With Heel-Lead instead of Toe-Lead, and danced without a smile in Victorian formality, **International Tango** has precise, unforgiving movements, graded for correctness with no spontaneity. Visual emphasis is on the proud torso and head. Control of the lady is minimal except for flicking her head by use of his knee. Still, all kinds of the **Tango**s are danced flat, and usually with a similar hold.

6.   COUPLEDANCER'S REFERENCE DATA for TANGO

Abrazo: (*ah-BRAH-tho*, Spanish for *embrace* or *hug*.) See Embrace(2).

Abrupt: Two Leadable variances; each is a Coupledance **Adorno** Action suitable for all **Tangos**, and each variance has a characteristic Tango look, an Accent.
From Promenade Position, one variance is an **Abrupt** body-Turn to Closed then immediately Recovering to Promenade Position; no Footwork. With a **Knee-Lead**, either the Man's Knees or all Knees shift Toward each other then spring back Toward Line-of-Direction. Timing is *And Quick*.
The other variance is, from a Low Stance in a Closed Position, an brusque Body-Turn to Promenade Position. No Footwork, but all Knees and both Heads **Abruptly** shift toward Line-of-Direction. Normally, Timing is *Quick*.
Similar to **Head-Flick**, **Head-Fan**, and **Tick**. (See Five-Step, Salute, and Head-Flick-Link. Also see Flourish, and Gesture.)

Adelante: (*ah-day-LAHN-tay*, Spanish for *forward*.) A Coupledance Term, or two Leadable, Basic Movements or Actions, Left or Right Foot, Mirror-Image Opposite.
The Free-Foot advances in the direction the Upper-Body is Facing, or, the Free-Foot Moves **Forward** to or past Supporting-Foot, with or without Change-of-Weight. Or, to Move ahead in the direction the Man is Facing. Or, Movement ahead in the direction In-Front of the dancer.
Generally, Forward Steps are with Push-Off Rearward with Weight well Forward over Balls; not of one reaching ahead with Foot, (except for how Man does in Argentine Tango.)
"Most of us don't put our best foot forward until we get the other one in hot water." -- Anonymous
Opposite of **Backward**. (See Walk, Step-Out, Foot-Movements, Sideward, DiagForward, DiagForwardRise, ForwardCheck, DiagForCheck, ForwardHold, DiagForHold, ForwardClose, Forward-Rise, ForwardTouch, ForTouch, DiagForTouch, ForTurn, and DiagForTurn. Also see Forward-Walk, Walking-Step, Normal-Walking-Cadence, Brisk-Walk, Swing-Time, Body-Rhythm, March, Classical-Walk, Ballet-March, Strut, Stroll, Skate, Skim, Ramble, Meander, Trot, Jog, and Run. Also see Control, Balance, Center-of-Balance, and Press. Also see Forward-Twostep, Forward-Foxtrot, Heel-Marching-Step, and Kiki-Walks.)
Note: **Forward** also refers to the Placement of one's Feet and Weight, etc.

Adorno: (*ah-DOR-no*, Spanish for *adorn* or *embellish*.) A General Latin Coupledance Genre, Performed for visual effect, and meaning to enhance, decorate, or increase the beauty of some particular dance Action or Movement.
There are all the **Argentine Tango Adornos**. Of these, there is the **Firulete** Genre of **Moving Adornos**, that includes the **Rulo, AnkleTrip, KneeFlick, LaLlevada, Castigada, Cucharita, Gancho, Golpes, Picados**, and the **Amague** Genre that includes the **Frappe**(1). And then there is the **Dibujo** Genre of [Stopped] **Parada** Adornos, that includes the **Lapiz, ShoeShine, Puntada-del-Pie, Caricias, Lustrada, Chiche, Fanfarron, Golpecitos, Zapatazo, Levantada**, and the **Enganche**.
The **Adorno** is almost the same as **Flourish**, and **Gesture**. [See Corte(2).] (Also see Abrupt, Head-Flick, and Samba-Tic.)

Aficionado or **Afficionado:** (*ah-fe-the-o-NAH-do*, Spanish for *liking, amateur, fancier.*) A General Argentine Coupledance word for an enthusiastic admirer or follower; a devotee or Fan of the **Argentine Tango.**

Similar to a **Milonguero**(1), **Tanguero**, Dedicated-Dancer, Fan(4), and Danceaholic. (See Dance-Mania, and Dance-Craze.) [Much from *Tango Terminology*, *www.tangoafficionado.com.*]

Amague: (*ah-mah-GAY* is Spanish for *hint.*) The **Amague** is an **Argentine Tango** Coupledance Action, an Adorno (Flourish), a Quick Embellishment, a threatening Gesture or sign to Partner, and it is almost always Executed by the Man.

Ed Loomis [www.batango.com/loomis] describes this **Amague** as follows:
"*... To make a threatening motion as a feint: An amague is used as an embellishment either led or done on one's own, and may be used before taking a step. An example of an amague may be a beat* [**Frappe**(1)] *before taking a step.*"

The most common **Amague** is the **Frappe**(1). Some others are the ShoeShine, Puntada-del-Pie, and Levantada. (Also see AnkleTrip, KneeFlick, Abrupt, LaLlevada, Castigada, Cucharita, Gancho, Golpes, Picados, Rulo, and Frappe; all are the Firulete Genre of Adornos Performed while Moving.) (Also see **Cuatro**, Stomp, and Heel-Strike.)

American Competition Tango: See Tango American-Style.

American-Start: In 2/4 Cut-Time, for **Argentine Tango** Coupledancing, the Leadable **American-Start** can be the first two of several Moves to completion of the Resolucion, or of the Natural-Resolution. A two-Measure long Figure, Rhythm Timing is either *Slow Slow, Slow Slow*; or, *Slow Slow, Quick Quick Slow*. The **American-Start** Starts in Closed Position Argentine Tango, both Start with their Feet Together. Lady's Head is often Open. Then with Man's Right Foot, both Step-Thru then Sideward.

Man Steps *CrossThruInFrontHold* then *widesideturn1/4CWhold*.
Lady, Following, Steps *crossthruinfronthold* then **SideTurn1/4CWHold*.
Notes: 1) * Lady's second Step is Shorter than Man's.
          2) Their second Step can be either the **Basic-Start** as noted, or the **Double-Start**.
          3) May be followed by the Basic-Step, Pepito, or the Salida.
Similar to **Backward-Start.** (See Eight-Step-Basic-Tango.)

American Tango(1) or **New-French-Tango:** A Rhythm, Traveling-Coupledance. The **American Tango**(1), an American interpretation of the original, is much less complex than the rapidly Flexing and Swiveling **Argentine Tango** Genre. Also, it is much less formal and has more gentle Movement than has the similar twins, the **American Tango**(2) and the **International Tango**. [The extremely different **American Tango**(2), better known as the **Tango American-Style**, is a Competition dance and is almost identical to the **International Tango**.]

The following is from *Dancing and Dance Bands* - [http://nfo.net/usa/dance]:

"[Maurice] *Mouvet created many new dance steps... . Many dance historians also feel that Mouvet is the innovator of the `American' Tango, as it is still danced today, - both in America (and in Argentina too). ...*

"*The Tango had gained great popularity after WW1. While Maurice was in Paris, he met a group of South Americans who were dancing their native Argentine Tango. He studied their dance steps, returned to the U.S. and began performing them in front of audiences, as well as teaching the dance to students at his own studio. It was only after WW1 that the Tango was standardized and simplified. Contra body movement, and the step now called the `Tango Draw' or `Tango Close' were introduced. His version is still referred to as the `American Tango' and is widely popular in the United States, Argentina, and the rest of the world.*"

This simplified **American Tango**(1) has both pronounced CBM and Body-Flight. It has both languid and contrasting crisp Movements, and, with its structure correlated to its musical Phrasing, is easier to Coupledance than any other Tango. **American Tango**(1) is danced in Closed Position Informal and in various other extravagant Positions, at 30 to 34 MPM.

The history of the **American Tango**(1) begins with Tango's second introduction into the U.S., this time from Europe. Mainly France had continued to import their Tango interpretations from the Argentine well into the early 1920s. Europe developed rules, including some Dancefloor Traveling. American high society embraced this **New-French-Tango**, or the **Continental Tango**, beginning about 1926. Further simplified, the resulting **American Tango**(1) was an easier and tamer version, but still electric and extremely romantic. This subject **American Tango**(1) Genre later had its own offshoots, such as the **Valentino Tango**, and the **Contest Tango**.

"*Blue Tango* times *Deep Purple* equals *Mood Indigo*." -- Anonymous

See **Tango-American-and-Continental Step-Listing**, and **Continental Tango**. [Also see Tango, Tango-Music, Five-Step-Basic-Tango, Argentine Tango, Argentine Tango Step-Listing, International Tango, American Competition Tango, and International Tango Step-Listing. Also see Basic-Step(4).]

American Tango(2): See Tango American-Style.

American-Tango-Basic: See Five-Step-Basic-Tango.

AnkleTrip or **Trip** or **Tripping** or **The Trip:** A Man's Unleadable **Adorno** Movement, either danced Singularly or while Coupledancing. Two *Quick* Beats long, and suitable for all **Tangos**, **PasoDobles**, and **Flamencos**, among other dances. **AnkleTrip** is most often Performed as the Man Steps-Thru from Promenade Position.

An Accent having a characteristic Tango look, Dramatic and on the verge of comic, the Man purposely **AnkleTrips** himself in an embellishment for effect.

The Man may prepare by first Flashing from Closed to Promenade Positions, with no Foot Movement. After secondly Stepping Slowly *forward*, the Man, Tilting Forward, starts to Totter then catches himself. He Performs this by momentarily Hooking his Right Toe Behind his Left ankle, thereby beginning to fall Forward. He then catches himself by Stepping *Forward*. He has immediately released his Right Toe to Check his Forward fall. *"Tripped by the light fantastic."* -- Anonymous

Note: His Lady may dance a **KneeFlick** with her Inside-Leg immediately prior to the Man's **AnkleTrip**.

(See Rulo, Abrupt, Levantada, LaLlevada, Castigada, Cucharita, Gancho, Golpes, Picados, Amague, and Frappe; Firulete Adornos all Performed while Moving.) (Also see Flourish, and Gesture.) (Also see Out-of-Balance, Tips, Lean, Incline, Pitch, Toddle, and Clumsy.) (Also see Toe-Stab, Toe-Tap, Toe-In, and Toe-Touch.) (Also see LockBehind, and CutBehind.) (Also see Comedy.)

Apache Dance or **Dance-of-the-Underworld:** (*ah-PAHSH* or *ah-PO-shay*) A violent Coupledance originated by the Parisian underworld, Performed to Waltz or Tango music, and popular as early as 1902 or 3. French reporter Emile Darsey applied the name, **Apache**, (after American Indian Apaches,) to Parisian criminals and ruffians; street gangs who created their own dance.

The following is from *Dancing and Dance Bands* - [http://nfo.net/usa/dance]:
"... *very popular dance team of Maurice Mouvet and Florence Waltron* [which] *began presenting the infamous `Apache', and all through the 1910s and `20s, this would become one of* [their] *most successful ballroom, theater, and Club exhibition acts. In 1907, Mouvet danced his version of `L`Apache' at the Cafe de Paris in France, and in 1910 he did it, with partner Madeleine D`Harville, at New York's Cafe de L`Opera. ...*"

This **Apache Dance** was a Showdance in which skilled Couples acted out their story in Pantomime. The **Apache Dance** portrayed their uninhibited passions, by the female Partner (prostitute) being gladly flung about, dragged by her hair, kicked then she crawls back to him to be kicked again then strenuously embraced with fervor. Wearing rough or ragged clothes or perhaps a striped shirt, neck scarf and barette, the Apache Man (pimp) entertainer violently spins his Prone Lady across the Dancefloor in the 1950s French Nightclubs, demanding her earnings. There was no set Routine, but the Couple would often Break-Apart from certain Closed Positions. Perhaps a knife would be drawn, simulating a fight between lovers. They would probably end by both rolling around upon the Dancefloor.

The **Whirlwind-Waltz**, created in 1907, was said to have similarities with the **Apache Dance**, in that in one part, each Partner would alternately swing the other by the arms in a Circle to Waltz Time. The **Apache Dance** also had some similarities with the early **Canyengue-Tango** from Buenos Aires, in that some subservient woman would literally Cling to the Man and gladly render herself up into his complete control. Some found similarities in the **CanCan** in that both dances were scandalous and free from propriety. The **Apache Dance** happened to be the first known to use the **Break-A-Way** form of dancing. In the 1920s, "*The Apache Dance*," probably a Waltz, and "*Apache Dance Piano Solo*" Sheet Music were published, both by a *J. Offenback*.

(See Apache-Spin, Texas-Tommy, Swing-Out, Apache-Whip, Apache-Whip-from-Shake-Hands, Apache-Whip-then-Freeze, Apache-Whip-then-Rollout, HugMe-then-Apache-Whip, HugMe-Apache-then-Continuous-Whip, HugMe-Apache-Whip-then-Double-Rollout, HugMe-Apache-Whip-then-Freeze, and HugMe-Apache-Whip-then-Rollout. Also see Layout, Airplane, Floor-Sweep, Pot-Stir, and Belt-Buckle-Floor-Sweep. Also see Lindy-Hop.) [Much data from Sonny Watson's StreetSwing.com]

Arch: Two different Unleadable Coupledance Styling Actions or Stances, of one's Feet upon their Closing, Left to Right or Right to Left, relative to all **Tangos**, and possibly useful in other dances.

An **Arch** is the Closing-Together **Position**ing of one's Feet at a Natural-Resolution, i.e., Closed-Finish at the Ending of a Tango Pattern or a complete dance.

With Feet Closed, **parallel** and staggered, an **Arch** is where the Inner Ball of one's Free-Foot **fits**, closely Touching inside the **Arch**, i.e. Instep, of one's Supporting-Foot. One may or may not Change-Weight with an **Arch**.

For Tango, both Man's and Lady's Free-Foot always Closes staggered **Trailing** one's Supporting-Foot Instep.

The Lady's **Arch** is almost always Mirror-Image Opposite her Man's Arch.

This **Arch** Foot Positioning is often instantaneous with a **Brush-Tap**; the "Brush" Executed to this **Arch**.

(See Close, Tango-Close, Tango-Draw, CloseTouch, Tango-Tap, The-Break, Backward-Close-Finish, and Natural-Resolution.)

Argentine Tango or **Tango Argentino** or **Tango-Arrabalero** or **Baile-Nuestro:** A Leadable, intricate Coupledance. This is the original, authentic Tango, the Tango that modern Argentines Coupledance in Buenos Aires. "*El Alma del Tango*," (anonymous,) Spanish, meaning "*The Soul of the Tango*." Languid and romantic, this Tango is often referred to as the "*Dance-of-Love*". Tango origins go back to about the 1870s, before a constant state of evolution. There is the Tango that immigrant men Coupledanced in the working-class suburbs outside the city of Buenos Aires in the 1920s, when men outnumbered women sometimes by as many as twenty-to-one. They had the saying, *sin las ninas, no es Tango*, (without women, there is no Tango.)

Of Tango origins, it is believed that the Tango has been mostly influenced by the Spanish Gypsy **Milonga**, but also by the Afro-Argentine **Candombe**, the **ContraDanza-Spanish**, and by the Cuban **Habanera** dances. Their name Arrabalero seems to refer to the Bolero. The original Tango could possibly have been a hybrid between the Haitian and Cuban **Tanango** and this **Habanera**.

Ed Loomis [www.batango.com/loomis] describes **Argentine Tango** history as follows:
"*TANGO Popular music from the Rio de la Plata region dating back to 1885-95, defined by a 2/4 rhythm until the 1920s when a 4/8 rhythm became common. A popular dance originating in the mid 19th century which descended from the Candombe, Habanera, Milonga, and (by some tango scholars) the Tango Andaluz. The exact origins of Tango are a historical mystery.*"

Following extracts from *Re: [TANGO-L] tango/milonga* [http://pythia.uoregon.edu/]:
"*The presence of Candombe in the early tangos would depend on how much that particular expression of African culture rubbed up against the cultures of sailor, gaucho, and European immigrant.*
"*There may be some dispute over which word came first but it is generally accepted that milonga preceded tango as a dance form and greatly influenced it in the early stages.*"

Being wrapped up in Tango vastly influenced the Tango's participant's Way-Of-Life, in that living it came with a certain Mode-of-Dress-and-Behavior. They also had the saying, "*The Tango is not a dance but an obsession.*" -- Anonymous. All **Argentine Tangos** are typically danced to Music from the Bandoneon, piano, violin and bass. In particular, and with deep emotion, the sound of this **Bandoneon** has given the Argentine Tango its notable melancholic and nostalgic air.

This **Argentine Tango** has been a brooding, earthy, tense, dramatic, sensual yet meditative, low, and Flat Tango. "*The Tango is the vertical expression of a horizontal desire.*" -- Anonymous. Many Figures are danced with head-to-head and chest-to-chest contact, as dramatic leg-Flicks and other Embellishments are slickly Performed, such as a Close-Embrace mixed with Open-Embraces. This Tango has been characterized by its passionate Hold, by complex leg Movements, by Circling and Flicking, by Flaring Feet and with rapid changes of Position. "*Is one supposed to dance it standing up?*" -- Countess Melanie de Pourtales asked. Still, this **Argentine Tango** is presently danced Sedately, Smoothly and effortlessly. Steps are Small, purposeful and precise. With a feline quality, one's Body Pauses its Movement as one's Foot is Positioned; then one's Feet Pause in Movement as one's Body relocates over the newly Supporting-Foot. "*El tango no esta en los pies. Esta en el corazon.*" (Anonymous.) This is Spanish for, "*Tango is not in the feet. It is in the heart.*" In Buenos Aires, and in other parts of Argentina and in Uruguay, methods for dancing their "*Tangos*" are extremely individualistic to each Coupledancer. Categorization of their beloved **Argentine Tango** by broad Stylistic Terms is unacceptable to them. Their **Tango** is their "*way of life*". Even in the Buenos Aires city neighborhoods and other local places, their basic **Argentine Tango** differs considerably. But rough commonalities still remain in spite of their myriads of dancing differences. (Continued)

Argentine Tango: (Continued)

The two overall **Argentine Tango** types of dance are the **Linear-Tango** and **Rotary-Tango** methods, and their two overall **Argentine Tango** Styles are the **Show-Tango** and the **Tango-de-Salon**.

This **Tango-de-Salon** originated basically from the **Canyengue-Tango**, that developed then changed or became mostly influenced by the **Petroleo-Tango** in the 1940s. This **Petroleo-Tango** is a Tango with many differences, and can be broken down into the following Styles (as well as many others): The **Tango-Orillero, Tango-Apilado, Milonguero-Tango, Club-Style Tango, Tango-Nuevo**, and the **Liquid-Tango** Styles.

For this **Tango-de-Salon** Genre, there are no "*correct*" Dancefloor alignments, except for the fact that modern Argentines from Buenos Aires Travel-Coupledance Counter-Clockwise if the Dancefloor is sufficiently large. In their **Linear-Tango** method, these Argentines dance with long, soft, loving, gentle, hesitently Slow, Stalking Steps, intently Following the Music's broken Rhythm. Their dance also includes extensive Pauses.

After Leaning-Into-EachOther in a Close-Embrace, (see Tango-Lean,) Partners may alternately Open-Embrace in order to break into intricate leg Movements for a type of **Rotary-Tango**, with Movements that include many Ganchos and Ochos. These **Rotary-Tango** portions of their dance are not often danced upon extensive Dancefloors; instead, this **Rotary-Tango** method is usually danced in bars and NightClubs having minimal floorspace. Such small Dancefloors require increased Couple-Rotation and also force each Partner to Turn more often individually.

A completely different Style is used for Exhibitions and while On-Stage; Argentines necessarily Choreograph Flashy Routines for such occasions using their famous **Show-Tango** Style.

The **Argentine Tango** is really a Sequence of short dances, each consisting of the Start, through to their Natural-Resolution. All **Argentine Tangos** are normally danced on a ragged One-Beat Rhythm-Station, in 4/4 Time at 27 to 33 MPM, (played at 108 to 132 BPM.) Others say at 16 to 32 MPM, and ideally at 20 to 25 MPM for any Social Tango. The Man dances Forward, Rearward, and Sideways. The Man often, sometimes continually, wraps his Right arm completely around her waist, with his Right elbow drooped Down almost against her waist. Often his Weight is back upon his Heels, causing his Steps to Step Under-His-Lady. The Man's Forward Steps are with **Ball-Steps**, (Toe-Leads,) except he has no Body-Rise. He Extends each Foot Forward in the Balletic fashion, slightly before his Body Moves over the Foot. This characteristic is possible since there happens to be no Driving or Swinging Movement for **Argentine Tango**. His Left Toe Points Slightly Outward as it Slides Forward, into a general slight Left Turn.

His Lady's Weight remains well Forward as she Coupledances, whether in Closed or in Promenade Position. [See Embrace(2), and Tango-Lean.] For awhile, she may constantly press either of her cheeks against his Right cheek. Her Left wrist is often wrapped about his neck. The contact of their Upper-Bodies is relaxed, while their Lower-Bodies immaculately Perform Swiftly with accurate Movement. "(The Tango) *is a sad thought that you can dance*." - said Enrique Santo Descepolo.

See the **Argentine Tango Step-Listing**. (Also see Milonga, Tango y Milonga, Milonga-Candombera, Milonga-Portena, Candombe, and Tango. Also see Argentine Tango Basic-Step, American-Start, Backward-Start, Basic-Start, Five-Step-Basic-Tango, and Eight-Step-Basic-Tango. Also see Posterior-Protrusion, and Sway-Back.)

Argentine Tango Masters Association or **ATMA**: (*www.elmundodeltango.com*) This is a regional organization of the **America First Tango University**, which presents syllabuses for the **Argentine Tango** Genres, **Milonga**, and **Vals** Coupledances. Coupledance Levels are for both Amateur and Professional; Bronze Associate, Silver Licentiate, Gold Fellow, and Star Master. Appropriate tests are set by this **ATMA**.
    (See Argentine Tango.)

Argentine Tango Step-Listing: Various **Movements, Figures and Patterns,** (or Steps,) are listed together below. Types of Argentine Tangos and corresponding Terms are also included. All items listed below are described elsewhere in this book.
    See **Tango-American-and-Continental Step-Listing.** (Also see International Tango, American Competition Tango, and International Tango Step-Listing.)
    The following **Argentine Tango** items are listed in alphabetical order:
Abrazo, Abrupt, Adelante, Adorno, Aficionado, Amague, American-Start, American Tango, AnkleTrip, Arch, **Argentine Tango**, Argentine-Walk, Argentine-Waltz, Around-the-World, Around-the-World-ContraCheck, Arrastre, Arrepentida.   Back-Flick(1), Backward-Start, Backward-Start-with-Circle, Bailarin, Bailongo, Balanceo, Baldosa, Ballroom-Tango, Bandoneon, Barrida, Basic-Start, Basic-Step(4), Behind-Gancho-to-Weighted-Foot, Bird-of-Paradise-ContraCheck, Body-Alignment, Boleo.   Cabeceo, Cadena, Cadencia, Cafe Tango, Caida, Calecita, Caminando, Caminar, Caminata, Candombe, Cangrejo, Canyengue-Tango, Carancanfunfa, Caressing-the-Floor, Caricias, Carousel(2), Carpa, Castigada, Chair, Chair-Forward-Poised Position, Chase(5), Cheek-to-Cheek Position, Chiche, Closed Position Argentine Tango, Close-Embrace-Tango, Club-Style Tango, Codigo, Confiteria-Tango, Contest Tango, Continental Tango, Continuous-Ganchos, Corrida, Corrida-del-Pie, Corrida-Garabito, Corte(2), Cortina, Cruz, Cruzada, Cruzara, Cuadrado, Cuatro, Cucharita, Cunita, Cut-Ocho. Desplazamiento, Develope, Dibujo, DobleCruz, Doble-Ochos, Double-Start, Drape Position, Drop, Drop-Hinge.   Eight-Count-Basic, Eight-Step-Basic-Tango, ElAmericano, Elevadas, Embrace(2), Enganche, Enrosque, Entrada, Entregarme, Espejo, European-Start, Exhibition-Tango.   Fanfarron, Fantasia, Figure-Fore, Finnish-Tango, Firulete, Five-Step-Basic-Tango, Flare, Flick(2&3), Flourish, Frappe(1), French Tango, Freno, Front-Hook.   Gancho, Gauchos, Gesture, Giro, Golpecitos, Golpes.   Habanera, Hamaca, Harvest-Moon Tango, Head-to-Head Position, HeelBrush.   Indicate, Intrusion.   Junta.   KneeFlick, Knee-Up Position.   LaCobra, LaCruz, Lady's-Behind-Gancho, LaLLevada, LaMarca, LaMilonguita, Lapiz, Latigazo, Leaning-Into-EachOther, Left-Behind-Ganchos, Left-Inside-Ganchos, Leg-Crawl Position, Leg-Crawl-with-Flare, Leg-Stretch-on-Arm, Levantada, Linear-Tango, Liquid-Tango, Lunfardo, Lunge, Lustrada.   Maneges, Marcacion, Media-Luna, Media-Vuelta, Milonga, Milonguero(1&2), Milonguero-Tango, Molinete, Mordida-Alto.   Natural-Resolution, NightClub Tango.   Ocho-Abierto, Ocho-Cortado, Ocho-Milonguero, Ochos(1&2), Ochos-Adelante, Ochos-Defrente, Ochos-en-Espejo, Ochos-Largos, Ochos-para-Atras, Ochos-Picante, On-the-Side, Open-Finish-Gancho, Orillero-Tango.   Parada, Parallel-Rocks, Partial-Step, Pasada, Paseo, Paso, Pecho-Argentino, Pepito, Petroleo-Tango, Picados, Pickup, Pista, Planeo, Pocket, Practica, Press-Line, Private-Milonga, Progressive-Back-Fans, Progressive-Side-Step, Progressive-Tango-Rocks, Promenade-Sway, Promenade-to-Counter-Promenade, Promenade-to-Left-Outside, Promenade-Vine, Puntada-del-Pie, Pyramid(2).   Quartas, Quebrada, Quebrada Position, Quick-Open-Telemark.   Rabona, Reclining-Lady, Reclining-Lady-with-Develope, Resolucion, Reverse-Mordida, Revolucion, Right-Behind-Ganchos, Right-Foot-Outside Position, Right-Inside-Ganchos, Rock-Turn, Ronde, Ronde-Aerial, Ronde-Floor, Ronde-Forward, Ronde-Rearward-and-Slip, Ronde-Rudolph, Ronde-Rudolph-and-Slip, Ronde-Split, Rotary-Tango, Ruade, Rulo. Sacada, Salida, Salida-Cruzada, Salida-de-Gato, Salida-Modified, Salon-Tango, Sandwich,
(Continued)

Argentine Tango Step-Listing: (Conitiued)
Seguidillas(2), Sentada, Sentado-Hinge Position, Sentado-Line, Serpiente, Shift-Weight, ShoeShine, Shoulder-Lead(1), Show-Tango(1), Side-Cadencia, Side-Chase, Side-Corte, Side-Thru, Sidewards-Cunitas, Slip, Snap-Change, Spicy-Ochos, Spiral, Stairs, Stealth, Step-Thru, Stork(1&2), Sube-y-Baja, Suspension, Switch, Switch-Rock, Swivel, Swivel-Point.   Tanda, Tango, Tango-Apilado, Tango-Argentino, Tango-Arrabalero, Tango-Club-Style, Tango-de-Salon, Tango-Hustle, Tango-Lean, Tango-Liso, Tango-Milonga, Tango-Nuevo, Tango-Orillero, Tango-Rhythmic-Style, Tango-Stepping, Tango-Switches, Tango-Vals, Tanguero, Telemark-from-Left-Outside-to-Semi-Closed, Telemark-to-Semi-Closed, Tijera, To-Dance-Inside, To-Dance-On-The-Side, To-Dance-Outside, Toe-Tap, Trabada-Step, Track-the-Floor, Traspie, Tres-Ochos, Turning-Mutual-Boleos.   Valentino Tango, Vals-Criollo, Vals-Cruzado, Vals-Porteno, Viborita, Villa-Urguiza-Tango, Vine, Vuelta.   Whisk.   Zapatazo, Zarandeo.

Argentine-Walk: See Progressive-Side-Step.

Argentine-Waltz or **Vals** or **Vals-Criolo** or **Vals-Cruzado** or **Crossed-Waltz** or **Tango-Waltz** or **Tango-Vals:** The **Argentine-Waltz** completes the trio of currently popular Argentine Social-Dances; the Tango, the Milonga, and this **Vals**. This **Vals** is a charming Variation of the Slower Argentine Tango, in which the same identical Steps are danced at the Buenos Aires Milonga hall to the Faster 3/4 Time Rhythm of the Viennese Waltz, but without Pauses. Featured prominently in dancing the **Vals** are its Turning Figures. Similar to the Hesitation-Waltz, this **Argentine-Waltz** basic key Patterns are Executed in Tango-de-Salon Style, with Smooth and Elegant Waltz Steps based on Walking. **Vals** can include Variations based on Orillero and Fantasia Styles.

The **Vals**, as with the Argentine Tango and Milonga dances, all Travel around the Dancefloor Counter-Clockwise, with the most speedily Traveling Couples using the outer ring of the Milonga Dancefloor. The Couples' Embrace(2) is essentially the same for all of this trio of dances, i.e., Close-Embrace mixed with Open-Embrace. For this **Vals** (only), each Step is taken only on the first of each three (ONE-two-three) Counts, with one exception; occasionally a *Quick Quick Quick* Three-Steps' Chasse, or perhaps a ZigZag, is Stepped on its every Beat of the three.

The following is from **Vals-Cruzado:** [www.elmundodeltango.com]

   "The Waltz is the joyful one of the trio of the Argentine social dances (Tango, Milonga and Vals) and it was the first dance to reach the Rio De La Plata in 1816. Waltz was derived and assimilated from Vals Criollo, brought by those persons both in South America of European parents, from persons of a mixed/Amerindian heritage and from people of the interior and rural areas. Also, the Waltz was mixed with the Vals Porteno, from the inhabitants of the port of Buenos Aires.

   "By taking the shape of Grand-Mother Milonga and Father Tango, Mother Waltz developed her own way, escaping from any other influences to receive the name of Vals Crusado." -- Ive Simard

Ed Loomis [www.batango.com/loomis] describes the **Vals** as follows:

   "VALS Argentine waltz: Sometimes referred to as Vals Criolo or Vals Cruzado, and danced to what is arguably the most beautiful dance music anywhere (editorial bias)."

With regards to this **Vals Basic-Step**, the **Vals** music Beat may sound Faster than that for Argentine Tango music, but the Time between the first note of each **Vals** Triplet is typically the same or longer than between each Beat of an Argentine Tango song.

[See Tango-Orillero, and Show-Tango(1).] (Also see Vals-Criollo, and Vals-Porteno. Also see Lead/Follow-for-Tango, and Palm/Finger-Lead-in-Closed.)

Around-the-World: A Flashy, partially Leadable, General Coupledance Circular Figure, Performed with artful Balance. Suitable for the Slow-**Foxtrot**, Slow-**Waltz**, all **Tangos**, **Rumbas**, the **Bolero**, and other dances such as **Cabaret**. Around-the-World is Performed in Loose-Closed Position except for Feet, arms and Hands. Timing varies.

Lady Sweeps Around-the-World by Bending at her waist to her Right, then she is Led Sweeping Clockwise from her waist in a half Circle. While thus Sweeping Circularly, she also Slowly makes a Sweeping Sway with her Head and eyes rolling across the ceiling from her looking to her **Right** to looking to her **Left**.

While Sweeping, the Lady has either both Feet together, or she has her Left leg Front-Hooked around the Outside of her Partner's Right calf. Also, the Lady has, either her hands Grasping her Man's shoulders, or she has her arms Raised Straight-Arm and spread high.

Man holds his Lady loosely but securely by either of two methods: (1) With both of his Hands at her waist and hips, his Thumbs spread; or, (2) With both of his Hands at her back, flat against her wings or waist. Man sinks Well into his Knees to place his Center-of-Balance enough Rearward to Counter-Balance his Lady's Backward Bend; his Right Knee and Foot are Forward between his Partner's Feet; he may also extend his Toes Outward for Stability in Supporting her, as in Fifth-Position-Extended.

(See Rag-Doll, Around-the-World-ContraCheck, Bird-of-Paradise, Bird-of-Paradise-ContraCheck, and Sway-ContraCheck.)

Around-the-World-ContraCheck: A Flashy, partially Leadable, General Coupledance Circular Figure, Performed with artful Balance. Suitable for the Slow-**Foxtrot**, Slow-**Waltz**, all **Tangos**, **Rumbas**, the **Bolero**, and other dances such as **Cabaret**.

The Man, after first Lowering by Softening his Right Knee, Moves Forward into The Lady, and the Couple assumes a Figure identical to the normal **ContraCheck** Position, except as follows:

Lady, either with her Hands Grasping her Man's shoulders, or with her arms Raised Straight-Arm and spread, Bends at her waist to her Right, then she is Led to Sweep Clockwise from her waist in a half Circle. She also slowly makes a Sweeping Sway with her Head and eyes rolling across the ceiling from her Right to Left, as she Sweeps Circularly, (her eyes rolling Opposite that for **Sway-Contracheck**.)

Man holds his Lady loosely but securely by either of two methods: (1) With both of his Hands at her waist and hips, his Thumbs spread; or, (2) With both of his Hands at her back, flat against her wings or waist. Man sinks Well into his Knees to place his Center-of-Balance enough Rearward to Counter-Balance his Lady's Backward Bend; his Right Knee and Foot are Forward between his Partner's Feet; he may also extend his Toes Outward for Stability in Supporting her.

Similar to **Sway-ContraCheck**. (See Around-the-World, Bird-of-Paradise-ContraCheck, Bird-of-Paradise, and Rag-Doll.)

Arrabalero: A General Argentine Coupledance word for a Man of the slums (*arrabal*) and of low social status; a simple Man of direct ways who speaks plainly with coarse language.

Similar to a **Compadrito**. (See Canyengue-Tango.) [Mostly from *Tango Terminology*, *www.tangoafficionado.com*.]

Arrastre: (*ar-RRahs-tray*, Spanish for *to drag*.) A General Coupledance Action or Movement of **Dragging**, perhaps one's Foot or Feet, or of hauling one's Partner; e.g., displacing the Partner's Foot some distance while dancing Straight or while Turning. A sample basic **Arrastre** would be to simply Drag the Partner's Foot with one's own Foot.

Same, but more Generalized than **LaLlevada**, and even **Barrida**. Similar to **Sacada**, and **Desplazamiento**. [See Drag(2), Constant-Tug, Draw, Slide, and Biomechanics.]

Arrepentida or **Repentant:** (*ar-rray-pen-TE-dah*, Spanish for *repentant*.) An **Argentine Tango** Coupledance Genre Term for a changing of the Man's mind. A variety of Movements or Figures which allow the dancing Couple to avoid collision with another Couple, especially upon short notice when Crowded-Floor Dancing.

(See Freno, Balanceo, Cadencia, Side-Cadencia, Check, Pause, Hesitation-Change, and Change-of-Direction.)

Back-ContraCheck: A partially Leadable Coupledance Picture-Figure, suitable for the Slow-**Foxtrot**, Slow-**Waltz**, both **Rumbas**, the **Bolero**, and **International Tango**. **Identical to ContraCheck** except the Man and Lady have switched roles.

Lady, after Lowering by first Softening her Right Knee, then Leading with her Right shoulder and Softened Left Knee, her hips are led Forward by her Partner, as he Softens his Supporting Right Knee positioned behind his Left leg, with his Left shoulder Rearward. All legs are Crossed High at thighs and all four Feet are In-Line in Fifth-Position-Extended. She views him but he has Head-Closed.

(See BackwardCheck, and BackwardHold.)

Back-Corte(1): A Leadable **International Tango** Coupledance Pattern. Four Steps in 1 1/2 Measures, 2/4 Rhythm Timing is *Slow Quick Quick, Slow*. In Closed Position International Tango throughout. The Couple-Rotates a Quarter-Turn Counter-Clockwise total.

Man dances *backward BackTurn1/8CCW diagforturn1/8CCW, Close.*
Lady Steps *Forward forturn1/8CCW DiagBackTurn1/8CCW, close.*

Back-Corte(2): See Corte.

Back-Flick(1): An Unleadable Coupledance Movement suitable for all **Tangos**; where, in Left-Open-Facing Position with both Touching Sideward to the Man's Right, the Lady **Back-Flicks** before both Step-Thru. She does this by **Flicking** with her Left leg as she Quarter-Turns Clockwise.

Similar to **Flick**(3). [See Boleo, Latigazo, Ruade, Ochos-Picante, Mulekick, Flick(2), and HeelBrush.]

Back-Flick(2): See Flick, and Mulekick.

Back-Open-Promenade: A partially Leadable **International Tango** Coupledance Pattern. Four Steps in 1 1/2 Measures, 2/4 Rhythm Timing is *Slow Quick Quick, Slow*.

Couple dances from Promenade Position. Man (only) Half-Turns Clockwise to Closed Position #1 for International Tango, then Couple dances into Back-Contracheck Position.

Man dances *diagforward ThruSwivel1/2CW diagbackward, BackCheck.*
Lady Steps *DiagForward shortthru DiagForward, forcheck.*

Back-Twinkle: A partially Leadable, one-Measure, **International Tango** Coupledance Figure, where 2/4 Rhythm Timing is *Quick Quick Slow*. Performed Mirror-Image in Promenade Position. The Tap is with the Heel; the Touch is with the Inner-Ball.

Man dances *backward CloseToLeftInstep tapdiagfortouch*.

Lady Steps *Backward closetorightinstep TapDiagForTouch*.

(See Twinkle.)

Backward-Close-Finish: A Leadable Coupledance Ending Figure that is suitable for all **Tangos**, and is especially suitable for the American and Continental Tangos. One 2/4 Measure long, Rhythm Timing is *Quick Quick Slow*. **Backward-Close-Finish** is danced entirely in Closed Position for a Tango.

Opposite of The-Break, the Man dances the Lady's part and visa-versa. The **Backward-Close-Finish** itself, consisting of a Rearward half of a Box-Step, encompasses a **Tango-Draw** to a **Tango-Close**, (similar to a CloseTouch,) to an **Arch**, (with possibly a Brush-Tap.) (See Tango-Tap.)

Man dances *Backward brushsideward DrawTouchArch*.

Lady, Following, dances *forward BrushSideward drawtoucharch*.

Same as **Backward-Tango-Close**. (Also see Five-Step-Basic-Tango, Step-and-Drag, and Natural-Resolution.)

Backward-Start or **Retroceso** or **Reverse-Start:** In 2/4 Cut-Time, for the **Argentine Tango** Genre and **Milonga** Coupledancing, the Leadable **Backward-Start** can be the first two of several Moves to completion of the Resolucion, or of the Natural-Resolution. A two-Measure long Figure, Rhythm Timing is either *Slow Slow, Slow Slow*; or, *Slow Slow, Quick Quick Slow*. The **Backward-Start** Starts in Closed Position Argentine Tango, both with their Feet Together. Lady's Head is usually Open.

Man Steps *ShortBackwardHold* then *backbrushwidesidewardhold*.

Lady, Following, Steps *forwardhold* then *ForBrush*SidewardHold* into Facing-Offset Position.

Notes: 1) * Lady's second Step is Shorter than Man's.

2) Their second Step can be either **Basic-Start**, as noted, or the **Double-Start**.

3) Similar to the American-Start, and to the Retroceso-con-LaRonda.

4) May be followed by the Basic-Step, Pepito, or the Salida.

Caution: The Man Stepping Back against the Line-of-Dance can collide with Forward-dancing Couples.

(See Eight-Step-Basic-Tango.)

Backward-Start-with-Circle or **Retroceso-con-LaRonda** or **Reverse-Start-with-Circle:** In 2/4 Cut-Time, for **Argentine Tango** Coupledancing, the Leadable **Backward-Start-with-Circle** can be the first two of several Moves to completion of the Resolucion, or of the Natural-Resolution. A two-Measure long Figure, Rhythm Timing is *Slow Slow, Quick Quick Slow*. The **Backward-Start** Starts in Closed Position Argentine Tango, both with their Feet Together. Lady's Head is usually Open.

Man Steps *ShortBackwardHold* then *backbrushsidewardscribefullCCWcircle*.

Lady, Following, Steps *forwardhold* then *ForBrushSidewardHold* into Facing-Offset Position.

Notes: 1) * Man's Left Toe scribes a small circle on the Dancefloor. The Man views his Toe as his Lady impatiently waits.

2) Similar to the Backward-Start.

3) May be followed by the Basic-Start, the Double-Start, or the Revolucion.

Backward-Tango-Close or **Back-Tango-Close:** Two partially Leadable, General Coupledance Figures, Left or Right. First, the Man Steps Rearward; upon his Left Foot to Close his Left Ball against his Right Arch, or Rearward upon his Right Foot if for visa-versa. Next, he Tango-Closes as described under Tango-Close. His Lady Follows.

Same as **Backward-Close-Finish**. (See Tango-Draw, Arch, Paseo, Five-Step-Basic-Tango, and CloseTouch.)

Bailar: (*bah'e-LAR*, Spanish for *to dance*.)

Bailarin: (*bah'e-lah-REEN*, Spanish for *dancer*.) A Coupledance Term for a professional or a very accomplished dancer.

Bailongo: (*bah'e-LAWN-go*, Spanish for *a milonga*.) A Coupledance slang Term for an **Argentine Tango** Genre dance spot in Buenos Aires. **Bailongo** is a Lunfardo word for describing a place where people dance.

(See Milonga.)

Balanceo: (*bah-LAHN-thay-o*, Spanish for *balance*.) An **Argentine Tango** Coupledance Term for to Check deeply then replace.

(See Freno, Arrepentida, Cadencia, Pause, and Check.)

Baldosa: (*bahl-DO-sah*, Spanish for *flat paving-stone*.) A Leadable, Walking **Argentine Tango** Coupledance Box-Step Pattern, probably of six Steps that form the shape of a square, rectangle, or parallelogram. The **Baldosa** is named after checkerboard tile Dancefloors common in Buenos Aires.

Similar to the **Cuadrado**. [See Box-Step(1), Basic-Box, Touch-Box, Jazz-Box, Left-Turning-Box, and Right-Turning-Box.]

Ballroom-Tango: A very General Amalgamation of various **Tangos**. **Ballroom-Tango** is defined and described well under *Wikipedia Tango (dance)* - *http://en2.wikipedia.org/wiki*, as follows:

"*Ballroom tango, divided in recent decades into the `International' and `American' styles, is descended from the tango styles that developed when the tango first went abroad to Europe and America. The dance was simplified, adapted to the preferences of conventional ballroom dancers, and incorporated into the repetoire used in International Ballroom dance competitions.*

"*Subsequently the International Tango evolved mainly as a competitive dance, while the American Tango evolved as an unjudged social dance. As a result, the American Tango is believed by some to be inferior, and some American Tango teachers have introduced elements of technique borrowed from the International Tango. In International tango, sequences of figures and even entire dances are choreographed instead of improvised. This makes the dance less dependent on lead-follow technique and allows for more separation between the dancers. International tangos also use different music and styling from Argentine tangos, with more staccato movements and the characteristic `head snaps'.*"

[See Tango, International Tango, American Tango(1), Tango American-Style, Continental Tango, American Competition Tango, Valentino Tango, Contest Tango, Argentine Tango, and Milonga.]

Ball-Step or **BallFlat** or **Toe-First** or **Toe-Lead** or **Toe-Heel** (*TH*): A General Coupledance Action of the **Foot-Leads** Genre, stressed in Standard, Modern and Smooth dancing. The Ball-of-Foot Touches the Dancefloor first, prior to Lowering the rest of the Foot.

A Forward, **Toe-First**, **Ball-Step** is taken with one's Heel almost **not in contact** with the Dancefloor, then followed by the Lowering of one's Heel, causing very Slight Body-Rise then a Lowering as the Foot Flattens.

For **Argentine Tango**, the Man dances Under-His-Lady; i.e., his Forward Steps are **Ball-Steps**, (Toe-Leads,) except there is no Body-Rise. He Extends each Foot Forward in the Balletic fashion, before his Body Moves over the Foot. This characteristic is possible since there is no Driving or Swinging Movement required for **Argentine Tango**.

Opposite of **Heel-Lead**. (See Foot-Positions-on-Floor, Ball-of-Foot, Toe-Movements, Tip-Toe, Flat-Step, and Flat-of-Foot. Also see Sending-Foot, and Receiving-Foot.)

Bandoneon or **Fueye**: A small accordion-like musical instrument, intimately associated with and played accompanying most all **Argentine Tango** Genre and **Milonga** Coupledancing. Originally of German manufacture, the beloved "*heart-and-soul*" sounds from this "*button-box*" have defined the **Argentine Tango** since about 1899.

(See Tango-Music.)

Barrida: (*bar-RRAY-dah*, Spanish for *sweep*.) A **Foot-Sweep**. An **Argentine Tango** Coupledance Embellishment or Flourish, Performed by either Partner. The **Barrida** Action is that of one Partner's Foot Pushing to relocate the other Partner's Foot along the Dancefloor.

Ed Loomis [www.batango.com/loomis] describes this **Barrida** as follows:

"*A swoop; a sweeping motion: One partner's foot sweeps the other's foot and places it without losing contact. Barridas are done from either the outside or the inside of the foot of the receiving party. the technique is different for the inside and outside barridas.*"

Same, but more explicit than **Arrastre**, and more Generalized than **LaLlevada**. Similar to **Sacada**, and **Desplazamiento**. [Some data from http://nfo.net/dance/tango.]

Basico: (*bei'-SEE-ko*, Spanish for *basic*.) A General Argentine word for a **Basic** Coupledance Figure or Pattern. An example is the Eight-Step-Basic-Tango.

[See Basic(1)&(2). Also see ChaCha-Basic, and Bolero-Basic.]

Basic-Reverse-Turn-Closed-Finish: A Leadable, two-Measure Coupledance Pattern, suitable for the **International Tango**. Rhythm with 2/4 Timing is *Quick Quick Slow, Quick Quick Slow*.

Begins and ends in the Closed Position For Tango, with Man Locking in-between. Consists of six Steps with a 3/4-Turn Counter-Clockwise total Couple-Rotation.

Man dances *forturn1/4CCW* with CBM *DiagForTurn1/4CCW lockinfront, BackTurn1/4CCW diagforward Close*.

Lady dances *BackTurn1/4CCW* with CBM *sideturn1/4CCW Close, crossinfronturn1/4CCW DiagBackward close*.

Similar to **Open-Reverse-Turn-Closed-Finish**.

Basic-Start: For **Argentine Tango** Genre and **Milonga** Coupledancing, the Leadable **Basic-Start** is a 1/2- or one-Measure Movement and is Stepped to Man's Left. Rhythm Timing is either *Slow* or *Slow Slow*, in 2/4 Cut-Time. In Closed Position Argentine Tango, both might Start with their Feet Together. Lady's Head is usually Open. Starting with Man's Left Foot, both Step *Sideward*. Man's Step is wide while Lady's Step is Shorter than Man's.

Similar but simpler than the **Double-Start**. Usable in the Backward-Start, and American-Start. May be preceded by the Retroceso-con-LaRonda, or the Media-Luna. May be followed by the Basic-Step, ElAmericano, Pepito, or the Salida. (See Drop-Hinge, and Eight-Step-Basic-Tango.)

Basic-Step: In 2/4 Cut-Time, a Three-Measure Pattern for the **American Tango** Style of Coupledance.

This Basic-Step is in common with that for the Valentino Tango, and it is Patterned upon the Man taking the Five-Step-Basic-Tango, (three Forward Walking Steps, a Right Sideward-Step, a Tango-Draw then a Tango-Close.) Basic-Step Rhythm Timing is *slow Slow, slow Quick Hold, slow Hold*. The Tango-Close finish without Weight can have several Foot Stylings, (see Brush-Tap.) This subject Basic-Step is danced Starting in Closed, Banjo, or in Promenade Positions; the Lady is Picked-Up from being in these last two Positions.

(See Valentino Tango.)

Behind-Gancho-to-Weighted-Foot: In **Argentine Tango** Coupledancing, four different Unleadable Figures; Man's Left or Right, and Lady's Left or Right. Banjo or Sidecar, one Partner's Lunge is held, while the other Flicks Behind Partner's Weighted-Foot.

(See Gancho, and Open-Finish-Gancho.)

Bien-Parado: (*be-EN pah-RAH-do*, Spanish for *well stood.*) A General Argentine Coupledance Term for Standing Straight.

Similar to **Pinta**. (See Postura, Derecho, and Eje.) [Mostly from *Tango Terminology*, *www.tangoafficionado.com.*]

Bird-of-Paradise: A Flashy, partially Leadable, General Pose or Figure, Performed with artful Balance. Suitable for many Coupledances, including **Cabaret**, **Tango**s, both **Rumba**s, and the **Bolero**. Bird-of-Paradise is Executed in Loose-Closed Position except for arms and Hands. Timing varies.

Lady lays far Backward from her waist, with her arms Softly outstretched High, with Palms **Outward** in a **Lyre-Arms Position**, and as described in **Free-Hand-Fashioning-Raised-Wrist**. She looks Up and to her Left.

Man holds his Lady loosely but securely by either of two methods: (1) With both of his Hands at her waist and hips, his Thumbs spread; or, (2) With both of his Hands at her back, flat against her wings or waist. Man sinks Well into his Knees to place his Center-of-Balance sufficiently Rearward to Counter-Balance the Lady's Backward Bend; his Right Knee and Foot are Forward between his Partner's Feet; he may also extend his Toes Outward for Sideward Stability in Supporting her.

(See Bird-of-Paradise-ContraCheck, Around-the-World, Around-the-World-ContraCheck, Rag-Doll, and Sway-ContraCheck.)

Bird-of-Paradise-ContraCheck: A Flashy, partially Leadable, General Coupledancing Picture-Figure, Performed with artful Balance. Suitable for the Slow-**Foxtrot**, Slow-**Waltz** and all **Tangos**, and as an ending for other dances, such as all **Quicksteps**, **Rumbas**, the **Bolero**, and **Cabaret**.

The Man, after first Lowering by Softening his Right Knee, Moves Forward into the Lady, and the Couple assumes a Figure identical to the normal **ContraCheck** Position, except as follows:

Man Grasps his Partner's waist with both Hands, and Turns his Toes Outward for Sideward Stability. He Supports her as she lays Backward, by placing his Center-of-Balance sufficiently Rearward to Counter-Balance the Lady's Backward Bend.

Lady lays far Backward from her waist, with her arms Softly outstretched High, with Palms **Outward** in a **Lyre-Arms Position**, and as described in **Free-Hand-Fashioning-Raised-Wrist**. She looks Up and to her Left.

(See Bird-of-Paradise, Sway-Contracheck, Around-the-World-Contracheck, and Around-the-World.)

Body-Alignment: See Placement.

Boleo or **Voleo:** (*bo-LAY-o*, Spanish for *bowling-green*; from verb *bolear, to throw*; derived from the *boleadoras* used for tripping cattle.) A series of Unleadable **leg Whipping Actions**, Left or Right, useful while Coupledancing in the Rotary-Tango type of the **Argentine Tango** Genre. These off-the-floor Embellishments are (rarely) useful also in the Milonga and Argentine-Waltz.

Usually from a sudden Change-of-Direction, the **Boleo** is a **Circular Swinging of one's Free-leg Behind and Crossward** of the Supporting-leg; e.g., a Rearward Cross-Kick, usually High, in which the dancer's leg is Extended Backward and Crossed Behind the Knee with CBMP. The leg's inertia for to continue in its original Movement is exaggerated into this **Boleo** Swinging Action. Besides perhaps being High and Straight Sideward Behind, this Rearward **Boleo** usually is Low and Circular. The **Boleo** might begin by tracing an Arc upon the Dancefloor with the Toe that continues Behind one.

Ed Loomis [www.batango.com/loomis] describes this **Boleo** as follows:

"A boleo may be executed either high or low. Keeping the knees together, with one leg back, swivel and return on the supporting leg with a whipping action of the working leg."

Tango York [www.bakers64.freeserve.co.uk/] describes this **Boleo** as follows:

"An ornament. Throwing or swiveling one leg with the knees locked together, usually one behind the other. A boleo may be done with the toe touching the floor or higher. And may be executed either high or low. Keeping knees together, with one leg in back, swivel on the supporting leg."

Following is extracted from *Learn the Tango* [http://markov.iworkforfood.net/] by [eero@bergentango.no]:

"Boleos require the woman to stand in her axis in perfect balance with a `loose' foot. Both should be able to distinguish between linear and circular systems of lead, (many do without recognizing the difference). The man must be able to recognize the exact position of the woman's axis, and he must be able to execute a change of direction precisely around this axis. The woman must be able to disassociate between her upper body and her hip while responding to a change of direction. Both must remain soft for the whole boleo, which requires high precision. Both should have enough balance to be able to choose/change the direction of exit.

"There are huge differences when people are ready to do proper boleos. But in general I would say it happens between 2 and 4 years of weekly dancing/training. ..."

On a crowded Dancefloor in a Milonga, to avoid Kicking others, the dancer's Boleo Movements need to be shrunk and miniaturized. If any, instead of a gigantic Boleo, tiny and Soft Shakes and Wiggles are in order.

Similar to the **Latigazo, Ruade, Mulekick, Flick**(2), and a **HeelBrush**. [See Flick(3), and Back-Flick(1). Also see Tango-Liso, and Tango-de-Salon. Also see Figure-Fore, Fan(1), and Flare.]

[Some data from http://nfo.net/dance/tango.]

Brush-Tango-Tap: See Brush-Tap.

Brush-Tap or **Brush-Tango-Tap:** Two partially Leadable **International Tango** Coupledance Actions, that may also be suitable for American and Continental Tangos. Free-Foot is Brushed then **Tango-Tapped** within a half-Measure. Timing is *And Slow*.

Either Left or Right, Mirror-Image Opposite, one dances *BrushDiagForTouch*. After Brushing against the **Arch** or Inner-Edge of one's Supporting-Foot, one's Free-Foot is swept Slightly DiagForward on its Inner-Edge, with its Heel barely off the Dancefloor, and with its Knee veering Inwards. Toes point parallel, and only a Slight Weight ends upon this Inner-Edge.

(See Change-Feet-Tap, Touch, Promenade-Tap, Represa, Abrupt, Tick, Tango-Close, Tango-Draw, Spanish-Drag, Progressive-Link, and Head-Flick-Link. Also see The-Break, and Backward-Close-Finish.)

Bumper: A weird item worn by American Ladies while Coupledancing in the United States about 1912-14. The Tango was introduced twice in America, first by the Argentineans and secondly from France in 1926. Due to the close and sexy Tango's nature, the subject **Bumper** came (only) with Tango's first introduction. "*The Tango*" [www.showgate.com/] states:

"*Even the Americans were doing it, although some ladies were given to wearing 'bumpers' to protect themselves from rubbing a bit too closely against their male partners.*"

On the same subject of discouraging intimacy upon the Dancefloor, "*You Should Be Illegal*" [www.annabellemagazine.com/] states:

"*Forget about dancing close to your sweetheart in Utah, where there must be daylight (yes, daylight!) visible between the two desiring bodies. A town in Washington practically forbids women from leading, they can only make backward steps while dancing.*"

Cabeceo: (*kah-bay-THAY-o*, Spanish for *nod* or *shake of the head*.) An **Argentine Tango** and **Milonga** Coupledance Term, referring to the Traditional Technique Argentines use for selecting a dance Partner from a distance in the Buenos Aires Milongas. Either the Man or Lady uses eye contact with Head Movements as described under **Milonga**.

(See Codigo.) [Much from www.batango.com/loomis.]

Cadena: (*kah-DAY-nah*, Spanish for *chain*, *series*, or or *enchainement*.) An **Argentine Tango** Term for a Genre of Steps Coupledanced in the **Rotary-Tango** and **Show-Tango**(1) Styles. All are partially Leadable and Performed in the **Open-Embrace-Tango** Style.

LaCadena is also a **ContraDanza-Cubano** Figure.

The following is from *Tango Terms* [www.tangoberretin.com/alex]:

"*Cadena: Literally 'a chain' three or four steps involving changes of direction that repeats itself.*"

Tango York [www.bakers64.freeserve.co.uk/] describes **LaCadena** Genre as follows:

"*Cadena Chain. A movement of two people across the floor in a circular motion. One partner displaces the other partners leg and rolls across the front of their body. The other partner continues the motion. Must be seen to be appreciated.*"

Ed Loomis [www.batango.com/loomis] describes **LaCadena** Genre as follows:

"*An athletic and very theatrical turning figure which moves rapidly across the floor turning left, in which the couple alternate amagues (cuatros) or ganchos. Another variation involves the man stepping outside left in crossed feet and leading the lady in a change of direction to keep her in front of him as he turns to the left, alternately going around her and bringing her around him.*"

For still another Variation of **LaCadena**, see **Turning-Mutual-Boleos**. (Also see Amague, Cuatro, and Gancho.)

Cadence or **Cadencia** or **Steps-per-Minute:** A Basic Coupledance Term. Rhythmic Movement; Timing, Count, e.g., even Steps danced to music Beats-per-Minute (BPM).
"*Music is an invisible dance, as dancing is silent music.*" -- Anonymous
"*Dance is a sort of silent rhetoric.*" -- Canon Thoinot Arbeau
(See Normal-Walking-Cadence, Beat, Tempo, Rhythm, Rhythm-Stations, Timing, Two-Beat Timing, Down-Beat Timing, Rhythm-Pattern, Body-Rhythm, Slow-Motion, Syncopate, A-Tempo, Ad-Libitum, Dance-Count, Speed-It-Up, Speed-Wobble, Sway-Control, and Slow-Down.)

Cadencia: (*kah-DEN-the-ah* is Spanish for *cadence*.) **La-Cadencia** is an **Argentine Tango** and **Milonga** Coupledance Term for the musical **Phrasing**. **Cadencia** is Rhythm, Beat, the regular repetition of sound and Movement; e.g., the subtle shifting of Weight, the accentuated or subtle Sway of their Bodies as part of or their interpretation of the Beat. **Cadencia** can simply be the Basic, Leadable Coupledance Figure of **Stepping twice, or four times, In-Place.** **La-Cadencia** is useful for when trapped upon a crowded Dancefloor.
Ed Loomis [www.batango.com/loomis] describes **Cadencia** as follows:
"*CADENCIA A deep check and replace, usually led by the man as he steps forward left. Useful for avoiding collisions and making direction changes in small spaces. May also refer to subtle shifting of weight from foot to foot in place and in time with the music done by the man before beginning a dance to give the lady the rhythm he intends to dance and to ensure that she will begin with him on the correct foot.*"
Same as **Mark-Time.** [See Balanceo, Sur-Place, Side-Cadencia, Chase(5), and Side-Chase.]

Cafe Tango or **NightClub Tango** or **French Tango:** A **Continental Tango** Free-Style of Coupledance, preferred by the more advanced dancer, and related to the **American Tango** Free-Style.
"*The Cafe and Night Club styles features closed position, sharp progressive movements and intricate footwork. Here the music is more dramatic in character and the interpretation more intimate. The man is more dominant in this interpretation and here you are always conscious of his lead and styling, rather than a series of framed Picture poses characteristic of the Harvest Moon version. Each version has its uses and its adherents.*
"*---- and the sharp Cafe, or so-called French style, is preferred by the advanced dancer.*"
-- [From www.geocities.com/danceinfosa.]
Same as **Milonguero-Tango,** and **Tango-Apilado.** (See Petroleo-Tango, Valentino Tango, and Contest Tango.)

Caida: (*kah-EE-dah*, Spanish for *fall*.) An **Argentine Tango** and **Milonga** Coupledance Figure.
Ed Loomis [www.batango.com/loomis] describes this **Caida** as follows:
"*A step in which the man steps backward, sinks on his supporting leg, and crosses his working leg in front without weight while leading the lady to step forward in outside position, sink on her supporting leg and cross her working leg behind without weight. Caida may be done to either side.*"

Calecita or **Carousel**(2) or **Stork**(2): (*kah-lay-SEE-tah,* Spanish for *carousel* or *merry-go-round.*) A partially Leadable Coupledance Pattern, suitable for the **Argentine Tango**. The Man, supporting his Lady, Pivots her upon her one leg by Stepping in a complete **Circle around his Lady**.

Assuming that, in Varsouvienne or Skirt-Skaters Position throughout, the Man takes five Forward Curving Steps, *slow Slow quick Quick slow* for the **Argentine Tango**, and assuming that the Man is Rotating the Lady for a Full-Turn Clockwise. And assuming that the Lady's Left is her Supporting-Foot; then her Right Foot is Held In-Front of her Softened Left Knee with her Right Knee Held Outwards. Her Head remains far Left.

Ed Loomis [www.batango.com/loomis] describes the **Calecita** as follows:

"A figure in which the man places the lady on one foot with a lifting action of his frame and then dances around her while keeping her centered over, and pivoting on, her supporting leg."

The Man must use care to retain the Lady's Balance, by Slightly increasing and/or decreasing his dancing radius as needed.

Very similar to the **Ballerina-Wheel**, and to the **Tornillo-Wheel**. (See Planeo.)

Caminada: See Caminata.

Caminando: (*kah-me-NAHN-do,* Spanish for *walking.*) A Leadable Coupledance Pattern used in the **Argentine Tango, Milonga,** and in the **Argentine-Waltz**.

Ed Loomis [www.batango.com/loomis] describes **Caminando** as follows:

"CAMINANDO A crossing and walking step which the man initiates at 3 of basico [Step 3 of Eight-Step-Basic-Tango] *as he steps forward right in outside right position, pivoting to his right on his right foot and leading the lady to pivot on her left foot, stepping side left (side right for the lady) and drawing his right leg under him with weight (the lady mirroring with her left). The man then steps forward left in outside left position, pivoting to the left on his left foot, stepping side right and drawing his left foot under him with weight (as the lady dances the natural opposite). The man returns to outside right position and either continues the figure or walks the lady to the cross."*

Caminar: (*kah-me-NAR,* Spanish for *traveling, walking,* or *moving along.*) A Leadable, Progressive Coupledance Movement, Figure, or activity, special to the **Argentine Tango** Genre. Both Feet are usually kept close to the Dancefloor, with at least one Foot-part always in contact.

It is an **Argentine Tango** fundamental that when dancing the Tango, one must "*caminar el Tango,*" which means "*walk the Tango,*" (meaning within the Beat.)

Larry E. Carroll [http://home.att.net/~larrydla/basics_1] notes as follows about **Caminar:**

"*... there is surprising complexity behind this apparently simple activity.*"

ToTango [www.totango.net] describes **Caminar** as follows:

"*... the walk is similar to a natural walking step but the ball of the foot touches before the heel. The body and leg must move as a unit so that the body is in balance. Walks should be practiced for balance and fluidity.*"

Ed Loomis [www.batango.com/loomis] describes **Caminar** as follows:

"*CAMINAR To walk: The walk is similar to a natural walking step, but placing the ball of the foot first instead of the heel. Sometimes taught that the body and leg must move as a unit so that the body is in balance over the forward foot. Another style requires stretching the working leg, placing the foot, and then taking the body over the new supporting foot regardless of direction. Walks should be practiced both forward and backward for balance, fluidity, and cat like gracefulness.*"

Similar to **Walk(1)**, and to the **Caminata**. [See Paso, Prominade(8), and Paseo.]
[Much from www.clubdetango.com.ar; and www.tangocanberra.asn.au]

Caminata or **Caminada:** (*kah-me-NAH-tah,* Spanish for *a walk.*) A simple, Basic Coupledance Pattern Genre of the **Argentine Tango** that has several **Walking Steps** Variations, including the **Paseo**, the **Chase(5)**, **Side-Chase**, and the **Backward-Start**.

Similar in meaning to **Caminar**. (See Paso, and Paseo.)

Candombe (*can-DOME-bay*)**:** An Afro-Argentine Coupledance in vogue in Buenos Aires about 1915, danced by descendents of their black slaves, which is thought to have influenced in the evolution of the **Argentine Tango**. **Candombe** was also a place where blacks danced. Also, **Candombe** is drummed Tango music with a marked Rhythm.

Tourists in Montevideo, Uruguay have often been drawn by the **Candombe** Music, along with *candomble*, the worship from which it derived. There, the best time to experience **Candombe** is during Carnival, which usually begins in late January or early February and lasts more than a month.

The following is from *Drumming Away in Uruguay*; [www.aarpsegundajuventud.org]:

"Uruguay's Candomble began among African slaves, first brought by Spaniards in 1750. The Africans retained their belief in their orishas (gods) by matching them to Catholic saints. The priests would see the slaves praying to a saint, while they were secretly practicing their African religion. Candombe music originated with the drumming, singing, and dancing that accompanied Candomble ceremonies. Later, candombe music was performed at family parties and the annual Carnival.

" 'In the early years, candombe was played exclusively by blacks, ... This expressed their rage.' Uruguay's white elite initially shunned and even banned the African music, considering it a threat to public morals and sometimes punishing participants harshly. ...

" 'A lot of Uruguayans saw candombe as a music of poor people, or barefoot people and children begging in the streets,' says Da Luz. 'It took a long time to win acceptance here.'

"The music became widely popular in the late 1960s, when musicians fused it with canto popular, a folk style featuring singers and guitars. During Uruguay's military dictatorship (1972 to 1984). Candombe became the music of political resistance. 'With time,' says Prieto, 'white people became interested and the doors opened. Now there is no race, no class, no gender in playing candombe.'

"In fact, today it is Uruguay's national music, along with la murga and tango."

The following is an excerpt from *Music of Uruguay*; [www.absoluteastronomy.com]:

"Candombe originates from the Rio de la Plata, where African slaves brought their dances and percussion music. The word tango then referred to the traditional drums and dances, as well as the places where dancing occurred. Candombe rhythms are produced by drum ensembles, known as cuerdas, which include dozens of drummers and feature three drum sizes: tambor repique, tambor chico and tambor piano."

Ed Loomis [www.batango.com/loomis] describes the **Candombe** as follows:

"CANDOMBE   A type of dance originallly danced by the descendants of black slaves in the Rio de la Plata region. Music of African origin with a marked rhythm played on a `tamboril' (a kind of drum)."

The following are extracts from *Re: [TANGO-L] tango/milonga* [http://pythia.uoregon.edu/]:

"CANDOMBE is a strong folk tradition in Uruguay, and presumably dates back to African rhythms and dances of the 1800s. I would assume that early forms of Candombe took place on both sides of the river. I would NOT assume that Candombe was part of the tango development (except in an oblique way) until it became obvious in those milongas candombera in the 1930s.

"The presence of Candombe in the early tangos would depend on how much that particular expression of African culture rubbed up against the cultures of sailor, gaucho, and European immigrant.

"Candombe existed as a separate dance long before tango and milonga but it too evolved as it became incorporated into the milonga over the years."

(Continued)

Candombe (Continued)
(See Tango y Milonga, Milonga, and Milonga-Candombera.)
[Some data from http://nfo.net/dance/tprimer. Much from www.aarpsegundajuventud.org.]

Candombeada-Milonga: See Milonga-Candombera.

Cangrejo: (*kahn-GRAY-Ho*, Spanish for *crab*.) A Leadable Figure or repetitive Pattern suitable for the **Argentine Tango** Genre and the **Milonga** Coupledances.
The **Cangrejo** is a Figure consisting of two Steps, danced in either Open-Embrace or in the Tango-Lean, Facing Partner from waist up with CBM. Partners Travel Sideways to the Man's Left. Man Steps *sideward CrossInFront*. Lady Follows Mirror-Image Opposite.
Desplazamientos: Displacing the Lady's Left Foot Crossing by the use of the Man's Right Foot Crossing, the Man "helps her Foot along" in its Travel as they dance. This is a Sacada.
The **Cangrejo** Figure is normally repeated again and again.
Ed Loomis [www.batango.com/loomis] describes the **Cangrejo** as follows:
"*CANGREJO   A repetitive pattern of walking steps and or sacadas in which the man advances turned nearly sideways to his partner.*"
Similar to **Side-Cross-In-Front**. (See Crab-Walk, Corrida, and Corrida-del-Pie.)

Canyengue-Tango: (*kahn-JEN-gay* or *kahn-YENN-gay*, Spanish for *rhythmical walk*.) An early Style of the **Argentine Tango** Genre that had become fully developed by the early 1930s. It was a **Rotary-Tango** type of Coupledance that has few writeups found, so there are only word-of-mouth descriptions.

This typically Well Bent-Kneed **Canyengue-Tango**, of the introverted Inwards-and-Downwards-Style, was Coupledanced with a Macho Swagger, and with a strong Hold by the Man. Their constant Frame was an offset **Close-Embrace Tango-Lean.** With both Partners gazing Downwards, their Clasped Hands were in his coat Left pocket or against her Right hip. Dress fashion in the 1920s and early 30s was long tight skirts, which restricted the Lady's Movements. Consequently, shortened Steps were employed. Crossing of the Lady's legs was minimal. Footwork was emphasized by Syncopated legs interlocking; i.e., with Quick, reciprocating Ganchos and the like. The "*old guard*" Music was in the Syncopated 2/4 Time of the 1920s.

This historical **Canyengue-Tango**, currently danced, may not be reproduced accurately by its practitioners. Some modern Coupledancers exaggerate their Bodily Movements for accent.

The following is from *Daniel Trenner*, *www.dancetraveler.com*:

"*Canyengue, refers to the late twenties and thirties neighborhood styles. Dancers tell of how the canyengue died out and the forties social style tango took hold.*"

The following is from *www.batango.com/loomis*:

[Canyengue is] "*a very old style of tango from the 1900s to the 1940s. The music from this era had a faster or peppier 2/4 tempo so the dance had a rhythmic flavour similar to that of modern milonga. A very close embrace was used as well as some unique posture and footwork elements.*"

The following is from *Tango Terminology*, *www.tangoafficionado.com*:

"*Canyengue ... The tango of the arrabal. A lunfardo word with several meanings. It refers to somebody or something from the slums, i.e. low class. It also describes a gathering where people from the slums dance. It is also a certain way to perform or dance the tango with a slum attitude. Finally, it is a rhythmic effect created by Leopoldo Thompson by hitting the string of the contrabass with the hand or the arch of the bow.*"

The following is from *Lunfardo Dictionary*, *www.todotango.com*:

This describes **Canyengue** as something or someone from the outlying suburbs, or a manner of dancing Tango with breaks and cuts.

The following is from *Ney Homero da Silva Rocha*, *www.bardetango.com*:

[Describes Canyengue as] "*the porteno tango dance, which uses cortes (the man leads the woman to a stop) and quebradas (there is a breaking movement of the body) which give the dance a more informal identity.*"

Compare against the later **Petroleo-Tango.** (See the still later Salon-Tango, and the Show-Tango. Also see Arrabalero, and Compadrito.)

[Some data from www.tejastango.com, and www.tangocanberra.asn.au.]

Carancanfun: See Carancanfunfa.

Carancanfunfa or **Carancanfun:** (*kah-rahn-kahn-FOON-fah*, Spanish.) A Coupledance slang Term of the **Argentine Tango** Genre.

Tango York [www.bakers64.freeserve.co.uk/] describes **Carancanfunfa** as follows:

A Coupledance slang Term "*in the lingo of the compadritos* [compadres, friends], *the dance of tango with interruptions (cortes) and also those who dance it that way in a very skillful manner.*"

[See Parada, and Corte(2). Also see Tanguero, and Milonguero(1).]

Caressing-the-Floor: A popular Coupledance saying by Dancers in love with their special Dancefloors, in that there was no longer the need for Feet Raising from dirt surfaces in dancing. With wood or smooth floors, dancers could now "Use-the-Floor," Sliding their Feet for more comfortable dancing.

[See Elevadas, and Press(1).]

Caricias: (*kah-REE-the-ahs*, Spanish for *caresses*.) A Flourishing Movement or Figure; an Adorno or Embellishment used in the **Argentine Tango** Genre of Coupledances.

Ed Loomis [www.batango.com/loomis] describes **Caricias** as follows:

"*A gentle stroking with the leg or shoe against some part of the partner's body. They can be subtle or extravagant.*"

Either Partner can Caress the other. One can place their leg between their Partner's non-reacting legs (*Entrada*) and further, Hooking it behind their Partner's farthest leg at the Knee, then **slide calf-to-calf.** In response, the Entrada leg can be Sandwiched then the other Partner could be Caressed by a **slide calf-to-calf.**

Caution: A Caress could cause the instigator to be shunned or slapped if too intimate, or cause the Partner to even fall if too violent.

(See the others of the **Dibujo** Genre of [Stopped] **Parada Adornos**, that includes the **Lustrada, ShoeShine, Puntada-del-Pie, Lapiz, Chiche, Fanfarron, Golpecitos, Zapatazo, Levantada,** and the **Enganche.**) (Also see Flourish, and Gesture.)

Carousel(*kah-ro-SELL*): A partially Leadable **Argentine Tango** and **Milonga** Coupledance Pattern, in which the Man dances in a complete **Circle around his Lady**, as described in **Calecita.**

Tango York [www.bakers64.freeserve.co.uk/] describes **Carousel** as follows:

"*The lead steps in a circle around the follower - keeping them on their own axis.*"

Ed Loomis [www.batango.com/loomis] describes **Carousel** as follows:

"*A term used for molinete con sacadas to the man's left, the lady's right, with ochos and or cortado to exit.*"

[Some from http://nfo.net/dance/tprimer.]

Less explicit than **Calecita.** (See Molinete, and Sacada. Also see Horse-and-Cart, Ballerina-Wheel, and Tornillo-Wheel.)

Carpa: (*KAR-pah*, Spanish for *the tent*.) Used in the **Argentine Tango** and **Milonga** Coupledances, a Leadable, intimate **Position** while dancing, in which the **Lady Partner Leans Inward** Toward her Man.

Ed Loomis [www.batango.com/loomis] describes the **Carpa** as follows:

"*The tent: A figure created when the man leads the Lady onto one foot as in calecita and then steps back away from her, causing her to lean at an angle from her foot to his frame.*"

[See Tango-Lean, Milonguero-Style, Quebrada Position, Leaning-Into-Each-Other, Calecita, Embrace(2), and Lean.]

Castigada: (*kahs-te-GAH-dah*, Spanish for *punishment*.) A Flourishing Movement or Figure; a **Firulete Adorno**; an Embellishment used in the **Argentine Tango** and **Milonga** Coupledances.

Ed Loomis [www.batango.com/loomis] describes the **Castigada** as follows:

"A lofting of the lady's working leg followed by flexing at the knee and caressing the working foot down the outside of the supporting leg. Often done as an adorno prior to stepping forward, as in parada or in ochos."

Similar to the **Cucharita**. (See AnkleTrip, KneeFlick, Abrupt, Levantada, LaLlevada, Gancho, Golpes, Picados, Amague, and Frappe; all Performed while Moving.) (Also see Flourish, and Gesture.)

Chair (*chr*) or **Sit:** A Leadable Coupledance Checking Movement for all **Foxtrots, Waltzes, Tangos, Eastern Swing,** and **Jive.** Also suitable for other dances.

From Semi-Closed Position, Partners dance one Forward Thru Lunge Step with Inside-Feet, Lady Trailing, and with Lady's Left Knee only Slightly Inside of Man's Right Knee, in order to facilitate his next Lead. Partners may Lower either only minutely or considerably, simulating seated. All Feet are in Third-Position-Extended. Body-Weights are either upon Inside- or Outside-Feet as directed. Both look Inside and Behind. A **Chair** is a nice dance Tag Ending.

See **Knee-Lead** for Man's next Lead. (See Chair-and-Slip, Chair Position, Chair-Forward-Poised Position, and Sit-Line.)

Chair-Forward-Poised Position: Favored by most over the (original) **Chair Position.** A Leadable Coupledance possible Ending Position for all **Foxtrots, Waltzes, Tangos, Eastern Swing,** and **Jive.** Also for other dances. From Semi-Closed Position, Partners have danced a Forward Thru Lunge Stepped with Inside-Feet. With a Strong Checking Action and Deeply Softened Knees, their Body-Weights are Forward over their Inside-Feet, or optionally distributed over both Feet. All Feet are in Third Position Extended. Both are looking Inside and Behind.

(See Chair, Chair-and-Slip, and Sit-Line.)

Change-Feet-Tap or **Change-Feet-Tango-Tap:** A partially Leadable **International Tango** Coupledance Movement, that may also be suitable for American and Continental Tangos. Changes Supporting-Foot to Free-Foot in a half-Measure. Timing is *And Slow.*

Either Left or Right, Mirror-Image Opposite, one dances *CloseLower DiagForTouch.* The Moving Foot Closes Flat and Staggered Rearward, then the Free-Foot **Tango-Taps** slightly DiagForward on its Inner-Edge, with its Heel barely off the Dancefloor, and with its Knee veering Inwards. Toes Point parallel, and Weight ends upon Inner-Edge of new Supporting-Foot.

(See Brush-Tap, Touch, Change-Feet, Kick-Step, Kick-Ball-Change, Tango-Close, Promenade-Ending, Counter-Promenade, and Promenade-to-Counter-Promenade.)

Change-Feet-Tango-Tap: See Change-Feet-Tap.

Change-of-Sway: A Leadable Coupledance Ending Action; often a Tag for all **Foxtrots, Waltzes, Tangos, Swings** and **Jive.** Without Stepping, changing from one to a different Sway Position. Couple reverses their Side-Stretch, shoulders and Head Positions from some other Sway Position, such as an Oversway or a Side-Lunge-Left or -Right, to the Opposite Side-Stretch, shoulders and Head Position.

(See Oversway-Change-of-Sway, Side-Lunge-Change-of-Sway, and Picture-Figure.)

Change-Point: An Unleadable Basic Movement used in International, Modern and Smooth Coupledancing, and in Latin Rhythm Coupledancing. Changing Touching Foot from one to the other. One's Free Foot is Closed to the Supporting Foot and as a part of the same Motion, the new Free Foot is Pointed Sideward and Touches the floor, all in one Quick Movement.

(See Jete-Point.)

Chase(1): A partially Leadable **International Tango** Coupledance Pattern, similar to Hairpin without its first and last Steps. Timing is *Slow Quick Quick, Quick Quick*, 1 1/2 Measures long. Begins in Promenade Position, then a Pickup, a Sideward Step for both with a **Tick** for the Lady and/or Man, a brisk 1/4- to 3/8-Turn Clockwise to Feathered Position, recovering in Feathered Position or to Closed Position International Tango.

Man dances *diagforward StepThru sideward, ForTurn1/4CWCheck recover*.

Lady Follows with *DiagForward stepthrucross SidewardFlick, backward* with CBM *RecoverForward*.

Chase(2): Two Simple, Basic, Leadable **Argentine Tango** Coupledance Figures, Forward or Rearward, each one Measure in length in 2/4 Cut-Time. Danced entirely in Closed Position Argentine Tango; Timing for the two **Chase** Steps involved is *Slow Slow*.

If the Man dances *forward Close*, then the Lady, Following, dances *Backward close*. Or, if the Man dances *Backward close*, then the Lady, Following, dances *forward Close*.

Two or more **Chases** might be danced in sequence. The **Chase** may Turn. Two or more **Chases** in sequence become one of the **Caminata** Pattern Variations.

Similar to **Side-Chase**. (See Cadencia.)

[Data from http://64.33.34.112/.dance/tangels]

Chasse (*shah-SAY*) or **Chassez** or **Chasser** or **Sashay** or **Chassay** or **Chassee:** (French for *chased*. From *Pas Chasse* in the Classic **Ballet**.) A Gliding, Sliding Figure in which one Foot literally Chases one's other Foot out of its Position and displaces it. After a Preparatory-Step, the dancer's Free-Foot is Slid Outward with Weight applied. The other Foot is then Drawn along the Dancefloor to Close to it, followed by a fourth Step.

Ten different Basic Coupledance Figures, partially Leadable, each four Steps in length. Performed in various ways, and suitable for the Slow-Waltz, the **Foxtrots**, **Tangos**, both **Swings** and Jive, and other dances. All are danced *Slow, Quick And Slow,* or, *Slow, Quick Quick Slow,* with second and third Steps on Balls, and with Feet Closing or partially Closing on the third Step.

The ten Chasses are as follows:
1) *forward, Forward close Forward*
2) *Forward, forward Close forward*
3) *CrossInFront, diagforward Close diagforward*
4) *CrossInFront, sideward Close sideward*
5) *CrossBehind, diagrearward Close diagrearward*
6) *Rearward, rearward Close rearward*
7) *rearward, Rearward close Rearward*
8) *crossbehind, DiagRearward close DiagRearward*
9) *crossinfront, Sideward close Sideward*
10) *crossinfront, DiagForward close DiagForward*

The second Step Moves Toward the Direction-of-Dance, the third Step Closes, and the fourth Step Moves in the same direction as the second Step.

Note: Some say the Chasse is a series of (usually) Sideward Steps where the Free-Foot never Passes one's Supporting-Foot. Others say the Chasse is only that portion of the Steps, *Sideward* and *Close* into Third-Position.

(See Chasse-Roll, The-Change, Gallop, Shuffle, Touch-Step, Step-Ball-Change, Coaster-Step, Rabona, Change-Step, Chasse-Turn, Anchor-Step, Forward-Hitch, Backward-Hitch, and Triples. Also see Forward-Twostep, Backward-Twostep, Sideward-Twostep, Forward-Foxtrot, Backward-Foxtrot, and Sideward-Foxtrot.)

Cheek-to-Cheek Position or **Dancing-Cheek-to-Cheek:** An American informal and romantic way of Coupledancing. Mostly in the 1930s and 1940s, Together in an otherwise Loose-Closed Position, Partners of the same Height often danced **with right facial cheeks touching**, dancing usually to the Medium-**Foxtrot**. The Lady would hold her forehead against his cheek if the Partners were nearly the same Height. If the Lady was very short and her Man was tall, she then would often place and hold her cheek, usually her Right, against his chest while they danced. Both **Slow-Dancing** and the **Argentine-Tango** are now currently often danced **Cheek-to-Cheek**.

[See Head-to-Head Position, and Over-the-Heart-Hand-Hold. Also see Loose-Hug Position, Cuddle Position(1), Shadow-Enfold Position, and Crush-In-Closed. Also see Embrace(1), Cuddle, Enfold, Hug, Squeeze, Bundle, Snuggle, Envelop, Clasp, Clutch, Grasp, and Cling. Also see Milonga, and Tango-Lean.]

Chest-Lead(1):   A Coupledance Movement for the Man in Leading his Lady. This **Chest-Lead** is used the most in the American **Tango**. For a sample in the American **Tango**, in two Measures with his 4/4 Timing being *Hold quick Quick slow Slow, quick Quick slow Slow Hold*, the Man would Execute two **Chest-Leads**; each of his first of his two *quicks* is a **Chest-Lead**. From their initially Closed Position, as he Quickly Steps Forward upon his Left Foot, the Man simultaneously protrudes his **Chest-Lead** into his Lady's chest, bouncing her Body Rearwards and Apart into a very Loose-Closed Position, twice. Then, twice, he Recovers her into a full Banjo Position as he Steps Back *Slow*ly upon his Left Foot. (Twice, the Lady is Outside-Swiveled and Picked-Up.)   This **Chest-Lead** for the first time may be a surprise for her.

Chest-Lead(2): See Lead/Follow-for-Tango.

Chiche: (*che-CHAY*, Spanish for *hisses*.) A Flourishing Movement or Figure; a **Dibujo Adorno**; an Embellishment used in the **Argentine Tango** and **Milonga** Coupledances.
        Ed Loomis [www.batango.com/loomis] describes **Chiche** as follows:
        "*Small ornamental beats done around the supporting foot with the working foot in time with the music, either in front or in back as desired.*'
        Similar to **Golpecitos, Fanfarron**, and **Golpes**. (See Lapiz, ShoeShine, Puntada-del-Pie, Caricias, Lustrada, Zapatazo, Levantada, and Enganche; all Performed during a Parada.) (Also see Flourish, and Gesture.)

Closed Position Argentine Tango or **Open-Embrace-Tango** or **Right-Foot-Inside Position** or **Ballroom-Hold** or **Waist-Hand-Hold:** This is the Traditional Position suitable for the **Argentine Tango** Genre of Coupledances, although only its **Tango-Nuevo** and **Show-Tango**(1) versions of the **Salon-Tango** Genre must be danced in this subject **Open-Embrace**d Position.
        Partners Face, perhaps Leaning Slightly Inward, close in Standing-Stance. Offset substantially to their Right, with Right Feet Pointing between Feet. Shoulders may be Forward Contrabody, although shoulders are kept fairly parallel. Man's Right arm wraps around her waist for Leading, while Lady's Left Hand placement is optional, (but no Salute.) His Left Hand holds her Right Hand at her Shoulder-Level, or he may vary this by Lowering her Right Hand to his Left hip. Elbows are Lowered in and her Head is often Open, Torqued to her Right. Man's Head is to his Left or he looks at her.
        This **Open-Embrace** Position essentially becomes a **Close-Embrace-Tango** when the Man increases the Embrace and the Lady **Tango-Lean**s, applying Cheek-to-Cheek. The following **Salon-Tango** Genre Styles either may or must be Coupledanced **Close-Embrace**d: The Tango-Orillero, Tango-Apilado, Milonguero-Tango, Club-Style Tango, and the Liquid-Tango.
        Same as the less-explicit **To-Dance-Inside**. Similar to **Right-Foot-Outside Position**. (See Milonga, Linear-Tango, and Rotary-Tango. Also see Closed Position, Closed Position Bolero, Closed Position Country, Closed Position Informal, Closed Position International Standard, Closed Position International Tango, Closed Position Layback Swing, Closed Position Lively Swing, Loose-Closed Position, and PasoDoble-Hold. Also see Argentine Tango Step-Listing.)

Closed Position International Tango or **International-Tango-Hold** or **Tango-Stance:** Related but **more compact** than for the Closed Position International Standard. Both Partners' Left hips and Shoulders are Turned CCW Slightly more than for the Closed Position International Standard, allowing the Man to Hold his Lady further around her waist. The Man's Left Hand is brought Slightly more inward.

Partners Face strongly Patched and Offset substantially to their Right, Knees Well Softened, with Right Feet Pointing between Feet, and with both Heads Proud to their Left with Head-Space. Leg muscles are Tensed for strength but not for Rigidity. Neither party smiles. Shoulders-Parallel are Spaced Shoulders-Away from each other. Joined Lead Hands are at her Shoulder-Level with Man's Left elbow Slightly Raised from neutral. Man's Right arm is Well wrapped around her waist with fingertips to her spine, which allows Lady's Left Palm and forearm to be straight and parallel with the Dancefloor, and her Left Thumb near to being under his Right armpit. Her Left index finger applies upward pressure under his Right wing. This is called her `Tango-Salute'.

Closed-Promenade: A Leadable **International Tango** Coupledance Pattern, that may also be suitable for American Tango. Consists of four Steps in 1 1/2 Measures. Timing is *Slow Quick Quick, Slow*.

Begins in Promenade Position and ends in Closed Position International Tango. Lady rides Man's hip until completing her Swivel. First two Steps have Heel-Lead for both, also for Man's third Step. During Heel-Leads, Feet of both continually Point in parallel, angled Toward Partner. Both have CBMP on Step-Thru. Feet Close Flat and Slightly staggered.

Man dances *diagforward StepThru diagforturn1/8CCW, Close*.

Lady dances *DiagForward stepthruswivel1/2CCW PickupTurn1/8CCW, close*.

Same as **Open-Promenade**, except ends Close instead of ForwardFeathered. (See Promenade-Link, Promenade-Ending, Quarter-Beats, Promenade-Tap, Progressive-Link, Head-Flick-Link, Counter-Promenade, and Promenade-to-Counter-Promenade.)

Close-Embrace-Tango: See Tango-Lean, and Embrace.

Club-Style Tango or **Pecho-Argentino:** One Style of the **Tango-de-Salon** Coupledance, which is part of the **Argentine Tango** Genre.

During the 1950s, this **Club-Style Tango** which was danced in the suburbs of Buenos Aires was **very similar to** the **Milonguero-Tango** of central Buenos Aires. For instance, both this **Club-Style Tango** and the **Milonguero-Tango** incorporated the **Ocho-Cortado**. Both were likely to have originated from their older **Tango-Orillero** Style.

This **Club-Style Tango** is constantly danced **only** in a **Close-Embrace**, as fully described under "Tango-Lean." This **Linear-Tango** type of dance Travels CCW upon the Line-of-Dance.

[Much from www.tejastango.com.]

Codigo: (*KO-de-go*, Spanish for *code of behavior*.) An **Argentine Tango** and **Milonga** Coupledance Term, referring to the codes of behavior and the techniques for selecting a dance Partner in the Buenos Aires Milongas. The **Cabeceo** is one such technique.

(See Milonga.) [Much from www.batango.com/loomis.]

Compadre: (*kom-PAH-dray*, Spanish for *friend.*)   A General Argentine word for a responsible, brave, well-behaved, honorable Man of the working class who dresses Well and is very Macho.

(See Genteel, Gentleman, Charm-and-Courtesy, Charm-and-Finesse, Etiquette, Code-of-Conduct, and Manners. Also see Macho, and Gusto.)

[Much from *Tango Terminology, www.tangoafficionado.com.*]

Compadrito: (*kom-pah-DREE-to*)   A General Argentine word for a "*Dandy; hooligan; street punk; ruffian: They invented the Tango.*"

Similar to an **Arrabalero.** (See Dandy, Costume, Mode-of-Dress-and-Behavior, Making-a-Show, and Stand-Out.) [From *Tango Terminology, www.tangoafficionado.com.*]

Compas(1): (*kom-PAHS*, Spanish for *measure* or *regulate.*)   A General Argentine word for the "*Beat, as in the beat of the music.*"

Same as the **Beat**(1). [See **Ritmo**, and Yumba. Also see Beats-per-Measure, Beat-Value, Steady-Beat, MPM, BPM, Underlying-Beat, Tempo, Time-Signature, Metronome, Cadence(1), Normal-Walking-Cadence, Time, Timing, Lagged-Timing, On-the-Beat, Lose-the-Beat, Four/Four-Time, Three/Four-Time, Two/Four-Time, Rhythm, Rhythm-Pattern, Body-Rhythm, A-Tempo, Ad-Libitum, Ahead-of-the-Beat, Rush-the-Start, and Slow-Motion.] [Much from *Tango Terminology, www.tangoafficionado.com.*]

Confiteria-Bailable: (*kon-fe-tay-REE-ah bah'e-lah-BL*)   A General Argentine Coupledance Term for "*A cafe like establishment with a nice atmosphere where one can purchase refreshments and dance tango. A nice place to meet friends or a date for dancing.*"

(See Milonguero-Tango, Tango-Liso, Milonga, and Confiteria-Style.) [Mostly from *Tango Terminology, www.tangoafficionado.com.*]

Confiteria-Style: A General Argentine Coupledance Term. "*May refer to a smooth and simple Salon Style as in Tango Liso or to Milonguero Style.*"

(See Milonguero-Tango, Tango-Liso, Milonga, and Confiteria-Bailable.) [Mostly from *Tango Terminology, www.tangoafficionado.com.*]

Confiteria-Tango: (*kon-fe-tay-REE-ah*, Spanish for *pastry shop.*) See Milonguero-Tango.

Contest Tango or **Harvest-Moon Tango:** An **American Tango** Style of Coupledance, often danced in **American Tango** Free-Style Competitions.

"*Contest Tango is a more wide open Tango, with many steps originating from Promenade Position. Here, kicks by the lady, Rondes and Oversways are extensively used, and the whole dance concentrating on picture-type figure that features the lady in a variety of framed postures.*" -- [From www.geocities.com/danceinfosa.]

(See Valentino Tango.)

Continental Tango or **Show-Tango:** A Rhythm, Traveling-Coupledance. Made famous in spectacular shows around the world in the 1930s and later, this Tango has almost no resemblance to its authentic Tango origins in Buenos Aires. This Tango is danced at 32 to 34 MPM, (played at 128 to 136 BPM.) The history of the **Continental Tango** begins with Tango's introduction into France. Tango became very popular in Europe about 1915, after first coming into only limited and temporary vogue in the U.S. Europe, mainly France, continued to import their Tango interpretations from the Argentine well into the early 1920s. Europe developed rules, including some Dancefloor Traveling. Tango was often danced Head-to-Head in Europe, and even danced while kissing with arms entwined. Americans called the resulting **Continental Tango,** "this **New-French-Tango.**" Offshoots in Europe included the **Cafe Tango.**

The following is from *Ballroom Dancing:* [www.colleenmurray.com]

[The Argentine Tango's] "*importation into the upper classes of Western Europe was catalysed by France's greatest music-hall star: Mistinguett, who gave the first ever demonstration in Paris in 1910. Interest in the dance rapidly exploded as a "Tangomania", initially through Paris then London and New York. THe first world war did nothing to cool this interest, with Rudolph Valentino popularising the Tango further in his film "The Four Horsemen of the Apocalypse" (1921).*"

The following is from *Holland Masters 2003 Dance History:* [www.danceplaza.com]

"*The Tango was introduced in Europe, actually in Paris in the Argentine community. Until 1907 the Tango was not accepted in London, the dance was too erotic and had many opponents. After some stylistic changes the Tango was accepted by Paris and London. That was the time (1912) of the tango-parties, tango-teas and tango-soupier with professional tango demonstrators.*"

See <u>**Tango-American-and-Continental Step-Listing**</u>, and **American Tango**. (Also see Tango, Milonga, Argentine Tango, Argentine Tango Step-Listing, International Tango, American Competition Tango, and International Tango Step-Listing.)

Continuous-Ganchos: Various partially Leadable, **Argentine Tango** Coupledance Figures or Patterns, two or more Measures long.

Continuous-Ganchos are **Enganched** (Flicked) by both Partners, but one at a time. Of the many different ways to Flick **Ganchos**, each may be reciprocated by the Partner, followed by still another **Gancho** and again reciprocated, etc.

(See **Gancho** for the different kinds. Also see Front-Hook, and Enganche.)

Figure 1. **ContraCheck**

ContraCheck (*contra ck*): Performed with artful balance, a Leadable Coupledancing Picture-Figure suitable for the Slow-Foxtrot, Slow-Waltz, both **Rumbas**, the **Bolero**, and the **International** and **American Tangos**, and as an ending for other dances, such as both **Quicksteps**. Begins in a Loose-Closed Position. Timing varies.

After first Lowering by Softening his Right Knee, Lowering her to allow her lengthy Stride Rearward, the Man Moves Forward into the Lady, and the Couple assumes a Contrabody Position with Right shoulders Forward and all four Feet In-Line, as in **Fifth-Position-Extended**. If the Lady Strides Slightly off from straight Rearward, she can imbalance her Man. To protect against this imbalance, the Man should have his Left Toe rotated Outward.

Man's Center-of-Balance is over his Flexed but Supporting Left leg, with his hips Up to his Lady, and with his back straight and vertical, (no Posterior-Protrusion.) All legs are crossed high at thighs. Finally, Man draws his Right Knee to touch his Left Knee, which allows Lady more freedom to lay Backward. Man views Lady, who's Head is Well Closed and Up. Lady's Supporting Right Knee is well Flexed and her hips are Up to her Partner. No Rise for Man at Ending, although Lady may Rise Slightly. Both are on their own Center-of-Balance. The Heel of her Supporting Right Foot should not Touch the Dancefloor.

(See Figure 1.) (See ContraCheck-and-Switch, Sway-ContraCheck, Back-ContraCheck, No-Hands-ContraCheck, Bird-of-Paradise-ContraCheck, Around-the-World-ContraCheck, Around-the-World, Traveling-ContraCheck, ForwardHold, and ForwardCheck.)

ContraCheck-and-Switch: A Leadable Coupledancing Figure or Pattern, suitable for the Slow-Foxtrot, Slow-Waltz, both **Rumbas**, the **Bolero**, and the **International** and **American Tangos**, and for other dances, such as both **Quicksteps**. Timing varies.

To ContraCheck: Follow the ContraCheck description as given above.
Note: Lady's Head must remain Well Closed in order to assure a successful **Switch**. (See Figure 8.)

To Switch: First, In-Place, Man Recovers Back on Right as Lady Recovers Forward on her Left, then **all four Feet Swivel a Half-Turn Clockwise In-Place**, or at least a 3/8-Turn followed by a 1/8-Turn Clockwise. Ends in Closed Position with Man's Weight Forward on Right and with Lady's Weight Back on her Left Foot.

(See Sway-ContraCheck, Back-ContraCheck, No-Hands-ContraCheck, Bird-of-Paradise-ContraCheck, Around-the-World-ContraCheck, Around-the-World, Traveling-ContraCheck, ForwardHold, and ForwardCheck.)

Corrida: (*koR-RREE-dah*, Spanish for *run*.) A Progressive Running Sequence of Steps, most often referred to for the **Argentine Tango** Genre and **Milonga** Coupledances.
Tango York [www.bakers64.freeserve.co.uk/] describes **Corrida** as follows:
"A running step used in milonga, a series of small steps in double-time."
The shortest **Corrida** would be two *Quick* Forward Steps. Four **Corridas**, a **Run**, would have eight short and **Quick Forward Steps**, if for music two Measures long with 2/4 Rhythm Timing of *Slow Slow, Quick Quick Slow.*
Same as **Corrida-del-Pie**. (See Corrida-Garabito, and Cangrejo.)

Corrida-del-Pie: (*kor-RREE-dah del pe-AY*, Spanish for *foot race* or *running*.) A Spanish Coupledance Term for a short sequence of Running Steps. Also, an alternate name for **LaLlevada**.
Same as **Corrida**. (See Corrida-Garabito, and Cangrejo.)

Corrida-Garabito: (*kor-RREE-dah gah-rah-BEE-to*, Spanish for *running scrawl*.) A Leadable four-Step Figure or Pattern used in the **Argentine Tango**, **Milonga**, and in other Coupledances. Beginning in a Semi-Closed Position, Partners Step-Thru and Step Side to Face, then Pivot two Steps Clockwise in a Closed Position.

Ed Loomis [www.batango.com/loomis] describes the **Corrida-Garabito** as follows:

> "*A milonga step in which the couple alternately step through between each other, the man with his right leg and the lady mirroring with her left, then pivot to face each other as they step together. May be repeated as desired.*"

Corte(1) (*KOR-tay*, Spanish for *cut*) or **Back-Corte:** A Leadable Coupledance Movement, useful in American and Argentine **Tangos**. The **Corte** retains a Closed Position.

For the **Back-Corte**, the Man, after Striding Rearward on Left Foot, Dips Backward-and-Sideward, Lowering with a Softened-Left-Knee for a Slow-Count. His Right leg remains Extended Straight with Toe Touching. The Lady is brought Forward, into him, on her Right Foot into a Contrabody Press-Line.

(See Dip, Plie, Lunge, Advanced-Corte, Hover-Corte, Reverse-Corte, Three-Step-Reverse-Corte, and Side-Corte.)

Corte(2): (*KOR-tay* is Spanish for *cutting edge, cut, expedient*, or *notch*.) The **Corte** Genre is an **Argentine Tango** Coupledance Term for an unforseen and sudden **halt** in the dance.

The **Parada** Stop is a **Corte**. The Lady's hanging **Quebrada** is a **Corte**. The "*cutting*" Term refers to **Holding** up the dancing for several music Beats. Many Tango Moves are improvised, which at times create conflicts of intention between Partners, thus the **Corte**.

Upon the **Corte** (stop), the Man then sometimes clarifies his intentions to his Lady, while she may show signs of expectation irritation at the halt. Doodling, the Man might Perform the **Lapiz**, the **ShoeShine** or some other **Dibujo**, and/or his Lady might respond with a **Puntada-del-Pie**, or the **Levantada**. These signs are often Executed simply as Flourishes, for visual effect during down-time.

Ed Loomis [www.batango.com/loomis] describes the **Corte Cut** (Parada) as follows:

> "*In tango, corte means cutting the music either by syncopating, or by holding for several beats. May refer to a position in which the torso is erect over a flexed supporting leg with the working leg extended forward to a pointe with the knees together which the man assumes when touching the lady's foot with his in parada. The lady moves to the same position from parada as the man closes over her working foot in mordida, and pivots on her supporting foot in this position whenever the man leads an outside barrida. May also refer to a variety of dramatic poses featuring erect posture, flexed supporting legs, and extended dance lines by both dancers, used as a finale. See Quartas.*"

This **Corte**(2) Pausing Genre is the Opposite of the **Firulete** Genre with its uninterrupted dancing flow. Within this **Corte**(2) of the **Dibujo** Genre of [Stopped] **Parada Adornos**, the Caricias, Lustrada, Chiche, Fanfarron, Golpecitos, Zapatazo, Levantada, and the Enganche, are also included. (See Pause, Hold, Freeze, Collect, Hesitation, Break, Suspension, Freeze-and-Melt, and Hover. Also see Quartas, and Quebrada Position.)

Cortina: (*koR-TEEN-a,* Spanish for *curtain.*) That which conceals or hides something. **Cortina** is the name for a brief Interlude of non-Tango music; i.e., non-danceable music that is played between "**Tanda**" Dance-Sets, separating **Tandas** at an Argentine **Milonga** (place-of-dance). A **Cortina** signals the end of a **Tanda** and acts as a cue for escorting the Lady back to her seat.

In Buenos Aires, most everyone deserts the Dancefloor, to return to their seats, while the **Cortina** is playing. And they wait; they do not again begin dancing upon the first music note of the next **Tanda**.

(See Milonga for more etiquette details, and Tanda.) [Much from www.dancetraveler.com, www.batango.com,loomis, and www.tangonadamas.com/abouttango.]

Counter-Promenade: A Leadable **International Tango** Coupledance Pattern, that may also be suitable for American and Continental Tangos. Consists of three Steps and a Change-Feet-Tap in 1 1/2 Measures. Rhythm for 2/4 Timing is *Slow Quick Quick, And Slow.*

Danced entirely in **Reverse-Promenade Position** with Lady continually riding Man's hip. No Turn. Feet continually point in parallel, angled Toward Partner. Both have Heel-Lead on first three Steps. Both have CBMP on Step-Thru. Feet Close Flat and staggered Rearward. Each Outside-Foot **Tango-Taps** Slightly DiagForward and on Inner-Edge, with Heel barely off the Dancefloor, and with Outside Knees veering Inwards. Both their Weights end on Inner-Edge of Inside-Feet.

Man dances *DiagForward stepthru DiagForward, closelower DiagForTouch.*
Lady dances *diagforward StepThru diagforward, CloseLower diagfortouch.*
(See Promenade-Ending, Promenade-to-Counter-Promenade, Reverse-Semi-Closed Position, Promenade-Tap, Closed-Promenade, Open-Promenade, Quarter-Beats, Promenade-Link, Progressive-Link, and Head-Flick-Link.)

Coupling: See Enrosque.

Cradle(1)(Verb): Basic Coupledance Movements. Leadable means to achieve two Basic Coupledance arms crossed In-Front, Partners Side-by-Side Figures; either the Lady or Man is Cradled or Left-Cradled. Only the two Figures for the Lady to be Cradled are delt with here. To Cradle or Left-Cradle the Lady is to Position her so that the **Lady's Right arm becomes crossed <u>underneath</u>**. There are two ways to **Cradle** or Left-Cradle the Lady, (and two ways to **Wrap** or Left-Wrap the Lady):

1. To **Left-Cradle** the Lady **from Left-Open** Position: With Hands at Waist-Level, the Lady Rolls-In a Full-Turn to the Man's Left side. Taking her Left Hand results in the Lady's **Right arm** becoming crossed **underneath**. By switching her to his Right side while in this Stance, the Lady is placed in **Cradle** Position, with the Lady's **Right arm**, again, remaining crossed **underneath**. (The same as for Spaghetti #2.)

2. **Outside**-Turning the Lady from Butterfly Position, by Raising her Left Hand, to **Cradle** Position, results in Lady's **Right arm** becoming crossed **underneath**; or to **Left-Cradle** Position, which results in Lady's **Right arm** becoming crossed **underneath**. (See Spaghetti #2.)

(See Wrap.)

Cradle(2): See Cunita.

Cradled Position: A Leadable, General Coupledance Position, suitable for all **Waltzes**, **Twosteps**, **Tangos**, **Rumbas**, **Boleros**, **ChaChas**, **Mambos**, **Sambas**, **Polkas**, **Discos**, **Hustles**, **Swings**, **PasoDobles**, **Onestep**, **Cajun-Jittergug**, and other dances.

When the Lady is **Cradled**, the Lady's arms are crossed In-Front, **Left** on top. Man Shadows with Lady to his Right. Lady's Right and Man's Left Hands are Clasped In-Front; Man's Right Hand around Lady Clasps her Left Hand.

Similar to **Wrapped Position** where Lady's **Right** arm is on top. (See Left-Cradled Position, and Rolling-Cradle.)

Criss-Cross: A Leadable, two-Measure Coupledance Pattern, suitable for the **American Tango**, and other Tangos. Rhythm 2/4 Timing is *Quick Quick Slow, Quick Quick Slow.*

Begins in Promenade Position, then to Reverse-Semi-Closed, Pickup, and ends in some Closed Position for Tango.

Man dances *diagforward StepThru Swivel1/2CW* Inward, *stepthruswivel1/2CCW* Inward *DiagForward* Pickup *drawclosetouch.*

Lady, Following, dances *DiagForward stepthru Swivel1/2CCW* Inward, *StepThruSwivel1/2CW* Inward *forswivel1/2CCW* Across Man *CloseTouch.*

Cross (*X*) or **Crossward** or **Cross-Sideward:** (*cruzar* is *to cross*, and *cruze* is *the cross* in Spanish.) Four Leadable, Basic Coupledance **Movements** or **Figures**, Left or Right Foot, In-Front or Behind, Mirror-Image Opposite.

Consists of two Beats or Steps, half a Cross-Step. With pronounced Shoulder-Lead, with one's Body almost Sideways to Direction-of-Travel, either the Left or Right Foot is drawn Across either In-Front of or Behind the Supporting-Foot and Well beyond. Cross is Stepped either *Sideward CrossInFront*, or *Sideward CrossBehind*, with a Change-of-Weight.

Some say **Cross** consists of only one Beat or Step, (only the second Step above,) where the dancer Steps either *CrossInFront*, or *CrossBehind.*

Note: Comparing "**Cross**" to "**Lock**", Locking Crosses tighter. **Cross** more likely means to Cross-In-Front, and rarely means to Cross-Behind. To Lock, one first Steps Forward or Backward. Lock Travels a shorter distance.

Similar to **Croise**, and **Dessus**. (See En-Croise, and Dessous. Also see DiagCross-In-Front, and ForCrossCheck. Also see DiagCross-Behind, and BehindCrossCheck. Also see Crossed-Feet Stance, Cross-Touch, Cross-Touch-In-Front, and Cross-Touch-Behind. Also see Crossward-and-Angular, Crossward-and-Sideward, Crossward-and-Perpendicular, Cross-Wind, and Cross-Unwind. Also see Pas-de-Basque, Fifth-Position, Sur-le-Cou-de-Pied, Cross-Foot-Across-Ankle, Cruzara, Cut, and Lock. Also see Foot-Movements.)

Crossed-Waltz: See Argentine-Waltz.

Cross-Turn: A Leadable, General Coupledance Figure, Forward or Rearward **Turning**.

The **Cross-Turn** consists of three Steps, where one's Feet are Crossed Tightly upon the second or third Step, either In-Front or Behind. The **Cross-Turn** facilitates a tighter Turn. An example is the Viennese-Lock in the Viennese-Turn.

(See Cruzada, and Cruzara.)

Crush: A Leadable, General Coupledance Holding Action;   an affectionate Movement of Clasping each other around each Body using all arms, **Pressed** in a close **Embrace**(1). A **Crush** is sometimes employed as the Ending Movement of the entire Coupledance.   But in some Closed Positions, the Lady might complain that she does not like it; complaining that she feels **Crushed**.

Same as or similar to **Hug, Cuddle, Enfold, Squeeze, Bundle, Snuggle, Envelop, Clutch, Grasp,** and **Cling**. (See Cuddle Position, Loose-Hug Position, Shadow-Enfold Position, Slow-Dancing, Cheek-to-Cheek Position, Head-to-Head Position, Over-the-Heart-Hand-Hold, and Crush-In-Closed. Also see Tango-Lean.)

Cruzada(1) or **Trabada:** (*kroo-THAH-duh*, Spanish for *crosswise* or *crossed*.) Two Leadable, Mirror-Image Coupledancing Figures, Turning-Left and Turning-Right, both suitable for the **Argentine Tango** and the **Milonga**. Both Figures begin and end with Feet-Together in Closed Position Argentine Tango [Embrace(2)]. Two Measures long in 2/4 Cut-Time, both **Cruzada** Figures consist of four Steps plus a CloseTouch (Tango-Close). Rhythm Timing for each Figure is *Slow Slow, Quick Quick Slow.*

For the **Cruzada-Turning-Left;**

Man Steps *sideward Cross&Cut, backturn1/4CCWforward ForTurn1/4CCW tangoclose*.

Lady Steps *Sideward cross&cut, Turn1/4CCWBackward waybackturn1/4CCW TangoClose*.

All Steps are Opposite for the Mirror-Image **Cruzada-Turning-Right.**

Notes: 1) The **Cruzada** is the way most Argentines initially Start their Tango.

2) Dancers' Feet normally Cross Tightly In-Front, but may Lock Tightly Behind.

3) Dancers' Softened-Knees Rise Straight-Kneed after Tango-Closing.

Ed Loomis [www.batango.com/loomis] describes the **Cruzada** as follows:

"A cruzada occurs any time a foot is crossed in front of or in back of the other. The lady's position at 5 of the 8 count basic [Eight-Step-Basic-Tango]."

Similar to **Trabada-Step,** and to the more General **Cruzara**. (See Cut-Step, FrontCut, CutBehind, Cut, LockBehind, Lock, Cross-Turn, and Resolucion.)

[Much data from http://nfo.net/dance/tango, and http://64.33.34.112/.dance/tangels.]

Cruzada(2): A General Argentine Coupledance word. *"Crossed feet occurs whenever the couple are stepping together on his and her right feet and then on his and her left fee, regardless of direction. The opposite of parallel feet."* (Opposing-Feet.)

[From *Tango Terminology*, www.tangoafficionado.com.]

Cruzar: See LaCruz.

Cruzara: (*kroo-THAR-uh*, Spanish for *to cross*.) With Knees Softened, a General Coupledance Movement. A **Cruzara** is a Step taken by the dancer's Foot being **Crossed Tightly In-Front** of or Behind the other Foot.

Similar to the more explicit **Cruzada**. (See Cut-Step, FrontCut, CutBehind, Cut, LockBehind, Lock, and Cross-Turn. Also see Salida-Crusada.)

Cuadrado: (*koo'ah-DRAH-do*, Spanish for *square*.) A Leadable **Argentine Tango** Coupledance Box-Step Pattern, that is danced primarily in the Milonga, Club-Tango, and Canyengue-Tango Styles.

Similar to the **Baldosa**. [See Box-Step(1), Basic-Box, Touch-Box, Jazz-Box, Left-Turning-Box, and Right-Turning-Box.]

Cuatro: (*koo'AH-tro*, Spanish for *four*.) Two Unleadable, General Spot-Coupledance Figures or Movements, Right or Left. Snappy looking; appears as if one is waving an unhinged leg back and forth. Often used in the **Argentine Tango**.

The Free-Leg is Crossed-In-Front of the Supporting-Leg, and is kept off of the Dancefloor. The Toe Points Down as the Free-Leg shin parallels the Dancefloor; both of one's legs thereby form the **Figure-Four** numeral at this instant.

Ed Loomis [www.batango.com/loomis] describes this **Cuatro** as follows:

"*A figure created when the lady flicks her lower leg up the outside of the opposite leg, keeping her knees together, and briefly creating a numeral 4 in profile. This can be led with a sacada or with an arrested rotational lead like a boleo, or it can be used, at the lady's discretion, in place of a gancho or as an adornment after a gancho.*"

Same as **Figure-Fore**. (See **Amague**.)

Cucharita: (*koo-char-EE-tah*, Spanish for *little spoon*.) A Flourishing Movement or Figure; a **Firulete Adorno**; an Embellishment used in the **Argentine Tango** and **Milonga** Coupledances.

Ed Loomis [www.batango.com/loomis] describes **Cucharita** as follows:

"*A lifting of the lady's foot with a gentle scooping motion by the man's foot to the lady's shoe, usually led during forward ochos to create a flicking motion of the lady's leg.*"

Similar to the **Castigada**. (See AnkleTrip, KneeFlick, Abrupt, Levantada, LaLlevada, Gancho, Golpes, Picados, Amague, and Frappe; all Performed while Moving. Also see Flourish, and Gesture.)

Cunita(*koo-NEE-tah*) or **Cradle** or **Hamaca**(*ah-MAH-kah*): As if rocking a cradle, **LaCunita** is a Leadable Coupledance Pattern that is danced in the various **Argentine Tangos** and in the **Milonga**. **LaCunita Gently Rocks and Pauses**. **LaCunita** dances two Measures in length in 2/4 Cut-Time; Rhythm Timing is *Slow HoldAnd, Slow HoldAnd*, consisting of two Steps plus two Taps total.

The **LaCunita** Pattern, in four Cadence Beats, is danced entirely in a Facing-Offset Position with the Lady's Head-Open. Except, from Closed Position Argentine Tango, Partners usually Couple-Rotate a 1/8 Turn Counter-Clockwise on their very first Step into their Facing-Offset Position. Partners may finally Couple-Rotate a 1/8 Turn Clockwise on their final multi-Pattern Step to return into Closed Position [Embrace(2)]. Otherwise, any Couple-Rotation, CW or CCW, while dancing the **LaCunita** Pattern, is optional.

Together, Partners Move Forward then Toe-Tap, then they Move Rearward then Toe-Tap. Upon the second and fourth Cadence Beat, Partners either **Toe-Tap-Crossed-In-Front** (Rocked Forward), or **Toe-Tap-Crossed-Behind** (Rocked Rearward), relative to their own Supporting-Foot, **without Weight** thereby applied.

Man, looking at Lady, Steps *forwardhold* Weight Forward *Toe-Tap-Crossed-In-Front*, *BackwardHold* Weight Rearward *toe-tap-crossed-behind*.

Lady, Following, Steps *BackwardHold* Weight Rearward *toe-tap-crossed-behind*, *forwardhold* Weight Forward *Toe-Tap-Crossed-In-Front*.

Pattern may be repeated and repeated.

Ed Loomis [www.batango.com/loomis] describes the **Cunita** as follows:

"A forward and backward rocking step done in time with the music and with or without chiches, which is useful for marking time or changing direction in a small space. This movement may be turned to the left or right, danced with either the left or right leg forward, and repeated as desired."

Similar to **Waltz-Balances-Forward-and-Backward** (with Points), and **Rock-with-Feet-Crossed**. [See Rock-Turn(1)&(2), Rock-Steps, Rock-Steps-Four, Rock-Back-and-Forth, Rock-Diagonally, and Forward-Rock.]

Note: May be preceded by the Pepito.

Cut-Ocho: See Ocho-Cortado.

Derecho: (*day-RAY-cho*, Spanish for the *right way; straight.*) A General Argentine Coupledance name for Standing Straight and erect.

Similar to **Postura**. (See Pinta, Eje, and Bien-Parado.) [Mostly from *Tango Terminology*, www.tangoafficionado.com.]

Desplazamiento: (*dess-plah-tham-E-en-to*, Spanish for *displacement.*) An **Argentine Tango** Coupledance Movement, **Rotary-Tango** Style. **Desplazamiento** is Displacing the Partner's leg or Foot by the use of the dancer's own leg or Foot.

(See Sacada. Also see LaLlevada, Viborita, and Arrastre.)

Develope or **Developpe** (*dayv-law-PAY* or *dev-lo-PAY*, French for *unfold* or *developing movement*): General, Unleadable, Smooth and Graceful Coupledance and Ballet Actions or Picture-Figures, normally of One-Measure duration. **Developes** are Performed by the Lady in the **Bolero**, Slow-Foxtrot, Slow-Waltz, **International Tango**, **International Rumba**, in **Roundance** Routines, in **Ballet**, and in other dances.

There are several ways to **Develope**; initially, the Free-Foot is drawn Up to the Knee of the Supporting-Leg, where there is a Forward or Sideward or even a Rearward Movement, of an unfolding and straightening of the Lady's Free-Leg En-l'-Air, followed by a Hold of this Extended leg, then a Slower Recovery. Often the Timing is *Slow And Slow*.

In **Ballet**, the Free-Foot is drawn Up to one's Supporting-Knee, then from there, it is unfolded Smoothly to Point its Toe En-l'-Air, where its leg is attempted to be Straight and parallel with the Dancefloor, but may reach only 45 degrees, and where this leg is held for perfect Control. Hips remain level and square with the direction one is Facing.

One Coupledance sample Develope is Performed as follows: Begins in Semi-Closed Position and ends in Feathered Position.

a) Lady Steps *CrossBehind*; Knee Softened, Lady's Right Ball Supports her Weight;

b) She Swivels a Quarter-Turn Counter-Clockwise;

c) She draws Up her Left Foot Outer-Heel to the Outside of her Right Knee, (sole to Inside for Ballet);

d) She Kicks, (without showing sole,) by first Waist-Level Knee-Up with Pointed Toe, then Straight-Knee with Pointed Toe;

e) Straightening her Supporting-Leg, she Holds her Left leg as straight and parallel with Dancefloor as she can;

f) She smoothly Recovers Closed.

Her Man has Stretched his Right side and Stepped *crossbehind*, applied Weight to Left Foot, Stretched Left side and views Lady's Foot Action, (with Man's chin past his shoulder.)

Inverse of **Envelope**. (See Ronde, Rond-de-Jambe, En-Dedans, En-Dehors, and Pas-de-Cheval. Also see Bicycle, and Adagio.)

Developpe: See Develope.

Dibujo: (*de-boo-HO*, Spanish for *sketching*.) Executed simply as a Flourish, the **Dibujo** is a Coupledance **Adorno** Genre of various Actions or Movements, Performed within the larger dancing **Argentine Tango** Genre.

A **Dibujo** might be Performed by either Partner during a **Corte**(2) such as a **Parada** Stop. A **Dibujo**, Executed by the dancer's Toe is doodling, squibbling or scribbling upon the Dancefloor, as if sketching Circles or other small Toe Movements.

The **Dibujo** Genre of [Stopped] **Parada Adornos**, includes the Lapiz, ShoeShine, Puntada-del-Pie, Caricias, Lustrada, Chiche, Fanfarron, Golpecitos, Zapatazo, Levantada, and the Enganche.

(See Flourish, and Gesture.)

Dip: (*dp*) Several Leadable, General Coupledance Movements or Figures, where the Free Leg Extends Forward with thighs parallel, the Knee and ankle forming a straight line from the hip, and the Toe normally Touches the Dancefloor.

(1) A Slight to severe Supporting Knee-Bend, **sinking to a Sitting Position.**

(2) A Slow **lowering of the Lady's** Body by the Man's Lead, with the Lady supporting her own Weight by use of one Supporting-Leg Rearward.

(See Corte, Curtsy, Plie, Sit-Break, Sit-Line, Chair, Drop, and Death-Drop.)

Dip-Deep: A Leadable, General Coupledance Movement or Figure, where the Man Dips his Lady Deeply. Here, the Lady is usually Dipped so Deeply that she is unable to Support her own Weight. Such a Dip looks and feels very awkward unless Skillfully Performed. The Lady should not weigh more than five-eighth the Man's Weight.

"*Ludicrusly they deep-dip, as if in sheep dip.*"   Anonymous

DobleCruz: A Leadable, Six-Measure Coupledance Pattern suitable for **Argentine** and **American Tangos.** Beginning in Promenade Position, Partners Step-Thru and Man Locks Behind as Lady Serpientes, then a Pickup and a Tango-Close.

Man dances Abrupt *diagforward* AnkleTrip *Thru sideward* toward Line-of-Dance to Loose-Closed Position *CrossBehindHoldHoldHoldHold sideturn* to Pickup *DiagForward close.*

Lady dances Abrupt *DiagForward* KneePop *thru Sideward* to Face Center-of-Hall *crossbehind FanToCrossBehind sideward CrossInFront fantocrossinfront SideTurn* to Pickup *diagbackward Close.*

Man's Timing is *Slow Slow, Quick QuickHold, HoldHold, HoldHold, HoldHold, Slow Quick Quick.*

Lady's Timing is *Slow Slow, Quick Quick Slow, Slow Quick Quick, Slow Slow, Quick Quick Slow, Slow Quick Quick.*

(See Serpiente.)

Doble-Ochos (*doe-blay-O-CHOss*) or **Double-Eights** or **Double-Ochos** or **Ochos-en-Espejo:** (*O-chos en ess-PAY-Ho*, Spanish for *eights in the mirror.*) Mainly suitable for Coupledancing the **Argentine Tango**, and possibly other Tangos and also PasoDobles. **Doble-Ochos** is one Measure long in 2/4 Cut-Time, and is only partially Leadable. Total Couple-Rotation is a Quarter-Turn Counter-Clockwise.

The Lady dances her **Ochos**(1) throughout this Figure with no change, while, as described as follows, her Man joins in and dances **Ochos** with his Lady. With Partners Moving into a very Loose-Closed Position, and Swiveling on Ball, the Man joins her as he feels his Lady begin to Turn at her **Ochos** beginning. Man's Rhythm Timing is *And slow and Quick And.*

Man, beginning with his Feet Closed, dances *Swivel1/4CCW* Shoulders-Parallel *backpoint weightback Close PickuptoFace.* Man eyes his Lady throughout the Figure, or else he looks in the directions his Lady is about to Turn.

Ed Loomis [www.batango.com/loomis] describes the **Ochos-en-Espejo** as follows:

"*The man and the lady execute forward or back ochos simultaneously, mirroring each others movement.*"

Similar to **Ocho-Abierto.** See **Tres-Ochos** for a continuation of the **Doble-Ochos.** (Also see Ochos(2), Ochos-para-Atras, Ochos-Largos, and Revolucion. Also see Salida-Modified.)

Note: May be preceded by ElAmericano.

Double-Closed-Promenade: A Leadable, two-Measure **International Tango** Coupledance Pattern, consisting of six Steps. Rhythm for 2/4 Timing is *Slow Quick Quick, Quick Quick Slow.*

Begins in Promenade Position, to Closed Position International Tango, to Promenade Position, back to the Closed Position with a Pickup. CBM on Step-Thru.

Man dances *diagforward StepThru diagforward, StepThru diagforward Close.*

Lady Follows with *DiagForward stepthru DiagForward, stepthruswivel3/8CCW Pickup close.*

(See Closed-Promenade, and Double-Open-Promenade.)

Double-Ochos: See Doble-Ochos.

Double-Open-Promenade: A Leadable, two-Measure **International Tango** Coupledance Pattern, consisting of six Steps. **Identical to Double-Closed-Promenade** except ends in Feathered Position, with Man Stepping *Forward* Outside Partner, instead of Closed Position Pickup.
(See Closed-Promenade.)

Double-Ronde: A partially Leadable, Spot-Coupledance Figure, one Measure long, suitable for International **Tango** and other dances.
Begins and ends in Closed Position International Tango. On Left Ball, Man Fans an extra-long Forward-Ronde, Sweeping his **Right** leg, as his Lady Flares a Rearward-Ronde, Sweeping her **Left** leg, then she Runs around him. All individual and Couple-Rotations and Rondes are Counter-Clockwise. Man has 3/4-Rotation total while his Lady has 1 3/4-Rotations total. Man's Timing is *longslow Quick*; Lady's Timing is *Slow quick And quick*.
Man dances *forswivel3/4CCW Close*.
Lady dances *BackTurn1/4CCW insideturnronde1/2CCW DiagForTurn* around Man *forswivel1/2CCW* to Face.
Note: Figure is usually followed by a **Man's-Ronde-Turn**.

Double-Start: In 2/4 Cut-Time, for **Argentine Tango** Coupledancing, the Leadable **Double-Start** can be the first three of several Moves to completion of the Natural-Resolution.
Danced in Closed Position Argentine Tango, both Partners Start with their Feet Together. Lady's Head is usually Open. A one-Measure long Figure, Rhythm Timing is *Quick Quick Slow*. For both Partners, the **Double-Start** is a *Quick* Sideward Touch with a *Quick* draw back, then the **Basic-Start** Side Step is Stepped.
Man Steps *touchsideward* then *recovertouch*, all in one Beat, then he Steps *widesideward* (Basic-Start) to Man's Left.
Lady, Following, Steps *TouchSideward* then *RecoverTouch*, all in one Beat, then she Steps *Sideward* (Basic-Start) to Man's Left. Lady's last Step is Shorter than Man's.
Similar but more complex than the **Basic-Start**. Usable in the Backward-Start, and American-Start. May be preceded by the Retroceso-con-LaRonda, or the Media-Luna. May be followed by the Basic-Step, ElAmericano, Pepito, or the Salida. (See Drop-Hinge.)

Double-Telemark or **Double-Open-Telemark** or **Double-Telemark-to-Semi-Closed:** A Leadable Coupledance Pattern, suitable for the Slow-**Foxtrot**, Slow-**Waltz** and **International Tango**. Consists of two Measures, seven Steps. Of the three possible Timings, one is *Slow Quick Quick, And Quick Quick Slow*.
Total Couple-Rotation is at least 1 3/4 Turns Counter-Clockwise. Begins in Closed Position International Standard or Tango, and ends in Semi-Closed (Promenade) Position.
Consists of **two Telemarks-to-Semi-Closed Figures**, except, instead of the 3/4-Turn, these are increased to a 7/8-Turn each, (Counter-Clockwise). Also, there is this "*And*"-across, where both Quickly Step-Thru and Across Left, for her Pickup to Closed Position, ready for the second Telemark-to-Semi-Closed Figure. It is best for the first Telemark to complete one Full-Turn.
(See Telemark series, and Quick-Open-Telemark.)
Note: The other two Timings are *Slow Quick Quick, Quick Quick Quick Quick*; and *Quick Quick Quick Quick, Quick Quick Slow*.

Drag(1)(*drg*) or **DrawClose:** Two Leadable, Basic Coupledance Actions, Left or Right. Drawing the Free-Foot **Slowly** Toward or to Closing with one's Supporting-Foot, **without a** Change-of-Weight.

CloseTouch is same except Movement is **Faster.** Similar to **Tango-Close.** (See Draw, Step-and-Drag, Slide, TowardClose, TurnClose, and Fan. Also see Spanish-Drag, and Spanish-Drag-with-Knee-Climb.)

Drag(2): (*Arrastre* in Spanish) A General Coupledance Action; to Pull, draw or haul along the Dancefloor, especially by force, (do not do); or, reluctant or difficult Movement; or, to prolong or retard Movement.

Same as **Arrastre.** (See Constant-Tug, and Biomechanics.)

Drape Position: A General, Leadable Coupledance Position, suitable for **Bolero, PasoDoble**, all **Rumbas**, and all **Tangos**, among other dances.

A Lay-Back for the Lady with her arms, Head and legs drooping. The Lady is **Draped**, with extreme Bending at the waist either backwards or forwards, Dead-Weight over and Across her Partner's bent forearm, with her Toes barely Touching the Dancefloor. It is very difficult for the Man to Support the fully relaxed Lady for long.

(See Lift-Bent.)

Draw (*drw* or *dr*) or **TowardClose:** Two Leadable, Basic Coupledance Actions, Left or Right, of Movement of the Free-Foot in the direction of one's Supporting-Foot. The Free-Foot is Slid without Weight toward the Supporting-Foot **without Closing.** There is **no Change-of-Weight.**

After a Step, the Free-Foot is Drawn, in at least two Counts Slow Motion, with the Free-Toe Pointed Slightly Away from the Supporting-Foot, approaching but **not quite Closing** with one's Supporting-Foot. The Free-Toe retains contact with the Dancefloor.

Similar to **Slide**(1). (See Drag, Constant-Tug, CloseTouch, TurnClose, Tango-Draw, and Fan. Also see Arrastre, Spanish-Drag, and Spanish-Drag-with-Knee-Climb.)

Drop: A Leadable, General Coupledance Action or Movement, suitable for all **Tangos**, for International **Rumba** and **Bolero**, for **DiscoCha, DiscoSwing** and all **Hustles**, and possibly for other dances.

A **Drop** is the sharp Lowering of a Body, usually the Lady's, in a Staccato fashion. In addition, a **Drop** is where the Lady's Body Weight is caught and supported by her Man, while usually some Body-part of the Lady has remained in contact with the Dancefloor.

(See Death-Drop, and Dip.)

Drop-Hinge or **The-Chair** or **Sentado-Hinge** or **LaSentada:** (*lah-sen-TAH-dah* is Spanish for *sedate*.) A possibly Leadable Coupledance Picture-Figure, at least one-Measure long, suitable for American and Argentine **Tangos**, for Slow **Waltz**, for all **Rumbas** and the **Bolero**, among other dances. Timing varies.

Man, if from a Closed position, first Steps *Backward* a Quarter-Turn Counter-Clockwise; but if from Semi-Closed position, the Man first Steps *Crossward* Thru. His second Step* is wide *sideward* and Slightly *forward*, and he applies a Softened Left Knee. Man partially Supports Lady with this Left Knee, (hence **The-Chair**.) His hips are then eased Contrabody into his Lady as he views her face. **Man Flexes his Right Knee against his Left Knee as his body Rotates Counter-Clockwise, which Leads Lady to Cross her leg.**

Lady Following, first Steps either *forward* or *crossward* Thru. Her second Step is a wide *SideTurn1/4CCW*; her third is a *crossbehind* as she continues Turning with CBM. This last Step is Well under her Body with her Left Knee Bent to Support her Weight. Her Head is Closed with chin Up, and her hips are Well Up. Then Lady's Free-Knee of her Right leg is Raised to Cross her Left Knee; her Right Free-Foot is Across against Outside of the Knee of her Left Supporting-Leg.

Similar to **Hinge**. (See Sentado-Line, Sentado-Hinge Position, Foot-Across-Knee, Foot-Across-Ankle, Hinge-with-Shape, Hinge-Line, and Hinge Position.)

Note: * May be the Basic-Start or Double-Start if dancing Argentine Tango.

Drop-Oversway-from-Closed: A partially Leadable, 1 1/2 Measure Coupledance Picture-Figure, suitable for **International Tango**. From Closed Position International Tango, begins with an approximate 3/4-Turn Counter-Clockwise in two Steps. Rhythm for 2/4 Timing is *Quick Quick Slow, Slow*.

In the first two Steps, the Man dances *forturn1/4CCW ForSwivel1/2CCW*, his Lady dances *BackTurn1/4CCW heelturn3/8CCW*.

The Staccato Picture-Figure *Slow, Slow* portion follows:

Man dances Semi-Closed and Flat *diagforward*, bending his Left Knee and Stretching Left side, with CBM to reach for Patch. Partners Facing, he views Lady, his Right Toe remains Extended and Pointed.

Lady, Striding Low, is to dance one lengthy Right Step, reaching with her Right Knee to touch the Inside of Man's Left Knee; her Step is *DiagForTurn3/8CCW*, with her Supporting Right Knee bent and her Right side Stretched. Her Left Toe is Extended and Pointed. She looks Well to her Left and Up.

(See Throwaway-Oversway.)

Eight-Count-Basic: See Eight-Step-Basic-Tango.

Eight-Step-Basic-Tango or **Eight-Count-Basic** or **European-Start:** Suitable for all **Tangos** except for the International Tango. A Leadable, Basic, Forward-Traveling Coupledance Pattern that is widely danced in Europe, especially in Finland, where it tends to be preferred over the Five-Step-Basic-Tango.

Begins and ends Facing with Feet-Together, in Closed Position, Informal or Argentine Tango. Three Measures long in 2/4 Cut-Time, and Slightly Curving CCW, this **Eight-Step-Basic-Tango** consists of a **Backward-Start** (Steps 1&2), a **Salida** (Steps 3,4,5), then a **Resolucion** (Steps 6,7,8). Rhythm Timing is *Slow Slow, Quick Quick Slow, Quick Quick Slow*.

For the **Backward-Start**, Man dances *ShortBackward backbrushwidesideward*; Lady, Following, dances *forward ForBrushSideward*, into Facing-Offset Position.

For the **Salida**, Man dances *BrushForward* Outside no Turn *forturn1/8CCW ForClose*; Lady, Following with Head-Open throughout, dances *sidebrushbackward LongBackTurn1/8CCW* Shoulders-Parallel *crossinfront* Trabada-Step.

For the **Resolucion**, Man ends dancing *forturn1/8CCW LongForTurn1/8CCW sidedrawclose* at Arch with Weight, straighten. Lady, with Head-Open, ends dancing *CrossBackTurn1/8CCW longdiagbackturn1/8CCW SideDrawClose* at Arch with Weight, straighten.

Ed Loomis [www.batango.com/loomis] describes **Eight-Step-Basic-Tango** as follows:
"*8 COUNT BASIC The first figure usually taught to beginning students after the walking steps. The 8 count basic includes elements which are used throughout the dance, although the complete figure itself is not much used socially. The name refers to counts in music, however the man is not constrained to rigidly mark a step on each count or beat of the rhythm. He is free to hold or to syncopate, or cut the beat, as the music moves him or as space on the floor around him allows. Also the figure may be danced into or out of at various points and is not always entered at the beginning. There are also shortcuts within the 8 count basic. For instance, the man may lead the lady from the cruzada at 5 directly to 2, or he may close his left foot to his right without weight on 7 and step side left directly to 2. So in actuality the positions which the dancers move through at each step are numbered as reference points. In closed dance position, they are as follows;*

"*1. The man steps back right, the lady forward left*[Backward-Start]. *Or, variations: the man settles his weight on his right leg, placing the lady on her left and holds. Also, the man may settle on his right leg, placing the lady on her left, quickly extending his left leg to his left side to point then closing back to his right leg without weight, as the lady mirrors his action with her right leg*[Double-Start]. *Or the man may step through with his right leg between the partners, leading the lady to mirror his action (espejo) by stepping through with her left leg, remaining in closed position although briefly resembling promenade position*[American-Start].

"*1. The man steps side left, the lady side right, with the man stepping slightly further than the lady*[Basic-Start].

"*2. The man steps forward right in outside right position keeping his upper body turned toward the lady in contra-body, the lady back left paralleling the man and also in contra-body. This is a common point of entry to the figure which the ladies should be aware of.*

"*3. The man steps forward left, the lady back right stretching slightly more and seeking the man's center.*

"*4. The man closes his right foot to his left with weight and rotates his upper body to face forward, leading the lady to cross her left foot in front of her right with weight (cruzada) as she finishes moving back in front of the man. Many variations for the lady begin from this position.*

(Continued)

Eight-Step-Basic-Tango: (Continued)
            "5.   The man steps forward left inside his partner (to her center), the lady back right.

            "6.   The man steps side right, the lady side left.
            "7.   The man closes his left foot to his right with weight, the lady her right foot to her left."

        Tango Primer [http://nfo.net/dance/] describes **Eight-Step-Basic-Tango** as follows:
            "*8 Step Basic Tango Start: (often called the European Start)*
            "*The so called `Eight Step Basic Tango Start' is of European origin, and somewhat ridiculed by native born Argentineans. However, there is really nothing wrong with it, but it is a `Tango Phrase and a Half' in length, and so does need a little care in dancing. If one is comfortable with it, stay with it. It is as good a Tango Start as any other start.*

            "*This 8 Step Start is also very widely used in Finland, - where the Tango is virtually the national dance. The Finnish Tango may be defined as a sub-gerne distinct from the Argentinean model. It embodies more influences from the music of the Old World perhaps than from South America. Musically the Finnish Tango tempo is slower, while the music is burdened with predominant minor keys and Slavically flavored melodies - very much in the vein of the German `schlager' Tango. Did you know that Finland has more than 2000 tango clubs? (The Japanese and some Zambians are also enamored of the dance. We have not mentioned it, but there is also a so-called `European' sub-genre of the Tango.)*"

        [See Five-Step-Basic-Tango. Also see Caminata, Paseo, Step-and-Drag, Tango-Draw, Tango-Tap, Natural-Resolution, Backward-Close-Finish, Backward-Tango-Close, Paso, and Arch(2). Also see Basic-Step(4), Continental Tango, Valentino Tango, Contest Tango, and Cafe Tango.]
        [Some data from http://nfo.net/dance/tango.]

        Eje: (*ay-HAY*, Spanish for the *axis* or *balance*.)   A General Argentine Coupledance name for the Body-Straight-and-Slim.
        Similar to **Postura**. (See Pinta, Derecho, and Bien-Parado.)
        [Mostly from *Tango Terminology*, www.tangoafficionado.com.]

        ElAmericano (*el-ah-MAY-ree-kah-no*): **ElAmericano** is an **Argentine Tango** Coupledance Figure, one Measure long in 2/4 Cut-Time.
        Mostly Leadable, its Travel to the side is useful when one's way ahead is blocked. Begins in Closed Position Argentine Tango, except just prior to Starting **ElAmericano**, the Man has Led his Lady into taking as **wide** a Step as his, to his Left.
        ElAmericano Travels shortly to the Man's Left of the direction the Man originally faces. Turning Mirror-Image, each Partner Taps first an Eighth-Turn in one direction then each Swivels a Quarter-Turn Opposite, then both Partners Step-Thru. The Figure ends with his Lady Swiveling to Face.
        Man's Timing is *Slow and Slow*, while his Lady's Timing is *slow And slow and*.
        Man dances *CrossBehindToeTapRaiseFoot* **swivel1/4CCW **StepThru*.
        Lady, Following, dances *crossbehindtoetapraisefoot* **Swivel1/4CW **stepthru **swivel1/4CCW* to Face.
        Notes: 1) * Raise Foot to where one's calf is parallel with Dancefloor.
                    2) ** Danced with one's Knees tightly Together.
                    3) May be preceded by the Basic-Start or Double-Start, as modified above.
                    4) May be followed by the Doble-Ocho.

        Elevada: (*ay-lay-VAH-dah*, Spanish for *elevation*.) See KneeFlick.

Elevadas: (*ay-lay-VAH-dahs*, Spanish for *elevated*.) A Coupledance word used by Argentines about their former dancing, before the 20th century, when they had only dirt surfaces to dance upon. **Elevadas** means dancing with Feet Raised, rather than Slid along, from the surface.

Ed Loomis [www.batango.com/loomis] describes **Elevadas** as follows:

"Dancing without keeping the feet on the floor. This was the style before the turn of century when tango was danced on dirt surfaces in the patios of tenements, low-class taverns, and on the street. Once tango went uptown enough to actually be danced on floors (wood, tile, marble) the dancers fell in love with the floor, thus we now refer to `caressing the floor'."

[See Caressing-the-Floor, and Press(1).]

Embrace or **Abrazo** or **Dance-Hold:** (*ah-BRAH-tho*, Spanish for *embrace* or *hug*.) The General Term used by Argentine Coupledancers for their various Closed Positions, when dancing their Genre of **Argentine Tango**, their **Milonga**, **Argentine-Waltz**, and other dances. Besides the famous **Close-Embrace**, there also is the **Open-Embrace**. There are Changes in the **Embrace** within the dance, as described under **Tango-Lean**.

Some people describe the **Abrazo** as "*a modified hug*", [www.totango.net/gavitowork]. [www.tangoshow.com] says "*El Tango es el baile del abrazo*", meaning "*Tango is the dance of the embrace*".

Same as **Close-Embrace-Tango**, and **Open-Embrace-Tango**. (See Argentine Tango, Milonga, and Argentine-Waltz. Also see Cuddle, Enfold, Crush-In-Closed, Loose-Hug Position, Cuddle Position, and Slow-Dancing. Also see Argentine Tango Step-Listing.)

Enganche: (*en-GAHN-chay*, Spanish for *hooking, coupling, ensnaring,* or *the little hook*.) A Flourishing Action or Movement or Figure; a **Dibujo** or **Firulete Adorno**; a teasing Embellishment used in the **Argentine Tango** and **Milonga** Coupledances.

Enganche is an Action during either Movement or Stopping (Parada), where Partners talk with their Feet, and where the Man may teasingly work his Lady over. **Enganche** is the verb for various Coupledance "*hooking*" Actions of one leg around another; a Quick, partially Leadable Genre in the **Rotary-Tango** Style. **Enganche** is a verb whereby either the Man or his Lady wraps his or her leg, from inside or outside, around their Partner's leg.

Ed Loomis [www.batango.com/loomis] describes **Enganche** as follows:

"Occurs when a partner wraps a leg around the other's leg, or uses a foot to catch and hold the other's foot or ankle."

Similar to the **Gancho** Genre. [See **Gancho** for the different kinds. Also see Continuous-Ganchos, and Front-Hook. There is the Firulete Genre of Moving Adornos, that includes the Rulo, AnkleTrip, KneeFlick, LaLlevada, Castigada, Cucharita, Gancho, Golpes, Picados, and the Amague Genre that includes the Frappe(1). And then there is the Dibujo Genre of (Stopped) Parada Adornos, that includes the Lapiz, ShoeShine, Puntada-del-Pie, Caricias, Lustrada, Chiche, Fanfarron, Golpecitos, Zapatazo, Levantada, and the Enganche. Also see Flourish, and Gesture.]

Enrosque (*en-ros-KAY*, Spanish for *to twist* or *to coil*.) or **Hooking** or **Coupling:** A Coupledance Pattern for the **Argentine Tango**, danced by the Man. While his Lady Executes **Molinetes** Circling around him, the Man Performs an **Enrosque**; e.g., the Man Spins upon one Foot, Hooking then Dragging his Free-Foot Behind, or around In-Front of his Supporting-Foot. The Man is the Hub and the Lady is the Rim.

(See Hook-Wind, Hook-Unwind, Vine, Vine-Eight, and Corkscrew. Also see Figure-Fore, and Giro.) [Much from http://nfo.net/dance/tprimer; and www.batango.com/Loomis]

Entrada or **Intrusion**: (*en-TRAH-dah*, Spanish for *entrance*; *in-TROO-the-ON*, Spanish for *intrusion*.) Terms used in Coupledancing the **Argentine Tango** Genres and the **Milonga**. **Entrada** and **Intrusion** Terms are **Adornos** where the instigating dancer places a leg or Foot between their Partner's non-reacting legs.

This **Entrada** purpose is perhaps for a Caress (*Caricia*) or a Quick Kick (*Gancho*), or perhaps to Touch or even to Push against their Partner's Foot or leg. An **Entrada** sets a format for play and emotion, all Performed using Feet and legs only. Having Stopped dancing (*Parada*), the instigator could portray tenderness, playfulness, mischievousness, or anger; while the Partner might counter with annoyment, brazeness, tenderness, shyness, playfulness, or the like.

Ed Loomis [www.batango.com/loomis] describes the **Entrada** as follows:

"Occurs when a dancer steps forward or otherwise enters the space between their partners legs without displacement."

Entregarme: (*en-tray-GAR-may*, Spanish for *surrender* or *deliver*.) A Term used in Coupledancing the **Argentine Tango** and the **Milonga**.

Ed Loomis [www.batango.com/loomis] describes **Entregarme** as follows:

"To give oneself up to the leader's lead."

(See Following, and Leading.)

Envelop: A General Coupledance Holding Action; to cover, wrap, or enclose one's Partner.

Same as **Enfold**. [See Embrace, Cuddle, Squeeze, Bundle, Snuggle, Hug, Clasp, Clutch, Grasp, Cling, Cuddle Position, Loose-Hug Position, Shadow-Enfold Position, Slow-Dancing, Cheek-to-Cheek Position, Head-to-head Position, Over-the-Heart-Hand-Hold, and Crush-In-Closed. Also see Carpa, Tango-Lean, Leaning-Into-Each-Other, and Milonguero(2).]

Envelope: (*env-law-PAY* or *en-VEL-o-pay*) General, Unleadable, smooth and Graceful Coupledance and Ballet Movements, Right or Left active leg, normally of One-Measure duration. **Envelopes** are Performed by the Lady in the **Bolero**, Slow-**Foxtrot**, Slow-**Waltz**, **International Tango**, **International Rumba**, in **Roundance** Routines, in **Ballet**, and in other dances.

There are several ways to **Envelope**; all involve a **pedalling backwards**, as on a bicycle. Rhythm and Timing varies.

One sample Envelope is Performed as follows: Begins in Semi-Closed Position and ends in Feathered Position.

a) Lady Steps *CrossBehind*; Knee Softened, Lady's Right Ball Supports her Weight;

b) She Swivels a Quarter-Turn Counter-Clockwise to Cross lower legs;

c) To smoothly **pedal backwards**, the Lady **Swipes** her Left Pointed Toe Well Forward from the Dancefloor until Knee is Straight, followed by a Lift and Knee-Bend of her Left Free-Foot to Knee-Level with Toe Pointing Down. Her Free-Foot is then Lowered to Tightly Cross her Right Foot at the ankles, where she Cuts Flat to Free Rearward her Right Foot.

Inverse of **Develope**. (See Football-Kick, and Bicycle.)

Escondido (*es-cone-DEE-do*): (Spanish for *conceal*.) In Fast Waltz Rhythm, a pursuit dance and one of the Argentine **Gato** Amalgamation of dances. The Lady is Choreographed to amorously "hide" from the Man in this **Escondido** dance.

Similar to **Fimeza**, **Bambuco**, and **Jarabe**. (See Gato-con-Pelaciones.)

Espejo: (*ess-PAY-Ho*, Spanish for *mirror*.) See Mirror-Image.

Eternal-Dance: A General Coupledance Term for Tango.

Walter Sorell writes: "*As the dance is born with man, it will exist as long as man exists. As it exists in life and nature everywhere in thousands of disguises, it will even survive man and stand at the cradle of what may come after him. Since nothing stands still but is in eternal flow whose rhythm is the universal pulsebeat of movement, the dance will be when the world will no longer be and another world will take its place.*"

Havelock Ellis writes: "*Dancing as an art, we may be sure, cannot die out, but will always be undergoing a rebirth. Not merely as an art, but also as a social custom, it perpetually emerges afresh from the soul of the people.*"

European-Start: See Eight-Step-Basic-Tango.

Exhibition-Tango: See Show-Tango, and Tango-Argentino.

Fallaway (*falwy* or *flwy*): Two Leadable, General Coupledance Movements. Beginning in Semi-Closed or Reverse-Semi-Closed Position, both Partners **Fallaway** by Stepping Backward with either Inside-Feet or Outside-Feet, carefully retaining their Body Position.

(See Left-Fallaway, Right-Fallaway, and Fallaway Position.)

Fallaway-Four-Step: A Leadable, one-Measure **International Tango** Coupledance Figure of four Steps. Rhythm with 2/4 Timing is *Quick Quick Quick Quick*. In total, there is essentially no Couple-Rotation. Begining in Closed Position International Tango, Partners Fallaway into Semi-Closed Position.

Man dances *forward* with CBM *DiagBack1/16CW* into Fallaway Position *backward* with CBM in Semi-Closed *Close* Right Slightly Rearward of Left Foot. Ends with Left Knee In for Inside Ball Touch.

Lady Steps *Backward* with CBM *diagbackspiral3/8CW* into Fallaway Position *Backward* with CBM in Semi-Closed *close* left Slightly Rearward of Right Foot. Ends with Right Knee In for Inside Ball Touch.

Similar to **Four-Step**, **Four-Step-Change**, and **Five-Step**.

Fallaway-Promenade: A Leadable, two-Measure Coupledance Pattern, suitable for the **International** and **American Tango**s. Consisting of six Steps, Rhythm with 2/4 Timing is *Slow Quick Quick, Slow Quick Quick*.

Man Quarter-Turns Clockwise then Eighth-Turns Counter-Clockwise; from Promenade Position to Reverse-Semi-Closed Position then back to Promenade Position. Lady Eighth-Turns Counter-Clockwise then Eighth-Turns Clockwise.

Man dances *diagforward StepThru* with CBM *sideturn1/4CW* to cut her off, *BackBehind* with CBM in Fallaway *backturn1/8CCW* with CBM *TangoClose*.

Lady, Following, dances *DiagForward stepthru* with CBM *SideTurn1/8CCW* toFace, *backbehind* with CBM in Fallaway *BackTurn1/8CW* with CBM *tangoclose*.

Fan: Several partially Leadable, General Coupledance Actions, suitable for all **Tangos**, **Rumba**s, **Boleros**, **ChaChas**, **Mambos**, **Foxtrots**, **Waltzes**, and for other dances. A **Fan** is a Circular Motion by the dancer's Free-Foot as the Body Turns.

Fanning can be either Rearward or Forward, and Performed by either or both Partners, and with either Foot. Fans consist of Swiveling on one Foot with the other Extended and Skimming in continual contact with the Dancefloor ('Track-the-Floor') to Fan completion. As required, the Fan may Sweep in a wide arc with Supporting Knee Well Bent, or the Free-Leg may Swing with a whip-like Movement in a small arc with legs closer Together.

(Tracking-the-Floor, in French, for Ballet, is "*a terre.*")

(See Flare, Ronde, Drag, and Draw. Also see Boleo, and Ruade.)

Fanfarron: (*fahn-faR-RRON*, Spanish for *hector* or *braggart.*) A Flourishing Movement or Figure; a **Dibujo Adorno**; an Embellishment used in the **Argentine Tango** and **Milonga** Coupledances.

Ed Loomis [www.batango.com/loomis] describes **Fanfarron** as follows:

"*A rhythmic tapping or stomping of the foot in time with the music for dramatic and emotional effect. Boisterous behavior.*"

Similar to **Golpecitos**, **Chiche**, and **Golpes**. (See Lapiz, ShoeShine, Puntada-del-Pie, Caricias, Lustrada, Zapatazo, Levantada, and Enganche; all Performed during a Parada. Also see Flourish, and Gesture.)

Fantasia: See Show-Tango(1).

Feathered-Reverse-Turn-Closed-Finish or **Open-Reverse-Turn-Closed-Finish:** A Leadable, two-Measure Coupledance Pattern used in **International Tango**. Begins and ends in Closed Position International Tango, with Feathered Position in-between. Six Steps with a 3/4-Turn Counter-Clockwise total Couple-Rotation. Rhythm with 2/4 Timing is *Quick Quick Slow*, *Quick Quick Slow*.

Man dances *forturn1/4CCW* with CBM *DiagForTurn1/4CCW backfeather* with CBM, *BackTurn1/4CCW diagforward Close*.

Lady dances *BackTurn1/4CCW* with CBM *sideturn1/4CCW ForwardFeather* with CBM, *crossinfronturn1/4CCW DiagBackward close*.

Similar to **Basic-Reverse-Turn-Closed-Finish**.

Figure-Eight: General Coupledance Term for Movements or Figures, where either or both Partners Step Steps or simply Rotate hips, in fashions that form the numeral eight.

(See Forward-Roll, Shimmy, Knee-Drape, Up-and-Over-the-Top, Arm-Waves, Body-Wave, Body-Ripple, Side-Body-Waves, Broken-Sways, Hip-Waves, Washing-Machine, Hip-Rocks, Hula-Dance, Side-Lift, Side-Rise, Body-Lift, Cuban-Hip, Cuban-Motion, and Hip-Lift.)

Figure-Eights: See Ochos.

Figure-Fore or **Four:** Two Unleadable, General Spot-Coupledance Figures or Movements, Right or Left. Snappy looking; appears as if one is waving an unhinged leg back and forth. Often used in the Argentine **Tango**, and in **Swing** and **Country-Western** dancing; also suitable for other dances.

Performed Apart from Partner, by either Partner, or by both at once in concert in Butterfly or Loose-Closed Positions. Partners Leaning-Into-EachOther throughout the Figure. Weight is never Transferred from the Supporting-Foot. Rhythm Timing is *Slow Slow.*

The Free-Leg is Crossed-In-Front of the Supporting-Leg, and is kept off of the Dancefloor. The Toe Points Down as the Free-Leg shin parallels the Dancefloor; both of one's legs thereby form the **Figure-Four** numeral at this instant.

1st *Slow:* Begins by **Swiveling** a Quarter-Turn Outward, Away from one's Free-Foot, with both Feet Pointing in one Twisted-Waist direction. The Free-Leg is Swinging Forward as a pendulum, with the Free-Toe **Brushing** then Passing the Supporting-Foot Instep, to a slight Knee-Up.

2nd *Slow:* The Supporting-Foot is **Swiveled** a Half-Turn, so that both Feet are now Pointed in the Opposite Twisted-Waist direction, forming the **Figure-Four.** The same Free-Foot is then again Swung Forward as a pendulum, with its Outer-Edge **Brushing** then Passing the Supporting-Foot Outer-Edge.

The Figure may be repeated by, again, Swiveling a Half-Turn Outward, Away from one's Free-Foot, (never transferring Weight from the Supporting-Foot.)

Same as **Cuatro**. Similar to **Curls.** (See Figure-Four Position, and Spiral-Hook.)

Finnish-Tango: See Eight-Step-Basic-Tango.

Firulete: (*fee-roo-LET-ay*, Spanish for a *quick flourish.*) An adornment, decoration, Embellishment. The **Firulete** is a General Latin Coupledance Movement Genre, most often used in the **Argentine Tango** Genre of dancing.

A Quick Gesture (Adorno) Performed between Steps, and Executed simply as a Flourish for visual effect, a **Firulete** does not interrupt the flow of the dance. A **Firulete** is complicated or Syncopated Movements Performed by the dancer, demonstrating Skill and music interpretation.

The **Firulete** Genre is the Opposite of the **Corte** (Dibujo) Genre with its interrupted dancing flow. (See Rulo, AnkleTrip, KneeFlick, Abrupt, Levantada, LaLlevada, Castigada, Cucharita, Gancho, Golpes, Picados, Amague, and Frappe; all **Firuletes** Performed while Moving. Also see Arm-Flail, Fluffing, Shoulders-Shudder, and Tick. Also see Finger-Styling, and **Finger-Flourishes**, which include Finger-Snaps, Fingers-Flick, Flaring-Fingers, Flinging-Fingers, Shaking-Fingers, Spirit-Fingers, and Circle-Hands. Also see Adorno, Flourish, and Gesture.)

Five-Step: A Leadable, 1 1/2 Measure **International Tango** Coupledance Pattern. Rhythm with 2/4 Timing is *Quick Quick Quick Quick, AndHold.* Consists of four Steps then a Body-Turn. There is only 1/8 to 1/4 total Couple-Rotation Counter-Clockwise.

Begins in Closed Position International Tango, Feathers, then Banjo, then ends with a brusque Body-Turn, where all Knees and both Heads **Abrupt**ly shift to Promenade Position.

Man dances *forward* with CBM *DiagBackward* Feathered *backward* with CBM *ShortBackward* in Banjo, *AbruptTap.* Man's Body Slightly Turns CCW, nil, CW, CCW, then Swivels In-Place 1/8 CW to open Lady. Ends with Left Knee In for Inside Ball Tap Position.

Lady Steps *Backward* with CBM *diagforward* Feathered *ForOutside* with CBM *forclose* in Banjo, *AbruptTap.* Lady's Body Slightly Turns CCW, nil, nil, nil, then Swivels In-Place 1/4 CW to Promenade Position. Ends with Right Knee In for Inside Ball Tap Position.

Similar to **Four-Step, Fallaway-Four-Step,** and **Four-Step-Change.**

Five-Step-Basic: See Five-Step-Basic-Tango.

Five-Step-Basic-Tango or **Five-Step-Basic** or **American-Tango-Basic** or **Tango-Phrase:** A Leadable, Basic Coupledance Pattern that is used in **all Tangos.** Begins and ends Facing with Feet-Together, in Closed Position Informal, Argentine Tango, or in International Tango. Two Measures long in 2/4 Cut-Time, this Basic Pattern consists of four Steps plus a CloseTouch (Tango-Close); i.e., Patterned upon the Man taking three Forward Walking Steps, a Right Sideward-Step, a Tango-Draw then a Tango-Close. Rhythm Timing is *Slow Slow, Quick Quick Slow*; (or, *slow Slow, slow Quick Hold, slow Hold.*) The Man Leads with two Ball-Steps Forward, Straight or Slightly Curved, followed by **The-Break** (Tango-Close-Finish).

Man dances *forward Forward, forward BrushSideward drawtouch* at Arch.

Lady dances *Backward backward, Backward brushsideward DrawTouch* at Arch.

[See Caminata, Paseo, Step-and-Drag, Tango-Tap, Resolucion, Natural-Resolution, Backward-Close-Finish, Backward-Tango-Close, Paso, and Arch(2). Also see Eight-Step-Basic-Tango. Also see Basic-Step(4), Continental Tango, Valentino Tango, Contest Tango, and Cafe Tango. Also see Backward-Start, Basic-Start, Double-Start, and American-Start.]

[Some data from http://nfo.net/dance/tango.]

Flare *(flr):* Several sometimes Leadable, General Coupledance Actions, suitable for all **Tangos, Rumbas, Boleros, ChaChas, Mambos, Salsas, Foxtrots, Waltzes,** and other dances.

Flaring can be either Rearward or Forward, and Performed by either or both Partners, and upon either Foot. **Flares** consist of Swiveling on one Foot with the other Extended and **Raised off the Dancefloor** to Flare completion. As required, a **Flare** may Sweep out in a wide arc with Supporting Knee Well Bent, or the Free-Leg may Swing with a whip-like Movement in a small arc with legs closer Together. Some beautiful **Flares** are as High as Hip-Level. Partners Flaring together need to **Flare** to the same Height for Styling beauty, to avoid *"flailing the air with flares."*

In **Country-Western** dancing, a **Flare** is simply a Low Kick that Skims the Dancefloor. (Aerial Flaring in French, for Ballet, is *En-L'Air.*)

(See Fan, Brush-Flare, and Ronde. Also see Leg-Crawl-with-Flare. Also see Boleo, and Ruade.)

Flat-Step or **Flat** or **Heavy-Footed:** A Basic Coupledance Movement, Stepped with No-Float. In the difficult but pure sense, **Flat-Step** is where the entire underside of one's Shoe is placed or bottomed to the Dancefloor simultaneously, as in a Stealth fashion. But in the practical sense, **Flat-Step** is Down, Bent-Kneed and Stepped Slightly Toe-First as Stepped the comedian, Groucho Marx; or, Up, Stepped Flat with a very slight Heel-Lead, Straight-Kneed like the Frankenstein monster in casts.

(See Flat-of-Foot, Low-to-the-Floor, Foot-Positions-on-Floor, Level-Progression, Tip-Toe, Step, Stamp, Stomp, and Foot. Also see Tango-Stepping.)

Flick(1) or **Back-Flick:** General, Unleadable Coupledance Actions. A **Flick** is a Quick and Light Backward Movement of the Free-Foot. A Sharp Kick Rearward with Pointed Toe and Flexed Knee.

Less Kick than **Mulekick.** More Kick than a **HeelBrush.** More explicit than a **Boleo, Latigazo, Ruade,** or a **Flicker.** [See Flick(2), and Back-Flick.]

Flick(2): Two quick, partially Leadable Coupledance Movements, Left or Right, suitable for both International and American **Tangos,** among other dances, and Performed by either the Lady or Man or both, using their Outside-Feet.

After a Forward Half-Turn Swivel on the Inside-Foot, the Opposite Toe is Extended Straight, Touching Dancefloor, then Slid to Close against Supporting-Foot, with or without Weight applied.

An option is to Mulekick then Close.

Similar to **Back-Flick.** (See Flicker, Fan, and Flare.) [Also see Boleo, Latigazo, Ruade, Mulekick, Flick(1), and HeelBrush.]

Flick(3): See Gancho, and Flicker.

Flourish or **Embellishment:** An Unleadable, Singular or Leadable with Partner, General Coupledance Genre of Actions or Movements, for visual effect. A Dramatic Gesture; or, a bold, Sweeping Movement; or, a Waving in the air; or, a Showy display.

The **Flourish** is almost the same as the **Adorno,** and **Gesture.**

(See Finger-Styling, and **Finger-Flourishes,** which include Finger-Snaps, Fingers-Flick, Flaring-Fingers, Flinging-Fingers, Shaking-Fingers, Spirit-Fingers, and Circle-Hands.) (Also see Arm-Flail, Fluffing, Shoulders-Shudder, Tick, and Samba-Tic.) (Also see ArmWork, and Free-Hand-Fashioning.) (Also see Abrupt, Head-Flick, Shrug, and Accent.) (Also see all the **Argentine Tango Adornos.** Of these, there is the **Firulete** Genre of **Moving Adornos,** that includes the Rulo, AnkleTrip, KneeFlick, LaLlevada, Castigada, Cucharita, Gancho, Golpes, Picados, and the Amague Genre that includes the Frappe(1). And then there is the **Dibujo** Genre of [Stopped] **Parada Adornos,** that includes the Lapiz, ShoeShine, Puntada-del-Pie, Caricias, Lustrada, Chiche, Fanfarron, Golpecitos, Zapatazo, Levantada, and the Enganche.)

Fluffing(1): A General Coupledance Action or Movement for visual effect. Either the Lady or the Man purposely Fluffs the Lady's skirt and/or petticoat Up during the dance.

(See Flourish.)

Fluffing(2): See KneeFlick.

Following or **Follow:** (*seguir* in Spanish) A **Follower** is one that **comes or goes after the Leader**, while a **Leader** invites the way by **going in advance**. Tenet number one for this Basic Coupledance Action is, "The Man is the Leader, but the Lady **completes** and **enhances**." Attuned, the Lady Follows her Partner's Timing, Technique, Movement and Figure Lead. First and foremost, the Lady must follow his Lead, for both Cadence and Figures, no matter the kind of contact Coupledance, Choreographed or not. She is never intent upon "dancing her own dance," even for a Choreographed Routine in a Closed Position.

Partners attempting to Coupledance but not accomplishing synchronized Cadence Together is not dancing, it's Offbeat. Coupledancing is one aspect in our modern world where the man alone does the Leading. The most difficult part in all contact Coupledancing is for the Man Partner. He must not only do his own dance, but must also Lead his Lady Partner through every inuendo of her own dance part. The Lady needs to cooperate with him fully, and Follow him as lightly and easily and unquestioningly as she can, because she depends upon him while "*Following light as a feather*." The Lady needs to correctly **react** to her Man's Movements and/or signals, either through Bodily Connections or by visual means. The excellent Lady Follower can almost instantly successfully ascertain her Leader's intentions, and then **react** accordingly. But the excellent Lady Follower does not anticipate or early guess her Leader's Lead. She waits and Follows, Attuned to her Man's intended Moves which he Communicates by his Body Lead, such as his Pitch-Point. Consequently and ideally, there is a minute delay in her **Following**, creating a Slight pressure or force exertion that is extremely important in Lead and Follow. All Steps the Lady takes must be at least a nano-second later than her Leader's Lead, otherwise she is the Leader.

The following are extracts from the *Tango-L Thread* [http://markov.iworkforfood.net/]; although written for Argentine Tango but essentially applies to most all Closed Coupledances:

"*... the leader leads with his chest and the follower follows the chest lead with her feet, or by turning her body, then the leader follows the direction of the leader with his step. For example to take a forward step for the leader, he begins with his weight clearly on his right foot, brings his upper body forward almost imperceptively, which causes the follower to step back on her right foot. He then follows her by stepping forward with his left foot. We call it the lead/follow/follow.*

"*To step to the side, ..., the leader moves his upper body very slightly to the left without twisting it or pivoting, causing his partner to step to her right; he then follows with a slightly larger step to the left with his left foot. The size of his initial upper-body movement should determine the size of the follower's step, which determines the size of his side step, which ideally will indicate the length of steps the leader plans to take in the rest of the dance.*"

There can be only one person with their hands on the steering wheel. There are many independent Ladies who won't be led by Men, not even on the Dancefloor. Such Ladies are not for any kind of Coupledancing, and this book does not pertain to them. Still, there are proper times when the Lady Partner will take over, but only for a moment and then she relinquishes her Lead. This can be helpful. She may temporarily Lead them clear of colliding with another Couple unseen by him. There are other exceptions; one is that the Lady may Lead the Man while crossing a minefield. Traditionally the Lady is the Follower, but in rare instances it is the Man that Follows his Lady. The Lady temporarily Leads whenever she is dancing **Forward**, in Closed Position in their Travel. This is because it is difficult and awkward to Lead for whoever is dancing Backwards. Also, there may some spot that suddenly creates trouble, where the Lady could conceivably take over the Lead **for an instant**, after which, her Man should immediately always say "*Thanks!*" to her in appreciation as he again takes the Lead.

(Continued)

<u>**Following**</u> or **Follow:**   (Continued)
   Follow the Man's Timing. Timing is crucial. The excellent Lady Follower is Skilled at Synchronizing to that of her Man's Rhythm. Her responsibility is to assure they dance always in **Unison**, as if they are a complete entity. She must comply with his Timing and Cadence (Rhythm), even if she prefers otherwise or considers it in error. *Perhaps he hears a different drummer. Let him step to what he hears, however measured and far away. (Anon.)* While "*tact amounts to taking a firm stand without stepping on the partner's toes*," perhaps leave it to a later session when a **Male** professional whom he respects can improve his Timing. His Partner sidekick is never his teacher, no matter how `good' she is; and visa-versa. In Roundancing, the Routine is really secondary to the Couple's Timing together, i.e., to her totally Following her Partner. Becoming lost in complex Routines sometimes causes the Follower to lose this essential point.

   Although the Lady has perhaps been thoroughly and excellently taught how to Follow, she may lack **experience** in Following. She may not have yet logged the necessary Floortime in her chosen art. With enough experience in Following Men dancers, she will undoubtably become the excellent dancer she has dreamed of achieving. This would be a true Coupledancer versus just a technician. *It is especially the man's timing that the expert lady dancer follows so well. (Anon.)* An Experienced-Dancer is an educated dancer; experience is compulsory education.

   In a Closed Position, the excellent Lady Follower does not present Limp-Arms. **Each Upper-Body must have Body-Tone** for successful Lead and Follow without Breaking-Frame. Also, a Lady viewing her Man's Feet is no help in **Following**; a beginner Lady would probably Follow better by viewing his eyes, (although not allowed in International Standard Dancing.)

   Avoid any verbal disapproval, criticism or even correction, especially during Workshop while learning Figures, Patterns, or Routines together. Even with your intimate dance Partner and certainly with a casual Partner, this is a word of caution for from either the finest to poorest of dance Partners. Instead, at the very least, there should be a smile to each other at the end of every Dance-Set, preferably with a "*thank you*" from each Partner, followed with something nice to say about their dance just danced.

   A soldier must be a good follower in order, later, to be a good leader. It is identically the same for dancers. -- Anonymous

   Following is the inverse of **Leading**. (See Frame, Poise, Togetherness, Anticipation, LaMarca, Indicate, Following-the-Follower, Lead/Follow-for-Tango, Palm-Finger-Lead-in-Closed, and Pitch.)

<u>**Following-the-Follower:**</u> A General Coupledance Term referring to cases in which the Man finds he must, perhaps momentarily, **Follow the Lady's Lead**.
   Perhaps the Lady Partner Follows poorly; perhaps she is both a stranger and a Beginner to Coupledancing, and assuming she mis-interprets the Man's Lead. Here, the surprised but Skilled Leader compensates by changing the Figure(s) he had in his mind in order to accommodate her wrong Movement(s). This tests the Man's improvisation Skills for continuous Smooth dancing, and usually entails momentarily **Following-the-Follower**.
   The Leader should estimate what his Follower is able to handle then keep their dance within her handleable boundaries, i.e., he should avoid Out-Shining his Partner.
   (See Leading, Following, and Lead/Follow-for-Tango.)

Foot-Across-Ankle or **Cross-Foot-Across-Ankle** or **Cross:** Two Unleadable, General Coupledancing Stances, Left or Right, suitable for **Tango**, **Country-Western**, and other dances.

Free-Knee is Forward. Free-Foot is held slightly Raised, Across and against Outside of ankle of Supporting-Foot.

Similar to **Wrapped Position**(2), **Sur-le-Cou-de-Pied**, and **Foot-Across-Knee**. (See Cou-de-Pied, Sous-Sus, Cross-Touch, Crossed-Feet Stance, Coupe, and Cut. Also see Drop-Hinge, Pas-Croise, Sentado-Line, Sentado-Hinge Position, and Knee-Up Position.)

Foot-Across-Knee or **Cross-Foot-Across-Knee** or **Cross:** Two Unleadable, General Coupledancing Stances, Left or Right, suitable for **Tango**, **Country-Western**, and other dances.

Free-Knee Up with Free-Foot Raised Across and against Outside of Supporting-Foot Knee.

Similar to **Foot-Across-Ankle**. (See Drop-Hinge, Sentado-Line, Sentado-Hinge Position, and Knee-Up Position.)

Forward-Ochos: See Ochos(2).

Forward-Rock: Two Leadable, one-Measure, three-Step, General Spot-Coupledance Figures, Left and Right. Rhythm Timing is usually *Quick Quick Slow*.

Rocking Movements, danced in a Closed Position, with Man's Weight twice Moving Forward as Lady's Weight twice Moves Rearward. No Turning. Not more than 75 percent of one's Weight is Transferred when Rocked Forward. No Foot Position change after first Step, (last two Steps are Weight-Changes In-Place,) although Feet may Lift slightly off the Dancefloor.

For **Forward-Rock-Left**, Man Steps *forward Backward forward*, as Lady Steps *Backward forward Backward*.

For **Forward-Rock-Right**, Man Steps *Forward backward Forward*, as Lady Steps *backward Forward backward*.

Opposite of **Rock-Back**. (See Planted-Foot, Rock-Back-and-Forth, Rock-Diagonally, Rock-with-Feet-Crossed, and Rock-Side-to-Side. Also see Rock-Steps, Rock-Steps-Three, Rock-Steps-Four, And Rock-Apart. Also see Rock, Rock-Steps, Rock-Turn, Electric-Kicks, Rock-the-Boat, and Rocking-Chair.)

Four-Step: A Leadable, one-Measure **International Tango** Coupledance Figure of four Steps. Rhythm with 2/4 Timing is *Quick Quick Quick Quick*. In total, there is usually no Couple-Rotation.

Begins in Closed Position International Tango, Feathers to Banjo, then ends in Promenade Position with Feet Closed.

Man dances *forward* with CBM *DiagBackward* Right-Side-Lead *backward* with CBM in Banjo *CloseBackTurn1/16CW*. Ends with Left Knee In for Inside Ball Touch.

Lady Steps *Backward* with CBM *diagforward* Left-Side-Lead *ForOutside* with CBM in Banjo *diagbackturn1/4CWclose* to Semi-Closed. Ends with Right Knee In for Inside Ball Touch.

Similar to **Fallaway-Four-Step**, **Four-Step-Change**, and **Five-Step**.

Four-Step-Change: A Leadable, one-Measure **International Tango** Coupledance Figure of four Steps. Rhythm with 2/4 Timing is *Quick Quick Quick Quick*, or *Quick Quick And Slow*. Begins and Ends in Closed Position International Tango. There is 1/4 total Couple-Rotation Counter-Clockwise.

Man dances *forward* with CBM *swivel1/4CCWDiagBackward* Right-Side-Lead in Closed *close* Left Slightly Forward of Right *ShortSlipBackTurn1/16CCW*.

Lady Steps *Backward* with CBM *Swivel1/4CCWdiagforward* in Closed *Close* Right Slightly Rearward of Left *shortslipforturn1/16CCW*.

Similar to **Four-Step**, **Fallaway-Four-Step**, and **Five-Step**.

Frappe: (*frah-PAY*, French for a *frozen sherbert*.) The **Frappe** is a Coupledance Action, an Adorno or Flourish. The **Frappe** is an **Amague** useful in all **Tangos**. The **Frappe** is a **harsh Stamp** to the Dancefloor, Executed by the Man immediately preceding the Couple's next Dramatic Movement or Action. His **Frappe Stamp** warns or announces of a coming Move that will be severe or powerful in nature.

(See Stomp, and Heel-Strike.) (Also see AnkleTrip, KneeFlick, Abrupt, LaLlevada, Castigada, Cucharita, Gancho, Golpes, Picados, and Rulo; all are the Firulete Genre of Adornos Performed while Moving.) (Also see Fanfarron, Chiche, Puntada-del-Pie, and Golpecitos.)

Free-Tango: See Neo-Tango.

Freeze-and-Melt: A General Coupledance Term that refers to the varying of one's Rhythm Timing, for that estatic interplay between dancers and music. Possibly Leadable.

Freeze-and-Melt is a moment of complete in-Action, and then a Sharp, Clean Action or Movement, Smartly Performed.

"*The sparkling contrasts between posed immobility and sudden flashing action.*" [From "TAP!" by Rusty E. Frank]

Similar to **Suspension**, and **Light-and-Shade**. (See Hold, Pause, Hesitation, Pose, Hover, Collect, Break, Respite, Ooze, and Positura. Also see Start, Flashy, Individual-Style, Showmanship, Charm-and-Finesse, Charisma, Panache, Beat-Foot-Forward, and Flash-and-Pzazz.)

French Tango: See Cafe Tango.

Freno: (*FRAY-no*, Spanish for *brake* or *stop and hold*.) See Balanceo, Arrepentida, Pause, and Check.

Front-Hook: An Unleadable, sexy, General Coupledance Action, suitable for all **Tangos**, the **Bolero**, both **Rumbas**, **Cabaret**, and others. Facing, the stabilized Man normally places his Right leg Forward, to which his Lady **Front-Hooks** her Left leg around the outside of his ready calf, Toe Down. The Man may Turn his Toes Outward for stability to Support her.

(See Around-the-World. Also see Ganchos, Continuous-Ganchos, and Enganche.)

Front-Ochos: See Ochos(2).

Fueye: See Bandoneon.

Full-Weight: A General Coupledance Action or Term. **Full-Weight** is when the dancer's complete Weight is applied.

(See Partial-Weight, Change-of-Weight, Body-Weight, and Partial-Step.)

Fundamentals-of-a-Dance or Rudiments-of-a-Dance or Basics-of-a-Dance: General Coupledance Terms. Every dance has topical items that can be noted, such as a certain dance's characterizing Footwork, Holds, Postures, Leading, Following, arm and Body Styling, hip Motions, Head use or positions, directional Movements, etc.

Gancho (*GAHN-cho*, Spanish for *hook* or *ensnarement*.) or Flick or Hook or Leg-Hook or Hook-and-Recover: A Gancho is a Coupledance Firulete Adorno "*hooking*" Action of one leg around another; a Quick, partially Leadable Argentine Tango Action or Movement in the Rotary-Tango Style. There were Ganchos Flicked in Buenos Aires before 1978.

A Bending-at-the-Knee Gancho is a sharp and rather harmful-looking Swipe or Hooking Action by one's Foot, Low, catching around the Partner's ready Leg, (see Enganche.) One Partner's Gancho is usually followed by a reciprocating Gancho from the other Partner. Partners must cooperate in Executing Ganchos to avoid hurt. There are Inside and Outside Ganchos, either Right or Left-Footed, and around either a Weighted-Foot or a Free-Foot. (See Front-Hook.)

The following is from *Tango Terms* [www.tangoberretin.com/alex]:

"*Gancho: Literally `a hook' where one person flicks the leg between the legs of his/her partner*."

Ed Loomis [www.batango.com/loomis] describes Gancho as follows:

"*The hook: Occurs when a dancer hooks a leg sharply around and in contact with their partners leg by flexing the knee and releasing. May be performed to the inside or outside of either leg and by either partner.*"

The following are nine different Argentine Tango Gancho Coupledance Figures, with twelve different ways to Flick:

Examples 1-4: Behind-Gancho-to-Weighted-Foot (see Open-Finish-Gancho),
Example 5: Right-Behind-Ganchos (or Open-Reverse-Double-Gancho),
Example 6: Left-Behind-Ganchos,
Example 7: Right-Inside-Ganchos (see Corte-Double-Gancho),
Example 8: Left-Inside-Ganchos,
Example 9: Lady's-Behind-Gancho.

Similar to Enganche. (See Continuous-Ganchos.) (Also see Picados, Golpes, Rulo, AnkleTrip, KneeFlick, Abrupt, Levantada, LaLlevada, Castigada, Cucharita, Amague, and Frappe; all Firulete Adornos Performed while Moving.) (Also see Flourish, and Gesture.)

Note: At times, Ganchos are inappropriate at a Milonga, and it is best to remain unpretentious.

Gato (*GAH-toe*): (Spanish for *cat*.) A type of Argentine Folkdance Amalgamation, each Performed by two or more Couples, and characterized with much finger snapping. Music is a type of very Fast Waltz in steady quarter notes.

Similar to Chacarera, and Jarana. (See Gato-con-Pelaciones, and Escondido.)

Gato-con-Pelaciones (*GAH-toe-cone-pay-lah-see-OWN-nay-es*): (Spanish for *cat with stories*.) An Argentine Fast Waltz Genre of dances, each Performed by two Couples. Their "stories" have a diversified content; either amorous, philosophical, or political.

(See Gato, and Escondido.)

Gauchos or **Gaucho-Turn** (*gcho trn*): A Leadable 2 1/2-Measure, nine-Step Coupledance Pattern, suitable for Argentine and American **Tangos**. In a Closed Position throughout, **Gauchos** are Counter-Clockwise Rocking Turns, a Half-Turn total Couple-Rotation. Timing is *Quick Quick Quick Quick, Quick Quick Quick Quick, Slow.*

Man dances *rockforturn1/8CCW LatinCrossBehind rockforturn1/8CCW LatinCrossBehind, rockforturn1/8CCW LatinCrossBehind forward Sideward, tangoclose.*

Lady Following, dances *RockBackTurn1/8CCW latincrossinfront RockBackTurn1/8CCW latincrossinfront, RockBackTurn1/8CCW latincrossinfront Backward sideward, TangoClose.*

Gaucho-Turn: See Gauchos.

Giro or **Giro-Turn:** (*HEE-ro*, Spanish for *turning round.*) A **Giro** is a **Turning Step or Figure**; a normally Leadable, Basic Coupledance Pattern Genre of the **Argentine Tango** that has several Variations. **Giros** are various Patterns where Movement sequences from the Man to the Lady and vice-versa. **Giros** are without Opposition-Footwork, but not especially upon Same-Feet. The most common of the **Giro** Genre are the many different **Ochos**.

Several other **Giro** Patterns are as Follows: While his Lady Performs **Molinetes** Circling around him, the Man may Circle CW or CCW, perhaps Sharply, perhaps Slowly; or instead, perhaps the Man Executes an **Enrosque**. And sometimes the Man will Spiral placing his Free-Toe In-Front, (see Figure-Fore.)

The combined **Giro** and **Molinete** both appear and feel out-of-this-world! But, for both Man and Lady, such Patterns are difficult to learn and Perform Well. They say Balance, Timing, Musicality, width and direction all enter into its perfection. The Man is the Hub and the Lady is the Rim.   (See Media-Vuelta. Also see Vine, Vine-Eight, Cross-Wind, Cross-Unwind, Hook-Wind, Hook-Unwind, and Corkscrew.) [Much from http://64.33.34.112/.dance/tangels; www.tangocanberra.asn.au; www.batango.com/loomis; and http://nfo.net/dance/tprimer.]

Giro-Turn: See Giro.

Giving-Weight: A General Coupledance Action, referring to when two dancers allow each other to Support perhaps a fourth of their Body Weight, especially during Couple-Rotations. **Giving-Weight** could be acceptable if for safety and/or mutual enjoyment, although Weighing Down one's Partner can be unacceptable.

Similar to **Weight-Connection**, and **Support**. (See Counter-Balance, Counter-Movement, Counter-Sway, Leaning-Into-EachOther, Leaning-Away-from-EachOther, Constant-Tug, Stable, and Steady. Also see Hanging-On, and Clinging-Vine. Also see Frame, Poise, Posture, Stance, Position, and Basic-Hold.)

Golpecitos: (*GOL-pay-SEE-tohs*, Spanish for *tiny toe taps.*) A Flourishing Movement or Figure; a **Dibujo Adorno**; an Embellishment used in the **Argentine Tango** and **Milonga** Coupledances.

Ed Loomis [www.batango.com/loomis] describes **Golpecitos** as follows:
"*Rhythmic tapping done with a flat foot on the ball or underside of the toe as an adorno.*"

Similar to **Chiche, Fanfarron**, and **Golpes**. (See Lapiz, ShoeShine, Puntada-del-Pie, Caricias, Lustrada, Zapatazo, Levantada, and Enganche; all Performed during a Parada. Also see Flourish, and Gesture.)

Golpes: (*GOL-pays*, Spanish for *toe taps*.) A Flourishing Movement; a **Firulete Adorno**; an Embellishment used in the **Argentine Tango** and **Milonga** Coupledances.
Ed Loomis [www.batango.com/loomis] describes **Golpes** as follows:
"*With a tilted foot tap the floor with the toe and allow the lower leg to rebound keeping the knees together.*"
Similar to **Picados**. Also similar to **Golpecitos, Chiche**, and **Fanfarron**. (See Rulo, AnkleTrip, KneeFlick, Abrupt, Levantada, LaLlevada, Castigada, Cucharita, Gancho, Amague, and Frappe; all Performed while Moving. Also see Flourish, and Gesture.)

Grace-Fluidity-and-Purpose: A Coupledance saying for describing "*the dance*" in General; a marvelous Performance attained with an intended and desired effect.
"*The music's sound, the rhythmic dance,   The happy faces flushed, the feet*
Time keeping to the music's beat,   The lovely limbs, the tender glance!
O what more beautiful than this?" -- Arthur Peterson
"*When you dance, it seems to me   As if, in a tall wood   A thousand birds of dawn*
Awake to greet the day   Outgoing one another there   With lovely things to say." --
Anonymous
Similar to **Elegance-of-Movement**, and **Esthetic-Effect**. (See Graceful, Elegante, Fluidity, Skillful, Articulation, Audience-Appeal, Confidence, Strike-Ability, Class-Act, Clapping, and Flash-and-Pzazz. Also see Con-Amore, Amoroso, Delicado, Mignon, and Dolce.)

Grapevine or **Vine** or **Weave:** **Vine** is abbreviation for **Grapevine**. These are various Leadable, General Coupledance Figures or Patterns, danced Continuously Left or Right, Traveling Sideward, delineating a Zig-Zag or Weave-type Pattern with the Feet. Suitable for many dances.
A **Grapevine** is Basically a series of four Steps; (1) *Sideward*, (2) *CrossBehind*, (3) *Sideward*, and (4) *CrossInFront*. The **Grapevine** may begin with any one of these four Steps. Most begin *Sideward*, then a *CrossBehind* or *CrossInFront*, another *Sideward*, then a *CrossInFront* or *CrossBehind* (Opposite prior Stepped), etc. Series may be repeated and repeated.
Some say a **Grapevine** Moves to the Right or Left, having a Sideward Step, one Step Crossing Behind, plus another Sideward Step, then an Ending such as a Kick, Brush or Scoot.
The same people say the Grapevine becomes a **Weave** when there are two or more Sideward Steps plus two or more Crossing Steps, In-Front and Behind alternating, or visa-versa.
(See Weave, Quick-Vine-Eight, Vine-Behind, Front-Vine, Open-Vine, Vine-Apart-and-Together, Vine-Three, Vine-Four, Vine-Six, and Vine-Eight.)

Habanera or **Havanaise:** (*ah-bah-NAY-rah*, Spanish for *a Cuban dance.*) The **Habanera** was an outgrowth of **Danza-Habanera**, which had been imported into Cuba from Spain about 1825. From about 1850, the **Habanera** was a Traditional Cuban **Folk** Contra-Dance in 2/4 Time, Duple-Meter. The **Habanera** music theme is Syncopated with a fragile, Swaying Rhythm, and varies greatly.

About 1900, the **Habanera** developed into the Cuban **Habanera-del-Cafe**, which became popular about 1915. The **Habanera-del-Cafe** is thought to have influenced in the evolution of the **Argentine Tango,** noted as follows:

Ed Loomis [www.batango.com/loomis] describes the **Habanera** as follows:

"A side together side together stepping action entered with a side chasse, commonly used by the man as he leads backward ochos for the lady in crossed feet. An Afro-Cuban dance from the mid 19th century which contributed to tango."

(See Milonga. Also see ContraDanza-Spanish, ContraDanza-French, ContraDanza-Cubano, Danza, and Danzon.)

Half-Moon: See Media-Luna.

Hamaca: See Cunita.

Harvest-Moon Tango: See Contest Tango.

Head-Fan: A Leadable, General Coupledance Movement. A Sharp Turn of one's Head in the Opposite direction then back again.

Similar to **Head-Fkick**. (See Abrupt, and Tick.)

Head-Flick: A Leadable **International Tango** Coupledance Half-Measure Action. In Promenade Position with Lady's Head Open, both abruptly look at each other, or even more of a Head Turn, then Heads Turn Quickly back to Open-Her-Head. Timing is *And Quick.*

Man may Flick his Lady's Head by a Lead from his Knee, by a Light, Quick Motion then releasing. He Flicks the inner side of his Left Knee to his Right against the outside of her Right Knee, which in turn Flicks her Head. In combination with his Knee-Lead, the Man also Torques his Upper-Body Clockwise and glances Clockwise. Or the Lady may do her own **Head-Flick**.

Similar to **Head-Fan, Abrupt,** and **Tick**. (See Salute, Staccato, Knee-Lead, and Head-Flick-Link.)

Head-Flick-Link: A Leadable, crisp and Dramatic Coupledance Figure, suitable only for the **International Tango.** Timing is *Quick Quick and Quick,* one-Measure, two Steps.

Changes from Closed Position International Tango to Promenade Position. The first Step for both is with CBMP.

Second Step places both their Weights on Inner-Edges of Inside-Feet. Each Outside-Foot is Slightly DiagForward and parallel with one's Inside-Foot, and with Inner-Edge Touching, but with Heel Slightly off the Dancefloor, and with Outside Knees veering Inwards. Their Stance is Low. Lady is **Tango-Saluting** and riding Man's hip, and their Knees are intertwined.

Head-to-Head Position or **Forehead-to-Forehead Position:** An American informal, sometimes comical and perhaps romantic Coupledancing Stance. Leadable, Facing Partners touch foreheads Eye-to-Eye, if Partners are nearly the same Height. **Head-to-Head Position** is assumed mostly during the dancing of the **Onestep**, but also during **Medium-Foxtrot** and the **Argentine-Tango.**

The Couple is spaced Apart some four to twelve inches at their waists, but with normal Offset of Feet. They dance with Softened-Knees, and his Left Hand Lightly holds her Right fingertips Low below their waists. The Man's Right Hand holds his Lady at her side. Often this Pose is Travel-Coupledanced with extreme alternate Shoulder-Lead by both Partners.

[See Cheek-to-Cheek Position, Loose-Hug Position, Cuddle Position(1), Over-the-Heart-Hand-Hold, Slow-Dancing, Envelop, Clasp, Clutch, Grasp, and Cling. Also see Carpa, Tango-Lean, Leaning-Into-Each-Other, and Milonguero(2).]

HeelBrush or **Heel-Scuff** or **Back-Brush:** Two General, Unleadable Spot-Coupledance Actions, Left or Right, Mirror-Image Opposites.

The **Right-HeelBrush** is danced by first Smartly Brushing **Rearward**, one's Right Heel against the Dancefloor, immediately followed by one's Right Toe Brushing and a Slightly Raised Right Knee. All is Performed next to one's Left, Supporting-Foot.

The **Left-HeelBrush** is danced Mirror-Image Opposite.

Less Kick than a **Mulekick,** or even a **Flick**(1). More explicit than a **Boleo, Latigazo,** or a **Ruade.** [See Flick(2), and Back-Flick.] (Also see Well, Clean, Swing-Time, Riff, and Shuffle.)

Heel-Strike or **Heel-Floor-Strike:** An In-Place, General Singular or Coupledance Movement, particularly for the **Tango, PasoDoble** and **Flamenco.** **Heel-Strike** is also a **Tap-Dance Genre** Movement, useful in **Line-Dancing** and in other dances.

With Feet Together, as in the **Tangos,** one might **Heel-Strike** one Heel once to the Dancefloor with a Stamp sound while Standing, preperatory to immediately Stepping-Out with the same Foot.

Heel-Strike is almost the same as, and is an alternate for the **Hit-Heel.** Similar to **Stamp.** (See Heel-Raps, Heel-Drop, Choppy, Dropping-the-Heel, Heel-Marching-Step, Marcando, Taconeo, and Zapateado. Also see Heel-Lead, Step, Flat-Tap, and Stomp. Also see Stampers.)

Hijacking or **Stealing-the-Lead** or **Lead-Stealing:** General Coupledance Terms for a Basic Coupledance Action by the Follower. **Hijacking** has occurred whenever the **Follower temporarily assumes the Lead** from the Leader, **consciously,** and at times with the Leader's approval.

The following is an excerpt from *Raper's Dance Dictionary,* [www.dancedictionary.com]:

"***Hijacking:*** *The follower takes control of a step pattern and extensions* [Pattern(1)] *to execute some advanced interpretive styling. When the follower has completed their moves they will turn the lead back over to the leader -- similar to placing a period at the end of a sentence. During the Hijacking sequence the leader will normally do something that will not interfere with or detract from the follower's material. Also see Funk Swing.*"

Similar to **Back-Lead,** and **Aggressive Following.** [For Hijacking aproveable to the Leader, see Shine, Break-Endings, Break-A-Way Glossary for Break-A-Way(3), SugarPush-Fancy, Break-Pattern, Challenge-Step, and Dummying. Also see Following-the-Follower, Anticipation, Nip-and-Tuck, Under-Lead, Over-Lead, Leading, Following, Seguir, Suivre, and Lead/Follow-for-Tango.]

Hooking: See Enrosque.

Incline or **Penche** or **Penchee** (*pahn-SHAY*): Various possibly Leadable, General, Coupledance Actions. To **Lean** or slant **Out-of-Balance**, usually on one leg with one's other leg Raised, possibly Performed by one Partner. Or, to **Bend** one's Head or Body as in a Nod or Bow.
(See Tilt, Over-Balance, Tips, AnkleTrip, Sway, Sway-To-and-Fro, and Totter.)

Indicate: Referring most often to the Man's unique method for Leading Argentine Coupledancing, i.e. **LaMarca**, especially for the **Argentine Tango** and **Milonga**. When Leading either of these two dances, the Man first **Indicates** to his Lady what Move she is to make. As the Lady makes that Move, then the Man Follows to complete that Move. In an Embrace, the Man **Indicates** mainly both with his Upper-Body Movement and with his Right Hand, but at times also by his Change-of-Weight.
(See LaCruz for an example. Also see Lead/Follow-for-Tango, Palm/Finger-Lead-in-Closed, Leading, and Following.)

Individual-Style: A General Coupledance Term regarding the Style of an individual dancer. This dancer may have a complimentary Charm-and-Finesse, even Charisma, or there may be a derogatory overall Style that is detrimental to that dancer's own interest; perhaps a display of conspicuous, ostentatious, or gaudy dancing.
(See Flash-and-Pzazz, Panache, Shine, Class-Act, Audience-Appeal, Light-and-Shade, Smartly, Ooze, Freeze-and-Melt, Expand, Confidence, Constant, Impact, Juice, Bring-Down-the-House, Strike-Ability, and CareFree-Way.
On the other hand, see Making-a-Show, Out-Shining, Flaunting-It, Austere-Line, Breaking-Frame, Posterior-Protrusion, Slumped-Torso, Round-Shouldered, Chicken-Wings, Limp-Arms, Stiffness, Straight-Kneed, Head-Bowed, Tilted-Head, and Affectation.)

Inertia: A Basic Coupledance Term; the tendency of the body to Resist acceleration; or, Resistance to Movement, Action or Change.
(See Biomechanics.)

Intensity: A General Coupledance Term; the depth of feeling of an Action or Movement; or, the relative degree of Force or strength.
(See Pulse, Heavy, and Lightly.)

International Dance: An Amalgamation, consisting of the International Standard and Modern Smooth Coupledancing, and the International Latin and Rhythm Coupledancing Genres. Of these, the Modern Smooth and Rhythm Coupledancing Genres are the American versions of International Dance, when relating to Competitions.
(See International Style, International Standard Division, International Latin Division, English-Style, Costume, and Blackpool.)

International Standard-Style or Standard Dances or International Standard Division or International Ballroom Division or International Modern or International Smooth or International Modern Smooth or Modern Dances or Modern-Style-Ballroom-Dancing: All are Competition Coupledance classification Terms for the same thing; most are obsolete. The Term, "Standard Dances" supercedes the former Term "Modern Dances" that had been in use since the 1920s. International Standard-Style is a sub-heading under International Style, (see same.)

International Standard-Style Figures, Patterns, and Technique have been agreed upon and formalized by the ISTD. International Standard, American Smooth, International Latin, and American Rhythm, are all Terms used to describe and broadly categorize their different Styles of Competitive Coupledancing. Techniques for these four overall Styles have seen many changes throughout the years. All of these Styles are further categorized by placing each in either a Closed-Division or in an Open-Division, and then, for fairness, still further categorized in detail as to the Style and Skill level of each participating couple, i.e., the ISTD Syllabus is essentially divided into Bronze-Level, Silver-Level, and Gold-Level, (see Competition-Levels, and International System.) Every Competing couple chooses and signs up accordingly.

Wearing Tail-Suits and Ball-Gowns, International Standard refers to the five Competition Traveling-Coupledances; the Rhythm Styles of International Slow-Waltz, International Tango, International Viennese Waltz, International Slow-Foxtrot, and the International Quickstep. All five of which are technical and precise, and are required to be danced almost exclusively in a Closed Position. These Standard Dances all Progress Counter-Clockwise around the Line-of-Dance.

Highly Stylized and intimidating to some dancers, Figures and Patterns for the International Standard-Style are sacrosanct with no deviation allowed. They are characterized by very precise elements of Technique, such as in Footwork, Rise-and-Fall, and amounts of Turn. With unique Elegance-of-Movement and with popularity throughout the world, the International Standard-Style is similar to the American Smooth-Style except Partners must remain Closed. Also, Tempo is normally Slightly Slower. These five dances require quite different Skills than those for the corresponding International Latin-Style of dances.

(See Competition-Categories, International System, Disciplined, Structured, and Travel-Dancing. Also see ABC, CID, DSFR, DTV, ICAD, ICBD, IDO, IDSF, ISTD, JDSF, NCA, NCDTO, NCSG, NDCA, NSD, NTA, RDTA, SGA, UCWDC, URDC, USABDA, USDSC, WD&DSC, and WSDC.)

International Tango or **Tango International** or **English-Tango:** A highly Disciplined, Rhythm Traveling-Coupledance, that has been lumped together with the International-Style of Standard Traveling-Coupledances at Competitions. This Formal, Competitive, distinctively structured, **International Tango** differs greatly from the many other Tangos, except for its similar **Tango American-Style** cousin. For instance, compared with the Soft Argentine Tango's emphasis on complex leg Movements, the **International Tango** has the Staccato Action emphasizing the proud Torso and Head.

During 1920 and 1921, the Continental Tango was standardized at a conference in London, and during the 1930s the staccato actions merged into the **International Tango** Choreography.

Danced at DanceSport events, the **International Tango** includes Slow-Foxtrot and Slow-Waltz Figures, with pronounced CBM but with no Body-Flight. This Tango is certainly NOT the *dance of love*. The required Tango Hold is quite different than that for the other International-Style of Standard Traveling-Coupledances, (see Salute.) It creates a tighter Hold for Quick Staccato Action. Intense, brittle and unsmiling, this dance is characterized by precise, Abrupt Head and Body Movements, which are then contrasted with very Slow, Stiff but catlike Movements, with dramatic Poses. These Staccato impressions apply a "punch" in the right places, e.g., a Staccato-like application to each Quick-Lead Step and Turn entry.

In 2/4 or 4/4, or sometimes 4/8 Time, its Rhythms vary. Danced on the One-Beat only, with sometimes Split-Measures, ideally at 32 to 33 Bars per minute Tempo, (28 to 34). Except for the Chase(4), most every one of its Patterns or Figures Curves Counter-Clockwise.

See **International Tango Step-Listing**. [Also see **International Tango Competition-Step-List**; and Tango, American Tango(1), and Argentine Tango.]

International Tango Competition-Step-List: All Steps listed below are described elsewhere in this book. The following may be without ISTD or NCDTO approval. See **International Tango Step-Listing**.

Bronze: Walk, Progressive-Side-Step, Closed-Promenade, Rock-Turn, Reverse-Turn-Closed-Finish, Back-Corte, Progressive-Link, Reverse-Turn-Open-Finish, Progressive-Side-Step-Reverse-Turn, Open-Promenade, Forward-Rock-Left, Forward-Rock-Right, Natural-Twist-Turn.

Silver: Promenade-Link, Basic-Reverse-Turn-Closed-Finish, Back-Open-Promenade, Four-Step, Fallaway-Promenade, Outside-Swivel-Link, Outside-Swivel-and-Tap, Brush-Tap.

Gold: Fallaway-Four-Step, Oversway, Four-Step-Change, Chase.

International-Tango-Hold: See Closed Position International Tango.

International Tango Step-Listing: International Tango Movements, Figures and Patterns, (or Steps,) are listed together below.

All Steps listed below are described elsewhere in this book.

Some of the following listed Steps may be without NCDTO or ISTD accreditation.

See **International Tango Competition-Step-List.** (Also see Tango, American Competition Tango, and Argentine Tango.)

The following International Tango Steps are listed in alphabetical order:
Abrupt, Arch.   Back-ContraCheck, Back-Corte, Back-Flick, Back-Open-Promenade, Back-Twinkle, Backward-Close-Finish, Basic-Reverse-Turn-Closed-Finish, Brush-Tap.   Chair, Chair-Forward-Poised Position, Change-Feet-Tap, Change-of-Sway, Change-Point, Chase, Chasse, Closed Position for International Tango, Closed-Promenade, ContraCheck, ContraCheck-and-Switch, Counter-Promenade.   Develope, Double-Closed-Promenade, Double-Open-Promenade, Double-Telemark, Drop, Drop-Oversway-from-Closed.   Envelope.   Fallaway-Four-Step, Fallaway-Promenade, Fan, Feathered-Reverse-Turn-Closed-Finish, Five-Step, Flare, Flick, Forward-Rock-Left, Forward-Rock-Right, Four-Step, Four-Step-Change, Front-Hook.   Head-Flick, Head-Flick-Link.   Knee-Flick, Knee-Up Position.   LaPuerta, Leg-Crawl Position, Leg-Wrap Position, Link, Lunge, Lunge-Line.   Man's-Ronde-Turn, Mini-Telespin.   Natural-Pivot-Turn, Natural-Promenade-Turn, Natural-Twist-Turn.   Ochos, Ochos-para-Atras, Open-Promenade, Outside-Swivel-and-Tap, Outside-Swivel-Link, Oversway, Oversway-with-Extension.   Pickup, Progressive-Link, Progressive-Side-Step, Progressive-Side-Step-Reverse-Turn, Promenade-Ending, Promenade-Link, Promenade Position for Tango, Promenade-Sway, Promenade-Tap, Promenade-to-Counter-Promenade.   Quarter-Beats, Quick-Open-Telemark. Reclining-Lady, Reclining-Lady-with-Develope, Reverse-Fallaway-Slip, Reverse-Pivot, Reverse-Pivot-Half, Reverse-Turn-Closed-Finish, Reverse-Turn-One-Half, Reverse-Turn-Open-Finish, Rock-Back-Left, Rock-Back-Right, Rock-Turn, Ronde, Ronde-Aerial, Ronde-Floor, Ronde-Forward, Ronde-Rearward-and-Slip, Ronde-Rudolph, Ronde-Rudolph-and-Slip, Ronde-Split, Rumba-Cross.   Salute, Same-Foot-Lunge, Side-Corte, Side-Lunge-Change-of-Sway, Side-Lunge-Left, Spanish-Drag, Stairs, Stalking-Walks, Sway-ContraCheck, Syncopated-Whisk. Tango-Switch, Telemark-from-Left-Outside-to-Semi-Closed, Telemark-to-Semi-Closed, Telespin, Telespin-to-Semi-Closed, The-Break, Throwaway, Throwaway-Oversway, Traveling-Swivel.   Viennese-Turn.   Whisk.   X-Line Position.

Intrusion: (*in-TROO-the-ON*, Spanish for *intrusion*.) See Entrada.

Inwards-and-Downwards-Style: A General Coupledance Term. Here, the essence of one's Movements is introverted and inward-looking, where one's Relaxed Weight remains Down and Low, covering only a small space. One's arm Movements are Closed and Curved Inwards around one's Body. Ballet Training is helpful here but not necessarily required for satisfactory Performance.

Dance Style examples are: Spot-Dancing, Flamenco, Swings, Balboa, Hustles, Slow-Twostep, Salsa, Mambo, ChaCha, and Argentine Tango.

Opposite of **Outwards-and-Upwards-Style.** (See Spanish Dance, Pedestal-Dancer, Spot, Spot-Dancing, Cante Jondo, and Introverted-Dancer.)

Junta: (*hOON-tah*, Spanish for *bringing together* or *closing*.) A General Argentine Coupledance word.

The following is from *Tango Terminology*, *www.tangoafficionado.com*:

"*Junta: From juntar - to join or bring together (as in, one's feet or knees);*
Close: In Tango it is essential that the ankles and knees should come together or pass closely by each other between each step to create an elegant appearance, preserve balance, and to communicate clearly the completion of the step to one's partner. This applies equally to the man and the lady."

(See Tango-Stepping.)

KneeFlick(1) or **KneePop**(2): A **Kinesics**. An Unleadable, General Singular dance Movement. A Dramatic Accent having a characteristic Tango look, an embellishment for effect. A **KneeFlick** is a Quick horizontal Flicking of either one or both Knees. The nearly instantaneous **KneeFlick** Starts by its Cocking Slightly Inwards then Flicking Slightly Outwards and Slowly Returning to Neutral. **KneeFlicking** both Knees simultaneously is a rather ugly Movement.

[See Knees, Knee-Pop(1), Knee-Lead, Head-Flick, and Knee-Drape.]

KneeFlick(2) or **Fluffing**(2) or **KneePop**(2): A **Kinesics**. A Lady's Unleadable Action, either danced Singularly or while Coupledancing. Two *Quick* Beats long, and suitable for all **Tangos**, **PasoDobles**, and **Flamencos**, among other dances.

After the Lady may have prepared by first Flashing from Closed to Promenade Positions, with no Foot Movement, her **KneeFlick** is often Performed as the Lady begins to Step-Thru from Promenade Position. In Promenade, purposely, the Lady's Inside Knee is momentarily Flicked Up to toss and Fluff her skirt Up as she Steps. The Lady Performs a High Knee-Up with Toe Pointed Down, then her Inside Foot Quickly Steps to the Dancefloor.

Note: Her Man, in conjunction, may Perform an **AnkleTrip** one Beat after her **KneeFlick**.

[See Knees, KneeLift, Knee-Bend, Knee-Drape, and Knee-Up Position.]

LaCobra or **LeCobra:** Both an **Argentine** and **American Tango** Coupledance Pattern from two to six Measures long. This fun Step begins and ends in Semi-Closed Position for Tango, with a Step-Thru in-between. The Man Slinks Clockwise around his Partner with Forward-Swiveling Strides. The Man is the Rim-Partner while the Lady is the Hub-Partner.

Probably repeating, each actual **LeCobra** portion is two Measures long, with a Half-Turn Couple-Rotation, and consists of three Steps and a Hold, 2/4 Timed *Slow Slow, Slow Slow*.

The Man Dances *forstride ForCrossLowLongSwoop, Swivel1/2CWOnBallRise fortouchhold*.

Following, the Lady dances *ShortForward forcrosslowshortswoop, spiral1/2CWonballrise ShortForTouchHold*.

Note: The Man might Start the **LeCobra** Pattern with the Man's Football-Kick and a CW Swivel-half, after a Left Forward Step of his in Semi-Closed.

LaCruz or **Cruzar:** (*lah-KROOth*, Spanish for *the cross*. *Cruzar* means *to cross*.) Use of these words are often referring particularly to several different **Crossing-In-Front Movements** or Figures. There is **LaCruz** Left or Right, Executed while Coupledancing the **Argentine Tango** or **Milonga**, in which much **Crossing** is common for both.

When dancing either of these two dances, the Man first Indicates for his Lady to most often **Cruzar** her Left Foot In-Front of her Right Foot.

Some note that **LaCruz** is the Lady's Position at Count 5 of the Eight-Step-Basic-Tango. Same as **Trabada-Step**. (See Cruz, Cruzara, Cruzada, and Crusado.)

[www.batango.com/loomis; and www.tangocanberra.asn.au]

Lady's-Behind-Gancho: A partially Leadable, one-Measure **Argentine Tango** Coupledance Figure, in the **Rotary-Tango** Style. Begins after Man has **Sandwich**ed his Lady's Left Protruding Toe. Rhythm Timing is *Slow Slow And*.

Lady is first Led to Step Forward, onto her Right Foot, Across Man's Left Foot. Next, Man Checks her at her waist, preventing any Forward Stepping of Lady's Left Foot, causing Lady to Transfer her Weight Rearward, as Man, his Weight Rearward, Bends his weightless Left Knee and Freezes. With Lady's Knees Together, she Mulekicks her Right Foot Rearward, beneath her Man's Left thigh.

(See Gancho, and Flick.)

Note: May be followed by another **Sandwich** then the Ochos.

LaLlevada (*lah-zhay-VAH-dah*, Spanish for *to transport/carry*) or **Barrida** (*bar-RRAY-dah*, Spanish for *sweep*) or **Sweep** or **Corrida-del-Pie** (*koR-RREE-dah del pe-AY*, Spanish for *run of the foot*) or **Slide-of-the-Foot**: LaLlevada is an **Argentine Tango** Coupledance Adorno (i.e. Embellishment or Flourish) of the **Firulete** Genre and of other Figures; a Foot Lead Action Executed by the Man. LaLlevada is in the **Rotary-Tango** Style, and always ends as the **Parada** ended. The actual **Llevada** is relocating his Lady's leg by carrying, using his own leg, from one point to another, Traveling either on or off of the Dancefloor.

Ed Loomis [www.batango.com/loomis] describes this **Llevada** as follows:

"*Occurs when the Man uses the upper thigh or foot to `carry' the lady's leg to the next step. Barridas interspersed with walking steps in which the man takes the lady with him across the floor.*"

The following is one **Llevada** in detail:

One Measure long in 2/4 Cut-Time, Figure permits from 1/4- to 3/8-Turn total Couple-Rotation Clockwise. Man's Timing is *And slow Slow*. Lady's Timing is *hold Slow*.

Man dances *Swivel1/4CWtouch** Facing *widesideward* ***LeadSlideCrossTouch* in a CCW arc.

Lady, Eyeing Man and Following, at first is forced to *hold* her Position. ***Swivel1/4CWslidetouch*.

Notes: 1) * Man Sandwiches Lady's Left protruding Toe for an instant.

2) ** Man Swivels Lady with his Right Heel Slightly clear of floor. Lady allows Man to Slide her Left Foot to 1/4-Turn her.

3) **LaLlevada** is often repeated up to three times.

4) May be preceded by the Sacada.

5) May be followed by the Sandwich.

Same but more explicit than **Barrida**, and **Arrastre**. Similar to the **Sacada**, the **Desplazamiento** the **Cucharita**, and even to the **Castigada**. (See Levantada, Rulo, Castigada, Cucharita, Gancho, Golpes, Abrupt, Picados, Amague, and Frappe; all Performed while Moving. Also see Flourish, and Gesture.) [Some data from http://nfo.net/dance/tprimer.]

LaMarca or **Marcacion** or **The Mark** or **Mark:** (*lah-MAR-kah*, Spanish for *the lead, mark* or *sign.*) An **Argentine Tango** Coupledance Term. **LaMarca** is used **to transmit the Man's Lead**, (Movement, Direction, Timing, spacing,) immediately prior **to his Lady's Following** his various **Marcacion** methods.

The following is from *Illustrated Tango Dance Steps;*   http://nfo.net/dance/tprimer:

"*La Marcacion:*

"*Tango differs somewhat from the leading and following techniques of other dances in that there is something called `La Marcacion', or more simply `la Marca'. On occasion, a Tanguera (Tango-woman) will sometimes stop and simply wait. If asked why, she might reply, `No me Marcastes', I didn't get a `mark'. It is somewhat difficult to explain on a printed page.*

"*Often the leader will use his hands. The leader should have his right hand just under his partner's shoulder blade. When beginning a Turn, the leader may use a little pressure from the Heel of his hand to initiate a turn to his left, or pressure from his Fingers to initiate a turn to his right. When the Lady feels the Leader's hand pressing on the left side of her back, she knows that a turn to her right is being called for, - and vice versa.*

"*Mostly the leader's Upper Body sets the directions. Most `Marks' are given by the Leader's upper body.  For example, when the `La Resolucion' ends, both the Leader and follower are in the `start' position for the next dance figure.  The Leader might then just lift a shoulder over his Right foot (or LF if desired).  This is a `Mark' to the lady that he is not going to move, and she is free to do some `Adornos' -- ANY adornos that SHE chooses. When she is done, the man may drop his shoulder or adjust his Weight for the next figure. Sometimes, (signaling for an Ocho for example) the leader will slightly twist his upper body to indicate the direction of his (or her) next steps.*

"*Often the leader will use his Weight. For example, in the Body change above, the Lady was free to do some Adornos. When Done, the leader exhibits a Weight change from one foot to the other to start the next figure. This Weight change tells his partner that they are now about to move again.*

"*Lastly, it's important for a leader to know where he wants to go. Knowing this, it can be passed on to the partner, - even if only subliminally.*"

Same as **Indicate**, and **Lead/Follow-for-Tango**. [See Leading, Following, and Palm/Finger-Lead-in-Closed. Also see Embrace(1).]

Lame-Duck or **Castle-Lame-Duck:** A **Dipping Movement** that resulted in a **Novelty Fad** Coupledance popular about 1914, certainly in Utah and probably throughout the United States. Some say more than a hundred new Coupledances were invented between 1912 and 1914. **Vernon and Irene Castle** invented many of these, and one was this **Lame-Duck.**

Following is from *Lame duck (tango)* - [http://en.wikipedia.org/wiki/]:

*"The **lame duck** is a position in tango.*

"The dancers slightly separate, clasp hands, and face forward. The man steps forward with his right foot and the lady with her left, dipping with their right knee as they take the next step. The steps are repeated."

The actual **Lame-Duck** portion of this dance was **their Dipping Movement** that simulates lameness while the Couple Traveled Forward in a loose Promenade Position. Certainly the Right Knee was dipped, but it is uncertain whether or not the Left Knee was also dipped.

(See Merengue-Basic-Movement. Also see the Castle-Walk, Valse-Classique, Castle-Tango, Last-Waltz, Castle-Combination, and the Maxixe; all written by the Castles. Also see Animal-Dances, the Boston-Dip, Bunny-Hug, Gaby-Glide, Hug-Me-Close, Shiver-Dance, and Turkey-Trot; which were all novelty Fad dances in vogue in the 1910s. Also see Saltair Pavilion.)

LaMilonguita: See Milonga.

Lapiz: (*LAH-pith*, Spanish for *pencil*.) An Unleadable, Singular, General Coupledance Action for visual effect; a Dramatic gesture, a scribbling Movement for Showy display. The **Lapiz** is of the Dibujo Genre, usually Performed during a Parada [Corte(2) Stop]. The **Lapiz** may be used during various dances by either Partner, but usually by the Man.

For the **Argentine Tango** Genre, especially for the **Rotary-Tango** Style, the **Lapiz** is the Man-Partner's **Adorno** that he often Performs while Leading his Lady in a **Molinete**, as well as while dancing other Patterns. To Execute this **Lapiz**, the Man **Pauses to trace a Circle**, (or Circles, CW or CCW,) upon the Dancefloor with his Toe or with the inside edge of his Free-Foot, perhaps immediately after Swiveling upon his other Foot, all-the-while in some Closed Position. Or the Man may be actually Turning while Executing his **Lapiz.**

Ed Loomis [www.batango.com/loomis] describes the **Lapiz** as follows:

"Tracing of circular motions on the floor with the toe or inside edge of the working foot, while turning or waiting on the supporting foot. These may vary from small adornments done while marking time to large sweeping arcs which precede the lady as she moves around the man in molinete."

El Lapiz is an **Adorno** that is similar to a **Rulo**, and more explicit than a **Dibujo** or **Firulete.** (See ShoeShine, Puntada-del-Pie, Caricias, Lustrada, Chiche, Fanfarron, Golpecitos, Zapatazo, Levantada, and Enganche; all Performed during a Parada. Also see Flourish, and Gesture.)

LaPuerta or **Tango-Fan:** A Leadable, one-Measure Coupledance Figure, suitable for the American and International **Tangos.** Rhythm with 2/4 Timing is *Slow Quick Quick.*

Begins in Reverse-Semi-Closed or Left-Open-Facing Position; both Partners *StepThru* in CBMP with Inside-Feet, *Swivel* 1/2 Toward each other, then both *FlickStepThru* with new Inside-Feet, Ending in Promenade Step-Thru Position. Option is *FootballKick* instead of *Flick.*

(See Outside-Swivel-and-Tap.)

Latigazo: (*lah-TE-gah-tho*, Spanish for *whip*.) An **Argentine Tango** Term for describing a Whipping Action of the leg, as in a **Boleo**.
        [See Ruade, Mulekick, HeelBrush, Back-Flick, Flick(1)&(2), Ochos-Picante, and Shuffle.]

Lead/Follow-for-Tango or **Chest-Lead(2):** Although almost all is the same for most all other Closed Position **Lead/Follow** Techniques, certain particular **Lead/Follow** Technique is **unique** when assuming the **Close-Embrace** Position for Argentine Coupledancing. Argentine Coupledancing includes the **Argentine Tango** Genre, the **Milonga** Genre, and the **Vals** or **Argentine-Waltz**. Compare the **Leading** and **Following** writeups for general dancing, contained herein, with what follows.
        This first following portion of extracts from the *Tango-L Thread* [http://markov.iworkforfood.net/]; although written for **Argentine Tango**, still essentially applies to most all Closed Coupledances:
        "... the leader leads with his chest and the follower follows the chest lead with her feet, or by turning her body, then the leader follows the direction of the leader with his step. For example to take a forward step for the leader, he begins with his weight clearly on his right foot, brings his upper body forward almost imperceptively, which causes the follower to step back on her right foot. He then follows her by stepping forward with his left foot. We call it the lead/follow/follow.
        "To step to the side, as in what is generally called step 2, the leader moves his upper body very slightly to the left without twisting it or pivoting, causing his partner to step to her right; he then follows with a slightly larger step to the left with his left foot. The size of his initial upper-body movement should determine the size of the follower's step, which determines the size of his side step, which ideally will indicate the length of steps the leader plans to take in the rest of the dance.
        "All of this happens in a split second; it is almost imperceptible by either the follower or anyone watching, but the follower will do her part unthinking (that's the key!) unless she is determined not to. The technique presupposes good posture on the part of both dancers -- diaphragm up, forward and strong, shoulders relaxed, back and down, lower body grounded in the floor."
        Continuing with this second portion of extracts from the *Tango-L Thread* [http://markov.iworkforfood.net/] for the **Argentine Tango** Genre, which contains marked differences with most all other Closed Coupledances:
        "... the three most important rules for following are 1, the posture mentioned above, 2, maintaining as strongly as possible a parallel position to her partner with her upper body, and 3, la colocacion de los pies, the habit of bringing or brushing through the ankle bones and knees or thighs on each step and stopping with feet together and touching (or sandwiching her partner's foot if it is in the way.
        "Leaders ... indicating the lead and then following are the better dancers.
        "... we propose her a step, then she decides how and when the step is taken (just like in real life), then we followed her and try to step just a fraction of a second after her. This approach makes the worker appear smoother because the focus point is her step and not the worker's.
        "... this is leading by guiding: showing a way for the follower to move, then WAITING to see if and when the follower responded before initiating his ACCOMPANYING movement.

(Continued)

<u>**Lead/Follow-for-Tango:**</u>   (Continued)

"... *the leader initiates the movement, either as a `proposal' or `by showing the way' or doing precisely both by using the chest. Then the woman, the follower, executes the step and the man finishes the movement. The whole process takes fractions of seconds. ... the leader decides how big the step should be by stepping immediately and chronologically with her, guiding the length of the step and arriving at the end at the same time, many leaders will intend that the lady takes a slightly smaller step than his.*

"*The experienced leader is very gentle in his lead.*

"... *the man suggests the lead *and waits for the lady to follow.*

"*What we are talking about is to lead properly in the sense that: the leader feels the music, decides what move to execute as a corporal expression of the feelings that such music awakens in him, then he proceeds to communicate to the lady what he wants to do, she receives his message and moves, *then he completes the movement. The message is conveyed by the chest, and the frame.*

"*It is very interesting when a message to move is conveyed to the lady without any movement of the feet of the leader. An example of this happens when after a barrida of the man there is an `intention' a motionless lead for the woman to sweep (drag) back or when there is an indication for her to do a sacada after a sacada of the man. This `intention' conveyed by a motion of the upper body without moving the feet seems to be almost telepathic.*

"*There are many ways to lead, with the chest for instance, both partners crossing their arms at the back while there is contact at the upper chests, or similarly keeping contact only at the forehead.*

"*The lead should be initiated at the right moment, after the follower has placed her weight on the proper foot and not before. It should be gentle, also clear so that it is understood without any possible doubt, sufficient time should be allowed for the follower to complete the movement and express herself artistically.*"

Similar to or the same as **LaMarca**, and **Indicate**. (See Close-Embrace, Open-Embrace, and Off-Balance, under **Tango-Lean**. Also see Carpa, Leaning-Into-EachOther, Cheek-to-Cheek Position, and Closed Position Argentine Tango. Also see Palm/Finger-Lead-in-Closed, and Following-the-Follower.) [Also see Embrace(2).] (The Argentine Tango Genre consists of Linear-Tango, Rotary-Tango, Tango-de-Salon, Canyengue-Tango, Petroleo-Tango, Tango-Orillero, Tango-Apilado, Milonguero-Tango, Club-Style Tango, Tango-Nuevo, Liquid-Tango, and the Show-Tango. The Milonga Genre consists of Tango-y-Milonga, Milonga-Candombera, and Milonga-Portena.)

Leading or **Lead:** (*marcar, llevar,* and *guiar* in Spanish) A Basic Coupledance Action. Although the Timing is almost instantaneous, a **Leader** invites the way by **going in advance,** while a **Follower** is one that **comes after the other.** **Leading** is to Guide or Escort one's Partner is an Action traditionally delegated to the Man. The Man is in control of their Timing, Footwork and headings. In general, Coupledancing is dancing together in Unison, Moving as one, with his Lady being Attuned to him in harmonious accord. A healthy and socially rewarding Exercise, but not democratic. Coupledancing is innately autocratic, with a Leader and a Follower. Women cannot have it both ways; an independent woman is a woman who dances alone.

    Leading is non-verbal communication that Initiates and continues Movement, i.e., **Leading** is either physically Connected or there is visual communication of the Man's intended Action through his Bodily Movement. Guidance for his desired Direction or Rotation is Initiated and usually accomplished by his Body, Hands, fingers and/or arms. **Each Upper-Body must have Body-Tone** for successful Lead and Follow without Breaking-Frame.

    "The pants Lead the dance," since in Closed Position Travel-Dances, the **Lady dances mostly Backwards.** It is difficult and awkward for whoever is dancing Backwards to Lead. Coupledancing's tenet number one is, "The **Man is the Leader,** but the Lady **completes** and **enhances.**" As an indication of direction, the Man Invites and Directs his Partner into **Following** his Figure, Pattern or Routine. Communicating, the Man's Lead should be clear and firm, rather than aggressive by a rough Push or Pull.

    Partnered union consists of two Bodies Moving Together in harmony in the dance. In order to achieve harmony, it is not possible for both persons to be in control simultaneously of the functioning of the Partnership since each may have slightly different (or entirely different) ideas of the proper Direction and Tempo while only one Direction and Tempo in any case can prevail.

    Varying the Man's Lead: In Leading, the Man must remain aware of his Partner's need. He must always "invite" her. He must never force her to follow. Conversely, the Man must supply at least minimal Lead, so as to prevent his Lady from dancing off on her own, or to prevent her from taking the Lead unless he so desires.

    The man needs to vary his Lead according to his Partner's need:

    a) Depending upon the Lady - from a beginner dancer to the polished Follower, from the independent Lady who subconsiously leads to the timid lady who is afraid to step.

    b) Depending upon the type of dance - for instance, a Figure in impromptu Ballroom may be Led more than the same Figure in a Choreographed "Round" with which the Lady is very familiar.

    c) When the lady is unskilled or reticent at Following, or if she is attempting to Lead, it feels to the Man like he is driving a large vehicle without power steering. He will quickly tire due to sore arms. Instead, she should be "*light as a feather*" in his arms, attuned to his almost imperceptibly light Lead. Such resistance to being Led is a pain to both.

    The Man also sets the Pace: In addition to Following his Lead, the Lady needs to Follow the Timing set by the Man, which is his right, for their dancing a particular dance. Say the orchestra is playing a Waltz at about 100 BPM, (Slightly Slow.) Say our couple had Performed this identical piece before, dancing it precisely at its "Cadence locations" as prescribed if Competing, (Slightly Lagged on its Primary-Downbeat, etc.)

    (1) Now say the Man, just for fun, leisurely decides to substantially Lag its Primary-Downbeat until they almost fall back to the next proceding Beat behind. And say he also Lags all other Beats to where they just barely stay with the Count. A very Sedate fun state!

(Continued)

<u>Leading</u> or **Lead:**   (Continued)

(2) Or say the Man, just for fun, sprightly decides to dance this same Waltz up On-the-Beat, as if they were Marching it but with Float; dancing in Time with the music Cadence, where if their shoes had taps, the taps would Tap precisely at each constant background drumbeat. Exciting!

As a Competing Couple, they would be graded down considerably if they danced according to either (1) or (2), BUT, both are the Man's perogative to which the Lady is supposed to Follow, and to which an excellent Follower, in tune with her Man, CAN Follow.

In rare instances in Closed Position, it is the Lady that temporarily Leads, since it is that Partner **dancing Forward** that must Lead. It might be mentioned that a fresh Couple dancing Together is somewhat like a new marriage. Of course the Man is the Leader, **but---**. As each fancy Figure or Pattern is danced, there has to be a **concensus** between them in order to result in some reasonable success, some satisfaction for both, in their dance-of-the-moment. The Man must **compromise** if his Lady isn't capable of Following sufficiently; perhaps not enough Turn, even though he has Led it properly. Here, the Man would be required to Smoothly **Adjust** accordingly, in order for their successful mutual pleasure. In this sense, the **Man also Follows** a bit. **Agreement** is reached between them, with neither overpowering. Instead, the Man **Invites** his Lady-of-the-moment through his Repertoire of Moves.

There may some spot creating trouble, where the Lady could conceivably take over the Lead **for an instant,** after which, her Man should immediately always say *"Thanks!"* to her in appreciation as he again takes the Lead.

Avoid any verbal disapproval, criticism or even correction, especially during Workshop learning Figures, Patterns, or Routines together. Even with your intimate dance partner and certainly with a casual partner, this is a word of caution for from either the finest to poorest of dance partners. Instead, at the very least, there should be a smile to each other at the end of every dance set, preferably with a *"thank you"* from each Partner, followed with something nice to say about their dance just danced.

Leading is the inverse of **Following.** (See LaMarca, Indicate, Following-the-Follower, Pitch-Point, Frame, Poise, Togetherness, and Pitch.)

<u>Leaning-Into-EachOther</u>: A Leadable with cooperation, General Coupledance Action; Supporting each other by Leaning, usually in Butterfly Position, such as when dancing Sand-Step and in certain Patterns or Figures in ChaCha, Mambo and West-Coast-Swing.

A Couple assuming the **Close-Embrace** Position should be **Leaning-Into-EachOther** at times when dancing the Milongo, the Val, and most any of the Argentine Tango Genre. That is, in a different fashion, a Couple in a Closed Position can be **Leaning-Into-EachOther** for lengthy times while dancing such as the Argentine Tango, as described under **Tango-Lean.**

Similar to the **Tango-Lean.** Opposite of **Leaning-Away-from-EachOther.** (See Support, Counter-Balance, Giving-Weight, and Weight-Connection. Also see Embrace, and Carpa.)

<u>LeCobra</u>: See LaCobra.

<u>Left-Behind-Ganchos</u> or **Open-Natural-Double-Gancho:** A Leadable with cooperation, two-Measure **Argentine-Tango** Coupledance Pattern.

Man in Left-Outside Position on Right Standing-Foot; **Man Flicks** Behind Lady's Left Standing-Foot with his Left Foot and they Change-of-Weight, then **Lady Flicks** Behind Man's Left Standing-Foot with her Left Foot and they Change-of-Weight.

(See Gancho, and Flick.)

Left-Hip-to-Hip Position or **Left-Sombrero Position** or **Left-Waist-Swing Position:** A Leadable, Basic Coupledancing Stance, suitable for American **Tango**, **Rumba**, and the **Bolero**, and for other dances. Same as **Left-Outside Position except Left hips are touching**, Left arms are around Partner's waists. Right arms are Up above their Heads for Tango and Rumba, but spread horizontal for Bolero.

Similar to **Left-Star Position**, and to **Left-Hip-Turn Position**. Mirror-Image Opposite to **Hip-to-Hip Position**. (See Left-Outside Position, Left-Shoulder-to-Shoulder Position, and Left-Loose-Hug Position.)

Left-Inside-Ganchos: Two, Leadable with cooperation, two-Measure **Argentine-Tango** Coupledance Patterns, Lady's or Man's.

After a Forward-Check in Closed-Position, (no Contra,) both Recover and Hold with Weight on both legs and with Left Foot Forward. One Partner Flicks their Left Foot Inside the other's Left leg and they Recover, then the other Partner Flicks Inside the first Partner's Left leg and they either Hold or Recover.

(See Ganchos and Flick.)

Left-Outside Position: An **Argentine Tango** Coupledance Stance, Facing with Partner to one's Left, Left-Hip-to-Hip and with Shoulders-Parallel. Man Lowers her Right Hand, and there is CBMP since they look at each other.

Leg-Crawl Position: An Unleadable, Lady's Coupledance Stance, suitable for all **Tangos**, **PasoDobles**, **Rumbas**, **ChaChas**, **Mambos**, **Salsas**, and for the **Bolero** and other dances.

With Partners Facing, Except that her Man Quarter-Turns his Body Counter-Clockwise from Facing the Lady, so that she can **Slide** her Left Knee Up her Partner's Right leg, with his Left Side-Stretched and with his Head-Open. She may curl her Heel around to the Inside of his calf or Knee.

Similar to **Leg-Crawl-with-Flare**. (See Leg-Wrap Position, and Spanish-Drag-with-Knee-Climb.)

Leg-Crawl-with-Flare: An Unleadable, Lady's Coupledance Figure, suitable for all **Tangos**, **PasoDobles**, **Rumbas**, **ChaChas**, **Mambos**, **Salsas**, and for the **Bolero** and other dances.

Beginning in some Closed Position, the Lady partially Breaks-Apart from her Partner, Opening-Out perpendicular and Spreading her Left Free arm Away, perhaps horizontally. From this Position, the Lady Performs a High Forward Flare to Close with her Man, as her Man Quarter-Turns his Body Counter-Clockwise from Facing the Lady, so that she can **Slide** her Left Knee Up her Man's Extended Right leg, with his Left Side-Stretched. With his Right arm wrapped around her, she cuddles her Head on his chest and shoulder.

(See Flare, and Leg-Crawl Position. Also see Leg-Wrap Position, and Spanish-Drag-with-Knee-Climb.)

Leg-Stretch-On-Arm or **Splits-On-Arm:** An Athletic, **Cabaret**-Style, Unleadable, General Coupledance Stance, Performed mostly in Choreographed Argentine or American **Tango** expositions. The Lady, with both legs straight in a full **Splits** condition, hangs her (usually Right) leg in the crook of her Partner's (usually Left) arm.

[See Split, Supported-Splits, Extension(1), and Aerial-Splits. Also see Spanish-Drag-with-Knee-Climb.]

Levantada: (*lay-vahn-TAH-dah* is Spanish for *raised.*) The **Levantada** is an **Argentine Tango** Coupledance **Adorno** Movement, a doodling gesture, a sign to Partner, usually Executed by the Lady in exasperation during a **Corte**, (with their Feet Apart, they having abruptly stopped dancing.)

With her Knees remaining Together, the Lady Performs the **Levantada** by Raising her Free-Foot to where her shin parallels the Dancefloor. Then, **Swiveling** on her Supporting-Ball, she Slowly **Swipes her Free-Foot from Side-to-Side.** Most often, the **Levantada** is Executed as a Flourish, just for show. Instead, she might Perform the **Puntada-del-Pie** to show her irritation at the delay.

Of the **Argentine Tango Adornos**, there is the **Firulete** Genre of **Moving Adornos**, that includes this **Levantada**, the **Rulo, AnkleTrip, KneeFlick, LaLlevada, Castigada, Cucharita, Gancho, Golpes, Abrupt, Picados,** and the **Amague** Genre that includes the **Frappe**(1). And then there is the **Dibujo** Genre of [Stopped] **Parada Adornos**, that includes this **Levantada**, the **Lapiz, ShoeShine, Puntada-del-Pie, Caricias, Lustrada, Chiche, Fanfarron, Golpecitos, Zapatazo,** and the **Enganche.** (Also see Flourish, and Gesture.)

Level-Progression or **Flat-Dancing** or **Flat-Travel** or **No-Float:** General Terms, Coupledancing using level Movement **without Rise-and-Fall,** i.e., dancing Flat with absolutely no *Up-Down* Movement, i.e., dancing that emphasizes intricate Rhythms largely **Low-to-the-Floor.**

As with a glass of water Balanced upon the dancer's Head, **Level-Progression** is Low and Flat with Softened Knees and with Hesitant Body Movement, tentatively feeling its way, catlike. Maintaining a Level Movement throughout the dance requires Knees to be excessively Softened; down like Groucho!

(See **Tango** for No-Float example. Also see Horizontal Rhythm, Flat-Step, Skate, Stealth, Slink, Slither, Skim, and Flat-Turns. Opposite of Floating, Vertical Rhythm, and Bobbing.)

Light-and-Shade: A General Coupledance Term that refers to the varying of one's Rhythm Timing, for that estatic interplay between dancers and music. Possibly Leadable.

Light-and-Shade adds extra dimension to the Flow and Fluidity of Body-Rhythm, and is the ultimate experience sensed by Couples empowered by this **Light-and-Shade.** As with painting a picture, varied **Timing** creates a more **Light-and-Shade** effect to the dancer's picture. Not only are there *Slow*s and *Quick*s, but there are *And*s and *A'*-Steps for the dancer's use.

Light-and-Shade refers to this manner by which excellent dancers HighLight and Soften their marvelous Movements to blend with their music's fluctuations, including its melody. Onlookers are pleased to note that the Couple Freezes as the melody abruptly holds, and that they Accelerate and Decelerate in accord with music and melody.

Smartly is the "*light*" in **Light-and-Shade.** **Ooze** is the "*shade*" in **Light-and-Shade.** Similar to **Freeze-and-Melt.** (See Musicality-and-Expression, Impact, Juice, Syncopation, Individual-Style, Showmanship, Flashy, Charm-and-Finesse, Charisma, Panache, Flash-and-Pzazz, Beat-Foot-Forward, Break-Ending, and Guapa-Timing.)

Linear-Tango or **Walking-Tango:** There are two predominant **Styles** of the **Argentine Tango** Genre; the **Show-Tango**, and the **Tango-de-Salon** Genre. Within these two Styles, there are two types of Argentine Tango. One of these is the **Linear-Tango**, which is danced Slightly Curving Counter-Clockwise, following the Line-of-Dance about a more spacious Dancefloor than that for the **Rotary-Tango**, the second type.

The following are the **Linear** types of Argentine Tango: Petroleo-Tango, Milonguero-Tango, Club-Style Tango, and Tango-Apilado.

Each of the following is both **Rotary** and **Linear** types of Argentine Tango: Tango-de-Salon, Tango-Orillero, Liquid-Tango, and Show-Tango(1).

The **Linear-Tango**, although Travel-Danced in places such as Tango classes, clubs and saloons, is more of a formal Style than the other **Tango-de-Salon**, the **Rotary-Tango**. The Salidas, the Cunita, the various Ochos, and non-Turning Resolucions, might be included when dancing the **Linear-Tango**.

The following is from *Daniel Trenner*, www.dancetraveler.com:

"... *and the forties social style tango took hold. Then tango actually had two divisions: Salon, the walking dance, and Orillero, the one with the turns.*"

(See Pepito.)

Link: An **International Tango** Coupledance Leadable Action, for changing Positions from Closed (International Tango) to Promenade. Timing is an Abrupt *Slow*. Rhythm is *And Hold*.

A half-Measure Action with no Steps. Both their Weights end on Inner-Edges of Trailing-Feet, with Softened Inside Knees, and with Inner-Edges of Leading-Feet Touching.

Man dances *InPlaceTurn1/8CW*.

Lady, Following, dances *inplaceturn1/4CW*.

(See Progressive-Link, Promenade-Link, and Head-Flick-Link.)

Liquid-Tango: An outgrowth of the **Tango-Nuevo**, which is one Style of the **Tango-de-Salon** Coupledance, which in turn is part of the **Argentine Tango** Genre.

Being a combination of the **Linear-Tango** and **Rotary-Tango** types, the **Liquid-Tango**'s Body Positioning shifts between being an offset **Close-Embrace Tango-Lean** and an **Open-Embrace-Tango**, as they Coupledance. This principally allows for integration into their dance of the **Club-Style Tango** and **Tango-Nuevo**, as well as the other **Tango-de-Salon** Styles.

(See Tango-Liso.) [Much from www.tejastango.com.]

Llevada: (*zhay-VAH-dah*) See LaLlevada.

Loose-Hug Position: A Leadable, Basic Coupledance Position suitable for all **Latin Rhythm** dances and other dances. Facing with Softened-Knees and spaced Apart one to four inches at waists, with Slight **Offset**. Right Position is achieved by being Offset to Partner's Right. Shoulders-Parallel, the Man has his arms about his Lady's Upper-Body sides, and the Lady's arms are about his shoulders. Left Position is Opposite, Offset to Partner's Left.

[See Embrace(1)&(2), Cuddle, Enfold, Hug, Squeeze, Bundle, Snuggle, Envelop, Clasp, Clutch, Grasp, and Cling. Also see Cuddle Position(1), Crush-In-Closed, Shadow-Enfold Position, Cheek-to-Cheek Position, Head-to-Head Position, Over-the-Heart-Hand-Hold, Slow-Dancing, Forearm-Grasp, and PasoDoble-Hold. Also see Feathered Position, Shoulder-to-Shoulder Position, and Hip-to-Hip Position. Also see Feathered-Left Position, Left-Shoulder-to-Shoulder Position, and Left-Hip-to-Hip Position. Also see Carpa, Tango-Lean, Leaning-Into-Each-Other, and Milonguero(2).]

Low-to-the-Floor: A General Coupledance Term for **Level-Progression** or Flat-Dancing, i.e., dancing **without Rise-and-Fall**.
(See Flat-Step, Flat-Turns, and Horizontal Rhythm. Opposite of Floating, Vertical Rhythm, and Bobbing.)

Lunfardo: (*loon-FAR-do*, Spanish for *slang*.) A Coupledance Term for the Spanish slang of the Buenos Aires underworld, that is common in **Argentine Tango** dance terminology.

Lunge (*lun*): Several General, Leadable, one-Count Coupledance Movements, suitable for American **Twostep**, both **Foxtrots**, all **Waltzes**, all **Tangos**, **West-Coast-Swing** and other dances. Normally from some Closed Position, Pushing off with a Slight Spring, Weights are Transferred to a greatly Bent-Knee with the Free-Leg Straight and Extended.
A Checking Movement, the **Lunge** has a sudden plunge *Forward, DiagForward* or *Sideward*. All of one's Weight is applied. With Compression into the Moving-Leg, their Bodies are inclined from the ankle to the Head toward the Moving-Foot. A straight line is normally described from the Free-Foot Toe up and through the Inclined Body to the top of the Head. The Man Opens then Closes his Head.
(See Side-Lunge-Left, Side-Lunge-Right, Lunge-Basic, Lunge-Away, Same-Foot-Lunge, Lunge-Line, Lunge-Thru-and-Around, Right-Lunge-and-Slip, Lunge-Break, and Fence-Line.)

Lunge-Line: A Leadable Coupledance Position, **Lunge-Line** is suitable for American **Twostep**, both **Foxtrots**, all **Waltzes**, all **Tangos**, **West-Coast-Swing**, and possibly for other dances.
Without requiring to take the sudden plunge Step into the **Lunge**, Partners achieve the final position of the Lunge by Lowering by Compression into their Supporting Legs and assuming the Body Inclination characteristic to the **Lunge**.
(See Lunge for other Positions. Also see Line, Attitude-Line, Hinge-Line, Aida-Line, Eros-Line, Press-Line, Sentado-Line, and Sit-Line.)

Lustrada: (*loos-TRAH-dah*, Spanish for *to shine* or *polish*.) A Flourishing Movement or Figure; an Adorno or Embellishment used in the **Argentine Tango** Genre of Coupledances.
Ed Loomis [www.batango.com/loomis] describes **Lustrada** as follows:
"*A stroking of the man's pant leg with a shoe. May be done by the lady or by the man to himself but is never done to the lady.*"
The Lady can Perform a **Lustrada** in several ways. One way is when the Lady is doing **Ochos** beside her Man, even when they are **Ochos-Picante**.
An Adorno that is similar to **AnkleTrip**, and to the **Shoe-Shine**. (See the others of the **Dibujo** Genre of [Stopped] Parada Adornos, that includes the Lapiz, Puntada-del-Pie, Caricias, Chiche, Fanfarron, Golpecitos, Zapatazo, Levantada, and the Enganche.) (Also see Flourish, and Gesture.)

Macho or **Machismo:** A General Coupledance Term for an exaggerated sense of masculinity; the male animal. "*Jogging home from a vasectomy.*" -- Anonymous
(See Force, Aerial, Lift-Throw, and Lifts-to-Chest-or-Shoulder.)

Maneges: (Pronounced *man-EUSH. manege de chevaux de bois* is French for *merry-go-round*.) A Coupledance or Singular Term for a possibly Leadable Pattern, or series of Steps, that **Travels in a Circular Pattern** around the Dancefloor or Stage.
(See Circle, Curve, and Around.)

Man's-Ronde-Turn: A partially Leadable, Spot-Coupledance Figure, one Measure long, suitable for International **Tango** and other dances.

This Figure usually follows a **Double-Ronde.** Total Couple-Rotation is 7/8-Turn. Begins in Closed Position International Tango. On Right Ball, Man Fans an extra-long Rearward-Ronde, Sweeping his **Left** leg, as his Lady Strides four Steps around him, to end in Feathered-Left Position. Man's Timing is *LongSlow*; Lady's Timing is *Quick quick Quick quick.*

Man dances *Swivel7/8CCWtouch.*

Lady dances around Man *ForTurn1/8CCW forturn1/4CCW ForTurn1/4CCW forturn1/4CCW.*

Marcacion: See LaMarca.

Mark: See LaMarca.

May I Have This Dance?: A much-used General Ballroom Coupledance saying for an **Invitation-to-Dance**.

The following is from [www.dancetv.com/tips]:

"While traditional etiquette stipulates that the man asks the woman for a dance, it is becoming increasingly common for women to ask men. People who ballroom dance are there to do one thing: ballroom dance. In other words, you don't need to feel pressured into doing anything more than dancing. Tired of those silly one-liners? Well, in ballroom dancing there's only one one-liner, and it never gets old. The only pick-up line in ballroom dancing is `May I have this dance?' And ladies, you can ask the men to dance with this same one-liner. Pretty easy, isn't it?"

Same as **Shall-We-Dance?, Dance-With-Me, Let's-Dance**(2), and **Let's-Go-Trippin'**. [See the subtle method in "Milonga" for how to ask in Argentina. Also see Etiquette, Dance-Card, My-Card-is-Full, Social Dancing, Mixers, Dance Clubs, Dance Scene, Body-Exchange, and Pickup(6).]

Media-Luna (*MAY-dee-ah LOO-nah*, Spanish for a *half-moon*.) or **Half-Moon: Media-Luna** is an **Argentine Tango** Genre Coupledance Figure or Pattern in the **Rotary-Tango** Style. A typical Half-Turn **Media-Luna** Figure follows:

Ed Loomis [www.batango.com/loomis] describes the **Media-Luna** as follows:

"A sweeping circular motion of the leg similar to a ronde in ballroom but always danced in contact with the floor, never lifted. Usually danced by the lady and often led with a sacada to the lady's leg. May be used to bring the lady to an inside gancho."

The following is one sample **Media-Luna** Pattern in detail:

Four Measures long in 2/4 Cut-Time. Man's Timing is *Slow slow, Slow Hold, Slow Slow, Slow Hold.* Lady's Timing is *slow Slow, slow Slow, slow Slow And, slow slow.* Total Couple-Rotation is a Half-Turn Clockwise.

Begins in Closed Position Argentine Tango with a **Backward-Start,** both Cross their Feet then Lady Executes a **Parada.** Couple-Rotation is nil to this point. Man Swivels a Half-Turn twice then Closes, while his Lady Steps twice, Swivels, Points, then Steps to Face.

Man dances *Backward widesideward, MaxCrossBehind* Knees Flexed *Hold, Swivel1/4CW* to Face *Swivel1/4CW, Close Hold.*

Lady, Following, dances *forward WideSideward, crossbehind swivel1/4CWBackward* into "L" Position, *widesideward* to Face Square *StrideForward Swivel1/2CW* into "L" Position, *pointforward weightforwardswivelCCW* to Face Square.

Note: May be followed by the Basic-Start, Double-Start, or the Resolucion.

(See Track-the-Floor, Ronde, and Rond-de-Jambe.)

Media-Vuelta: (*MAY-dee-ah voo'ELL-tah*, Spanish for a *half-turn*.) A typical **Media-Vuelta** Figure used in the **Argentine Tango** follows:

With the Man's Right and his Lady's Left Feet Free, first the Man Steps *Forward*, causing Lady to Step *backward*, then the Man *Pivots1/2CCW*, causing his Lady to take two Steps.

Ed Loomis [www.batango.com/loomis] describes the **Media-Vuelta** as follows:

"*Usually done when the man's right foot and the lady's left foot are free. The man steps forward outside right (3 of 8 count basic)* [see Eight-Step-Basic-Tango], *leading the lady to step back left, then side right across his right leg, and forward left around him as he shifts weight first to his center, then onto his right foot as he then pivots on both feet half turn with his partner, the lady pivoting on her left foot. Media Vuelta is used by itself to change direction or manouver on the dance floor and as an entrance to many combinations.*"

[See Giro, and Molinete. Also see Half-Turn(1), and Demi-Tour.]

[Some data from http://nfo.net/dance/tango.]

Milonga or **Private-Milonga** or **LaMilonguita**: The Amorous **Milonga** was originally an Unleadable Spanish Gypsy **Folkdance** from Andalusia. Awhile before 1923, destitute Gypsy Flamenco-dancing immigrants from Spain, Coupledanced their **Milonga** in the Plata region of Buenos Aires. In lower dive cafes (Dancehalls), these Gypsies almost but never touched their Lady, but other poor immigrants grabbed their Ladies in a Closed Position. These other Argentine immigrants were from Italy and also from Spain, and were predominently men. Through them, a slowed down **Milonga** greatly influenced the evolution of the **Argentine Tango**.

The **Milonga** sub-Genre is composed of the early **Milonga-Candombera** and the later **Milonga-Portena**. In addition, there was the **Tango y Milonga** or **Tango-Milonga**, which was a middle step between the **Milonga-Candombera** and the actual **Tango**; i.e., the forerunner of the Argentine **Canyengue-Tango**.

The following is an excerpt from *Music of Uruguay*; [www.absoluteastronomy.com]:

"*The milonga was a South American style of song that was popular in the 1870s. The milonga was derived from an earlier style of singing known as the payada de contrapunto.*

"*The song was set to a lively 2/4 tempo, and often included musical improvisation. Over time, dance steps and other musical influences were added, eventually giving rise to the tango. Milonga music is still used for dancing, but the milonga dancing of today is derivative of tango.*"

The following is an excerpt from *Holland Masters 2003 Dance History*; [www.danceplaza.com]:

"*The Milonga is the forerunner of the Tango. The Milonga had already the characteristic head and shoulder movements that suddenly switched over to stillness. In the beginning of the 20th Century the Milonga was danced in small theatres for the High Society from Brazil. In that period the name was changed from Milonga to Tango, [since] the Milonga name carried too many memories from the ghetto's of Buenos Aires.*"

(Continued)

<u>Milonga:</u>   (Continued)

The following is an excerpt from *Tango Terminology*; [www.tangocanberra.asn.au]:

Milonga. *"... Milonga is a 'popular Argentine song and dance'. ... Cyber Tango* [www.cyber-tango.com] *says that it is the 'mother of Tango dance'... Also, ToTango* [totango.net] *notes that in the late 1800s (after 1872)* <u>Milonga</u> *had already acquired the meaning as the gathering place where one can dance (a Tango social dance), but that the word Milonga also is of African origin, from the word Mulonga, which meant word (or long story)! Nowadays, Milonga has several meanings: a music, a dance, and a place or gathering where one dances. The Milonga dance differs from Tango in that it is commonly referred to as peppy and cheerful (Bridge To The Tango). There's an interesting description of Milonga rhythm and Milonga music in an article by David Drake* [members.aol.com/tangero1] *where he refers to the 'spicy rhythms' of Tango, being 'sincopa' and 'milonga'."*

Milonga and **Argentine Tango** Music share a common origin. **Milonga** M usic has a March-like Rhythm with a light-hearted mood. This modern **Milonga, Tango y Milonga** or **Tango-Milonga One-Step** Coupledance, popular and currently danced in Argentina and also somewhat the world over, is a Traveling dance in Fast 2/4 Time, with *Quick Quick, Quick Quick* Rhythm *1 2, 1 2,* etc. One Step is taken for each music Beat. Triples and Adornos are rarely added because of its Fast 2/4 Timing. The Hold mostly used is described under **Argentine Tango, Embrace**(2), and the **Tango-Lean**. This **Milonga** dance incorporates almost all of the Steps and Techniques used in the Argentine Tango Genre, but it is normally danced fairly simply with happy, high-energy Swaggering and Bouncing. Yet this modern **Milonga** is a very Soft Coupledance with emphasis on leg Movements. The Close-Embrace is alternated with the Open-Embrace. There are no pauses, such as there are in Argentine Tango. Suggested **Milonga** Patterns are:

1) Backward-Start, Salida, Resolucion
2) Basic-Start, Salida, Cadencia, Resolucion
3) Turning-Forward-Cunita, Salida-Modified, Ochos, Turning-Backward-Cunita
4) Basic-Start, Salida, Stroll, Cadencia, Resolucion.

Typical of the **Private-Milonga**, (and of the Rotary-Tango,) there is an existing picture of a Couple in the **Closed Position Argentine Tango** as follows: The Man's Weight is upon his Forward Crossed Right Foot, while his contorted and shorter Lady appears to Perform Ochos. Above the waists, the Man Hugs his Lady to him, while below, Feet are some twelve inches far Apart from the Partner, and legs for both are Crossed at the Knees. Their shoulders are close together and almost parallel, while their hips Turn with CBMP to Semi-Closed. All elbows are Lowered. Off-Balance, the Lady's Left upper arm is well supported by her Left wrist being wrapped around his neck. His Right arm is wrapped High and completely around her upper Torso, Squeezing that portion of her against his chest. Assuming her Tango-Lean, her back arches with some Posterior-Protrusion while his Stance is more vertical, although he has some Tango-Lean. The Lady's Head is Open with her Left forehead pressed against his Right cheek. Clasped Hands are Held Slightly below Shoulder-Level.

In the 1800s, music of the Argentine Pampas was called "**Milonga**". It had an early rural dance-form that mutated (with other dances) into the early Tango about 1880. Currently, the Term "**Milonga**" has a second meaning in Argentina; e.g., "**Milonga**" also refers to some **Dancehall**(1), like "let's go to the *milonga* tonight."

(Continued)

Milonga: (Continued)

The following from *Types of Milongas in Buenos Aires* by *Janis Kenyon (from Tango-L)*:

"*Salon de Baile* - An atmosphere especially for dancing, predominately elegant attire, tables with tablecloths, where tango code is strictly respected, where they listen to tangos of the 40s with breaks of latin music. Older public with intermediate to high level of dancing.

"*Confiteria Bailable* - They have many of the same characteristics of the Salones de Baile, but also have a restaurant. The public is varied with lots of groups.

"*Club de Barrio* - The floors are basketball courts or the club restaurant; the caterer can be the dance organizer; predominately attended by the neighborhood families and married couples; the music is more varied.

"*Milonga Joven* - Informal atmosphere, young public, variety of dress. Live music and dance exhibitions. More relaxed standard and more diverse level of dancing; plan to listen to Piazzolla, some rock`n'roll as well as salsa and cumbia."

Much of the following is from *Daniel Trenner - Evening Etiquette at the Argentine Dance Hall*: [www.dancetraveler.com]

As for the Argentine **Milonga** place-to-dance ("*tango club*"), a casual **Practica** that includes teaching will begin at 8 or 9pm and end at 11 or 12. Then from midnight until perhaps 5am, the formal and highly structured **Milonga** occurs. Canned music is in Dance-Sets, **Tandas**, of four or five songs, such as four Tangos of similar Style in sequence. The next Set might be of four Argentine Waltzes, or of four or five **Milongas**. Other following Dance-Sets might be of Latins, Merengues, Salsas, Swings or Cumbias, then reverting back to Argentine music.

The customary invitation way to dance at an Argentine **Milonga** is by the following subtle method: It is a game of looking. Man or Lady, one lets one's gaze rest upon the person you want to dance with. That's the invitation when you catch each other's eyes. A smile and a nod at the Dancefloor is confirmation. The Man Moves toward her table as she waits for him at the Dancefloor edge, and they take a long moment to settle into an Embrace. (See Codigo, and Cabeceo.)

It is customary to dance the entire Dance-Set with one Partner, or at least a minimum of two dance-songs. Everyone normally sits down at their own table between each Set, while a short and undanceable Cortina is played. Here, one probably finds their next Partner for the next Dance-Set. It also is customary that if they plan to dance together the next Set, then one remains upon the Dancefloor and chats with that same Partner. The next Dance-Set music starts but everyone continues chatting. Then almost in Unison, each Man Raises his arms to invite the next Embrace, whereupon all Couples begin to Move, with no one in the way.

Upon finishing the Dance-Set to about the last note, if either Partner then says "*gracias*", they are indicating to end it. No "*gracias*" means that they want your Partnership for the next Dance-Set. With a "*gracias*", the Man always escorts the Lady back to her table.

Of the Tango, Milonga and Vals Cruzado... "*It is an internal power that develops a high degree of sensuality taking place between two bodies using a maximum expression in a minimum circular space and obeying the rules of atoms.*" -- Ive Simard

(See Argentine-Tango, Tango y Milonga, Milonga-Candombera, Milonga-Portena, Argentine-Waltz, ContraDanza-Spanish, Habanera, and Candombe. Also see Bailongo, Confiteria-Tango, and Confiteria-Style. Also see Invitation-to-Dance, and Body-Contact.)

Milonga-Candombera or **Candombeada-Milonga**: (*me-LAWN-gah kahn-dome-BAY-rah*) There are two Styles of **Milonga** dancing. This **Candombera-Milonga** was the earlier of the two types of **Milonga**; the later one being the **Milonga-Portena**. An early form of **Tango**, this **Candombeada-Milonga** melded first into the **Tango-Milonga**, which then developed into the earliest Style of **Tango**, the **Canyengue-Tango**.

The following are extracts from *Re: [TANGO-L] tango/milonga* [http://pythia.uoregon.edu/]:

"*CANDOMBE is a strong folk tradition in Uruguay, and presumably dates back to African rhythms and dances of the 1800s. I would assume that early forms of Candombe took place on both sides of the river. I would NOT assume that Candombe was part of the tango development (except in an oblique way) until it became obvious in those milongas candombera in the 1930s.*

"*It is my understanding that milonga (as we know it) did NOT predate tango. Rather that the music of the 1910s & 1920s had a generalized tango/milonga feeling. As tangos slowed down in the 1930s with the `de Caro sensibility', milongas sped up.*"

Different Variations of **Milonga** Rhythm are the Slower **Milonga-Campera** and the Faster **Milonga-Candombera**. This **Candombera-Milonga** was danced light and Fast to Syncopated Rhythms. Music was normally played at 2/4 Timing. Many of its Figures became Standard within the **Canyengue-Tango** and later **Tangos**. **Milonga** Rhythms provided the Buenos Aires impoverished with joyous moments of escape.

(See Argentine Tango, Tango y Milonga, Milonga, and Candombe.)

[Much from www.elmundodeltango.com/]

Milonga-Portena: (*me-LAWN-gah por-TAY-nah*) There are two Styles of **Milonga** dancing. This **Milonga-Portena** is the later one of the two types of **Milonga**; the earlier one being the **Milonga-Candombera**.

The following is an extract from an article by *Vittorio Pujia* in the *El Tanguata* magazine (April issue, Buenos Aires):

"*We know tango arose as a way of dancing, that dancers adopted milonga as their favorite rhythm to dance tango. Musicians adapted milonga to the needs of the dancers and so tango-milonga was born, from which tango and milonga portena came.*"

Milonguero(1): (*mi-lon-GAY-rro* is Spanish for a *male milonga dancer*.) Traditionally, a **Milonguero** was an afficionado of the **Milonga** and **Argentine Tango** Genre, who lived in Buenos Aires in the 1940s and 50s. He went dancing to the Milongas assidously.

Ed Loomis [www.batango.com/loomis] describes the **Milonguero** as follows:

"*MILONGUERO (feminine; Milonguera) Refers to those frequenting the milongas from the early 1900s to the present who were or are tango fanatics. A person whose life revolves around dancing tango and the philosophy of tango. A title given by other tango dancers to a man (woman) who has mastered the tango dance and embodies the essence of tango.*"

Similar to the **Tanguero**. [Much from http://nfo.net/dance/tprimer.]

Milonguero(2) or **Milonguero-Style:** (*mi-lon-GAY-rro* is Spanish for the *male milonga dancer's hold.*) A certain Coupledance **Hold** used dancing a particular type of **Argentine Tango.**

The **Milonguero's** Hold is "*the close embrace.*" Predominately popular in Buenos Aires while dancing the **Tango-Apilado**, this close Embrace (Abrazo) by the Man of his Lady is emphasized more than any complicated Footwork.

Ed Loomis [www.batango.com/loomis] describes the **Milonguero-Style** as follows:

"*Term originally given by Europeans and some North Americans to the style of dancing in a very close embrace; also referred to as confiteria style, club style, apilado style, etc. Usually used in the very crowded clubs frequented by singles in the center of Buenos Aires. Milonguero Style is danced in a very close embrace with full upper body contact, the partners leaning into each other (but never hanging on each other), and using simple walking and turning steps. This style relies on music of the more rhythmic type as characterized by orquestas like those of DaArienzo or Tanturi.*"

(See Carpa, Tango-Lean, Leaning-Into-Each-Other, and Lean.)
[Much from http://nfo.net/dance/tprimer.]

Milonguero-Style: See Milonguero(2).

Milonguero-Tango or **Confiteria-Tango:** (*mi-lon-GAY-rro* is Spanish for the *male milonga dancer's hold.*) One Style of the **Tango-de-Salon**, which is part of the **Argentine Tango** Genre, and was developed in the 1940s and 50s.

This **Milonguero-Tango** is constantly danced **only** in a **Close-Embrace**, as fully described under "**Tango-Lean.**" This **Linear-Tango** type of Coupledance Travels CCW upon the Line-of-Dance.

During the 1950s, this **Milonguero-Tango** of central Buenos Aires was **very similar to** the **Club-Style Tango** which was danced in the suburbs of Buenos Aires. For instance, both this **Milonguero-Tango** and the **Club-Style Tango** incorporated the **Ocho-Cortado**. Both were likely to have originated from their older **Tango-Orillero** Style. This dance Style is simpler than the Tango-de-Salon.

The following is from *Daniel Trenner*, www.dancetraveler.com:

"*... Also, some dancers were known best for their milongas. In the forties the word milonguero was not all that flattering, as it referred to one who was addicted to the night life, never worked, and was often begging for a loan.*

"*However, in the modern epoch Salon and Milonguero have become more interchangeable in describing the more vaguely defined styles of a now older generation. They are now allied in being contrasted to the stage fantasy tangos, inside and out of Argentina, and foreign social dance forms.*"

Same as **Cafe-Tango**, and **Tango-Apilado**. Similar to **Tango-Liso**. [See Petroleo-Tango. Also see Liquid-Tango, and Show-Tango(1).] [Some from www.tejastango.com.]

Mini-Telespin or **Checked-Telespin:** A Leadable Coupledance Pattern suitable for the Slow-**Foxtrot, International Tango,** both **Quicksteps** and Slow-**Waltz.** Timing for Foxtrot and Tango is *Slow Quick Quick, And Quick Quick Slow*; for Quickstep is *Slow Slow, Slow And Quick Quick, Slow*; and for Waltz is *Slow Slow Slow, And Slow Slow Slow*.

Begins and ends in a Closed Position, two or 2 1/2 Measures, for 1 1/4 Turns Counter-Clockwise. After second Step, Man is Hub-Partner, and Lady is Rim-Partner. By third Step, Man keeps Left Side Forward toward Lady, or he may Open Lady for a Whip sensation created by his Spinning. Lady's Head remains Closed.

Man dances *forward* with CBM *DiagForTurn1/4CCW Swivel3/8CCW* Point Left Toe and Open Lady, *spinonball3/8CCW continuespin1/4CCW Close.*

Lady Heel-Turns then takes Quick Forward Turning Steps; she dances *BackTurn1/8CCW* with CBM *Heelturn1/4CCW ForTurn1/4CCW* in Semi-Closed, *forturn1/4CCW* in CBM *ForTurn1/4CCW* Right-Side-Lead *closeturn1/8CCW* on Toes.

(See Telespin, and Telespin-to-Semi-Closed.)

Molinete: (*mo-le-NAY-tay,* Spanish for *wheel, windmill, windlass* or *turnstyle.*) A partially Leadable Coupledance Pattern for the **Argentine Tango,** danced by the Lady, Circling with a **Grapevine** about her Man, who is usually Executing an **Enrosque** in concert; e.g., a Box-Step Executed by the Lady around the Man, as the Man Performs a **Giro** or **Vuelta.**

Ed Loomis [www.batango.com/loomis] describes the **Molinete** as:

"... *a figure in which the lady dances a grapevine on a circumference around the man, stepping side-back-side-forward using forward and back ocho technique and footwork, as the man pivots at the center of the figure.*"

The combined **Giro** and **Molinete** both appear and feel out-of-this-world! But, for both Man and Lady, such Patterns are difficult to learn and Perform Well. They say Balance, Timing, Musicality, width and direction all enter into its perfection. The Man is the Hub and the Lady is the Rim.

(See Vine, Vine-Eight, Hook-Wind, Hook-Unwind, and Corkscrew. Also see Media-Vuelta, and Lapiz.) [Much from http://nfo.net/dance/tprimer; and www.tangocanberra.asn.au.]

Mordida: See Sandwich.

Mordida-Alto: (*mor-DEE-dah* is Spanish for *tiny bite,* or *to clutch*; *AHL-to* is Spanish for *high.*) A Genre of **Argentine Tango** Spot-Coupledance Figures in the **Rotary-Tango** Style. The **Mordida-Alto** is a Variation of the **Sandwich** (Mordida), whereupon, instead of a Foot, one dancer catches their Partner's **Knee** between their own Knees.

Natural-Fallaway-Whisk: A Leadable, one-Measure Coupledance Figure, suitable for Slow-**Foxtrot,** and **Argentine-Tango.** Rhythm Timing for both is *Quick Quick Quick Quick*.

Total Couple-Rotation is a Clockwise 3/4-Turn in four Steps; from Semi-Closed Position, into Closed, to Reverse-Semi-Closed, into Left-Whisk Positions.

Man dances *ThruTurn1/4CW* with CBM *diagbackturn1/4CW SideTurn1/4CW crossbehind* in CBMP.

Lady, Following, dances *stepthru* with CBM *Forward* between Feet *swivel1/2CWdiagbackward Turn1/4CWCrossBehind* in CBMP.

Natural-Pivot-Turn: A Leadable, four-Step, 1 1/2-Measure Coupledance Pattern, suitable for the **International Tango**. Rhythm with 2/4 Timing is *Slow Quick Quick, Slow*.

Turn is a Clockwise 7/8-Couple-Rotation total, that begins in Promenade Position and then continues in Closed Position International Tango.

Man dances *diagforward StepThruTurn1/4CW backpivot5/8CW, DiagForward*.

Lady, Following, dances *DiagForward stepthru ForPivot1/2CW, diagbackward*.

Identical to **Natural-Promenade-Turn** except ends in Closed Position.

Natural-Promenade-Turn: A Leadable, four-Step, 1 1/2-Measure Coupledance Pattern, suitable for the **International Tango**. Rhythm with 2/4 Timing is *Slow Quick Quick, Slow*.

Turn is a Clockwise 7/8-Couple-Rotation total, that begins in Promenade Position, Changes to Closed Position International Tango, then ends in Promenade Position.

Man dances *diagforward StepThruTurn1/4CW backpivot5/8CW, Forward*.

Lady, Following, dances *DiagForward stepthru ForPivot1/2CW, diagbackturn3/8CW*.

Identical to **Natural-Pivot-Turn** except ends in Promenade Position.

Natural-Resolution or **Resolution** or **Closed-Finish:** All are **Argentine Tango** Coupledance Terms for the Couple's Leadable, Gentle, 4-Step, alternate **Ending** for each Pattern or musical Phrase, or for the complete dance. Rhythm Timing is normally *Slow Slow, Slow Slow*; two Measures long in 2/4 Cut-Time. This **Natural-Resolution** (Ending) is perhaps as follows:

Man ends dancing *forward* Toe Outward *ForFeathered forward* Left Shoulder-Lead *Close* then Straight-Kneed.

Lady ends dancing *Backward* Weight Forward *backfeathered* with CBM *Backward* Right Shoulder-Lead *lockinfront* as she Leans against her Man.

Their **Natural-Resolution** might Half-Turn CCW or might not Turn at all.

See **Resolucion** for the most common Ending. (See Tango, Tango-Milonga, Gancho, Arch, Basic-Step, American-Start, Backward-Start, and Basic-Start.)

Note: Here, the word "Natural" has nothing to do with Clockwise.

Natural-Turn: A continual Clockwise Couple-Rotation (Natural-Turning) Executes easier while Traveling Counter-Clockwise about the Dancefloor, because if Traveled Clockwise about the Dancefloor, this Clockwise Couple-Rotation would require Overturning.

(See Outside-Turn, Lady's; and Natural-Right-Turn. Also see Direction-of-Turn.)

Natural-Twist-Turn: A Leadable Coupledance Pattern, suitable for the Slow-**Foxtrot** and **International Tango**. Also suitable for **American Tango**. In two Measures, six Steps for Lady and four Steps for Man. Rhythm with 4/4 or 2/4 Timing is *Slow Quick Quick, Slow Quick Quick*.

Total Couple-Rotation is a 7/8-Turn Clockwise. Begins in Semi-Closed or Promenade Positions. Inside-Feet are danced Thru with Man Turning to Closed Position, Man Locks Behind then Unwinds Clockwise, and ends in Semi-Closed Position. Man is Hub-Partner; Lady is Rim-Partner.

Man dances *diagforward StepThruSwivel3/8CW diagbackward, CrossBehind* with no Weight until near Unwound.

Lady dances *DiagForward stepthru Forward* in Closed, *forward* Feathered *ForOutsideSwivel7/8CW recovershortsideward* Unwinding her Man.

(See Natural-Turn, and Open-Natural-Turn.)

Neo-Tango or **New-Tango(2):** A series of Novelty **Fad** Coupledances, in vogue perhaps beginning about 1999 and covering a broad range of experimental Styles. With characteristics that are so Generalized, this Tango sub-Genre has various mini-Styles that have not yet been settled into any definitely defineable Tango dance Style. Still it can be said that all **Neo-Tangos** are of the **Rotary-Tango** type and are Generally part of the **Argentine Tango** Genre.

All of these **Neo-Tango** sub-Genre of Tango spinoffs often riles the Traditional Tango Purist who is normally very resistant to change. Such Purists often picture all of these hated **Neo-Tangos** as vulgar abominations of that which they love. With blasting Music in 4/4 Time, this **Neo-Tango** sub-Genre includes the **Swango,** so popular in 2005.

The following are excerpts from "*The New Tango Trades Cheek to Cheek For Hot, Fast Moves*"; [this is an article from the 8-29-05 Los Angeles Times by Kim-Mai Cutler.]:

"*Berkeley, Calif. - ... by about 4 am, ... with the traditional* [Tango] *crowd gone..., with the sort of modern, bass-heavy dance music that might be played in a hip nightclub... people in their twenties who remained switched over to a new kind of tango that had them lifting, twisting and ricocheting around the room. This is 'neotango,' a new millennium version ... booming all over the tango world.*

"*... in city after city across the U.S., a new generation of tango dancers is packing the floor again. They swerve and kick, not to the traditional violins ... but to the dub beats ... or wailing guitar lines... Formal wear is out; sneakers, low-rider jeans and halter tops are in.*

"*And the dance itself is different: faster, more fluid and requiring more floor space. While old-school dancers ... might press themselve heart to heart, the new version rotates over swaths of floor at high speed. Actually, there are many competing new versions. Some dancers borrow moves and music from electronica, swing and even martial arts.*

"*... DJ played gigs in Beijing, Washington D.C., and St. Louis this summer. ... hosts all-nighters in the San Francisco area and in other cities across the country, is emblematic of the new generation of dancers. ... Sept 11, 2001, ... At around the same time, **neotango** was growing increasingly popular in American and European dancing circles. It had its roots in the pounding club music, the experimental stylings of a few prominent Argentine dancers and modern fitness regimes: yoga, Pilates, martial arts and capoeira, ... While the traditional form of tango can be highly structured, neotango's early proponents believed dancers had to be free to experiment, and experiment they have.*

"*But when the neotango started picking up steam, the passionate tango community divided into cliques as arguments brewed over which kind of tango is best. Even as ... neotango events have swelled in popularity, some dancers ... have avoided ... events. When new-style dancers were dubbed the 'nuevo brats' for causing collisions on the floor with their flashy and sometimes haphazard moves ...*

"*Traditionalists simply long for the older styles: chest to chest, cheek to cheek, and eyes closed in what is known as the tango trance. 'Tango is very close to the heart,' ... 'that makes it really easy for crazy zealots to go in there and say that their style is **the** style and that's the only right style.' It isn't just the dance moves that are dividing the audience, it's the more beat-oriented music. ... The debate has even come home to Argentina. When neotango music first emerged, just one club in Buenos Aires would play ...*

"*Many people say it's not tango. ... But it's something new, something refreshing. ... It is abroad where the new dance has taken off and gone through endless mutations. ... 'Swango,' anyone? ... 'liquid tango' and 'free tango,' among an infinite assortment of names. By whatever name, it proves that ... Argentina doesn't have a lock on tango anymore.*"

See **Swango,** which is one of the **Neo-Tangos.** [Also see Tango-Nuevo, Liquid-Tango, Martial-Arts, and Capoeira. Also see Boleo, Gancho, and Sentada. Also see Traditional, Traditional-Dancing, Nuzzle-Dancing, and Tango-Trance. Also see Structured(1), Traditional-Dance-Doctrine, Accepted-Dancing-Mores, Innovating-Dancer, and Recalcitrant-Dancer.]

New-Tango: See Tango-Nuevo, and Neo-Tango.

NightClub Dancing or Club-Dancing or Dinner-Dance or Out-On-The-Town: Both Traditional and as of the 1990s, this General Term has been associated more with General Spot-Coupledancing on a Crowded-Dancefloor, and in a place of entertainment, normally with dinner and a FloorShow. These places usually provide drinking and did previously allow smoking. The General Coupledancing may be between shows, almost always to a combo, band or orchestra. Spot-Coupledancing encompasses mainly the American Medium Foxtrot and Waltz, the Onestep, **American Tango**, American Rumba and Bolero, American ChaCha and Mambo, American Samba and Merengue. Also, the Eastern and West-Coast-Swings, and Balboa, among other dances. These dancers may not be as Skilled as Ballroom-Dancers.
        (See Discotheque, Salsa, Ballroom Dancing, Big-Band-Dancing, Ballroom-Dancers, Social Dancing, Tea-Dance, Dance-Band, Combo, Dance-Set, and DanceSport.)

NightClub-Tango: See Cafe Tango.

No-Float: See Level-Progression.

No-Hands-ContraCheck: Performed with artful Balance, an Unleadable Coupledancing Picture-Figure suitable for the Slow-**Foxtrot**, Slow-**Waltz**, and **International Tango**, and as an ending for other dances, such as both **Quicksteps**, both **Rumbas**, the **Bolero**, and **Cabaret**.
        The Man, after first Lowering by Softening his Right Knee, Moves Forward into the Lady, and the Couple assumes a Figure **identical to the normal ContraCheck**, except that the Partners Perform the Figure **without Touching**. Instead, both spread their arms to match.

Oblique-Line: A General Coupledance **slanting Body Position**, deviating from vertical. Or, a series of Picture-Stances. Or, a Torso angle with greater than a ninety degree Bending but less than Straight, i.e., a Body Bent at an obtuse angle.

Ocho-Abierto (*O-CHO-ah-bee-AIR-toe*) or **Open-Eight**: Mainly suitable for Coupledancing the **Argentine Tango**, and possibly other Tangos and also PasoDobles. **Ocho-Abierto** is one Measure long in 2/4 Cut-Time, and is only partially Leadable. There is no Couple-Rotation.
        The Lady dances her Ochos(1) throughout this Figure with no change, while, as described as follows, her Man dances with his Lady. With Partners Moving into a very Loose-Closed Position, and Swiveling on Ball, the Man joins her as he feels his Lady begin to Turn at her **Ochos** beginning. Man's Rhythm Timing is *And slow and Quick And*.
        Man dancing In-Place, beginning with his Feet Closed and with Weight on his **Left** Foot, dances *swivel1/4CCW* Shoulders-Parallel *spiral1/2CW* Shoulders-Parallel *hold Close PickuptoFace*. Man eyes his Lady throughout the Figure, or he looks in the directions his Lady is about to Turn.
        Similar to **Doble-Ochos**. (See Ochos(2), Tres-Ochos, Ochos-Largos, and Ochos-para-Atras. Also see Salida-Modified.)

Ocho-Cortado or **Cut-Ocho** or **Ocho-Milonguero:** (*kor-TAH-do* is Spanish for *adapted cut.*) Two Leadable **Argentine Tango** Coupledance Movements, Left and Right, most suitable for the **Tango-Apilado.** As fully described under "**Tango-Lean,**" the Close-Embrace (Abrazo) by the **Milonguero** of his Lady is thereby maintained by this **Ocho-Cortado,** which is Performed as follows:

"*Instead of a pivot on the forward ocho, the lady, after her right foot forward, takes a side step, and is brought back via a cross on the next step.*"

Both the **Club-Style Tango** and the **Milonguero-Tango** incorporate this **Ocho-Cortado.** The **Ocho-Cortado** is one of the characteristic Figures of the **Milonguero-Tango** Style, due to its fine integration of the **Close-Embrace-Tango** with the music's Rhythm and feel.

[Much of above is from http://nfo.net/dance/tprimer, and www.tejastango.com.]

Ed Loomis [www.batango.com/loomis] describes this **Ocho-Cortado** as follows:

"*Cut eight: Occurs when a molinete or an ocho-like movement is stopped and sent back upon itself. Typical in club style where many such brakes are used to avoid collisions.*"

"*OCHOS CORTADOS Cut eights: A common figure in Milonguero or Club Style Tango which is designed to allow interpretation of rhythmic music while dancing in a confined space.*"

The following is from **Re: Ocho Cortado...** *http://pythia.uoregon.edu/*:

"*A `cut ocho' is one in which the open step of a giro is checked and reversed. Upon reversal, the leader often takes some of the follower's space, but always slightly displaces and pivots the follower, directing the follower's free foot to cross in front of the support foot. Typically returned to the leader's left, it can theoretically be returned to the right but be ready to also add a back ocho if the follower hooks instead of crossing in front. The leftward curvature of the line of dance makes the latter situation more uncommon and asymmetry in the frame will make it more challenging.*

"*It's very typical of the milonguero style because of it's rhythmic feel (the steps are three `quicks') and ease of execution in a crowd. ... During the check step the leader is pivoting, during the cross the follower is pivoting.*"

[See Ochos(2), Swivel-Point, and Ochos-para-Atras.] (Also see Ochos(1)&(2), Doble-Ochos, Tres-Ochos, Ocho-Cortado, Ocho-Abierto, Ochos-Largos, and Ochos-en-Espejo. Also see Salida-Modified.)

Ocho-Defrente: (*day-fay-REN-tay*, Spanish for *to the front.*) See Ochos(2).

Ocho-Milonguero: See Ocho-Cortado.

Ochos(1): (*O-CHOss* in Spanish is *eight*.) El **Ocho** is mainly suitable for Coupledancing the **Argentine Tango**, and possibly other Tangos and also PasoDobles. Only partially Leadable, El **Ocho** Figure is one Measure long in 2/4 Cut-Time. Performed by the Lady from a very Loose-Closed Position; here the PasoDoble-Hold is sometimes used. There is no Couple-Rotation.

Lady's Rhythm Timing is *and Slow And quick and.* Lady scribes a "figure eight" on the Dancefloor while Generally Facing her Man. Her Swivels are on Ball-of-Foot. She dances the entire Pattern as if her Knees were glued together. Her Free-Leg calf is held parallel with the Dancefloor during each of her Swivels. The Lady begins with Weight on her Left Foot Crossed InFront:

Lady dances *Raiseswivel1/4CCW ThruForwardWeight* Outside Man's Right *raiseSwivel1/2CW thruforwardweight swivel1/4CCW* to Face. Each *Weight* is a Delayed-Weight-Shift. Throughout her Figure, the Lady looks either in her Direction-of-Turn, or she eyes her Man.

While she dances, her Man simply remains Standing with Weight on his Right Foot. His Feet are either Closed or his Right Foot is Crossed-InFront or Crossed-Behind. If, instead, he dances Ochos with his Lady, the Pattern becomes the **Doble-Ochos**, or even the **Tres-Ochos**.

Similar to **Ochos**(2). (See Ocho-Abierto, Ochos-Largos, and Ochos-para-Atras. Also see Salida-Modified.)

Ochos(2) or **Figure-Eights** or **Ochos-Adelante** or **Ocho-Defrente** or **Front-Ochos** or **Forward-Ochos**: (*O-cho*, Spanish for *eight*. *ah-day-LAHN-tay*, Spanish for *forward*. *day-fay-REN-tay*, Spanish for *to the front*.) Forward Dance Steps plotting a "figure eight" on the Dancefloor. Two Leadable Coupledance Movements, Left or Right, suitable for all **Tangos**, the **Milonga** and **PasoDoble**.

A **Forward-Ocho** is Executed by a Forward Step with a Pivot and then another Forward Step. In all dances, three Ochos are normally performed; Timing is *Slow-, Slow-, Slow-.* Left and Right Half-Turn **Swivel-Points** in Sequence, one each, creates two **Ochos**, forming the "figure eight". The third **Ocho** allows for the Pickup(1).

Performed by the Lady from a very Loose-Closed Position; here the PasoDoble-Hold is sometimes used. Crossing In-Front (Step-Thru), her Forward Swivels are Quarter- or Half-Turns on Ball-of-Foot with Knees Together; her Free-Foot is Flared Rearward Knee-Bent, and Away from her Supporting-Foot.

Additions for when Performing **Argentine Tango** only: Lady's Knee is Raised to Hip-Level after each ForSwivel, as she Steps Forward Across Man's Right protruding Straight-Leg and Foot, while the Man Touches her Supporting-Foot with a side of his Right Toe after each Swivel, as she Steps Across.

Ed Loomis [www.batango.com/loomis] describes these **Ochos** as follows:

"*OCHO Eight (pl. ochos); Figure eights: A crossing & pivoting figure from which the fan in American tango is derived. Executed as a walking step with flexed knees and feet together while pivoting, ochos may be danced either forward or backward and are so designated from the lady's perspective. El Ocho is considered to be one of the oldest steps in tango along with caminada, the walking steps. It dates from the era when women wore floor length skirts with full petticoats and danced on dirt floors. Since the lady's footwork could not be directly observed the quality of her dancing was judged by the figure she left behind in the dirt after she danced away.*"

Similar to **Ochos**(1). (See Doble-Ochos, Tres-Ochos, Ocho-Cortado, Ocho-Abierto, Ochos-en-Espejo, Ochos-Largos, and Ochos-para-Atras. Also see Salida-Modified.)

Ochos-Adelante: (*ah-day-LAHN-tay*, Spanish for *forward*.) See Ochos(2).

Ochos-en-Espejo: (*O-chos en ess-PAY-Ho*, Spanish for *eights in the mirror*.) See Doble-Ochos.

Ochos-Largos: (*O-CHOss-lar-GHOss* is Spanish for *long* or *protracted eights*.) Mainly suitable for Coupledancing the **Argentine Tango**, and possibly other Tangos and also PasoDobles. **Ochos-Largos** is three Measures long in 2/4 Cut-Time, and is partially Leadable. There is Traveling and much CBM, but no Couple-Rotation.

Pattern Begins in a very Loose-Closed Position, with the Lady in a Trabada-Step, and with the Man with Feet Closed and Weight on his Right Foot. Rhythm Timing is *Slow Slow, Slow Slow, Slow Slow And*.

1) Man Steps *widesideward* as Lady dances *Raiseswivel1/4CCWThruForwardWeight*, ending with her Right Toe Touching Man's Right Instep or Toe

2) Man dances *swivel1/8CCWForStepThru* as Lady dances *Swivel1/2CWforstepthru* into Promenade Position for Tango

3) Man dances *Swivel1/4CWwidesideward* to Face as Lady dances *Raiseswivel1/4CCWThruForwardWeight*, ending with her Right Toe Touching Man's Right Instep

4) Man dances *swivel1/8CCWForStepThru* as Lady dances *Swivel1/2CWforstepthru* into Promenade Position for Tango

5) Man dances *Swivel1/4CWwidesideward* to Face as Lady dances *Raiseswivel1/4CCWThruForwardWeight*, ending with her Right Toe Touching Man's Right Instep

6) Man Steps *Close* and Pickup Lady to Face, as Lady dances *spiral1/8CWTouchClosed*.

Throughout the Pattern, the Man eyes his Lady, or else he looks in the directions his Lady is about to Turn; while the Lady looks either in her Direction-of-Turn, or she eyes her Man.

(See Ochos(1)&(2), Doble-Ochos, Tres-Ochos, Ocho-Abierto, and Ochos-para-Atras. Also see Salida-Modified.)

Ochos-para-Atras (*O-CHOss-PAH-rah-ah-TRAHss*) or **Backwards-Figure-Eights** or **Back-Ochos:** Rearward Dance Steps plotting a "figure eight". Two Leadable Coupledance Movements, Left or Right, suitable for all **Tangos** and **PasoDobles**. In all dances, three Ochos are normally performed; Timing is *Slow-, Slow-, Slow-*.

Performed by the Lady from a very Loose-Closed Position; here the PasoDoble-Hold is sometimes used. A **Back-Ocho** consists of two Rearward Steps with a Pivot in-between. Crossing Behind, her BackSwivels are Quarter- or Half-Turns on Ball-of-Foot; her Free-Foot is Flared Forward and Away from her Supporting-Foot.

Additions for when Performing **Argentine Tango** only: Lady's Knee is Raised to Hip-Level after each BackSwivel, as she Steps Rearward Across Man's Right protruding straight leg and Foot, while the Man Touches her Supporting-Foot with a side of his Right Toe after each Swivel, as she Steps Across.

There are many ways to dance **Back-Ochos**, whether Partners are in Open-Embrace or in Closed-Embrace, and all are appropriate at any Argentine Milonga. The Lady might dance them Smooth and sultry, or Whip them snappy and Rhythmical, or she might Embellish her **Back-Ochos** by Crossing her ankles.

(See Ochos(1)&(2), Doble-Ochos, Tres-Ochos, Ochos-Picante, Ocho-Cortado, Ocho-Abierto, and Ochos-Largos. Also see Salida-Modified.)

Ochos-Picante or **Spicy-Ochos:** (*O-CHOss pe-KAHN-tay*, Spanish for *piquant eights*.) *Piquant* means appealingly provocative, and these **Ochos** certainly are. **Ochos-Picante** are attractive Coupledance Adorno Actions, Performed usually by the Lady, while dancing any of the various **Argentine Tangos**, and possibly also the **Milonga** if Kicking another party can be avoided.

Ochos-Picante are Latigazos, Ruades, i.e., Back-Flicks(1) that are Performed by the Free-Leg at the height of each Ocho Pivot portion. Knees are held close during each and every Step-Thru and Swivel-Start, however at the point of one's direction reversal an **Ocho-Picante** can be Executed. The dancer's free lower-leg is **Quickly Bent at the Knee Pointing the Free-Toe straight Backward** with a Back-Flick in the air. The dancer's shin might momentarily become parallel with the Dancefloor or even Higher.

A **Lustrada** could be added immediately following the Back-Flick.

Caution: Avoid Kicking others.

Similar to **Picados**, and **Golpes**. [See Ochos(1)&(2), Doble-Ochos, Tres-Ochos, Ochos-para-Atras, Ocho-Cortado, Ocho-Abierto, and Ochos-Largos.]

On-The-Side: Several Generalized Coupledance Positions, Offset either Left or Right, and Partners either Facing in the same direction or else Opposed. (Not the same as To-Dance-On-The-Side.) (Less explicit than Banjo Position, Sidecar Position, and Side-by-Side Position.)

Ooze: A General Coupledance slang Term, predominately used in energetic dancing such as **Latin**. **Ooze** is a buzzword Couples use about **Decelerating from a brisk Movement**.

Excellent dancers HighLight and Soften their marvelous Movements to blend with their music's fluctuations, including its melody. Onlookers are pleased to note that the Couple Freezes as the melody abruptly holds, and that they Accelerate and Decelerate in accord with music and melody. **Ooze** is **Relaxing**, and **Beathing-Low** for an instant. After dancing a Movement Quickly, **Ooze** is suddenly Slowing and Softly seeping out a Step or two.

Ooze is the "*shade*" in **Light-and-Shade**. Inverse of **Smartly**. [See Freeze-and-Melt, Musicality-and-Expression, Impact, Juice, Syncopate, Guapa-Timing, Challenge(2), and Break-A-Way(3).] (Also see Showmanship, Class-Act, Audience-Appeal, Charisma, Panache, Charm-and-Finesse, Confidence, Strike-Ability, Presentation, Projection, Dynamics, Polished, Best-Foot-Forward, Individual-Style, Effervescence, and Expand.)

Open-Embrace-Tango: See Closed Position Argentine Tango, and Embrace.

Open-Finish-Gancho: An **Argentine Tango** Figure. One of four Behind-Gancho-to-Weighted-Foot Figures. Man holds Lunge-Right outside Partner while Lady Flicks Behind with Right Foot. Only partially Leadable.

(See Gancho, and Flick.)

Open-Promenade: A Leadable **International Tango** Coupledance Pattern, that may also be suitable for American Tango. Consists of four Steps in 1 1/2 Measures. Timing is *Slow Quick Quick, Slow*.

Begins in Promenade Position, then to Closed Position International Tango with Pickup, and ends in Feathered Position in CBMP after four Steps.

Lady rides Man's hip until completing her Swivel. First two Steps have Heel-Lead for both, also for Man's third and fourth Steps. During Heel-Leads for first two Steps, Feet of both continually Point in parallel, angled toward Partner. Both have CBMP on Step-Thru and on last Step.

Man dances *diagforward StepThru diagforturn1/8CCW, ForwardFeathered*.

Lady dances *DiagForward stepthruswivel1/2CCW PickupTurn1/8CCW, backwardfeathered*.

Same as **Closed-Promenade**, except ends ForwardFeathered instead of Close. (See Promenade-Ending, Quarter-Beats, Promenade-Link, Promenade-Tap, Progressive-Link, Head-Flick-Link, Counter-Promenade, and Promenade-to-Counter-Promenade.)

Orillero-Style: See Tango-Orillero.

Orillero-Tango: See Tango-Orillero.

Outside Position (Sidecar): A General Coupledance Position, similar to the various Closed Positions. One's Facing Feet are Closed and **to the Right and Outside of Partner's Feet**. Hand-Holds are various or none. Shoulders may be either Parallel or Feathered, and hips either Hip-to-Hip or not.

More explicit than **Offset-Facing-Opposed Position**. Same but less explicit than **Facing-Offset Position**, and **Feathered Position**. (See Dance Positions, Left-Outside Position, Butterfly-Left-Outside Position, Left-Open-Facing-Offset Position, Feathered-Left Position, Left-Star Position, Left-Shoulder-to-Shoulder Position, Left-Hip-to-Hip Position, Left-Loose-Hug Position, and [left] Spaghettis.)

Outside-Swivel(1): A Leadable, one-Measure Coupledance Figure, suitable for the Slow-**Foxtrot**, Slow-**Waltz**, both **Quicksteps**, and all **Tangos**. Rhythm Timing is *Slow Slow* (*Hold*) for all.

Beginning in Facing-Offset Position, the Man's Upper-Body 1/8-Turns Clockwise as his Lady Swivels a 1/2-Turn Clockwise. There is no Body-Sway.

Man Steps *backward* in CBMP *SkimCrossInFrontTouch* at Cou-de-Pied *hold*.

Lady, Following, dances *ForSwivel1/2CW* Toe-Spin in CBMP *brushtouchdiagback Hold*.

(See Outside-Swivel-and-Tap, and Outside-Swivel-Link.)

Outside-Swivel(2): See Outside-Swivel-and-Tap.

Outside-Swivel(3): See Outside-Swivel-Link.

Outside-Swivel-and-Tap or **Outside-Swivel**: A Leadable one-Measure Coupledance Figure, suitable for American and International **Tangos**. Rhythm with 2/4 Timing is *Slow Quick Quick*.

Begins in Closed Position International Tango, Feathers, Lady Flicks then to Promenade Position with Tap. No Turn for Man, Lady Swivels a Quarter-Turn Clockwise.

Man dances *backwardCrossInFrontTouch* at Cou-de-Pied with CBM *StepThru tapdiagforward*.

Lady dances *ForSwivel1/4CWflick stepthru TapDiagForward*.

(See Outside-Swivel-Link, Outside-Swivel, and Flick.)

Outside-Swivel-Link or **Outside-Swivel**: A Leadable one-Measure Coupledance Figure, suitable for **International Tango**. Rhythm with 2/4 Timing is *Slow Quick Quick*.

Begins in Closed Position International Tango, Feathers then to Promenade Position, Swivels to Closed Position #1 for Tango. The Man Quarter-Turns Counter-Clockwise; his Lady Half-Turns Clockwise then 3/4-Turns Counter-Clockwise.

Man dances *backwardCrossInFrontTouch* at Cou-de-Pied with CBM *StepThruTurn1/4CCW touchclose*.

Lady dances *ForSwivel1/2CW stepthruswivel3/4CCW TouchClose*.

(See Outside-Swivel-and-Tap, and Outside-Swivel.)

Oversway: A partially Leadable Coupledance Picture-Movement suitable for **Argentine** and **International Tangos**, both **Quicksteps**, Slow-**Foxtrot**, Slow-**Waltz**, and other dances. Timing varies. If begun from Closed Position International Standard, the Man initially Steps *BackTurn1/4* Counter-Clockwise, as his Lady Steps *forward*, into Promenade Position.

Man, from beginning in Promenade Position, takes one Left Step *diagforward*, first **Straightening then Flexing** his Left Knee for the **Oversway**. Keeping square with Lady, his Right Foot remains Pointed and Extended Sideward In-Place.

Lady, Striding with Energy, takes one lengthy *Sideward* Right Step with Head-Open, reaching with her Right Knee to touch the Inside of her Man's Left Knee, then Settling with her Supporting Right Knee Flexed.

Then with their Supporting Knees Softened, his Right and her Left sides Stretch Upward toward Joined and Raised Lead Hands, looking over Joined Hands in a High-Line Position. Both keep hips Up Toward Partner. Movement may end with a 1/8 Couple-Rotation Counter-Clockwise.

May also begin in Closed Position International Standard with Man's Left and Lady's Right Foot Free. (See Stride, Promenade-Sway, Oversway Position, and Oversway-with-Extension.)

Oversway-Change-of-Sway: A partially Leadable, Coupledance Ending Picture-Figure; suitable for **International Tango**, both **Quicksteps**, Slow-**Foxtrot**, Slow-**Waltz**, and others. Timing varies.

Beginning in Promenade Position, the Couple Performs the **Oversway** Movement, ending in the Oversway Position. The Couple then Performs the **Change-of-Sway** Action. (See Throwaway-Oversway, and Side-Lunge-Change-of-Sway.)

Oversway-with-Extension: A General Coupledance Position, suitable for the Slow-**Foxtrot**, Slow-**Waltz**, **International Tango**, both **Quicksteps**, and other dances.

Oversway-with-Extension is identical to the **Oversway Position**, with the addition of **Extending** the High-Line with an extreme Stretching of both Bodies.

(See Oversway, Throwaway Position, and Hinge-Line.)

Palanca: (*pah-LAHN-kah*, Spanish for *lever* or *leverage*.) A Basic Coupledance Action, referring to the Man's subtle assisting of the Lady, during her **Lifts** or **Jumps**, mainly in Argentine **Show-Tango**(1).

Same as **Lift**(3). [See Tango-Argentino. Also see Enlevement, Aerial(3), Flyer, Volta(1), Double-Work, Lift-Straight, and Lifts-to-Chest-or-Shoulder.]

Palm/Finger-Lead-in-Closed or **Right-Hand-Lead:** A Coupledance Term especially for Argentine Coupledancing, referring to **the Lead by the Man's Right Hand.** Argentine Coupledancing includes the **Argentine Tango** Genre, the **Milonga** Genre, and the **Vals** or **Argentine-Waltz.**

This also happens to be a General Lead for all Closed Position Coupledancing.

The following is from *Illustrated Tango Dance Steps;* http://nfo.net/dance/tprimer:

"*La Marcacion:*

"*Often the leader will use his hands. The leader should have his right hand just under his partner's shoulder blade. When beginning a Turn, the leader may use a little pressure from the Heel of his hand to initiate a turn to his left, or pressure from his Fingers to initiate a turn to his right. When the Lady feels the Leader's hand pressing on the left side of her back, she knows that a turn to her right is being called for, - and vice versa.*

(See LaMarca, Indicate, Lead/Follow-for-Tango, and Right-Arm-Lead.)

Panache: A complimentary General Coupledance Term for that special Quality that makes one dancer Stand-Out above another.

"*The essence of the art of dancing lies in the realm of the soul and heart; it is not the intellect but the emotions from which the dance takes off.*" -- Erika Hanka

Similar to **Charisma**. (See Showmanship, Stage-Presence, Flash-and-Pzazz, Shine, Scintillate, Class-Act, Audience-Appeal, Light-and-Shade, Smartly, Ooze, Freeze-and-Melt, Expand, Confidence, Constant, Impact, Juice, Stardom, Bring-Down-the-House, Strike-Ability, Charm-and-Finesse, Dance-the-Part, Best-Foot-Forward, Shine, Stand-Out, CareFree-Way, and Flaunting-It.)

Parada or **Stop:** (*pah-RAH-dah* is Spanish for *inactive*.) The **Parada** is a classic Spot-Coupledance Figure in the **Argentine Rotary-Tango** Style. The **Parada** brings the dancer's Lady-Partner to a **Stop**, while often simultaneously the Man places his Foot next to hers, In-Front, Sideward, or Behind, possibly in a **Sandwich** (between his Lady's Feet).

The following is from *Tango Terms* [www.tangoberretin.com/alex]:

"*Parada: Literally `stopped' - a step where the bodies stop and one foot of one person is adjacent to the foot of his/her partner. A foot-stop.*"

Ed Loomis [www.batango.com/loomis] describes the **Parada** as follows:

"*The man stops the lady, usually as she steps crossing back in back ochos or molinete, with pressure inward at the lady's back and at her balance hand with a slight downward thrust, preventing further movement. When properly led the lady stops with her feet extended apart, front and back, and her weight centered. The man may extend his foot to touch her forward foot as an additional cue and element of style or he may pivot and step back to mirror her position (fallaway).*"

A sample **Parada** follows:

Partially Leadable, there is no Couple-Rotation, although the Lady makes a Quarter-Turn Clockwise. The **Parada** begins after Partners have Executed a Basic-Start or a Double-Start.

The Man's Weight remains upon his Left Foot during the **Parada**'s *Slow Slow* one Measure long 2/4 Rhythm Timing. Man Leads Lady with his Right Ball-of-Hand. The Man retains his Stance throughout, but Slides his Right Ball-of-Foot to finally **contact** Lady's Left Ball-of-Foot.

Lady's Head remains Open. With shoulders Square to her Man's, the Lady is Led to Cross her Left Foot loosely Behind and apply Weight. Next, she Swivels a Quarter-Turn Clockwise on her Left Foot then Steps Backward on her Right Foot. Here, any further **Movement for her Left Foot is blocked by her Man's protruding Right Foot.** In "L" Position (To-Dance-On-The-Side), she ends her Figure with her Right Knee Softened and with her Left Leg Held Forward without Weight, Knees Together.

Man dances *hold SlideForCrossTouch* in a CCW arc.

Lady dances *crossbehind swivel1/4CWBackward.*

Note: Usually followed by LaLlevada, or the Sandwich.

(See Media-Luna.)

Parallel-Rocks: A Leadable, Spot-Coupledance Pattern suitable for the **Argentine Tango**. Three Measures long, Rhythm Timing is *And Slow Quick Quick, *Slow Quick Quick, Slow Slow.* Begins in Closed Position Argentine Tango. Flicks occur while Turning.

Man dances *backflickforward* to Facing-Offset *ForRock recoverbackward,* **ForSwivel1/2CWbackflick* to Left-Outside *forrock RecoverBackward,* *forswivel1/2CCWBackFlick* to Facing-Offset *Forward.*

Lady dances *ForFlickBackward* to Facing-Offset *backrock RecoverForward,* **backswivel1/2CWForFlick* to Left-Outside *BackRock recoverforward,* *BackSwivel1/2CCWforflick* to Facing-Offset *backward.*

Partial-Step or **Pressure-Step:** A series of Leadable, Basic Coupledance Movements, Left or Right Foot. These are Terms useful in describing an Action or Movement that is not a complete Step; i.e., a Movement of one Foot, taken in any direction, without Transferring any Weight. A **Pressure-Step** is taken with some Slight Pressure into the Dancefloor, but with **Partial-Weight** still being retained upon the Supporting-Foot.

This **Partial-Step** could be: (1) Forward, Sideward, or Rearward, or (2) at the Instep of the dancer's Supporting-Foot, or (3) by a Toe-Stab Instepward.

Similar to **Touch**. (See Step, Step-Touch, Foot, and Full-Weight.)

Partial-Weight or **Part-Weight:** A General Coupledance Action or Term. **Partial-Weight** is when the dancer's complete Weight is not applied.
(See Full-Weight, Partial-Step, Body-Weight, and Change-of-Weight.)

Pasada: (*pah-SAH-dah*, Spanish for *passage* or *passing over*.) The Lady's particular Movement while Coupledancing various kinds of **Argentine Tangos** at their **Milongas**. The Lady Steps Forward **over** her Man's Foot purposely in her way.
Ed Loomis [www.batango.com/loomis] describes the **Pasada** as follows:
"Occurs when the man has stopped the lady with foot contact and leads her to step forward over his extended foot. Used frequently at the end of MOLINETE or after a mordida. The lady may, at her discretion, step over the man's foot or trace her toe on the floor around its front. Pasada provides the most common opportunity for the lady to add adornos or firuletes of her own and a considerate leader will give the lady time to perform if she wishes."
(See Canyengue-Tango, Petroleo-Tango, Tango-de-Salon, Rotary-Tango, Tango-Orillero, Tango-Apilado, Milonguero-Tango, Club-Style Tango, Tango-Nuevo, Tango-Liso, Liquid-Tango, Show-Tango, Tango-Argentino, and the Continental Tango.)

Paseo: (*pah-SAY-o*, Spanish for *a stroll* or *a promenade*. **El-Paseo** is *the stroll*.) **Paseo** is a simple, Basic, Leadable, four-Count Coupledance Figure of the **Argentine Tango**, in which, from Feet-Together either in Closed Position Argentine Tango or in Banjo, the Man takes two Ball-Steps and a Touch. This Figure would be eight-Count when Half-Timed. Timing is either *Quick Quick Quick Hold*, or *Slow Slow Slow Hold*.
Man dances *forward Forward closetouch hold*.
Lady dances *Backward backward CloseTouch Hold*.
The **Paseo** may Turn. Two or more **Paseos** in sequence become one of the **Caminata** Pattern Variations. Up to five **Paseos** are sometimes Executed sequentially.
[See Paso, Tango-Draw, Tango-Close, Backward-Tango-Close, and Marque-Pied. Also see Caminar, Prominade(8), and Caminata.] [Mostly from http://64.33.34.112/.dance/tangels]

Paso: (*PAH-so*, Spanish for *a step*; *pisar* or *pasar* means *to step*.) A simple, Basic Coupledance Movement. A **Paso** is a single **Step** that the dancer takes.
(See Paseo.)

Pausa: (*PAH'oo-sah*, Spanish for a *pause* or *rest*.) A possibly Leadable, Spanish Coupledance Term for an in-Action. A **Pausa** is a momentary Hold; to cease dancing for a Time; or, a break in the dance; or, the duration of a musical note beyond its allotted period.
Same as a **Pause**. [See **Titubeo**, **Hold**(1), and **Freeze**(1). Also see Collect, Hesitation, Break(5), Suspension, Lull, Freeze-and-Melt, and Hover(1). Also see Arrepentida, Balanceo, and Freno.]

Pause-Step: A Leadable, General Coupledance Term for Pausing rather than Stepping one particular Step in Time. Perhaps Holding a Position for two or more Beats of music.
(See Balance, Hesitation, and Touch-Step.)

Pecho-Argentino: See Club-Style Tango.

Pepito (*pep-EE-toe*): The **Pepito** is an **Argentine Tango** Coupledance Traveling Pattern, two Measures long, in the **Linear-Tango** Style. Only partially Leadable. Total Couple Rotation is nil. Begins in Closed Position Argentine Tango, except both Partners' Feet are Spread, with Man's Weight on **his Left** Foot and Lady's Weight is on **her Right** Foot. Man's Timing is *Slow Slow, and slow Slow And.* Lady's Timing is *slow Slow, And slow Quick quick.*

Man dances *CloseTouch DiagForward, closetouch forward* Forward** Hold.*

Lady dances *crossbehindtouch Swivel1/8CW, Swivel1/8CCWclosetouch backward* StrideBackSwivel1/8CW crossinfront* Trabada-Step.

Notes: 1) * On Same-Feet.

2) ** On a line with Lady's Right Foot.

3) May be preceded by the Backward-Start, American-Start, Basic-Start, or the Double-Start.

4) May be followed by the Cunita.

Perform: A Coupledance Term, referring to the carrying out of a public presentation; or, executing a Movement, Figure, Pattern, or Choreography; or, the act or manner of a Performance.

Jean Baptiste Moliere writes: *"There is nothing so necessary for men as dancing... Without dancing a man can do nothing... All the ills of mankind, all the tragic misfortunes that fill the history books, the blunders of politicians, the miscarriages of great commanders, all this come from lack of skill in dancing... When a man has been guilty of a mistake, either in ordering his own affairs, or in directing those of the State, or in commanding an army, do we not always say: `So and so has made a false step in this affair'?... And can making a false step derive from anything but lack of skill in dancing?"*

(See On-Stage, Showmanship, Technique, Flash-and-Pzazz, Esthetic-Effect, Charm-and-Finesse, Charisma, Panache, Flashy, ShowGirl, Show-Stopper, Elegante, Pantomime, Articulation, Recital, and Stage-Struck. Also see Con-Amore, Amoroso, Delicado, Mignon, and Dolce.)

Petroleo-Tango: (*peh-TRO-lee-o*, Spanish for *slick* or *slippery*.) One Style of the **Argentine Tango** Genre that came into being in the 1940s. There was a Carlos Estevaz in the 1940s, whom Argentines called **Petroleo** for his strange new Style of Tango dancing. There were certain of his particular **Petroleo** Steps that came into vogue.

Comparing against the earlier **Canyengue-Tango,** of which this new **Petroleo-Tango** supplanted, the Couple's Stance here was more erect, with Knees barely Softened in **Open-Embrace** of the Outwards-and-Upwards-Style, with a Smooth Elegance-of-Movement. Being of the **Linear-Tango** type of Coupledance, it was Travel-Danced, CCW upon the Line-of-Dance, to Smoother music that had then become popularized. Lead and Follow were more refined and Lightly, with Turns added and with more subtle Footwork.

By the 1980s, this **Petroleo-Tango** had developed into the **Solon-Tango** Genre with its following types and Styles: The Rotary-Tango, Linear-Tango, the Tango-Orillero, Tango-Apilado, Milonguero-Tango, Club-Style Tango, Tango-Nuevo, and the Liquid-Tango.

(Also see the very different Show-Tango.)   [Much data from http://www.dancetraveler.com.]

Picados: (*pe-KAH-dos*, Spanish for *punctures*.) A Flourishing Movement; a **Firulete Adorno**; an Embellishment used in the **Argentine Tango** and **Milonga** Coupledances.

Ed Loomis [www.batango.com/loomis] describes **Picados** as follows:

> "*A flicking upward of the heel when turning or stepping forward. Usually done as an advanced embellishment to ochos or when walking forward.*"

Similar to **Golpes**, and **Ochos-Picante**. (See Rulo, AnkleTrip, KneeFlick, Abrupt, Levantada, LaLlevada, Castigada, Cucharita, Gancho, Amague, and Frappe; all Performed while Moving. Also see Flourish, and Gesture.)

Pickup (*pkup*) or **Close-Her-Up** or **Pick-Her-Up** or **Close-with-Her:** Two Leadable, Basic Coupledance Movements, from Man's Right or from Man's Left, Mirror-Image Opposite, suitable for all **Twosteps**, **Waltzes**, **Foxtrots**, **Quicksteps**, **Tangos**, **Onestep**, and other dances.

These Terms all mean for the Man to Close with his Lady-Partner in some fashion. Stepping-Thru with a **Pickup** from Man's Right is by far the most common method: One Step for both, with Inside-Feet from Semi-Closed Position (or from the Lady's Underarm-Turn). Short Step for Man, and with his Lead to her Left Wing, Lady Swivels a Half-Turn Counter-Clockwise, her Free-Foot Across her Man, to Closed Position.

(See Circle-Pickup, and Promenade-Close.)

Pinta: (*PEEN-tah*, Spanish for a *stain* or *spot*.) A General Argentine Coupledance slang Term for the dancer's appearance and Presentation. This includes the dancer's clothes, grooming, Posture, expression, and manner of speaking.

Similar to **Bien-Parado**. (See Postura, Derecho, and Eje.)

[Mostly from *Tango Terminology*, www.tangoafficionado.com.]

Pista: (*PISS-tah*, Spanish for *dancefloor*.) See Dancefloor.

Planchadora: (*plahn-chah-DOR-rah*, Spanish for *wallflower*.) See Wallflower.

Planeo: (*PLAH-nay-o*, Spanish for *pivot* or *glide*.) A Coupledance Figure or Pattern danced in the various **Argentine Tangos** and in the **Milonga**.

Ed Loomis [www.batango.com/loomis] describes the **Planeo** as follows:

> "*Occurs when the man steps forward onto a foot, usually his left, and pivots with the other leg trailing (gliding behind) as the lady dances an additional step or two around him. May also occur when the man stops the lady in mid stride with a slight downward lead and dances around her while pivoting her on the supporting leg as her extended leg either trails or leads. Can be done by either the man or the lady.*"

(See Calecita, Ballerina-Wheel, Tornillo-Wheel, Horse-and-Cart, Promenade-RunAround, and Right-Outside-RunAround. Also see Canyengue-Tango, Petroleo-Tango, Tango-de-Salon, Rotary-Tango, Linear-Tango, Tango-Orillero, Tango-Apilado, Milonguero-Tango, Club-Style Tango, Tango-Nuevo, Tango-Liso, Liquid-Tango, Show-Tango, Tango-Argentino, and the Continental Tango.)

Pocket: The Term "**Pocket**" is used in the Argentines for two Generalized Coupledance Feet Positions for the **Argentine Tango**, Left or Right. The Term "**Pocket**" refers to when one Tango dances on the Outside of Partner, either hip.

Less explicit than **To-Dance-Outside**.

Postura: (*pos-TOO-rah*, Spanish for *posture*.)   A General Argentine Coupledance word for "*Correct posture for tango is erect and elegant with the shoulders always over the hips and relaxed, and with the center carried forward toward the dance partner over the toes and balls of the feet.*"
     Same as **Posture**. (See Derecho, Eje, Pinta, and Bien-Parado.)
     [Mostly from *Tango Terminology*, www.tangoafficionado.com.]

Practica: (*prahk-tay-KUH*, Spanish for *practice* or *exercise*.)   **Practicas** is a General **Argentine Tango** Coupledance Term for **Practice-Sessions**.
     As for the Argentine **Milonga** place-to-dance ("*tango club*"), a casual **Practica** that includes teaching will begin at 8 or 9pm and end at 11 or 12. Then from midnight until perhaps 5am, the formal **Milonga** occurs.
     (See Workshop, Clinic, Seminar, Rehearse, and Walk-Thru.)

Practice: Practice and Practice, the three secrets to excellent Coupledancing.
Martha Graham writes: "*Practice is a means of inviting the perfection desired.*"
Beverly Sills says: "*There is no shortcut to anywhere worth going.*"
     Practice sessions or socials may be held for whatever type of Coupledancing the dancer is inclined to participate in. These may be daily, weekly, or monthly, and probably take various forms at various places. **Practicing** is repeating and repeating the elements and/or Techniques that have been taught; laboring through the Figures and Patterns, and/or complete dance Routines, so as to improve and progress. **Practicing** is not just standing, watching, talking, arguing, etc. It is working up the dancer's sweat.
     (See Rehearse, Practica, Walk-Thru, Disciplined, and Structured.)

Presentation or **Audience-Projection:** A General Coupledance Term, relating to how well the Couple Performs for an audience; to be formally seen. Without introversion or Strain, the Couple "sells" their dance to their audience, outwardly exuding joy and enthusiasm with Confidence in their Performance.
     Presentation is creating an attractive picture for the audience, by Performing clinically clear Lines whenever Striking-a-Pose. Just how the dancer uses the arms, legs, Shoulders, Torso, etc., are all important in **Presentation**.
     A **Presentation** example is, for Smooth and Standard International Dances in a Closed Position, the picture the Lady Presents by the Timing and manner in which the Lady Opens and Closes her Head. Some Ladies prefer Turning her Head Rightward as Moving into Promenade while others keep their Head Closed. Both are correct. Which looks better?
     Another important **Presentation** example is the selective use of fitting Facial expressions, after careful study.
     All Austere-Lines should be avoided, such as Breaking-Frame, Posterior-Protrusion, Slumped-Torso, Round-Shouldered, Chicken-Wings, Elbow-Droop, Limp-Arms, Stiffness, Straight-Kneed, Head-Bowed or Tilted, Wrist-Droop, and Affected-Fingers. Use care in Individual-Style when Making-a-Show.
     "*Do you not realize that dance is the pure act of metamorphosis?*" -- Paul Valery
     "*A good education consists in knowing how to sing and dance well.*" -- Plato, Laws
     "*Fine dancing, I believe, like virtue, must be its own reward.*" -- Jane Austen
     Similar to **Projection, Esthetic-Effect,** and **Audience-Appeal**. (See Stage-Presence, Showmanship, Essence-of-a-Dance, Elegance-of-Movement, Togetherness, Free-Hand-Fashioning, Style, On-Stage, Strike-Ability, Impact, Juice, Bring-Down-the-House, Flash-and-Pzazz, CareFree-Way, Facials, Pantomime, Articulation, Stardom, Class-Act, Light-and-Shade, Smartly, Ooze, Freeze-and-Melt, Clapping, Best-Foot-Forward, and Technique.)

Press-Line or Spanish-Line: A General Picture-Figure, mostly used in **Modern** and **Smooth** Coupledancing; usually the Man's Figure, Forward-Pressing his Right Foot. Also, **Press-Line** is two Coupledance Movements by either Partner, Right or Left. Suitable for **PasoDoble**, certain **Tangos**, both **Rumbas** and the **Bolero**, for West-Coast-**Swing**, and for General Ballroom and Roundancing, and for other dances.

One-half to three-quarters of one's Weight is Held Forward. One's Forward Pressing Knee is Bent with the Forward Foot Arched High on the Ball. One's Rearward leg is Held Straight with the Rearward Foot Flat to the Dancefloor.

Consists of the dancer directly **Forward-Pressing one Ball-of-Foot, then applying a Slight Twist with a Hold**. One's Body and Rearward Foot Twists 1/8 Clockwise if Left Foot is Forward, or Counter-Clockwise if Right Foot is Forward.

One-half to three-quarters of one's Weight is Held Forward. One's Forward Pressing Knee is Bent with the Forward Foot Arched High on the Ball. One's Rearward leg is Held Straight with the Rearward Foot Flat to the Dancefloor.

(See Foot-Pressure, Press, Line, Attitude-Line, Lunge-Line, Hinge-Line, Sit-Line, Sentado-Line, and Eros-Line.)

Pressure-Step: See Partial-Step.

Private-Milonga: See Milonga.

Progressive-Link or Link: A Leadable, crisp and Dramatic Coupledance Movement, Mostly used in the **International Tango**, but suitable for all Tangos. Timing is *Quick Quick*, two Steps, a half-Measure.

Changes from a Closed Position to Promenade Position. The first Step for both is with CBMP. The second Step can be overdone, less is best. With second Step, both their Weights end on Inner-Edges of Inside-Feet. Each Outside-Foot ends Slightly DiagForward and parallel with one's Inside-Foot, and with Inner-Edge Touching, but with Heel Slightly off the Dancefloor, and with Outside Knees veering Inwards. Lady ends riding Man's hip.

Man Dances *forward* Heel-Lead *InPlaceTurn1/8CW*.

Lady, Following, dances *Backward turn1/4CW*.

(See Link, Head-Flick-Link, and Promenade-Link.)

Progressive-Side-Step or Argentine-Walk: A Leadable, half-Measure Coupledance Movement suitable for International and American **Tangos**. Rhythm Timing is *Quick Quick*.

In Closed Position International Tango throughout. Both are on Inner-Edge of Foot upon second Step.

Man Steps *forward* in CBM *DiagBackward*. Lady Steps *Backward* in CBM *diagforward*.

Progressive-Side-Step-Reverse-Turn: A Leadable 3 1/2-Measure Coupledance Pattern, suitable for International and American **Tangos**. Rhythm with 2/4 Timing is *Quick Quick Slow, Slow Quick Quick, Slow Quick Quick, Slow*.

In Closed Position International Tango throughout. Total Couple-Rotation is a 3/4-Turn Counter-Clockwise. Pattern consists of a Progressive-Side-Step, half a Reverse-Turn, a Forward Rock, completing the Reverse-Turn and Close Ending.

Man dances *forward* in CBM *DiagBackward* on Inside-edge *forward* in CBM, *ForSwivel1/2CCW* Right Shoulder-Lead *backward* Left Shoulder-Lead *ForRock* Right Shoulder-Lead, *smallrecover* Left Shoulder-Lead *BackTurn1/4CCW* with CBM *diagforward*, *Close*.

Lady, Following, dances *Backward* in CBM *diagforward* on Inside-edge *Backward* in CBM, *backswivel1/2CCW* Left Shoulder-Lead *Forward* Right Shoulder-Lead *backrock* Left Shoulder-Lead, *SmallRecover* Right Shoulder-Lead *forturn1/4CCW* with CBM *DiagBackward*, *close*.

Progressive-Tango-Rocks: A Leadable, two-Measure Traveling-Coupledance Pattern suitable for both Argentine and American **Tangos**. Danced entirely in Closed Position International Tango, except Man usually holds Lady's Hand at his Left hip for first Measure. No Turning. Rhythm Timing is *Quick Quick Slow, Quick Quick Slow*.

Man dances in CBM, *forcheck BackRecover forward*, then with Hands Raised and in CBM, *ForCheck backrecover Forward*.

His Lady Follows.

Promenade-Ending or **The Promenade** or **Promenade-Quarter-Beats** or **Promenade:** A Leadable, Traveling-**International Tango** Coupledance Pattern, that may also be suitable for American and Continental Tangos. Consists of three Steps and a Change-Feet-Tap in 1 1/2 Measures. Timing is *Slow Quick Quick, And Slow*.

Danced entirely in Promenade Position with Lady continually riding Man's hip. No Turn. Feet continually Point in parallel, angled toward Partner. Both have Heel-Lead on first three Steps. Both have CBMP on Step-Thru. Feet Close Flat and Staggered Rearward. Each Outside-Foot **Touches** Slightly DiagForward and on Inner-Edge, with Heel barely off the Dancefloor, and with Outside Knees veering Inwards. Both their Weights end on Inner-Edge of Inside-Feet.

Man dances *diagforward StepThru diagforward, CloseLower diagfortouch*.

Lady dances *DiagForward stepthru DiagForward, closelower DiagForTouch*.

(See Quarter-Beats, Counter-Promenade, Promenade-to-Counter-Promenade, Promenade-Tap, Closed-Promenade, Open-Promenade, Promenade-Link, Progressive-Link, and Head-Flick-Link.)

Promenade-Link or **Pickup** (*pkup*): A Leadable **International Tango** Coupledance Figure, that may also be suitable for American Tango. Consists of two Steps with a Pickup and Touch in one-Measure. Timing is *Slow Quick Quick*.

Begins in Promenade Position and ends in Closed Position International Tango. Lady rides Man's hip until completing her Swivel. For the Steps, both have Heel-Lead, and Feet continually Point in parallel, angled toward Partner. Both have CBMP on Step-Thru, and their Touch is almost Closed.

Man dances *diagforward StepThru touch*. Man may 1/8-Turn Counter-Clockwise on Step-Thru.

Lady, Following, dances *DiagForward stepthruswivel1/2CCW PickupTouch*.

Similar to Promenade-Tap. (See Closed-Promenade, Open-Promenade, Progressive-Link, Link, Head-Flick-Link, Promenade-Ending, Quarter-Beats, Counter-Promenade, and Promenade-to-Counter-Promenade.)

Figure 2, **Promenade Position**

Promenade Position for Tango: A Basic Coupledance Position suitable for all **Tangos**, and for other dances.

Weight is on their Inside-Feet, and with Inside of Ball of Outside-Feet Touching Forward and spaced close. Pictured by some as Opened in a Vee as much as is Half-Open Position, but not so for any Tango. Shoulders-Parallel, or almost parallel is required, as in Closed Position International Tango; except, with both with CBMP, only hips and Heads are Slightly Open.

Lady's fingertips are at his shoulder seam, with her elbow Lightly resting, except for International Tango where she may Tango-Salute. But in all versions of Promenade Position, Weight is Well over Softened Trailing-Knees, Man's Left and Lady's Right Hands remain Clasped, and Inside-hips are in contact, with Lady's hip Behind Man's.

Essentially Mirror-Image Opposite to **Reverse-Promenade Position.** Similar to **Semi-Closed Position** for International Ballroom, Modern and Smooth. (See Semi-Closed Position for American Tango, Fallaway Position, and Promenade-Ending.)

Note: For sharp appearance, Lady's Head can remain Closed in this Position for American Tango, even with an Abrupt.

(See Figure 5.) (See Dance Positions.)

Promenade-Sway or **Challenge-Line:** A partially Leadable, General Coupledance Movement, suitable for the Slow-**Foxtrot,** Slow-**Waltz, Argentine** and **International Tangos,** both **Quicksteps,** and other dances. One-Measure long, Timing is *Slow Slow.*

Begins in a Closed Position; both Lower then Step *diagforward* to the Man's Left, on Balls of their Lead Feet, into a tight Semi-Closed Position, with a Slight Right face Turn through their Bodies. Then with their Supporting Knees Softened, Man's Left and Lady's Right sides Stretch Upward toward Joined and Raised Lead Hands. In a High Upright Poise, both look over Joined Hands in a High-Line Position. Their Free legs are behind, Straight. Movement may end with a 1/8 Couple-Rotation Clockwise or Counter-Clockwise.

(See Oversway, Broken-Sway, Side-Rise, Side-Stretch, Body-Lift, Hip-Lift, Swoop, Side-Lift, and Check.)

Promenade-Tap: A Leadable **International Tango** Coupledance Figure, that may also be suitable for American and Continental Tangos. Consists of two Steps and a Brush-Tap in one-Measure. Timing is *Slow Quick Quick.*

In Promenade Position throughout, with Lady continually riding Man's hip. No Turn. Feet continually Point in parallel, angled toward Partner. Both have Heel-Lead on both Steps. Both have CBMP on Step-Thru. Each Outside-Foot **Touches** Slightly DiagForward and on Inner-Edge, with Heel barely off the Dancefloor, and with Outside Knees veering Inwards. Both their Weights end on Inner-Edge of Inside-Feet.

Man dances *diagforward StepThru brushdiagfortouch.*

Lady dances *DiagForward stepthru BrushDiagForTouch.*

Similar to Promenade-Link. (See Promenade-Ending, Counter-Promenade, Promenade-to-Counter-Promenade, Closed-Promenade, Open-Promenade, Quarter-Beats, Progressive-Link, and Head-Flick-Link.)

Promenade-to-Counter-Promenade: A Leadable, Traveling-Coupledance Pattern suitable for all **Tangos**. Three Measures long, Rhythm Timing is *Slow Quick Quick, Slow Slow, Quick Quick And Slow*.

In Promenade Position the first three Steps, then Tango-Switching to Reverse-Semi-Closed Position, followed by three Steps and a Change-Feet-Tap. Lady continually rides Man's hip, first his Right then his Left.

Upon ending, Feet Close Flat and Staggered Rearward. Each Outside-Foot **Tango-Taps** Slightly DiagForward and on Inner-Edge, with Heel barely off the Dancefloor, and with Outside Knees veering Inwards. Both their Weights end on Inner-Edge of Inside-Feet.

Man dances *diagforward* Heel-Lead *StepThru* in CBM Heel-Lead *diagforward* Heel-Lead, *tangoswitchHold DiagForward* Heel-Lead, *stepthru* in CBM Heel-Lead *DiagForward* Heel-Lead *closelower DiagForTouch*.

Lady dances *DiagForward* Heel-Lead *stepthru* in CBM Heel-Lead *DiagForward* Heel-Lead, *TangoSwitchhold diagforward* Heel-Lead, *StepThru* in CBM Heel-Lead *diagforward* Heel-Lead *CloseLower diagfortouch*.

(See Promenade-Ending, Counter-Promenade, Tango-Switches, Promenade-Tap, Closed-Promenade, Open-Promenade, Quarter-Beats, Promenade-Link, Progressive-Link, and Head-Flick-Link.)

Promenade-to-Left-Outside: A Leadable, Traveling-Coupledance Pattern suitable for both Argentine and American **Tangos**. Four Measures long, 10 Steps, Rhythm Timing is *Slow Quick Quick, Slow Slow, Slow Slow, Quick Quick Slow*.

In Promenade Position the first four Steps, a Wing to Left-Outside Position, with looking at Partner and Lead-Hands Clasped Low at Man's hip, Four Forward Steps in this Position, with a Quarter-Turn Counter-Clockwise to Tango-Close in Closed Position International Tango, except Lady Locks Right Foot Behind.

Man dances *diagforward* on Inside-Edge *StepThru* in CBM *diagforward* on Inside-Edge, *ForCheckHold* in CBMP, *forward* in CBM *Forward* Right Shoulder-Lead, *forturn1/8CCW SideTurn1/8CCW close*.

Lady, dances *DiagForward* on Inside-Edge *stepthru* in CBM *DiagForward* on Inside-Edge, *stepthruswivel1/2CCWhold*, *Backward* in CBM *backward* Left Shoulder-Lead, *BackTurn1/8CCW sideturn1/8CCW LockBehind*.

(See Promenade.)

Promenade-Vine: A Leadable, Traveling-Coupledance Pattern suitable for both Argentine and American **Tangos**. Five Measures long, Rhythm Timing is *Slow Quick Quick, Quick Quick Quick Quick, *Quick Quick Slow, Slow Slow, Quick Quick Slow*. Lady dances Mirror-Image Opposite to Man.

Begins in Promenade Position. Partners dance Forward, Thru, Vine-Behind, Thru, *Vine-Behind, Chair, Back-Flick then to Reverse-Semi-Closed Position, BackTurn to Closed Position International Tango, Sideward then ends in Right-Tango-Closed.

Man dances *diagforward ThruTurn1/8CW* to Closed *sideward, CrossBehind sideturn1/8CCW* to Promenade *ThruTurn1/8CW* to Closed *sideward, *CrossBehind sideturn1/8CCW* to Promenade *CrossForwardChair, recoverbackward BackFlickswivel3/8CW, BackTurnCCW* to Closed *sideward Close*.

Lady dances *DiagForward thruturn1/8CCW* to Closed *Sideward, crossbehind SideTurn1/8CW* to Promenade *thruturn1/8CCW* to Closed *Sideward, *crossbehind SideTurn1/8CW* to Promenade *crossforwardchair, RecoverBackward backflickSwivel3/8CCW, backturnCW* to Closed *Sideward close*.

Puntada-del-Pie or **The-Foot-Tap:** (*poon-TAH-dah-del-pe-AY* is Spanish for *point-of-the-foot.*) The **Puntada-del-Pie** is an **Argentine Tango** Coupledance Movement, a doodling gesture, a sign to Partner, usually Executed by the Lady in exasperation during a **Corte**, (they having abruptly stopped dancing.)

The Lady Performs the **Puntada-del-Pie** by repeatedly Tapping her Free-Toe to the Dancefloor Behind her Supporting-Foot. Often, she does this during the time her Man does his **ShoeShine**. Most often, the **Puntada-del-Pie** is Executed as a Flourish, just for show. But instead, the Lady might Perform **Levantadas** to show her irritation at the delay.

The **Puntada-del-Pie** is similar to the **Golpecitos**, and even to the **Fanfarron**. It is more explicit than the **Dibujo**. (See ShoeShine, Lapiz, Caricias, Lustrada, Chiche, Fanfarron, Golpecitos, Zapatazo, Levantada, and Enganche; all Dibujo Adornos Performed during a Parada. Also see Flourish, and Gesture.)

Pyramid: See Tango-Lean.

Quartas: (Spanish for *poses.*) The name for various attractive Figure Poses that Couples assume in the **Argentine Tango**, **Argentine Waltz**, and **Milonga** Coupledances.

Ed Loomis [www.batango.com/loomis] describes the **Quartas** as follows:

"Dance lines struck and held as dramatic flourishes at the end of a song. Large dramatic ones are used for stage or fantasia dancing, smaller softer versions occasionally in Salon style, and not used in Milonguero style at all. See Corte."

[See Corte(2), and Picture-Figure.]

Quarter-Beats: A Leadable Spot-Coupledance Figure used in **International Tango**. Rearward then Forward, in Promenade Position throughout. Consists of three Steps and a Change-Feet-Tap in one Measure. Timing is *Quick And Quick And Slow.*

Tiny Steps with no Rise, Lady continually rides Man's hip.

Man dances *backward DiagBackward recoverdiagforward CloseLower touchdiagforward.*

Lady dances *Backward diagbackward RecoverDiagForward closelower TouchDiagForward.*

(See Promenade-Ending.)

Quebrada (*kay-BRAH-dah*) or **Break:** **Quebrada** is an **Argentine Tango** Coupledance Movement by the Man, in the **Rotary-Tango** Style. Begins with Lady in a very close Fan Position, to Man's Left.

Man Checks Lady, with her legs Spread fore-and-aft, as Lady Steps *Forward* Across Man. Now the **Quebrada** is Executed by the Man Placing his Right Foot without Weight between her Feet. The Man completes his Movement by Transferring his Weight Forward and Swiveling to Face her.

Note: May be followed by the similar **Sacada**.

Quebrada Position: (*kay-BRAH-dah*, Spanish for *break* or *broken*.) A Lady's Position for the **Argentine Tango** Coupledance. A **Corte**(2), the **Quebrada Position** is where, during their dance, the Lady Stands on one Foot as she hangs her Weight upon her Man. She relaxes her other Foot behind her own back, with its Toe normally Touching the Dancefloor.

Ed Loomis [www.batango.com/loomis] describes the **Quebrada** as follows:

"*A position where the lady stands on one foot with the other foot hanging relaxed behind the supporting foot. Sometimes seen with the lady hanging with most of her weight against the man. Also a position in which the dancer's upper body and hips are rotated in opposition to each other with the working leg flexed inward creating a broken dance line.*"

[See Tango-Lean, Tango-Apilado, Carpa, Milonguero-Style, Close-Embrace-Tango, and Embrace(2). Also see Lean. Also see Quartas, and Sentado Position.] [Some data from http://nfo.net/dance/tango.]

Quick-Open-Telemark: A Leadable Coupledance Figure, that is actually the **second half of the Double-Telemark**, including the added Step. Figure is suitable for Argentine and International **Tangos**, for Slow-**Foxtrot**, Slow-**Waltz** and both **Quicksteps**. There are at least three Timings: (1) *And Quick Quick Slow*; (2) *Quick Quick Quick Quick*; and (3) *Quick Quick And Slow*.

Begins and ends in Semi-Closed Position, with Loose-Closed Position in-between. One Measure, four Steps, total Couple-Rotation is 3/4- to 7/8-Turn Counter-Clockwise.

Man dances *CrossInFront* in CBMP *forturn1/8CCW Swivel3/4CCW* with Right Side-Stretch *diagforward* Left-Side-Lead.

Lady, Following, dances *diagforturn1/8CCW BackTurn1/8CCW* with CBM *heelturn3/8CCW DiagForward* Right-Side-Lead.

(See Telemark-to-Semi-Closed.)

Rabona: (*rrah-BO-nah*, Spanish for *tail*.) A Coupledance Figure danced in the various **Argentine Tangos** and in the **Milonga**.

Ed Loomis [www.batango.com/loomis] describes the **Rabona** as follows:

"*RABONA A walking step with a syncopated cross. Done forward or backward the dancer steps on a beat, quickly closes the other foot in cruzada, and steps again on the next beat. Adopted from soccer. See traspie.*"

Note: The **Rabona** could possibly be danced (with difficulty) as a Syncopated **Cross-Walk**.

Similar to the **Traspie**, to **Forward-Lock-Forward**, and to **Backward-Lock-Backward**. (See Latin-Cross-Forward, and Chasse. Also see Canyengue-Tango, Petroleo-Tango, Tango-de-Salon, Rotary-Tango, Linear-Tango, Tango-Orillero, Tango-Apilado, Milonguero-Tango, Club-Style Tango, Tango-Nuevo, Tango-Liso, Liquid-Tango, Show-Tango, Tango-Argentino, and the Continental Tango.)

<u>Reclining-Lady</u> or **Lean-Dip**: A Leadable Coupledance **Picture-Figure**, in which the Man Reclines his Lady Partner against his Right side. At least one-Measure long, suitable for **Cabaret**, all **Tangos**, all **Rumbas**, the **Bolero**, the Slow-**Foxtrot**, Slow-**Waltz**, and other Slow dances. Timing varies.

Begins in Skaters Position. Partners remain Side-by-Side throughout the Figure.

Man Head-Loops then releases Clasped Left Hands, laying Lady's Left arm about his own neck. Man Leads Lady's hip to against his hip, by his Right Hand at her Right hip or lower waist. Man widely Spreads his legs and Lunges Sideways by deeply Bending his Left Knee, with his Right leg Straight under her load, and with his Left-Side-Stretched. Man stabilizes his Lady throughout. Man views Lady's face and Extends his Left arm.

<u>Caution</u>: **Avoid Pressing Lady's rib-cage**; lightly Press below bottom rib, at her hip.

Lady, with her Left Foot remaining Parallel against Man's Right Foot, **Reclines** thusly: Lady Reclines Sideward to her Left, laying along and against Man's Right leg and side, holding Man's Right Hand safely Low to protect her rib. With extensive Left-Side-Stretch and keeping her left leg Straight, Lady views ceiling and Raises and Spreads her Right Knee, placing sole of her Right Foot against her inner Left calf.

Alternate beginnings are: (1) An Open-Impetus to a very open Semi-Closed Position; (2) From the first three Steps of a Telespin; (3) After an Open-Hip-Twist.

After Lady Raises, applying her Weight to her Right leg, their alternate Codas are: (1) Pattern ends in Semi-Closed Position; (2) Lady Rolls Forward into a normal Dip(1).

(See **Reclining-Lady Position**, and **Reclining-Lady-with-Develope**.)

<u>Reclining-Lady Position</u>: A Leadable Coupledance **Picture-Figure** Position, in which the Man has Reclined his Lady Partner against his Right side. Suitable for **Cabaret**, all **Tangos**, all **Rumbas**, the **Bolero**, the Slow-**Foxtrot**, Slow-**Waltz**, and other Slow dances.

Partners follow the above procedure for **Reclining-Lady** to achieve this Position.

(See **Reclining-Lady-with-Develope**.)

<u>Reclining-Lady-with-Develope</u>: A Leadable Coupledance **Picture-Figure** Pattern, in which the Man Reclines his Lady Partner against his Right side, followed by the Lady's Develope. At least two-Measures long, suitable for **Cabaret**, all **Tangos**, all **Rumbas**, the **Bolero**, the Slow-**Foxtrot**, Slow-**Waltz**, and other Slow dances. Timing varies.

Partners follow as above for **Reclining-Lady** to achieve the **Reclining-Lady Position**.

Lady Developes as follows: With Lady's Right Foot cocked against her inner Left calf, Lady Gracefully Kicks her Right Leg Toward the ceiling. Toe first, with a sudden initial Movement followed by a Slower Recovery, Lady Rises, applying her Weight to her Right leg.

Man stabilizes his Lady throughout, then Rises, Recovering with Weight on his Left leg. Pattern possibly ends in Semi-Closed Position.

<u>Repentant</u>: See Arrepentida.

Resolucion (*rray-so-LOO-the-own*) or **Resolution** or **Cierre** or **Closing-Finish:** All are **Argentine Tango** Genre and **Milonga** Coupledance Terms for the Couple's Leadable, Gentle, three-Step **Ending** for each Pattern or musical Phrase, or for the complete dance. Rhythm Timing for this Figure is *Quick Quick Slow*; one Measure long in 2/4 Cut-Time.

Same as Counts 6, 7, & 8 of the Eight-Step-Basic-Tango; an ending like a first half of an Arthur Murry Box-Step. Total Couple-Rotation is usually a Quarter-Turn Counter-Clockwise. Both Partners dance all three Steps *Ball-Heel*. Figure Ends Embraced, Blending Together in Closed Position Argentine Tango. This **Resolucion** is danced as follows:

Man ends dancing *forturn1/8CCW LongForTurn1/8CCW sidedrawclose* to Arch with Weight, straighten.

Lady, with Head-Open, ends dancing *CrossBackTurn1/8CCW longdiagbackturn1/8CCW SideDrawClose* to Arch with Weight, straighten.

Resolucion is the most used Ending; see **Natural-Resolution** for a less common Ending. (Also see The-Break, Backward-Close-Finish, Tango-Draw, Tango-Close, and CloseTouch.)

Note: May be preceded by the Media-Luna.

Reverse-Fallaway-Slip: A Leadable, one or 1 1/2-Measure, four-Step Coupledance Figure, suitable for the **International Tango**, Slow- and Medium-**Foxtrots**, Slow-**Waltz**, and both **Quicksteps**.

Timing for either International Tango or Slow-Foxtrot is *Quick Quick Quick Quick*, or *Slow Quick And Quick*, or *Slow Quick Quick And*. Timing for Slow-Waltz is *Slow Slow And Slow*, or *And Slow Slow Slow*, or *Slow And Slow Slow*, or *Slow Slow Slow And*. Timing for Quickstep is *Slow Quick Quick, Slow*, or *Slow Quick And Quick*, or *Slow Quick Quick And*.

Begins and ends in a Closed Position; Figure is danced in Semi-Closed on the Fallaway Crossing Step. Total Couple-Rotation is a 3/4 to Full-Turn Counter-Clockwise.

Man dances *forturn1/8CCW* with CBM *riseDiagBackTurn1/4CCW* with Right-Side-Lead *crossbehindlowerslip1/2CCW* in CBMP *StepInPlace*.

Lady, Following, her Head-Closed throughout, dances *BackTurn1/8CCW* with CBM *Risesideturn1/8CCW* with Left-Side-Lead *BackSlip1/8CCW* in CBMP *forswivel1/2CCW*.

(See Reverse-Fallaway-from-Closed.)

Reverse-Mordida: See Sandwich.

Reverse-Pivot or **Left-Pivot** or **Pivot-Slow-Left-Face:** A Leadable Basic, Swiveling Coupledance Figure, danced in two *Slow* Steps. **Couple-Rotation** for a Reverse-Pivot is one Full-Turn danced Counter-Clockwise, and always danced Traveling, never in one Spot.

Progresses either Forward or Backward. Executed in a tightly Closed-Contrabody Position; Left-Foot remains In-Front of Right-Foot for both while Left-Pivoting. Forward Left Steps between Partner's Feet. Heights are Lowered so that Knees interlock. Free-Legs alternate either Forward or Backward. Partners Swivel Half-Turns alternately on the Ball-Heel then Heel-Ball of the Feet.

(See Reverse-Pivot-Half, Singular-Pivot, and Pivot.)

Reverse-Pivot-Half or **Reverse-Half-Pivot** or **Left-Pivot-Half** or **Pivot-Half, Slow-Left-Face:** Two Leadable Basic Coupledance Movements, Swiveling one Step, either **Rearward** or **Forward**, and with either *Slow* or *Quick* Rhythm Timing. Suitable for the Slow-Foxtrot, Slow-Waltz, **International Tango**, both **Quicksteps**, and other dances. **Couple-Rotation** is 3/8- to 1/2-Turn **Counter-Clockwise**.

In a Closed-Contrabody Position, Left-Foot remains In-Front of Right-Foot for both during Pivot. Heights are Lowered so that Knees interlock. Free-Legs are Moved from either Forward or Backward, danced either Ball-Heel or Heel-Ball of the Foot. The Man may Step *BackSwivel* with Left Foot Forward, as his Lady Steps with Head-Closed *forswivel* with Right Foot Rearward; or, the Man may Step *forswivel* as his Lady Steps with Head-Closed *BackSwivel*.

(See Reverse-Pivot, Pivot-Half, Singular-Pivot, Closed and Contrabody.)

Reverse-Promenade Position or **Scorpion-Arms Position:** Names for a General Coupledance Position, suitable for many dances and often Performed as the Ending for various **Tangos**. **Scorpion-Arms** is essentially Mirror-Image Opposite to **Promenade Position**, except for arm configurations. **Scorpion-Arms** is a Position in which the Couple's Lead-Arms are Arched Vertically-Up into a curve not unlike a scorpion's tail and stinger.

Weight is on their Inside-Feet, Man's Left and Lady's Right; Weight is Well over Softened Trailing-Knees. The Inside of Ball of Outside-Feet are Touching Forward, normally Toward Reverse-Line-of-Dance. Spaced close, their Outside Knees are Slightly turned Inward.

Shoulders are almost Parallel, causing both Partners to have extreme CBMP; only their hips and Heads are Slightly Open. Inside-hips are in contact, with Lady's hip Behind Man's.

Lady's Left fingertips are at Man's Right shoulder seam; here, Man may assume a PasoDoble Hold with his Right arm, if Lady is short and/or buxom.

Man's Left and Lady's Right Hands remain Clasped, and, melded together, the Man has Raised his Lady's Right arm Arched vertically overhead into a curving arc.

(See Dance Positions, Counter-Promenade, Reverse-Semi-Closed Position, Left-Semi-Closed Position, and Left-Half-Open Position.)

Reverse-Sandwich: See Sandwich.

Reverse-Semi-Closed Position (*RSCP*) or **Counter-Promenade Position:** A Basic Coupledance Position with Lady on Man's Left. Suitable for the American Viennese and Medium-**Waltzes**, Country-Western Waltz, Period and Hesitation Waltzes, American **Quickstep** and Medium-**Foxtrot**, American **Onestep** and **Twostep**, Texas and Disco Twosteps, all **Tangos**, **Rumbas**, **Boleros**, **ChaChas**, **Mambos** and **Sambas**, the **Merengue**, **Polka**, **Cumbia** and **PasoDoble**, and other dances.

Opened Slightly in a Vee shape with both Upper-Bodies in CBMP, the Lady's Right and the Man's Left Inside-hips are in contact. Outside Toes Point Diagonally. Man's Left and Lady's Right Hands remain Clasped, and usually are Raised in a soft curve just over their Heads. Man's Right wrist is loosely around Lady's waist, or Man has taken a PasoDoble-Hold if Lady is short and/or buxom. With their Weights Forward, both Partners are ready for Stepping-Thru with Inside-Feet.

(See Reverse-Promenade Position, Left-Whisk Position, and Counter-Promenade.)

Reverse-Start: See Backward-Start.

Reverse-Turn-Closed-Finish: A Leadable, two-Measure, six-Step Coupledance Pattern, suitable for the Slow-**Foxtrot**, and for International and American **Tangos**. Rhythm Timing is *Slow Quick Quick, Slow Quick Quick* for Foxtrot; and *Quick Quick Slow, Quick Quick Slow* for the Tangos.

Begins either Feathered or in Closed Position International Standard or Tango, and Ends in Closed Position. Couple-Rotation is a 3/4 to 7/8-Turn total, Counter-Clockwise. Lady is Hub-Partner; Man is Rim-Partner.

Man dances *forturn1/4CCW DiagBackTurn1/4CCW backward* in Closed Position, *BackTurn1/4CCW diagforward Close*.

Lady, Following with Head-Closed, Lowers then dances *ShortBackTurn1/4CCW heelturn1/4CCW Forward* to Closed Position, *forturn1/4CCW DiagBackward close*.

(See Reverse-Turn-Open-Finish, Natural-Turn, and Walking-Turns.)

Reverse-Turn-One-Half: A Leadable, three Step Coupledance Figure, suitable for the Slow-**Foxtrot**, and for International and American **Tangos**. Timing is *Slow Quick Quick*.

Partners in Closed Position International Standard or Tango, Couple-Rotate 3/8 to a Half-Turn total, Counter-Clockwise in one Measure, with a Heel-Turn for the Lady. Lady is Hub-Partner; Man is Rim-Partner.

Man dances *forturn1/4CCW DiagBackTurn1/4CCW backward*.

Lady, Following with Head-Closed, Lowers then dances *ShortBackTurn1/4CCW heelturn1/4CCW Forward*.

(See Natural-Turn-One-Half, Double-Reverse Spin, and Four-Count-Turn.)

Reverse-Turn-Open-Finish or **Open-Reverse-Turn**: A Leadable, two-Measure, six-Step Coupledance Pattern, suitable for the Slow-**Foxtrot**, and for International and American **Tangos**. Rhythm Timing is *Slow Quick Quick, Slow Quick Quick* for the 4/4 Foxtrot; and *Quick Quick Slow, Quick Quick Slow* for the 2/4 Tangos.

Begins either in Feathered or in Closed Position International Standard or Tango, Blends to Closed Position, and Ends in Feathered Position. Couple-Rotation is a 3/4 to 7/8-Turn total, Counter-Clockwise. Lady is Hub-Partner; Man is Rim-Partner.

Man dances *forturn1/4CCW DiagBackTurn1/4CCW backward* Left-side Leading in Closed Position, *BackTurn1/4CCW diagforward Forward* Outside with CBM.

Lady, Following with Head-Closed, Lowers then dances *ShortBackTurn1/4CCW heelturn1/4CCW Forward* Right-side Leading to Closed Position, *forturn1/4CCW DiagBackward backward* with CBM.

(See Reverse-Turn-Closed-Finish, and Walking-Turns-with-Right-Parallel.)

Revolucion (*rray-vo-LOO-the-own*) or **Full-Turn:** The **Revolucion** is an **Argentine Tango** Coupledance Figure. In two Steps, one Measure in length, Rhythm Timing is *Slow Slow*. Total Couple Rotation is a Half-Turn Counter-Clockwise. The **Revolucion** perhaps begins in Closed Position Argentine Tango, Moves into Left-Outside Position, then ends Eye-to-Eye in Toe-to-Toe Position.

Danced on Same-Feet. With a Softened Supporting Right Knee, and Moving Left-Outside Partner, each Partner Points Forward to Touch Dancefloor, each with their Left Ball, with their Pointing Toes Turned Outward, Toward and near each others' Supporting Instep.

With a Gentle Lead, both Partners Transfer their Weight Forward onto their Left Feet, and both Swivel a Half-Turn Counter-Clockwise to Close Feet and Face, Straight-Kneed. Man ends with Weight on Right Foot, while Lady ends with Weight on Left Foot.

Man dances *fortouchhold swivel1/2CCWClose* to Face.

Lady, Following, dances *fortouchhold swivel1/2CCWCloseTouch*.

Notes: 1) May be preceded by the Backward-Start-with-Circle.
        2) Usually followed by the Doble-Ocho.

Rewards-of-the-Dance: A General Coupledance Term that refers to rewards received in recompense; rewards in return for one's merit or achievement in a dancer's world.

"The world of dance is a charmed place. Some people like to inhabit it, others to behold it; either way it is rewarding." -- Margot Fonteyn

"There's a reward in dancing that's indescribable... the mental and physical coming together. And when everything is right... there's no other feeling like it and you remember that and you'll do almost anything to feel that again." -- Robert Weiss

Rhythm or **Rhythmic-Structure:** (*el ritmo* in Spanish.) A Musical and Coupledance Basic Term, dealing with the elements of **Time** and **Energy**, and with Rhythm's relation to dancing. **Rhythm** is the element which gives meaning to the dance. The various kinds of Dance Music are defined by their unique Rhythms, and the Rhythm of each specific Music is defined by its underlying Beat, Pulsing, Accents, etc. Rhythm is a large factor, not only in the art of dancing, but in all **Movement**. **Rhythm** has been defined as *"the regular pulsation of music,"* and *"ordered Movement which runs through all beauty."*

Diane Mariechild writes: *"The dancer moves; she changes. Aware of her relationship to time and space, she moves through all dimensions, giving context and meaning to life. The dancer is the personification of our natural rhythm and creativity; she is the spark of creation itself."*

Maya Angelou said: *"Everything in the universe has rhythm. Everything dances."*

Helen PLotz writes: *"The rhythm of the universe, like the rhythm of our pulses, determines the rhythm of the dance."*

Angela Monet writes: *"Those who danced were thought to be quite insane by those who could not hear the music."*

Thomas "Fats" Waller said: *"Lady, if you got to ask, you ain't got it."* [On being asked to explain Rhythm].

"Only the wise can dance the rhythm of life." -- Anonymous

Rhythm may be Movement with a regular repetition of a Beat, Accent, Rise and Fall, or the like. In Music, the recurrent regular heavy and light accents conform to specific metered Timing. The flow of symmetrical Movement in regularly recurrent groupings can result in feelings of proportion and Forward Progression, according to Accent and Time values. One may find Rhythm wherever there is repetition, symmetrical groupings of form or ideas, formed by the regular recurrence of heavy and light accents, or by a methodical grouping of parts as a whole.

Rhythm is a common element in all forms of art, and it is an important element in all physical Skills, since every activity is Rhythmic. Movement that is pleasing to watch and feel has controlled Rhythm. Rhythm aids learning and adds pleasure and efficiency to Movement. Rhythm may assist in securing the greatest effect with a minimum waste of Energy, saving both physical and mental Energy.

Auditory Rhythm may be either expressed or perceived as sound. There are also visual and feeling Rhythms. In tactile sensation, there is the Rhythmic throbbing of the pulse, and one is able to recall the Rhythmic feel when repeating a Coupledance Pattern. Rhythm is a large part of habit, where one can take certain Actions without thinking.

Certain beginning dancers, individually Stepping to their own commonplace Rhythmic interval, (Walking,) will inadvertently disregard the music Beat played, rather than attempting to Coupledance to the Tempo being heard. This is most disconcerting to their Partner. One must make oneself listen to the Beat and be flexible. The Rhythm danced, not only synchronizes a Couple's physical Movements, but their moods and feelings as well.

Same as **Ritmo.** (See PolyRhythm, Rhythm-Pattern, Body-Rhythm, Step-Count, Blank-Rhythm, Throbbing, Rhythm-Stations, Time, Timing, Meter, Steady-Beat, Compas, Four/Four-Time, Three/Four-Time, Two/Four-Time, Time-Signature, Cadence, Metronome, Slow, Slow-Motion, Quick, And ---, A', Underlying-Beat, A-Tempo, Ad-Libitum, Count, and Counts. Also see Dance-Number. Also see Drum, and Clave.)

Right-Behind-Ganchos or **Open-Reverse-Double-Gancho:** A partially Leadable, two-Measure **Argentine Tango** Coupledance Pattern. Man in Facing-Offset Position on Left Standing-Foot; Man Flicks Behind Lady's Right Standing-Foot with his Right Foot and then they both Change-of-Weight, Man is DiagForward with Right Knee Bent, then Lady Flicks Behind Man's Right Standing-leg with her Right Foot and they Change-of-Weight again.
(See Gancho, and Flick.)

Right-Foot-Inside Position: See Closed Position Argentine Tango.

Right-Foot-Outside Position: This is the secondary Coupledance Position suitable for the **Argentine Tango** version.
Partners Face, Leaning Slightly Inward, Offset substantially to their Right, but close in Standing-Stance, and with Partner's Facing Feet to one's Right. Shoulders are Parallel, with no Feathering and not Hip-to-Hip. Man's Right arm wraps fairly Low around her waist for Leading, while Lady's Left Hand placement is optional, (but no Salute.) His Left elbow Slightly Outward, his Left Hand holds her Right Hand at her Eye-Level, or he may vary this by Lowering her Right Hand to his Left hip. Elbows are Lowered and her Head is often Open, Torqued to her Right. Man's Head is to his Left or he looks at her.
Same as the less-explicit **To-Dance-Outside**, and the **Offset-Facing-Opposed Position**. Similar to **Feathered Position**, and **Facing-Offset Position**. (See **To-Dance-On-The-Side**, Loose-Hug Position, Shoulder-to-Shoulder Position, Hip-to-Hip Position, Hip-Turn Position, and Star Position. Also see Argentine Tango Step-Listing.)

Right-Hand-Lead: See Palm/Finger-Lead-in-Closed.

Right-Inside-Ganchos or **Corte-Double-Gancho:** A partially Leadable, two-Measure **Argentine Tango** Coupledance Pattern. In Corte Position, on his Left Standing-Foot, Man Flicks his Right Free-Foot inside and Behind Lady's Right Standing-Leg and then they both Change-of-Weight, Man Bends Right Knee, then Lady Flicks inside and Behind Man's Right Standing-Leg and they Hold.
(See Gancho, Corte, and Flick.)

Ritmo: (*RRIT-mo*, Spanish for *rhythm*.) A General Argentine word for **Rhythm**. *"Refers to the more complex rhythmic structure of the music which includes the beat or compas as well as the more defining elements of the song. See compas."*
Same as the **Rhythm**. [See **Compas**, and Yumba. Also see Rhythm-Pattern, Body-Rhythm, Rhythm-Stations, Time, Timing, Meter, Steady-Beat, Four/Four-Time, Three/Four-Time, Two/Four-Time, Time-Signature, Cadence(1), Metronome, Slow-Motion, Underlying-Beat, A-Tempo, Ad-Libitum, Count, and Counts.] [Much from *Tango Terminology*, *www.tangoafficionado.com.*]

  Rock-Back or **Back-Rock** or **Backward-Rock:** Two Leadable, one-Measure, three-Step, Spot-Coupledance Figures, Left and Right. Suitable for International and American **Tangos,** for Americn **Twostep,** and for other dances. Rhythm Timing is usually *Quick Quick Slow.*

  Rocking Movements, danced in Closed Position International Tango or Informal, with all Feet in Third-Position-Extended, and with Man's Weight twice Moving Rearward as Lady's Weight twice Moves Forward. No Turning. No Foot Position change after first Step, (last two Steps are In-Place,) although Feet may Lift Slightly off the Dancefloor.

  For **Rock-Back-Left**, Man Steps *backward Forward backward*, as Lady Steps *Forward backward Forward.*

  For **Rock-Back-Right**, Man Steps *Backward forward Backward*, as Lady Steps *forward Backward forward.*

  Opposite of **Forward-Rock.** (See Rock, Rock-Apart, Break-Back, Rock-Step, Rocking-Maneuver, Rocking-Steps, Rock-Steps, Rock-Turn, Electric-Kicks, Rock-the-Boat, Hitch-Hike, and Rocking-Chair.)

  Rock-Back-and-Forth: Several usually Leadable, General Coupledance Spot-Movements; a Forward and Backward **Rocking** Motion with **Feet-Fore-and-Aft,** but remaining glued In-Place, in Fourth-Position of the Five Basic Foot Positions, with neither Heel nor Toe Lifting from the Dancefloor.

  Rocking-Back-and-Forth is with either the Left or the Right Foot Spread Forward, and Starts with either a Backward or Forward **Rocking. Rocking** is usually Slow and continuous several times, sequentially in each direction. Not more than 75 percent of one's Weight is Transferred when Rocked Forward; momentarily Into-the-Knees upon reaching Forward, and Full Weight is upon the Rearward Heel upon reaching Backward.

           Similar to **Sway-Back-and-Forth.** (See Planted-Foot, Zarandeo, Rock-Diagonally, Rock-with-Feet-Crossed, and Rock-Side-to-Side. Also see To-and-Fro, Coming-and-Going, and Approaching-and-Retiring. Also see Rock-Steps, Rock-Steps-Three, Rock-Steps-Four, And Rock-Apart. Also see Forward-Rock, and Rock-Back.)

  Rocking-Chair(1): Two Leadable, one-Measure, four-Step, General Singular or Spot-Coupledance Figures, Left or Right. Rhythm Timing is usually *Slow Slow Slow Slow.* Dance Positions vary.

  Rocking Movements, possibly danced in a Closed Position, with all Feet in Third-Position-Extended, and with Man's Weight Moving Forward as Lady's Weight Moves Rearward, and visa-versa. Normally no Turning. The Man's Right Foot and the Lady's Left Foot, or visa-versa, remain as the center (Home) point, **In-Place,** as Partners Rock Forward and Rearward. The Home Foot Raises In-Place.

  Rocking-Chair-Left is danced as follows:

  Man dances *forward RecoverHome backward RecoverHome.*

  Lady Follows accordingly.

  Rocking-Chair-Right is Mirror-Image Opposite.

  Similar to **Marchessi,** and **Corta-Jaca.** (See Electric-Kicks, Rock, Rocking-Steps, and Rock-the-Boat.)

  Rocking-Chair(2): A Leadable, General Coupledance Ending Figure; same as Chair except Figure has added Rocking back and forth by the Couple.

  (See Chair.)

Rocking-Maneuver: Various Leadable, Basic, Singular or Coupledance Movements, usually danced to two music Beats.

One's Feet are Spread in Third-Position-Extended and kept In-Place. On the first Beat, one's full Weight is upon either Foot in any Direction. One's full Weight is shifted to the Opposite Foot upon the second Beat.

Similar to **Rock-Step, Break-Back,** and **Rock-Apart.** (See Rock-Back.)

Rocking-Steps: See Rock-Steps.

Rock-Steps or **Rocking-Steps** or **Rocks** or **Rocking** or **Rock**(2): Actually more like **Weight-Changes, Rock-Steps** are one of the Leadable, Basic Coupledance Spot-Movements to be mastered. **Rock-Steps** may be initiated by either Foot, first Stepping in any Direction on the DownBeat. Movements for **Rock-Steps** are Executed in variable Positions, directions, and Rhythm Timing.

Connected usually by some Hand-Hold, Partners normally Transfer Weight simultaneously, **Rock-Stepping** either in Opposition or in conjunction with each other. Each person Rocks then Recovers in-Place, normally without a Change-of-Location. Feet might Raise from the Dancefloor, but they always return Home to their same spot if there is no Body-Turning.

One **Rock** is a single Rock then Recovering, (Change-Weight twice,) but usually **Rocks** are Executed in multiples. The dancer's Weight is shifted from one Foot to the other, for the amount of **Rocks** and Starting direction specified.

With each dancer's Feet Apart somewhat, **Rock-Steps** are Executed by Shifting one's Weight In-Place. **Rock-Steps** Can be Rocking Forward, Sideward, Backward, Crossward or Diagonally, from one Foot to the other, for a series of Rocking Movements. See **Rock-Back-and-Forth, Rock-Side-to-Side, Rock-with-Feet-Crossed,** or **Rock-Diagonally** Steps. Number of Weight-Changes is as indicated, but there are two or more Changes-of-Weight, each being in the Opposite direction from the preceding. Upon the initial **Rock-Step** portion, not more than 75 percent of one's Weight is Transferred, usually without the Heel Touching the Dancefloor.

Same as (more explicit) **Break-Back,** and **Rock-Apart.** Similar to **Rocking-Maneuver.** (See Forward-Rock, Rock-Back, Rock-Steps-Three, Rock-Steps-Four, Electric-Kicks, Rock-Turn, Rocking-Chair, RockAway, and Rock-the-Boat. Also see Spring-Action, Pulse, Pousette, and Accordion. Also see Counter-Balance, Counter-Movement, and Counter-Sway. Also see Left-Hand-Turn, Right-Hand-Turn, and Two-Hand-Turn.)

Rock-Turn(1): Two Leadable, General Spot-Coupledance Patterns, Right or Left, Couple-Rotation is either Clockwise or Counter-Clockwise, in Loose-Closed Position. Suitable for American **Onestep,** all **Tangos,** all-**Twosteps,** and other dances. Rhythm for Tango and Twostep is *Quick Quick Slow, Quick Quick Slow*; for Onestep is *Slow Slow SlowHold, Slow Slow SlowHold.*

Danced in a Closed Position. Feet are Apart with one ahead of the other. Weight is shifted (Forward and Backward) more than Steps are Stepped. Couple-Rotation is up to a Full-Turn, but usually a Half-Turn total. Lead-Hands may be held Low.

The **Clockwise Rock-Turn** is danced *diagbackturnCW ForTurnCW diagbackturnCW, ForTurnCW diagbackturnCW ForTurnCW.* The **Counter-Clockwise Rock-Turn** is danced *forturnCCW DiagBackTurnCCW forturnCCW, DiagBackTurnCCW forturnCCW DiagBackTurnCCW.*

(See Rock, Rock-Steps, Rocking-Steps, Forward-Rock, Rock-Back, Electric-Kicks, Rocking-Chair, Gauchos, and Rock-the-Boat.)

Rock-Turn(2): A Leadable, two-Measure, six-Step Coupledance Pattern used in **International Tango**. Rhythm with 2/4 Timing is *Quick Quick Slow, Quick Quick Slow*.
Danced in Closed Position International Tango throughout. The first Measure Quarter-Turns Clockwise; the second Measure Quarter-Turns Counter-Clockwise.
Man dances *backturn1/8CW ForTurn1/8CW recoverback, BackTurn1/8CCW sideturn1/8CCW Close*.
Lady dances *ForTurn1/8CW backturn1/8CW RecoverForward, forturn1/8CCW DiagBackTurn1/8CCW close*.

Rond (*rawn*): A General Coupledance Term meaning round or circular in French.
(See Ronde; Ronde, Forward; Ronde, Aerial; Ronde, Floor; Rond-de-Jambe; En-Dedans; En-Dehors; and Ballet.)

Rond-de-Jambe: (*rawn-duh-zhahnb*, French for *circling the leg* or *circular movement of the leg*.) (Spanish = *rodazan*) A series of Unleadable, General **Ballet** and Coupledance Movements in a half-circle Arc. **Rond-de-Jambes** are Movements in which the Free-Leg is worked to describe the letter "D" about one's Supporting-Leg. **Rond-de-Jambes** are often Practiced At-the-Barre. This is an exercise for Turning Outward one's leg in it's hip joint. One's Torso and Supporting-Leg remain stationary while Ronding.
A **Rond-de-Jambe** may be Executed with Left or Right leg, either **Forward** (**En-Dedans**) or **Rearward** (**En-Dehors**), Tracking-the-Floor (**Par-Terre** or **A-Terre**, *a-tehr*) or Aerial (**En-L'Air**, *ahn-lehr*), in either a **Demi** or a large (**Grande**) Arc in size. An Aerial Rond may be as High as 120 degrees from the Dancefloor.
(See Demi-Rond-de-Jambe; Grande-Rond-de-Jambe; Ronde; Ronde, Forward; Ronde, Aerial; and Ronde, Floor. Also see Adagio, and Exercices-a-la-Barre.)

Rond-de-Jambe-a'-Terre: See Ronde, Floor.

Rond-de-Jambe-en-Dedans: See Ronde, Forward.

Rond-de-Jambe-en-Dehors: See Ronde.

Rond-de-Jambe-en-L'air: See Ronde, Aerial.

Ronde or **Ronde, Rearward** or **Rearward-Ronde** or **Outward-Ronde** or **Rond-de-Jambe-en-Dehors:** Ronde = round. Two Leadable, Basic Coupledance Actions, Movements or Figures, Left or Right, suitable for **International Tango, Argentine Tango**, Slow-Waltz, Slow-Foxtrot, and for other dances. A **Ronde** is a Circling of one's Free-Foot and leg. Timing varies.
One Partner or both Lower with Feet-Together then **Ronde**, either simultaneously or Singularly. Free-Foot Sweeps Outward and Rearward from the hip, either Flaring or Fanning in a Circular arc, while Supporting-Knee is Bent till **Ronde** completion. Most commonly, Lady Sweeps her Right leg, and Man Sweeps his Left leg. Both work to keep Shoulders-Parallel. Arc may be extensive or tight, and Knee Bend amount varies, depending upon the Timing.
(See Ronde, Forward; Ronde, Aerial; Ronde, Floor; Rond-de-Jambe; En-Dehors; En-Dedans; and Barre. Also see Develope, Envelope, Ru-de-Vache, and Bicycle.)

Ronde, Aerial or **Rond-de-Jambe-en-L'air** or **Aerial-Ronde** or **Flare-Ronde** or **Ronde, Flare:** Four Leadable, Basic Coupledance Movements or Figures, Rearward (Outward) or Forward (Inward,) Left or Right, suitable for **International Tango**, **Argentine Tango**, Slow-**Waltz**, Slow-**Foxtrot**, and for other dances. Timing varies. Performed by one or both Partners, simultaneously or Singularly.

In French, in Classic Ballet, a **Rearward-Aerial-Ronde** is named **Rond-de-Jambe-en-L'air-en-Dehors** (Outward,) and a **Forward-Aerial-Ronde** is named **Rond-de-Jambe-en-L'air-en-Dedans** (Inward.) An extra-High Aerial-Ronde is named **Grand-Rond-de-Jambe-en-L'air.**

Beginning Lowered with Feet-Together, Free-Foot Sweeps off and above the Dancefloor in an arc while Supporting-Knee is Bent till Ronde completion. Flaring is either Rearward or Forward. In **Ballet**, the **Free-Leg** Sweeps parallel * to the Dancefloor. There is Swiveling on one Foot with the other Extended and Raised until Flare completion. Most commonly, Lady Sweeps her Right leg, and Man Sweeps his Left leg. Both work to keep Shoulders-Parallel. Arc may be extensive or tight, and Knee Bend amount varies, depending upon the Timing.

Similar to **Fan-Kick**. (See Aerial; Ronde; Ronde, Floor; Ronde, Forward; Rond-de-Jambe; Epaule; and Barre.)

Note: * The Free-Leg may Sweep as High as 120 degrees from the Dancefloor.

Ronde-and-Slip: See Ronde, Rearward-and-Slip.

Ronde, Floor or **Rond-de-Jambe-a'-Terre** or **Floor-Ronde** or **Fan-Ronde** or **Ronde, Fan:** Four Leadable, Basic Coupledance Actions, Movements or Figures, Rearward (Outward) or Forward (Inward,) Left or Right; suitable for **International Tango**, **Argentine Tango**, Slow-**Waltz**, Slow-**Foxtrot**, and for other dances. Timing varies. Performed by one or both Partners, simultaneously or Singularly.

In French, in Classic Ballet, a **Rearward-Floor-Ronde** is named **Rond-de-Jambe-a'-Terre-en-Dehors** (Outward,) and a **Forward-Floor-Ronde** is named **Rond-de-Jambe-a'-Terre-en-Dedans** (Inward.) A maximum Floor-Ronde with an exceedingly Bent-Knee is named **Grand-Rond-de-Jambe-a'-Terre.**

Beginning Lowered with Feet-Together, Free-Foot Sweeps in an arc while Supporting-Knee is Bent till Ronde completion. Fanning is either Rearward or Forward. There is Swiveling on one Foot with the other Extended in continual contact, Tracking-the-Floor, until Fan completion. Most commonly, Lady Sweeps her Right leg, and Man Sweeps his Left leg. Both work to keep Shoulders-Parallel. Arc may be extensive or tight, and Knee Bend amount varies, depending upon the Timing.

(See Ronde, Aerial; Ronde, Forward; Barre; Rond-de-Jambe; Epaule; and Ronde.)

Ronde, Forward or **Forward-Ronde** or **Inward-Ronde** or **Rond-de-Jambe-en-Dedans:** Two Leadable, Basic Coupledance Movements or Figures, Left or Right, suitable for **International Tango**, **Argentine Tango**, Slow-**Waltz**, Slow-**Foxtrot**, and for other dances. Timing varies.

Both Partners Lower with Feet-Together then Forward-Ronde, either simultaneously or Singularly. Free-Foot Sweeps Forward (Inward,) either Flaring or Fanning in an arc, while Supporting-Knee is Bent till Ronde completion. Most commonly, Lady Sweeps her Right leg, and Man Sweeps his Left leg. Both work to keep Shoulders-Parallel. Arc may be extensive or tight, and Knee Bend amount varies, depending upon the Timing.

(See Ronde; Ronde, Aerial; Ronde, Floor; Rond-de-Jambe; En-Dedans; and Barre.)

Ronde, Rearward: See Ronde.

Ronde, Rearward-and-Slip or **Ronde-and-Slip** or **Fallaway-Ronde:** A Leadable, Basic Coupledance Movement or Figure, suitable for **International Tango**, **Argentine Tango**, Slow-**Waltz**, Slow-**Foxtrot**, and for other dances. Rhythm Timing varies, usually *Slow Quick Quick*.

Both Partners Lower with Feet-Together then Rearward-Ronde simultaneously, Man Left and Lady Right, then Man Slips them Counter-Clockwise on *Quick Quick*. Both work to keep Shoulders-Parallel throughout.

(See Ronde, Rudolph-and-Slip.)

Ronde, Rudolph or **Rudolph-Ronde:** A one-Step, Leadable, Basic Coupledance Movement with no Weight Change; suitable for **International Tango**, **Argentine Tango**, Slow-**Foxtrot**, Slow-**Waltz**, both **Quicksteps**, and for other dances. Timing varies.

Man DiagForward Lunges Right and remains Low into Partner's crouch and side; Lady reacts with a Right Foot, Clockwise, Rearward-Ronde. Both work to keep Shoulders-Parallel.

(See Ronde.)

Ronde, Rudolph-and-Slip or **Rudolph-Ronde-and-Slip:** A Leadable, Basic Coupledance Movement or Figure, suitable for **International Tango**, **Argentine Tango**, Slow-**Foxtrot**, Slow-**Waltz**, both **Quicksteps**, and for other dances. Rhythm Timing varies, usually *Slow Quick Quick*.

Man DiagForward Lunges Right on *Slow*, and remains Low into Partner's crouch and side; Lady reacts with a Right Foot, Clockwise, Rearward-Ronde. Man then Slips them Counter-Clockwise on *Quick Quick*. Both work to keep Shoulders-Parallel throughout.

(See Ronde, Rearward-and-Slip.)

Ronde, Same-Foot: See Ronde, Split.

Ronde, Split or **Split-Ronde** or **Bomb-Shell** or **Ronde, Same-Foot** or **Same-Foot-Ronde** or **Wrong-Foot-Ronde:** An Unleadable, Basic, one-Step Coupledance Movement or Figure, suitable for **International Tango**, **Argentine Tango**, Slow-**Waltz**, Slow-**Foxtrot**, and for other dances. Timing varies.

Performed either in Loose-Closed Position or in Facing-Offset Position. Man Pauses as the **Lady Changes-Feet**. Simultaneously, each Partner begins their Ronde with Feet-Together. Both Lower then Rearward-Ronde Counter-Clockwise, each with their Left leg, while Couple-Rotating approximately a Half-Turn Counter-Clockwise.

Rotary-Tango or **Tango-with-Turns:** There are two predominant **Styles** of the **Argentine Tango** Genre; the **Show-Tango**, and the **Tango-de-Salon** Genre. Within these two Styles, there are two types of Argentine Tango, the **Linear-Tango** and this **Rotary-Tango** with its emphasis on the leg Movements.

The **Rotary-Tango** type is much more intimate and is the least formal of the two types. Rotating Partners Step intimate Patterns within each other's space as they encircle each other. The **Rotary-Tango** is Coupledanced with soft, loving, gentle, hesitently Slow, Stalking Steps, intently Following the Bandoneon's broken Rhythm. After possibly Leaning-Into-EachOther, (see Tango-Lean,) and with extensive Pauses, Partners may break into intricate legwork in their own special **Rotary-Tango** Style, which Normally includes Ganchos and Ochos. There are no "*correct*" Dancefloor alignments.

The following are the **Rotary** types of Argentine Tango: Tango-Nuevo, and Canyengue-Tango.

Each of the following is both **Rotary** and **Linear** types of Argentine Tango: Tango-de-Salon, Tango-Orillero, Tango-Liso, Liquid-Tango, and Show-Tango(1).

This **Rotary-Tango** method is normally not danced upon extensive Dancefloors; instead, it is mainly Spot-Danced in small bars, cafes and NightClubs. Small Dancefloors require increased Couple-Rotation and force Partners to individually Turn often.

The following is from *Daniel Trenner*, www.dancetraveler.com:

"*... and the forties social style tango took hold. Then tango actually had two divisions: Salon, the walking dance, and Orillero, the one with the turns.*"

The character of the Argentine **Rotary-Tango** method is of a very Soft Coupledance with visual emphasis upon leg and Foot Movements. For the **International Tango**, this characteristic was dramatically revised in Paris in the 1930s. In Paris, this **Rotary-Tango** method was combined with the Proud Torso of other British Ballroom Coupledances (mainly the Slow-Foxtrot), and given a Staccato action. This removed visual emphasis to the Head and Torso.

(See Parada, LaLlevada, Sandwich, Drop-Hinge, Media-Luna, Gancho, Quebrada, and Sacada.)

Ruade: (*RY-ad*, French for *kick* or *buck*.) General French **Ballet** Actions, off-the-floor Embellishments. A series of Unleadable **leg Whipping Actions**, involving a **Thrusting of one's leg Rearward**. A **Ruade** is a Rearward Kick, usually High, in which the dancer's leg is Extended most often Straight Backward from the Knee. Besides perhaps being High and Straight, this Rearward **Ruade** might be Low and Circular.

Similar to the **Latigazo, Boleo, Mulekick, Flick(2)**, and a **HeelBrush.** [See Ochos-Picante, Flick(3), and Back-Flick(1). Also see Fan(1), and Flare.]

Rulo: (*RRoo-lo*, Spanish for *curl*, *ball* or *bowl*.) An Unleadable, Singular, General Coupledance Action or Movement, suitable for the **Argentine Tango** Genre, the **Milonga**, and for other dances. The **Rulo** is for visual effect; a Dramatic gesture, a scribbling Movement for Showy display. The **Rulo** is of the **Firulete** Genre, usually Performed while Moving.

Ed Loomis [www.batango.com/loomis] describes the **Rulo** as follows:

"A curl: Used frequently at the end of molinete when the man, executing a lapiz or firulete ahead of the lady, curls his foot in around the lady and extends it quickly to touch...her foot."

"Tango Terminology" - [www.tangocanberra.asn.au] states:

"That the Rulo, as an adornment, normally accompanies a turn or change of face, and as the supporting leg and foot pivots, the other leg with foot and toe pointed marks out a curl (like a pigs tail) pattern on the ground with the whole motion of the turn, and that the foot drawing this pattern sharply (snappily) meets the other foot upon completion of the turn thus completing the curl."

An **Adorno** that is similar to a **Lapiz**, and more explicit than a **Dibujo**. (See AnkleTrip, KneeFlick, Abrupt, Levantada, LaLlevada, Castigada, Cucharita, Gancho, Golpes, Picados, Amague, and Frappe; all Performed while Moving. Also see Flourish, and Gesture.)

Rumba-Cross: A Leadable, four-Step Turning-Coupledance Figure, suitable for the Slow-**Waltz**, Slow-**Foxtrot**, International **Tango**, and both **Quicksteps**, (but not for Rumba). Timing for the Waltz is *Slow And Slow Slow*; for Foxtrot is *Slow Quick And Quick*; for Tango is *Quick Quick Slow, Slow*; and for Quickstep is *Quick Quick Quick Quick*.

In a Closed Position throughout the four Steps, except Lady's Head is Open for the first Step. Total Couple-Rotation is 5/8 to Full-Turn Clockwise.

Man, Head-Left dances long Low Heel-Toe *forturn1/8CW* with Right-Side-Stretch and Left-Shoulder-Lead Rising *LatinCrossBehindPivot3/8CW* Head-Left no Sway *diagbackpivot3/8CW* and Lower *Forward*.

Lady, Head-Open dances long Low Toe-Heel *BackTurn1/8CW* with Left-Side-Stretch and Right-Shoulder-Lead Rising *latincrossinfrontpivot3/8CW* Head-Closed no Sway *ForPivot3/8CW* between Man's Feet and Lower *backward*.

Sacada (*sah-KAH-dah*) or **Desplazamiento** or **Displacement:** The basic meaning here (in Spanish) for both **Sacada** and **Desplazamiento** is displacing (or moving) one's Partner's leg or Foot out of the way, using one's own leg or Foot. There are front, side and back **Sacadas**, among others. The **Sacada** Genre is about particular Displacing Movements by the Man in the **Argentine Tango** Coupledance **Rotary-Tango** Style.

One sample method by which the Man often Performs the **Sacada**, Displacing his Lady, is as follows. Assume it begins just after he Executes the **Quebrada:** Eying each other from the Embrace (Closed Position Argentine Tango), except that the Lady's Feet are Spread Side-by-Side, the Man Brushes his Right Foot as his Left Foot is Placed, Straight-Kneed without Weight, between the Lady's Feet and beyond. Performing the **Sacada**, the Man Transfers his Weight Forward, with the outside of his thigh High in contact with the inside of his Lady's Right thigh, forcing her to Rotate and Step Backward into a **Parada**. This may be followed by **LaLlevada**.

The following is from *Tango Terms* [www.tangoberretin.com/alex]:

"*Sacada: A displacement. Sacadas are the entering of the foot of one person between the feet of the partner with a displacement of the other's space.*"

Ed Loomis [www.batango.com/loomis] describes the **Sacada** as follows:

"*The most common term for a displacement of a leg or foot by the partner's leg or foot. Occurs when a dancer places their foot or leg against a leg of their partner and transfers weight to their leg so that it moves into the space of and displaces the partner's leg.*"

Planet Tango [www.planet-tango.com/tutorial] describes the **Sacada** as follows:

"*... a body displacement across the path of your partner to provoke a change of direction.*

"*Since a* <u>*sacada*</u> *involves leg action, it is not without sadness that we report that the cumbersome attempts of 'leg dancers' to execute secadas, cause more damage to the legs of their partners and their dance floor neighbours [than any other step].*"

(See Desplazamiento, LaLlevada, Viborita, and Arrastre.)

Caution: To avoid harm to Partner, only do **Sacadas** Foot-to-Foot, calf-to-calf, or thigh-to-thigh; the instigator must never apply one's ankle or Knee.

Salida or **Continuation-of-the-Start** or **Opening-Pattern:** (*sah-LEE-dah* is Spanish for *leave, go out, departure, outlet,* or *exit.* It also means *providing an opportunity* or an *option.*) **LaSalida** is an **Argentine Tango** Genre and **Milonga** Coupledance Term for the Leadable **Continuation-of-the-Start,** or **Opening-Pattern** of the Tango. **LaSalida** is the Start of a Step, Figure, or a Basic Walking Pattern.

The following is from *Tango Terminology*, *www.tangoafficionado.com*:

"<u>*Salida*</u>: *From salir.... The first steps of dancing a tango, or a tango pattern, derived from 'Salimos a bailar?' (Shall we [go out to the dance floor and] dance?.*"

LaSalida dances two Measures in length in 2/4 Cut-Time; Rhythm Timing is *Slow Slow, Slow Quick Quick,* five Steps total. (The **Salida** differs from the **Basic-Step.**)

LaSalida's first Measure of two Steps is either the **Backward-Start** or the **American-Start,** (possibly including the **Basic-Start.**) Description of **LaSalida**'s last three (*Slow Quick Quick*) Steps that follow, (beginning Embraced in the Closed Position Argentine Tango, and also known as "*Walking the Lady to the `crossa',*") are as follows:

Man dances *BrushForward* Outside no Turn *forturn1/8CW ForClose.*

Lady, Following with Head-Open throughout, dances *sidebrushbackward LongBackTurn1/8CW* Shoulders-Parallel **crossinfront.*

<u>Note</u>: * Upon her third, **Trabada-Step,** with her Knees Together but in a loose Cross, Lady Slightly Turns even more Clockwise Away from Man.

(See Salida-Modified, Salida-Crusada, Resolucion, and Ochos-Largos.)

Salida-Cruzada: A Leadable, one-Measure, two-Step Movement or Figure, suitable for many dances but named for use in the **Argentine Tango** Genre and **Milonga** Coupledances. Danced Facing in either Open-Embrace or Close-Embrace.

The beginning of a Pattern, the **Salida-Cruzada first Steps Sideward then Steps Behind.** The dancer Steps Side Left Crossing Right Foot Behind Left, or visa-versa; e.g., danced with a wide *Sideward* Step then a *CrossBehind* and beyond Step with a Slight Opening-Out.

This **Salida-Cruzada** is normally followed by a *CrossRecoverForward* Step by the original Foot, then possibly repeated Mirror-Image Opposite.

See Waltz-Balance-Sideward-Behind, DiscoSwing, Balancetes, Slow-Twostep, Pas-de-Basque, and Side-Cross-Hesitation; all of which also first Step Sideward then Step Behind.

Salida-de-Gato: See Salida-Modified.

Salida-Modified or **Salida-de-Gato:** In 2/4 Cut-Time, mainly suitable for Coupledancing the **Argentine Tango** Genre, the **Milonga**, and possibly other Tangos and also PasoDobles.

A Leadable Figure three Movements in length, the Man modifies the last (second) Measure of the **Salida** in order to Start some form of **Ochos**. Rhythm Timing is *Quick Quick Slow*. Only the last (*Slow*) Movement is the actual modification.

Man dances *Forward* Outside no Turn *forturn1/8CW softenswivel1/4CCW* with Right Foot Touching Rearward.

Lady, Following, dances *backward LongBackTurn1/8CW* Shoulders-Parallel *forwardoutside*.

Ed Loomis [www.batango.com/loomis] describes the **Salida-de-Gato** as follows:

"*... A variation on the basico in which the man steps side left, forward right outside the lady, diagonal forward left, and crossing behind right with a lead for forward ochos for the lady. The lady is led to step side right, back left, diagonal back right, and crossing forward left, beginning ochos on her left foot. This figure enters ochos without using cruzada.*"

Notes: 1) May be preceded by the Backward-Start or the American-Start.

        2) Followed by the Ochos, Doble-Ochos, Tres-Ochos, Ocho-Abierto, Ochos-Largos, or Ochos-para-Atras.

Salon-Tango: See Tango-de-Salon.

Saltarin: (*sahl-tah-REEN*, Spanish for *dancer* or *resless young rake*.) See Dancer.

Saltito: (*sahl-TEE-to*, Spanish for *a little jump*.) Same but smaller than a **Saltation**. See **Jump**.

[Also see Salto(2), and Saut(2).]

Figure 3, **Same Foot Lunge**

Salto: (*SAHL-to*, Spanish for *leap* or *jump*.) A very General Singular or Coupledance (Unleadable) Aerial Action or Movement; a **Leap, Jump,** or **Skip**; [see the same. Also see Saut(2), Saltation, and Saltito.]

Salute or **Tango-Salute:** An Unleadable **International Tango** Coupledance Stance for the Lady, where she Salutes with her Left Hand in Gripping her Partner; her Palm-Down, fingers together and horizontal under his Right wing. This readies her for an **Abrupt, Head-Flick, Tick,** or other crisp Movements, in that the Lady's Tango-Salute is her means of locking onto her Partner for stacatto, intertwined Tango! Lady's left palm and forearm are straight and parallel with floor, and her left thumb is near to being under his right armpit. Her left index finger applies upward pressure under his right wing.
(See Knee-Lead, and Head-Flick-Link.)

Same-Foot-Lunge: Both a Standard Modern and Smooth, and a Latin Rhythm, Leadable Coupledance Picture-Figure. Suitable for **International Tango,** Slow-**Foxtrot,** Slow-**Waltz,** both **Rumbas,** the **Bolero,** and for **International Samba,** and possibly other dances. Timings vary; other than for Timing, the Same-Foot-Lunge is Performed the same way in any dance.
Consists of one Step. Begins in a Closed Position or in Loose-Closed Position. Here, the Man's signal of Raising them both before Lowering, (Collecting,) is optional; but the Man must Lower them both before he Leads her with his Step. As he starts Leading Lady to Slightly Open Clockwise, the Man Steps *Sideward* broadly and slightly Forward as he looks Right then Left, with his Right Knee Well Softened, his hips Forward.
Lady Steps *CrossBehind* into CBMP, Well under her Body with her Right Knee Softened and Supporting her own Weight, with her Left upper thigh against Man's Right thigh, and with her Left Toe reaching toward the Man's Left Toe. She looks Left and High with her hips Raised.
There are various escapes from the Same-Foot-Lunge.
(See Figure 7.) (See Hinge, and Hinge Position.)

Sandwich or **Bite** or **Sandwiche** or **Sanguichito** or **Mordida** or **Mordita:** (*mor-DEE-tah* is Spanish for *tiny bite*, or *to clutch*.) The **Sandwich** is a Genre of **Argentine Tango** Spot-Coupledance Figures, in the **Rotary-Tango** Style, in which one Partner's Foot is **Sandwiched** between the other Partner's two Feet. A **Reverse-Sandwich** is when the receiving Partner's legs are Crossed.

A sample **Sandwich** follows, in which the Man first constricts his Lady then releases her:
One Measure long in 2/4 Cut-Time, the Man Swivels a Quarter-Turn twice, once on each Beat. The Lady does not Turn. Man's Timing is *Slow slow.* Lady's Timing is *Hold slow.*
Man dances *Swivel1/4CW** Facing *swivel1/4CWBackward***.
Lady, Following with Head Closed, at first is forced to *Hold* her Position. *forward*** on second Beat.

Notes: 1) * With legs straight, Man **Sandwich**es Lady's Left protruding Toe.
2) ** Man Steps Backward as Lady Steps Forward in a close Fan Position. Man ends with his Right Knee Softened, Knees Together, his Left Straight-Legged Touching Forward and with its Toe Outward.
3) May be preceded by the Lady's-Behind-Gancho, the Parada, or LaLlevada.
4) May be followed by the Ochos.
5) Upon a crowded Dancefloor, to remain unpretentious, or in order not to disturb their Closed-Embrace, the **Sandwich** might be Executed in miniature, not Opening their Frame.

Ed Loomis [www.batango.com/loomis] describes the **Mordida** as follows:
"One partner's foot is sandwiched or trapped between the other partner's feet. If the other partner's feet are also crossed it may be referred to as Reverse Mordida. Sometimes called Sandwiche, or Sanguchito."
[See Parada, and Corte(2).]

Sandwiche: See Sandwich.

Sanguichito: See Sandwich.

Seguidillas: (*say-ghee-DEE-l'yahs*, Spanish for *tiny successive*.) Particular Coupledance Steps used in certain kinds of **Argentine Tangos**, especially in the **Tango-Orillero** as danced in their **Milongas**.
Ed Loomis [www.batango.com/loomis] describes these **Seguidillas** as follows:
"SEGUIDILLAS Tiny quick steps, usually seen in orillero style."

Seguir: (*say-GHEER*, Spanish verb for *to follow*.)   A Basic Coupledance Action. The Man is the Leader, but the Lady **completes** and **enhances**. Attuned, the Lady **Follows** her Partner's Timing, Technique, Movement and Figure Lead.
Same as **Following**, and **Suivre.** (See Togetherness, Anticipation, LaMarca, Indicate, Following-the-Follower, Lead/Follow-for-Tango, and Palm-Finger-Lead-in-Closed. Also see Back-Lead, and Hijacking.)

Semi-Closed Position Tango for American Tango or Promenade Position: A rare Coupledance Stance, **with Lady's Head-Closed.** Lady's Head may remain Closed in this Position, even with an Abrupt. In fact, Lady's Head may remain Closed for their entire Tango dance; Her resulting CBMP creates a Dramatic embellishment for effect.

Weight is on their Inside-Feet, usually for readying to Step Forward with Outside-Feet. Forward Toes are spaced Close. Inside-hips are in contact, with Lady's hip Behind. Their Stance is Low, into their Knees. Man's Left and Lady's Right Hands remain Clasped and held at Lady's forehead Height, with Forward Elbows protruding Slightly.

(See Promenade Position, and other two Semi-Closed Positions.)

Sentada: (*sen-TAH-dah*, Spanish, from *sentar = to sit.*) **Sentada** is a General Genre of Coupledance Actions, Movements and Figures.

Ed Loomis [www.batango.com/loomis] describes **Sentada** as follows:

"A sitting action: A family of figures in which the lady creates the illusion of sitting in, or actually mounts, the man's leg. Frequently used as a dramatic flourish at the end of a dance."

(See Sentado, and Tijera.)

Sentado-Hinge: See Drop-Hinge.

Sentado-Hinge Position or LaSentada Position: (*sen-TAH-do*, Spanish for *Sedate.*) Two, possibly Unleadable, Lady's Coupledance Positions, Left and Right; suitable for American and Argentine **Tangos,** for Slow **Waltz,** for both **Rumbas,** and for the **Bolero,** among other dances. Knee up, Free-Foot is Across and against Outside of Weighted Knee.

For **Left Position,** Lady is on Man's Left with both Facing the same direction; Man partially Supports Lady with his Left Knee. His hips are eased Contrabody into his Lady and he is viewing her Face. His Right Knee is against his Left Knee. Lady's Head is Closed with chin Up, and her hips are Well Up. Her Free-Knee of her Right leg is Raised and Crosses her Left Knee; her Right Free-Foot is Across and against Outside of the Knee of her Left Supporting-Leg. An alternate here for the Lady's legs follows: With her Knees Together and with her Supporting Left-Knee Softly Bent, her Free-Leg Lays almost Straight.

Right Position (rare) is Mirror-Image Opposite.

Similar to **Hinge Position.** (See Drop-Hinge, Sentado-Line, Foot-Across-Knee, Foot-Across-Ankle, Hinge-with-Shape, and Knee-Up Position.) [Also see Sur-le-Cou-de-Pied, Cou-de-Pied, Wrapped Position(2), and Sous-Sus. Also see Sentada.]

Sentado-Line: A partially Leadable Movement into the Coupledance Picture Position for the **Sentado-Hinge.** Suitable for American and Argentine **Tangos**, for Slow **Waltz**, for both **Rumbas**, and for the **Bolero**, among other dances. Rhythm Timing is usually *Slow Slow.*

Man, from Closed, Steps widely *sideward* and he applies a Softened Left Knee. Man partially Supports Lady with his Left Knee. His hips are then eased Contrabody into his Lady as he views her face. Then he Flexes his Right Knee against his Left Knee as his Body Rotates Counter-Clockwise, which Leads his Lady to Cross her leg.

Lady, Following, Steps widely *Sideward* to Face him; then she Steps *crossbehind* with CBM, Well under her Body with her Left Knee Bent to Support her Weight. Her Head is Closed with chin Up, and her hips are Well Up. Then Lady's Free-Knee of her Right leg is Raised to Cross her Left Knee; her Right Free-Foot is Across and against Outside of the Knee or shin of her Left Supporting-Leg.

Similar to **Hinge-Line.** (See **Drop-Hinge,** Foot-Across-Knee, Foot-Across-Ankle, Pas-Croise, Hinge-with-Shape, Hinge, and Hinge Position.) [Also see Sur-le-Cou-de-Pied, Cou-de-Pied, Wrapped Position(2), and Sous-Sus. Also see Line(2), and Sentada.]

Serpiente (*serp*): A partially Leadable, three-Measure, six-Step Coupledance Pattern, suitable for **Argentine** and **American Tangos**, and for both **Rumbas**. Timing is *Quick Quick Slow, Slow Quick Quick, Slow Slow.*

Danced in Butterfly Position throughout. For both fans, the Man Fans Counter-Clockwise while his Lady Fans Clockwise. For both Partners, the first Fan Fans Rearward while the second Fans Forward. Each *QuickQuick* is one Beat, and each *FanFan FanFan* is two Beats long.

Man's Timing and descriptions are: *quickQuick fanfan, fanfan Quickquick, FanFan FanFan; andCross slow, slow Andcross, Slow Slow; sideward CrossBehind fantocrossbehind Sideward crossinfront, FanToCrossInFront.*

Lady's Timing and descriptions are: *Quickquick FanFan, FanFan quickQuick, fanfan fanfan; Andcross Slow, Slow andCross, slow slow; Sideward crossbehind FanToCrossBehind sideward CrossInFront, fantocrossinfront.*

(See Serpiente-for-Waltz, Serpiente-for-Bolero, and DobleCruz.)

Shift-Weight or **Weight-Shift:** A Leadable General Spot-Coupledance Movement. With **Feet Planted Apart** in any direction, (e.g., Feet-Fore-and-Aft, Feet-Crossed Stance, Feet-Diagonal Stance, or Feet-Side-by-Side,) and with Weight upon one Foot only, full or partial **Weight is Shifted onto the Opposite Foot.** There is no Travel in any direction.

(See Change-of-Weight, Planted-Foot, In-Place, and Stationary. Also see Shake, and Zarandeo.)

Shall-We-Dance?: A much-used General Ballroom Coupledance saying for an **Invitation-to-Dance**, usually offered to a Lady by the Man. But not always; presently the query "**Shall-We-Dance?**" can be heard said by the Ladies to Men.

In this world, there are still other customary ways to offer to Coupledance. For instance, see **Milonga** for the Argentinean's subtle means of inviting either a Lady or a Man to dance.

The following is from *Tango Terminology*, *www.tangoafficionado.com*:

"*Salida: From salir.... The first steps of dancing a tango, or a tango pattern, derived from 'Salimos a bailar?' (Shall we [go out to the dance floor and] dance?.*"

Same as **May I Have This Dance?, Dance-With-Me, Let's-Dance**(2), and **Let's-Go-Trippin'.** [Also see Etiquette, Dance-Card, My-Card-is-Full, Social Dancing, Mixers, Dance Clubs, Dance Scene, Body-Exchange, and Pickup(6).]

ShoeShine: The **ShoeShine** Adorno is an Unleadable, Singular, **Argentine Tango** Coupledance Action, doodle, or sign to Partner, usually Executed by the Man during a **Corte** [(2), Stop].

Let us say that they have abruptly stopped dancing, a Parada, and that the Man has become doubtful that his Lady is realizing which Foot to Move with next. By his Executing the **ShoeShine**, he can indicate to her which Foot he has free, i.e., with which Foot she is next to dance.

With his Supporting-Leg Slightly Softened, the Man does the **ShoeShine** by slowly rubbing his Free-Foot Up and Down behind the calf of his Supporting-Leg, as if **shining his shoe**. Then, when he is ready, the Partners resume their dance.

But most often the **ShoeShine** is Performed as a Flourish just for show.

An Adorno that is similar to the **Lustrada** and **AnkleTrip**, and is more explicit than a **Dibujo**. (See Lapiz, Puntada-del-Pie, Caricias, Lustrada, Chiche, Fanfarron, Golpecitos, Zapatazo, Levantada, and Enganche; all Performed during a Parada. Also see Flourish, and Gesture.)

Shoulder-Lead (*shldr ld*) or **Left-Side-Lead** or **Right-Side-Lead** or **Slice** or **Slicing** or **Crabbing:** Two Leadable, Basic Coupledance Actions, Mirror-Image Left or Right. Stepping *forward* with Left shoulder Forward, or *rearward* with Left shoulder Rearward. Or, Stepping *Forward* with Right shoulder Forward, or *Rearward* with Right shoulder Rearward. Not only the Shoulder, but normally the entire side of one's Body Leads in concert with the Moving-Foot, in advance of one's trailing side. Dancing literally as in Egyptian art, with legs uncrossed, toes and nose point Direction-of-Dance and the shoulder protrudes Forward, (not CBMP.)

Opposite of **CBM**. (See Egyptian-Pose, Lowered-Shoulder-Into-the-Break, and Mambo-Twist.)

Show-Tango(1) or **Fantasia** or **Exhibition-Tango** or **Tango-Argentino:** Though many more Styles are in Argentina, there are two distinct and predominant Styles of the **Argentine Tango** Genre. One of these is this theatrical **Show-Tango**, which is a variant for Stage-Dancing and is perhaps the most familiar to the world public. Consisting of an over-development of certain Tango Patterns for the stage, **Show-Tango** grew out from the combined **Tango-de-Salon** and **Tango-Orillero** Social-Dances in the 1950s.

The following is from *Daniel Trenner*, www.dancetraveler.com:

"Exhibition tango was first developed within the social vernacular. For the most part it was danced as a kind of loose warfare between different neighborhood schools, at the social dances, in breaks between the social dancing. In the fifties, Juan Carlos Copes led the development of tango for stage dancing, which culminated in Tango Argentino and modern show dancing. With this development, the tango style branched again, and the show dancers quickly broadened and evolved their vocabularies creating even more stylistic diversity."

Show-Tango consists of being of both the **Rotary-Tango** and **Linear-Tango** types of Argentine Tango. Always danced in the Open-Embrace-Tango, this **Show-Tango** is essentially Flashy Routines of exaggerated Movements; i.e., additional Balletic elements with showy Figures and Patterns, with a series of widely Striding Steps, large Sweeping Movements, many Ganchos, Boleos, Quebradas, Acrobatics and Solo Movements that require space to Perform. This **Show-Tango** is thereby most suited for the Stage or for Singular Ballroom Exhibition. Here, in this Stylized and breathtaking version of the **Argentine Tango**, the Couple is dressed in black and the Man perhaps wears a fedora.

(Continued)

Show-Tango(1): (Continued)
Ed Loomis [www.batango.com/loomis] describes the **Tango-Fantasia** as follows:
        "*TANGO FANTASIA This is a hybrid tango, an amalgam of traditional tango
steps, ballet, ballroom gymnastics, ice-skating figures, etc. This is what most people see when
they buy tickets for a tango show. The moves include all of the basic tango moves plus, ganchos,
sacadas, boleos of every kind, sentadas, kicks, leaps, spins, lifts, and anything else that the
choreographer and the performers think that they can get away with. Alas, this style of dancing
shows up from time to time at the milongas, usually badly performed by ill-behaved tango
dancers and frustrated tango performers who insist on getting their money's worth even if they
have to kick, step on, bump into, or trip every other dancer on the floor. This behavior is NOT
socially acceptable.*"
        The other predominant, and most popular, **Argentine Tango** Genre **Style** is the **Tango-
de-Salon**, a Genre in itself; versions of which can be usually seen in Tango classes, clubs and
saloons around the world.
        This subject **Show-Tango** is actually an extension of both the **Tango-de-Salon** and
Tango-Orillero, upon which it relies for its Basic-Steps. The Styles should not be blended,
because the Embellishments of the **Show-Tango** are inappropriate for crowded Social Dancing
or upon a small Dancefloor.
        (See Tango-Argentino.)

Show-Tango(2): See Continental Tango.

Side-Break: See Side-Cadencia.

Side-Cadencia or **Side-Break**: Two Leadable, Mirror-Image Spot-Coupledancing
Figures, Left and Right, suitable for the **Argentine Tango,** and for other dances. One Measure,
three Weight-Changes in length, Timing per Figure is either *Quick Quick Slow*, or *Slow Slow
Slow Hold.*
        These **Side-Breaks** are usually danced one in each direction, entirely in Closed Position
Argentine Tango (Embrace). A quiet Sideward Step on the Ball of either Foot is taken, with
only one quarter of one's Weight applied; *SideRock Recover Close.* The Lady Follows
Opposite. Perform with Supporting-Heel never Raising from the Dancefloor.
        Side-Cadencia is useful for when trapped upon a crowded Dancefloor.
        Same as **Cucaracha.** (See Cadencia, Side-Chase, and Time-Step.)

Side-Chase: A Simple, Basic, Leadable **Argentine Tango** Coupledance Figure, one
Measure in length in 2/4 Cut-Time. Danced entirely in Closed Position Argentine Tango;
Timing for the two **Side-Chase** Steps involved is *Slow Slow.*
        The Man dances *sideward Close*, and the Lady, Following, dances *Sideward close.*
        Two or more **Side-Chases** might be danced in sequence. The **Side-Chase** may Turn.
Two or more **Side-Chases** in sequence become one of the **Caminata** Pattern Variations.
        Similar to **Chase**(5). (See Cadencia.)
        [Data from http://64.33.34.112/.dance/tangels]

Side-Corte: A Leadable Coupledance Movement, suitable for all **Tangos** and other dances. Timing is *Slow Slow*.

Begins in a Closed Position, in which Partners Step *Sideward* Toward Man's Left, then, with Supporting-Knees well Flexed, both Quarter-Turn Upper-Bodies into Reverse-Semi-Closed Position, with Outside legs Extended parallel, their Toes Pointing and Touching Dancefloor. Both end up looking Toward Man's Right. Clasped Hands may be Raised.

(See Corte, and Dip.)

Side-Lunge-Change-of-Sway: A Leadable Coupledance Ending Picture-Figure suitable for **International Tango**, both **Quicksteps**, Slow-**Foxtrot**, Slow-**Waltz**, and others. Timing varies.

Beginning in a Closed Position, the Couple Performs the **Side-Lunge-Left** Movement, followed by the **Change-of-Sway** Action.

(See Oversway-Change-of-Sway, and Throwaway-Oversway.)

Side-Lunge-Left or **Left-Lunge:** A Leadable, General Coupledance Picture-Movement with one or more Counts. Suitable for **International Tango**, both **Quicksteps**, Slow-**Foxtrot**, Slow-**Waltz**, and others.

Man, from a Closed Position, Lowers himself and his Lady so that their Knees overlap, then he Leads her by Stroking one wide Left Step *sideward*; his Right Foot remains Pointed and Extended Sideward In-Place.

Lady Follows with Head-Closed, and with her Right Knee against the Inside of his Flexed Left Knee; she Strides Low, one wide Right Bent-Kneed Step *Sideward*, then her Torso Torques 1/8 Counter-Clockwise. Her Left Foot remains Pointed and Extended Sideward In-Place.

Next, they both Raise Slightly, their Supporting Knees remaining Softened, as his Right and her Left sides are Stretched; Aligning each Body Straight-Legged from Pointed Toe to Head, he remains looking Left as she looks to her Right.

(See Lunge, Lunge-Basic, and Side-Lunge-Right.)

Side-Lunge-Right or **Right-Lunge:** A Leadable, General Coupledance Picture-Movement with one or more Counts, particularly suitable for the Slow-**Foxtrot** and Slow-**Waltz**.

Man, from Closed Position International Standard, Lowers himself and his Lady so that their Knees overlap, then he Strokes one wide Right Step *Sideward*, Leading her with his Flexed Right Knee and his Body. His Left Foot remains Pointed and Extended Sideward In-Place, he remains looking Left and he has a Right Side-Stretch. His Torso may end Torquing 1/8 Clockwise, looking at his Lady.

Lady Follows with Head-Closed, and with her Left Knee against the Outside of his Flexed Right Knee; she Strides Low, one wide Left Bent-Kneed Step *sideward*. With Left Side-Stretch, her Right Foot remains Pointed and Extended Sideward In-Place. Her Torso may end Torquing 1/8 Clockwise, Opening her Head.

May be followed by a Hover-Roll. (See Lunge, Lunge-Basic, Right-Lunge-and-Slip, and Side-Lunge-Left.)

Side-Stairs: See Stairs.

Side-Thru: A Leadable, Basic Coupledance Movement or Figure, suitable for the Medium-Waltz, American **Twostep**, Argentine **Tango**, and other dances.

Both Partners Step to the Side, to the Man's Left, then either or both Partners **Step-Thru** and apply Weight.

(See Touch-Thru.)

Sidewards-Cunitas: (*koo-NEE-tahs*, Spanish for *little rocks*.) A Leadable Coupledance Figure that is danced in the various **Argentine Tangos** and in the **Milonga**.

Sidewards-Cunitas are **SidewardTouches**, one in each direction (left and Right). Executed either by one Partner or, more likely, by both Partners Stepping Sideways in Unison in some Closed or Facing Position. Each Side-Step, (Side-Left or Side-Right,) takes Weight and is followed by Touching Closed with the Opposite Foot.

Sidewards-Cunitas may be Continuous.

(See Cunita.)

SidewardTouch: Two Leadable, Basic Coupledance Movements, Left or Right Foot, Mirror-Image Opposite.

Either or both Partners Stepping Sideways in Unison, **taking Weight**, then Touching Closed with Opposite Foot.

Same as **Sidewards-Cunitas**. Similar to **DiagForwardTouch**, **DiagBackwardTouch**, and **SidewardHold**. (See Foot-Movements, Sideward, SideTouch, ForTouch, BackTouch, ForwardTouch, BackwardTouch, DiagForTouch, DiagBackTouch, and Cross-Touch. Also see SidewardClose, and Side-Step.)

Slice: See Shoulder-Lead.

Slicing: See Shoulder-Lead.

Slink: A probably Unleadable, General, Progressive Coupledance Movement. To Slowly Move across the Dancefloor in a Low, quiet, furtive, and sneaking manner.

Similar to **Slither**. (See Stealth, Skim, Skate, Level-Progression, Sweep, and Skid.)

Slip (*slp*): Several different Leadable, General Coupledance Movements, each normally Executed within one music Beat. Used in many dances but most suitable for the International **Tango**, Slow-**Foxtrot**, and Slow-**Waltz**.

A reversal of Movement after Checking. A *BackSwivel* for the Man to a Change-of-Direction. Both Partners Torque with CBM as they Sweep in Couple-Rotation in the direction of the Free-Foot, 1/8- to 1/2-Turn, most often Counter-Clockwise. A **Slip** Changes from several different Body Positions into either a Closed or Feathered Position.

(See Slip-Pivot, and Traspie.)

Slip-Pivot: A Leadable one-Measure, three Step, General Coupledance Figure, suitable for many dances, including the International **Tango**, both **Foxtrots**, and both **Waltzes**. Rhythm Timing for Foxtrot is *Slow Quick Quick*; Timing for Waltz is *Slow Slow Slow*.

Normally begins in Semi-Closed Position, and Slips a selected amount, between 1/8- and 1/2-Turn Counter-Clockwise Couple-Rotation, into either Closed Position or Feathered Position. Lady Pivots up to a Full-Turn.

Man dances *crossbehind* in CBMP *ShortSlipBackPivotCCW brushforward*.

Lady, Following, dances *ShortBackward diagforpivotCCW* to Man's Left Instep *Backward*.

(See Slip.)

Slither or **Slip:** A probably Unleadable, General, Progressive Coupledance Movement. Slowly Sliding one's Feet across the Dancefloor, Low, quietly and Stealthily.

Similar to **Slink**. (See Skim, Stealth, Sweep, Skate, Level-Progression, and Skid.)

Slow-Down or **Slow-Up:** A General Coupledance command, perhaps cautioning, for Slowing one's On-the-Beat dancing Cadence, in order to Lag to fit better or differently with the music, or to dance with Lagged-Timing. **Slow-Down** is a Deceleration (1) or (2).

Opposite of **Speed-It-Up**. (See Calando, Rallentando, Saunter, Slow-Motion, Timing, Tempo, Rhythm, Beat, Cadence, A-Tempo, Ad-Libitum, and Counts. Also see Loose-the-Beat, and Missing-a-Beat. Also see Ahead-of-the-Beat, and Rush-the-Beat.)

SlowHold: A series of Leadable, Basic Coupledance Movements; the Man Slowly Steps Omni-Directionally, applies Weight then maintains Position, usually for one Beat. The Lady Follows.

(See Tenuto.)

Snap-Change: A Leadable Spot-Coupledance Movement, suitable for the **Argentine Tango**, and other dances. Rhythm Timing is *Slow Slow*. Begins in Closed Position Argentine Tango. Couple-Rotation is a crisp, Clockwise Half-Turn total.

Man moves his Center-of-Balance Rearward, and his Lady's Forward, as he Steps *Backward*, then he *Swivels1/2CW* on both Balls-of-Feet, changing Weight to his Left Foot and Points *Forward*.

Lady Steps *forward*, then she Steps *ForSwivel1/2CW* between Man's Feet and Points *rearward*.

Note: Overall Line-of-Motion reverses after Figure is danced. (See Switch.)

Snuggle: A General Coupledance nestling or Cuddling Action; To **Snuggle** up and draw close Together.

Same as or similar to **Bundle, Cuddle, Enfold, Squeeze, Hug, Envelop, Embrace**(1), **Clasp, Clutch, Grasp,** and **Cling**. (See Cuddle Position, Loose-Hug Position, Slow-Dancing, Shadow-Enfold Position, Cheek-to-Cheek Position, Head-to-head Position, Over-the-Heart-Hand-Hold, and Crush-In-Closed.) [Also see Carpa, Tango-Lean, Leaning-Into-Each-Other, and Milonguero(2).]

Social-Tango: See Tango-de-Salon.

Softened-Knees or **Bent-Kneed** or **Into-the-Knees** or **Knee-Flex:** A Soft and Slight Bending of the Knee. A Leadable, Basic Action or Stance for Coupledancing Slow-**Foxtrot**, Slow-**Waltz**, **Viennese** and **Quickstep**, and in many other dances, such as when Appeling in the **PasoDoble**, and especially for Travel-Dancing. Even more-so for when dancing all **Tangos!**

Comparing Knee-Bend to the amount at normal Walking-Height, Knees while Travel-Dancing generally have a more pronounced Bend. One's own Knees Move closely together but normally do not touch. **Bent-Kneed**, the dancer partially absorbs shock from harsh Movements, adds Control, and improves speed and Balance.

Softened-Knees can mean Standing Neutral with both Knees Well Bent; or, in Closed Position, sufficient Lowering by the Couple results in their Knees engaging; or, Coupledancing Down, **Bent-Kneed** Stepping with Toe-First like Groucho Marx's Walk.

Softened-Knees help to give the dancer's Movements that **Ease-of-Movement** look, thereby eliminating any appearance of **Stiffness**.

Related to **Ease-of-Movement**. Inverse of **Knees-Pulled-Up**, and **Austere-Line**. (See Straight-Kneed, Head-Space, Ideal-Dance-Position, Body-Heights, Compression, Track, Plie, Deep-Into-Knees, Level-Progression, Scooping, Engagement-of-Knees, Flex, Stiffness, Knee-Cap-Room, Feet-Between-Feet, Posterior-Protrusion, and Knees-Back.)

Spanish-Drag or **Tango-Drag:** A Leadable Traveling-Coupledance Figure, suitable for the International and Argentine **Tangos**, and for other dances. Rhythm Timing is *Slow Slow And Slow*.

Begins in Closed Position International Tango, and possibly from a Side-Lunge-Right. There is no Couple-Rotation. Both Partners Step Sideward Together, often Down-Line, with Trailing legs Extended, then look Rearward while Dragging Insteps. With Torsos Low as Feet **Close**, both Change-Feet and crisply **Tango-Tap** DiagForward as they assume Promenade Position. Usually followed by a Promenade-Tap.

Man dances *sideward DragTowardClose* with Left Side-Stretch *CloseLower diagfortouch*.

Lady dances *Sideward dragtowardclose* with Right Side-Stretch *closelower DiagForTouch*.

Similar to **Spanish-Drag-with-Knee-Climb**. (See Tango-Draw. Also see Step-and-Drag, Drag, and Draw.)

Spanish-Drag-with-Knee-Climb: An Athletic, **Cabaret**-Style, partially Unleadable, General Spot-Coupledance Stance is assumed. This Pattern is Performed mostly in Choreographed Argentine, American, and International **Tango** expositions, but it is also used in other dances. Rhythm Timing is *Slow Slow And Slow*. There is no Couple-Rotation. Begins in some Closed Position, and begins possibly after a Side-Lunge-Right.

Both Partners Step Sideward Together Toward Man's Left, with Trailing legs Extended, but the Man Steps wider than the Lady, and Slightly Across his Lady's Line-of-Dance. Without helping, and with the Lady Dragging her Trailing Instep along the Dancefloor, the Man Lift-**Drags** his Lady partially Up his Trailing Right thigh, by use of his Right arm. Releasing Hands, the Lady grasps his Left shoulder and **Climbs** his Bent Left (Supporting) thigh, High with her Right fully Bent **Knee**. Whereupon her Man Holds and supports that Knee with his Left Hand. The Man eyes his Lady throughout this Pattern, while the Lady retains her Head-Closed condition until the last *Slow*, whereupon she looks Eye-to-Eye at him, almost touching nose-to-nose.

Man dances *widediagforward LiftDragUp* with Left Side-Stretch *hold graspKnee*.
Lady, Following, dances *SidewardBendBack dragfloor GraspShoulder KneeHigh*.
Similar to **Spanish-Drag**. (See Tango-Draw, and Leg-Crawl Position. Also see Step-and-Drag, Drag, Draw, and Leg-Stretch-On-Arm.)

Speed-It-Up or **Step-It-Up:** A General Coupledance command for correcting or changing one's too-Slow or Lagged-Timing dancing Cadence. Requesting a Thrust of Acceleration (1) or (2), in order to fit better with the music, or to change to dancing **On-the-Beat**.

Similar to **Acceleration**, both (1) & (2), and to **Shake-a-Leg**. Opposite of **Slow-Down**. (See **Accelerando**. Also see Allegretto, Alegria, Allegro, Con-Brio, Con-Calore, Cante Chico, Outwards-and-Upwards-Style, and Energico. Also see Smartly, Lightly, Amplitude, Active, and Lively. Also see Quick, Run, Agile, and Dart. Also see Timing, Tempo, Rhythm, Beat, Cadence, A-Tempo, Ad-Libitum, and Counts. Also see Ahead-of-the Beat, Rush-the-Start, Loose-the-Beat, and Missing-a-Beat.)

Spicy-Ochos: See Ochos-Picante.

Spiral-Hook (*sprl hk*) or **Spiral** or **Swivot** or **Torque-Turn** or **Serpentine** or **Spiral-Turn** or **Picture-Turn** or **Spiral-Pivot:** Two possibly Leadable, Basic Coupledance Movements, Left or Right, Clockwise or Counter-Clockwise, Mirror-Image Opposite. Performed Apart from Partner, by either Partner, or by both at once in concert. A **Spiral** is the Body's Rotation, accomplished by a Twisting Motion, simultaneously upon the Balls of both Feet. One's **Spiral** occurs after an initial Forward Step. The Free-Leg wraps around the Supporting-Leg.

With Feet Apart fore and aft, the Dancer is Turning Sharply upon the Ball-of-Foot, in the Opposite direction of the Forward Foot, while keeping the Rearward Foot In-Place, i.e., **Turning Toward one's other Foot.** Dancer **Spirals** on either Foot a Half- to a Full-Turn, until thighs Cross or until the Free-Foot Crosses over and forms a **Spiral** around this Weighted-Foot. Free-Toe may remain In-Place Touching Dancefloor, In-Front of and Crossing against the Weighted-Leg.

A **Spiral-Hook to one's Right** is taken by Turning on the Ball of one's Left Forward Foot.

A **Spiral-Hook to one's Left** is taken by Turning on the Ball of one's Right Forward Foot.

One always Steps Forward first for a **Torque-Turn.** Stepping Forward to **Spiral**, it is helpful to first Point **that** Toe Slightly in the Opposite direction of intended Turning.

Note: While remaining with Weight Standing on one Foot, one may Half-Turn in either of two directions; one direction is a **Spiral** while the Opposite direction is a **Swivel.** One Spiral then one Swivel can make one **Pivot.**

Opposite of **Swivel**(1). (See Figure-Four Position, Pivot, Swirl, and Chaine.)

Spiral-Pivot: See Spiral-Hook.

Spiral Position: See Figure-Four Position.

Spiral-Turn: See Spiral-Hook.

Split-Ronde: See Bomb-Shell, and Ronde, Split.

Splits-On-Arm: See Leg-Stretch-On-Arm.

Spot: A Coupledance Term describing a Movement, Figure, Pattern, Dance, etc., where Performance is restricted to a relatively small **Spot** on the Dancefloor, and not Progressing in any direction.

Opposite of **Traveling.** (See Spot-Dancing; and Inwards-and-Downwards-Style.)

Spot-Run: A General Coupledance Movement or Figure, in which the Partners Run around each other while in some dance position.

(See Spanish-Arms, Elbow-Swing, Waist-Swing, and Highland-Swing. Also see Windmill, Orbit, Wheel, Wagon-Wheel, Swing, Allemande, Reeling-Action, Paddle-Turn, Basket, Right-Outside-RunAround, Promenade-RunAround, Natural-Fleckerl, Reverse-Fleckerl, Horse-and-Cart, Wheel-Side-by-Side, and Buzz-Step, Partners.)

Spread: A Leadable, General Coupledance Action. **Spread** is wider than Second Foot Position. **Spread** is an instant when both Partners are Coupledancing Low Height with Feet widely **Spread** side-by-side, as in the second Step of a Waltz-Box or the Bolero Basic Side Step. This very wide Side-Step absorbs the time of a very Slow Beat without having to Pause.
(See Stretch, Stride, and Foot Positions.)

Spread-Your-Toes: See Press.

Spring: *"A time when boys feel gallant and girls feel buoyant."* -- Anonymous

Squeeze: A General Coupledance Action; to **Hug** Partner tightly; to crush, crowd or press Partner.
(See Clutch, Clasp, Grasp, and Cling.) [Also see Embrace(1), Cuddle, Enfold, Bundle, Snuggle, and Envelop. Also see Loose-Hug Position, Cuddle Position(1), Shadow-Enfold Position, Cheek-to-Cheek Position, Head-to-head Position, Over-the-Heart-Hand-Hold, Slow-Dancing, and Crush-In-Closed. Also see Carpa, Tango-Lean, Leaning-Into-Each-Other, and Milonguero(2).]

Stable: A General Coupledance Term, meaning Firmly In-Place, Balanced and fixed. **Stability** is the ability to maintain or restore one's Equalibrium when tended to be displaced.
(See Steady. Also see Support, Giving-Weight, Hanging-On, and Clinging-Vine.)

Stage-Tango: See Show-Tango(1), and Tango-Argentino.

Stairs: Two different Leadable Figures used in both Argentine and International **Tango** and in American **Twostep** Coupledances, usually in a Closed Position, and usually one-Measure long.
Each Figure has four Quick Steps per Measure. May Start as either Forward-Stairs or Side-Stairs, with Line-of-Dance for each being diagonally Forward to the Left. Man Steps with Left Foot then Closes with Right. His Lady Follows.

Stalking-Walks: A partially Leadable Coupledance Pattern, suitable for the **International Tango.**
With Man in Shadow Position with Left Hands Joined, Partners Stalk using Same-Foot, Starting with Left. They Stalk to *Slow And, Slow And, Slow And, Slow And* Timing. With Knees Well Bent, they gingerly Stride *diagforwardhalt, CrossInFrontHalt, diagforwardhalt, CrossInFrontHalt*. Both Partners may look Rearward every other Stride.

Stand-Out or **Show:** A General Coupledance Term for an Individual-Style of dancing, either good or bad. To **Stand-Out** is to be noticeable, even prominent; to appear in relief or in contrast to other dancers.
"Fortune favors the bold." -- Anonymous
(For complimentary, see Showmanship, Charisma, Panache, Charm-and-Finesse, Best-Foot-Forward, Strike-Ability, Bring-Down-the-House, Confidence, Juice, and Shine. For derogatory, see Making-a-Show, Flashy, Out-Shining, Flaunting-It, and Affectation.)

Steady: A General Coupledance Term, meaning **Stable** in Position, Firmly Supported, fixed, reliable and controlled in one's dance. Or, Moving or dancing with uniform regularity, unfaltering and constant.

(See Constant-Tug, Support, Giving-Weight, Hanging-On, and Clinging-Vine.)

Stealth: A Leadable, General, Progressive Coupledance Movement. Cautiously or carefully Stepping Forward, Low, with Flat-of-Foot, with one's Center-of-Balance Trailing.

"And now the stealthy dancer comes undulantly with catlike steps that cling." -- Arthur Symons

(See Flat-Step, Slink, Slither, Skim, Level-Progression, and Sweep.)

Step-Point: Two Leadable Basic Coupledance Movements, Left or Right Foot; a Single-Step followed by Pointing the Free-Toe in some direction with Knee Straight. No Change-of-Weight.

(See Step-Touch, Step-Swing, Step-Kick, and Step-Scoot.)

StepSwivel: Two Leadable, Basic Coupledance Movements, Left or Right, Mirror-Image Opposite.

Stepping In-Place then Quarter- to Half-Turning the body, on the same Foot Stepped, Outward, Away from one's other Foot. This process causes Rotation on that Ball-of-Foot, Counter-Clockwise for Left Foot and Clockwise for Right Foot. Free-Foot then only Touches Closed.

Similar to **ForSwivel**, and **BackSwivel**. (See SwivelStep, Turn, Swivel, Swivel-Walks, Circular-Swivel-Walks, Plait, Plait-Action, and Spiral-Hook.)

Step-Thru or **Thru** or **Through** or **Step-Thru Position:** Two Leadable, Basic Coupledance Movements, Right and Left Mirror-Image Opposite. Used in the Medium-**Waltz**, American **Twostep**, in Argentine **Tango**, and many other dances.

From a Closed, Semi-Closed, or Promenade Position, either or both Partners Cross-In-Front **Step-Thru** with their Inside-Foot, then they may or may not apply Weight.

Similar to **Touch-Thru**. (See Side-Thru, and Fallaway Position.)

Step-Thru Position: See Step-Thru.

Step-Touch: Two Leadable, Basic Coupledance Movements, Left or Right Foot. **Step-Touch** is a Single-Step followed by a light Touch by the Opposite Foot. This Touch could be: (1) at the Instep of the dancer's Supporting-Foot, or (2) by a Toe-Stab Instepward, or (3) Forward, Sideward, or Rearward. There is no Change-of-Weight.

Similar to **Partial-Step**. (See Step-Point, Step-Swing, Step-Kick, Step-Scoot, Touch-Step, and Balance-Touch.)

Stork(1): Two Unleadable, General Coupledance Movements, Left or Right Foot.

"Stork has none of the fun in bringing the babies." -- Anonymous

A **Stork** is where the dancer's Pointed Free-Foot is Raised and drawn Up against the inner portion of the Supporting-Knee.

Multiple Slow Forward Steps are sometimes Performed as in a Funeral-March, except with each Step being **Storked**. This **Storking** may be either with a Hop or else Flat with no Rise-and-Fall.

(See Knee-Up Position, Kneelift, and SugarPush-Lady's-Kneelift.)

Stork(2): See Calecita.

Straight: (*derecho* in Spanish) A General Coupledance Term for an Action, Movement, Figure, or Pattern. Coupledancing Forward, Backward, or Sideward with Steps forming a Straight Line. Or, the dancer's Straightened leg, arm, Body, fingers, or Head, etc.
Inverse of Curve.

Street-Dance: A General Coupledance Term. A Street-Dance is an informal dance form "grown in the streets" by the public, one that is "picked up" and copied through one's peers, and not one that is consciously developed in the learned studios through formal lessons by professionals or their like.
Street-Dance can mean that a certain Street-Dancer had newly hit upon some particular Basic-Step that he or she delightfully favored, and which then had been copied by local peers, perhaps imprecisely, and since then has become popular at local dances and perhaps beyond, and is commonly known by some particular name.
A Street-Dance is a "living" dance form that is forever changing, i.e., constantly developing, transforming, adapting and incorporating. A Street-Dance is one in which new Patterns, new Body Positions, and new Footwork Variations are developing. A Street-Dance is one that always allows for and encourages improvisation. It is one that has no set standards, is not an adjudicated dance form, and one that is not restricted by set rules.

Strike-Ability: A General Coupledance Term for an art of Partnership perfection; for the wonderful ability of Starting their dance with an explosive Audience-impact. Strike-Ability can result by the Couple having a peak precision level, apart from whether their dance is Fast or Slow.
Similar to Impact. (See Presentation, Projection, Esthetic-Effect, Constant, Confidence, Showmanship, Expand, Stand-Out, Shine, Juice, Light-and-Shade, Smartly, Ooze, Freeze-and-Melt, Bring-Down-the-House, Flash-and-Pzazz, Charisma, Panache, Charm-and-Finesse, Individual-Style, Class-Act, Grace-Fluidity-and-Purpose, Best-Foot-Forward, Grand-Entrance, Dance-the-Part, and Audience-Appeal.)

Sube-y-Baja: (*SU-bay ee BAH-hah*, Spanish for *to go up and down*.) A Coupledance Figure danced in the various Argentine Tangos and in the Milonga.
Ed Loomis [www.batango.com/loomis] describes Sube-y-Baja as follows:
"A milonga step in which the couple dance forward-together and back-together in outside right position with a pendulum action of the hips."
Similar to Coming-and-Going, and To-and-Fro. (See Forward-and-Back, and Zarandeo.)

Suspension: A Leadable General Coupledance Inaction then Action. Suspension is an immobile delay of the Couple's Movement, perhaps for several Counts or Measures, followed by a very Rapid Step, usually Progressive, and then continuing. Suspension is normally purposeful, interplaying with the music.
Similar to Freeze-and-Melt, Hold(1), and Freeze(1). (See Hesitation, Pause, and Collect.) [Also see Hover(1).]

<u>Swango</u>:   A Novelty **Fad** Coupledance of the **Neo-Tango** sub-Genre, in vogue beginning in 2005, that is a combination and blending of **Swing** (most often **West-Coast-Swing**) and the **Argentine-Tango**. Music is in 4/4 Time and is a Steady-Beat Slow Tango, or possibly Slow Swing Music.

The **Basic-Step** seems to be a **16-Count** Pattern: This **Swango** Step begins with one Basic Sugar-Push for the first six Counts then uses two Counts to blend to Loose-Closed Position.   With both Partners next Swivel-Stepping for Four Counts upon Same-Feet, both Step Left Feet to Sidecar, Swivel then Step Right Feet to Banjo, then repeat same. Next the Man Freezes as his Lady dances two Forward-Ochos for two Counts (still in Loose-Closed Position). Lastly, both use two Counts to blend to Butterfly preparing for a Sugar-Push again.

The following are **Swango** excerpts from www.hiphoplindy.com:

"Swango is a developing dance form that is an intoxicating and challenging mix of Swing (Lindy, West Coast, East Coast, Carolina Shag, whatever your thing is) and Argentine Tango.

"Danced to mellow Swing music. It is great for dancers ... At first glance you might think Swing and Argentine Tango appear totally different, well you'd be right, they are. However, their very differences make the transitions possible and it turns out they have surprising things in common! If you know some Argentine Tango take one of your favourite (mellow) swing tunes and just dance tango to it and see what happens. ..."

The following are **Swango** excerpts from www.swangoseattle.com:

"Dancing is our passion. And our skills in both West Coast Swing and Argentine Tango have allowed us to create a method to accelerate the process of learning to dance Swango. ...

"The exotic nuevo tango music is perfect for Swango. But Swango can also be done to much of the popular West Coast Swing music."

The following is a **Swango** excerpt from www.time2dance.com:

"rob and sheila: West Coast Classes & SWANGO dance at The Atrium on Wednesdays!!"

The following are **Swango** excerpts from www.usaswingnet.com:

"Swango dancing is hot!

"If you love the sexiness of Swing and the passion of Tango, 'Swango' may be a great new experience for you. It offers the best of both dance worlds."

The following are reviews of the Stage presentation, **"SWANGO"** [www.mainstage-mgmt.com]:

"'SWANGO' is hot! The music will have you groovin' in your seat, and a new script by Rupert Holmes kicks it up a notch. 'SWANGO' combines the passion of the tango with the sexy sizzle of swing in a new dance show that will leave you wanting to head for the ballroom or the bedroom! " -- The Scarsdale Inquirer

"As the title implies, the result is a magical synthesis. The dancers of both traditions are thrilling. Sensuous moves, beautiful spins and amazing lifts come one after another. Tango alternates with swing, couples switch with multiple pairs, and men and women have their times alone. It's all mesmerizing." -- The Journal News

With regards to mixing Swing with other dances in 16-Count Patterns in 4/4 Time, there are the three **Swango** "sister-dances", **Swalsa**, (Swing + Salsa,) **Swing-Rueda**, (Salsa-Rueda + Swing,) and **HipHop-Lindy**, (Swing + HipHop.) In addition, see the **Neo-Tango** sub-Genre, to which this **Swango** belongs.

Sway-ContraCheck or **Three-Dimensional-ContraCheck:** A partially Leadable Coupledancing Picture-Figure, Performed with artful Balance. Suitable for the Slow-**Foxtrot,** Slow-**Waltz** and **International Tango,** and as an ending for other dances, such as all **Quicksteps, Rumbas,** the **Bolero,** and **Cabaret.**

The Man, after first Lowering by Softening his Right Knee, Moves Forward into the Lady, and the Couple assumes a Figure **identical to the normal ContraCheck,** except as follows:

Upon the Couple settling into the normal ContraCheck Position, the Man Leads his Lady into a Slightly Torqued CCW Upper-Body Couple-Rotation. From there, the Lady Slowly makes a Sweeping Sway, with her Head and eyes rolling across the ceiling from her looking to her **Left** then looking to her **Right,** as she Sweeps through to the end of her **Sway-ContraCheck.** (Her eyes rolling Opposite than that for **Around-the-World.**)

The Man may Turn his Toes more Outward for stability to Support his Lady's Sway, and he Leads by Sweeping her Slightly from his Left to his Right.

(See Around-the-World-ContraCheck, Bird-of-Paradise-ContraCheck, and Rag-Doll. Also see ContraCheck-and-Switch, Back-ContraCheck, No-Hands-ContraCheck, and Traveling-ContraCheck.)

Switch(1): A Leadable General Coupledance Action oo Shifting Weight from one Foot to the other in a rapid Sliding Movement. One kind of **Switch** is for 1/4 to 1/2 Couple Rotation, a Quick Change in Facing Position is accomplished by a Swivel on the Supporting-Foot that Transfers Weight to the Free-Foot. For a **Switch** in a Loose-Closed Position with Feet Spread fore and aft and Weight distributed between both Feet, up to a Half-Turn Couple-Rotation can be made, Swiveling upon both Balls in the direction of the Trailing-Leg. Shortening the Spread during Swiveling helps.

(See Switch-Rock, and Snap-Change.)

Switch(2) (*swch*) or **Switch-Cross:** Two Leadable, Spot-Coupledance Figures, Left or Right, Mirror-Image Opposite, suitable for **Argentine Tango,** for both of each **Rumba,** each **ChaCha,** and other dances. Rhythm for Timing is *Quick Quick Slow* for Tango and Rumba, and *Slow Slow, Quick Quick Slow* for ChaCha. The Left Switch normally begins in Back-to-Back-Left Position, and ends with a Left-Step-Thru in either Butterfly or Left-Open-Facing Position. Either two or four Changes-of-Weight are made.

Man dances *forswivel3/8CCW* to Face *RecoverSideward* legs Spread *sidecrossinfront* (or *sidecrossinfront Close sidecrossinfront.*)

Lady, Following, dances *ForSwivel3/8CW* to Face *recoversideward* legs Spread *SideCrossInFront* (or *SideCrossInFront close SideCrossInFront.*)

Note: Overall Line-of-Motion reverses after Figure is danced, (see Switch-Rock, and Snap-Change.)

Switch(3): See Tango-Switch.

Switch-Rock: Two Leadable, one-Measure, Spot-Coupledance Figures, Left or Right, Mirror-Image Opposite, suitable for **Argentine Tango**, for each **Rumba**, each **ChaCha**, and for other dances. Rhythm Timing is *Quick Quick Slow* for Tango and Rumba, and *Slow Slow Quick Quick Slow* for ChaCha.

The Left Switch-Rock normally begins in Back-to-Back-Left Position, and ends in Left-Open-Facing Position. Either two or four Changes-of-Weight are made.

Man dances *forswivel3/8CCW* to Face *RecoverSideward* legs Spread *sideward* legs Spread (or *sideward Close sideward.*)

Lady, Following, dances *ForSwivel3/8CW* to Face *recoversideward* legs Spread *Sideward* legs Spread (or *Sideward close Sideward.*)

Note: Overall Line-of-Motion remains the same after Figure is danced, (see Switch.)

Swivel (*swvl* or *swiv* or *Sv*): Two possibly Leadable, Basic Coupledance Movements, Right or Left, Clockwise or Counter-Clockwise, Mirror-Image Opposite. Performed Apart from Partner, by either Partner, or by both at once in concert.

Upon Stepping, the Motion of the dancer's next Bodily Movement or Step produces Rotation. A **Swivel** is the Body's Rotation along the Vertical-Alignment of the Supporting-Leg, accomplished by Spinning either upon the Ball or Heel of the Supporting-Foot. **Turning Outward, Away from one's Free-Foot** causes the **Swivel**, which is usually for a Half-Turn. Even though this occurs on the Ball, one's Foot is kept fairly Flat to the Dancefloor.

Note: While remaining with Weight Standing on one Foot, one may Half-Turn in either of two directions; one direction is a **Swivel** while the Opposite direction is a **Spiral**. One Swivel then one Spiral can make one **Pivot**.

Opposite of **Spiral-Hook**. (See Turn, StepSwivel, SwivelStep, ForSwivel, BackSwivel, StrideTurn, SugarFoot, Sand-Step, Swivet, and Ramble. Also see Swivel-Walks, Circular-Swivel-Walks, and Plait.)

Swivel-Point: Two Leadable, General Coupledance Movements, Left or Right.

With a Softened Knee, the dancer Forward-Swivels a Quarter-Turn, or Half-Turn, or three-Quarter-Turn upon Ball-of-Foot; then the Free-Foot is Pointed, Straight-Kneed, Touching the Dancefloor, Sideward or Rearward and Away from the Supporting-Foot. For an alternate method, instead of Pointing, the Free-Foot is either Fanned or Flared.

Left and Right Half-Turn **Swivel-Points** in Sequence, one each, creates two **Ochos**, forming a "figure eight".

Swivot: See Spiral-Hook.

Syncopated-Whisk: A Leadable one-Measure, four Step Coupledance Figure, suitable for the **International Tango**, Slow-**Foxtrot**, Slow-**Waltz**, and other dances. Rhythm Timing for the Tango is *Quick And Quick Slow*; for Foxtrot is *Slow Quick And Quick*; and for Waltz is *Slow And Slow Slow*.

Begins in Semi-Closed Position or in Promenade Position, Turns to a Closed Position, then ends in Semi-Closed Position or in Promenade Position, except with Inside-Feet Stepped-Thru.

Man dances *StepThruTurn* to Face *close Sideward crossbehind.*

Lady, Following, dances *stepthruturn* to Face *Close sideward CrossBehind.*

(See Whisk, Whisk Position, Flat-Whisk, and Flat-Whisk Position.)

Taiwanese-Tango: The Tango as Coupledanced in Taiwan; one of the softest of all Tangos, almost a Foxtrot but still with some Tango flavor.

Tamara or **Latin-Bull:** (a verb) Achieving two Basic Coupledance Spaghetti Figures, Tamara or Left-Tamara, either by the Lady or by the Man. Suitable for American and Texas **Twosteps**, American **Tango, Four-Count, Polka**, the **Discos** and **Hustles, PasoDoble, Cajun-Jittergug,** and for other dances. The means for achieving the **Tamara** follows; the **Left-Tamara** being Mirror-Image Opposite.

Facing each other, Apart and Offset to their Right, the Partner to be Tamaraed places one's arms as follows: **Left arm is behind one's back while the Right arm is held High.** Then the other Partner Clasps Opposing-Hands. This Clasp is usually followed by the Couple Wheeling a Half-Turn Clockwise.

The following is from a 1986 pamphlet titled *Round Dance Manual*:

"*Tamara - The Tamara is usually entered into by joining the leading hands (M's L and W's R) and raising them as partners come to R hip position and join the M's R and W's L hands. Partners face first opposite direction with R hips adjacent. M's R arm crosses under W's R arm and holds her L hand at the small of her back with M's palm down and W's palm up and forearm parallel to the floor extended across behind her back. W's R hand is held slightly above her head with arm bent and elbow fwd, her palm up. M's L hand is raised to meet W's raised hand with his elbow bent and Fwd and his palm down, finger tips meeting. Joined M's L and W's R hands form a `Window' between them through which they can look at each other. Upon continuing the usual turn to face the other direction, the top hands release and M's R and W's L hands are held high as M's L is placed behind her back parallel to the floor and W places her R in his L hand at the small of M's back, palm positions reversed.*"

(See Tamara Position.)

Tanango or **Tanganya:** A Haitian and Cuban **Folkdance**, danced probably in the 1890s. (See Tango, and Argentine Tango.)

Tanda: (*TAN-da*, Spanish for *dance set*.) A **Tanda** is part of the formal and highly structured dancing at a **Milonga**. Canned music is played in Dance-Sets called **Tandas**, and each one consists of four or five songs. One **Tanda** is such as four Tangos of similar music Style played in sequence. The next **Tanda** (Set) might be of four Argentine Waltzes, or perhaps of four or five **Milongas**. Other following **Tanda** Dance-Sets might be of Latins, Merengues, Salsas, Swings or Cumbias, then all reverts back to Argentine music again.

It is customary to dance the entire Dance-Set with the one same Partner, or at least a minimum of two dance-songs. Everyone normally sits down at their own table between each **Tanda** (Set), while a short and undanceable **Cortina** is played.

Ed Loomis [www.batango.com/loomis] describes **Tanda** as follows:

"*TANDA A set of dance music, usually three to five songs, of the same dance in similar style, if not by the same orquesta. The tandas are separated by a brief interlude of non tango music called `cortina', or curtain, during which couples select each other. It is customary to dance the entire tanda with the same partner unless the man is rude or very disappointing as a dance partner, in which case the lady may say gracias (thank you) and leave.*"

(See Milonga for more etiquette details, and Cortina.) [Much from www.dancetraveler.com, and www.tangonyc.com]

Tanganya: (African) See Tanango.

Tango: *"You can't untie it."* An amorous Spot-Coupledance of sensually entwined bodies, drama and varying Rhythms. In Syncopated 2/4 or 4/4, or sometimes in 4/8 Time, Tango music is unique. When in 2/4 Time, *Slows* take one Beat of the music, while *Quicks* take a Half-Beat. All the various Tangos are danced on the One-Beat Rhythm-Station, and are danced with often Split-Measures at 32 Bars per minute Tempo, (28 to 34.) **Tango** may have been the first of the world-wide "Latin" dances.

Passionate, glamorous, Elegant Tango is not a simple dance. Low and Flat with Softened Knees, Curving Steps are placed with Hesitant Body Movement, tentatively feeling their way, catlike. There is Ho-Hum Tango, a very sedate Tango, just another dance; and then there is the **Tango!** A way of life! The Stance for Ho-Hum Tango is the same as for most other dances. The Stance for **Tango!** is unique and immediately recognizable, even by Novices. But a word of caution about any Tango: *"Only a shadow of difference between the sublime and the ludicrous."* -- Anonymous

Tango was born from poor European immigrant men in the 1910s; there was a report of Tango in Buenos Aires in July of 1910. Men danced with Macho to the music of the Bandoneon or guitar in Buenos Aires, attempting to impress the very few women available there at that time. They had no basic Figures or Patterns, except that all was inclined to be Macho for impression. They would dance by their own means, Leading some woman in a small area, through innovated complex Movements and Steps. Men would group and teach each other their ideas, outside on the streets, Kicking and intermingling their legs.

Tango origin is believed to have been influenced mostly by the Spanish Gypsy **Milonga**, but also by the Afro-Argentine **Candombe**, the **ContraDanza-Spanish**, and by the Cuban **Habanera** dances. The original Tango could possibly have been a hybrid between the Haitian and Cuban **Tanango** and this **Habanera**.

The following is from *Tango Terminology*, *www.tangoafficionado.com*:

"Tango: Popular music from the Rio de la Plata region dating back to 1885-95, defined by a 2/4 rhythm until the 1920s when a 4/8 rhythm became common. A popular dance originating in the mid 19th century which descended from the Candombe, Habanera, Milonga, and (by some tango scholars) the Tango Andaluz. The exact origins of Tango are a historical mystery."

Some say Argentines danced this dance originally on pebble-strewn dirt floors of caves with low ceilings, hence that characteristic Stance and creeping of all Tangos. Gingerly Stepping Bent-Kneed like a cat on a wet surface, Emoting, they danced Flat-Footed and low, their Bodies locked in *The Dance of Love*. (See Level-Progression.)

Being wrapped up in Tango vastly influenced its participant's Way-Of-Life, in that it came with a certain Mode-of-Dress-and-Behavior. (See Mimicry-En-Masse.)

Tango became very popular in Europe about 1915, after first coming into only limited and temporary vogue in the U.S. Europe, mainly France, continued to import their Tango interpretations from the Argentine well into the early 1920s. Europe developed rules, including some Dancefloor Traveling. Tango was often danced Head-to-Head in Europe, and even danced while kissing with arms entwined. American high society embraced this **New-French-Tango**, or **Continental Tango**, beginning about 1926. Maurice Mouvet learned this Tango in Paris and introduced it in New York in 1911. The resulting American Tango was an easier and tamer version, but still electric and extremely romantic. (Also see Contest Tango, and Cafe Tango.)

Since then, Tango has become at least three completely different Coupledances, danced in many Styles but always Low, sleek, Stealthy and recognizable as **Tango!** One family of Styles is the **International Tango**, the Modern and Smooth, Standard, Classic Coupledance; another Style is the **American** and **Continental Tangos**; and the third, original Style is the **Argentine Tango**.   (Continued)

Tango: (Continued)
Even cars Tango: *"Cars Tango the freeway with their wheels intertwined."* -- Anonymous
          (See **International Tango Step-Listing, Tango-American-and-Continental Step-Listing,** and **Argentine Tango Step-Listing.**)

Tango-American-and-Continental Step-Listing: Various **Movements, Figures and Patterns,** (or Steps,) are listed together below.
          All Steps listed below are described elsewhere in this book.
          The following listed Steps may be without NCDTO or ISTD accreditation.
          See **American Tango, Continental Tango,** and **Argentine Tango Step-Listing.** (Also see Tango, Argentine Tango, International Tango, American Competition Tango, and International Tango Step-Listing.)
          The following **American Tango and Continental Tango** Steps are listed in alphabetical order:
AnkleTrip, Arch, Around-the-World, Around-the-World-ContraCheck.   Back-Flick, Backward-Close-Finish, Brush-Tap.   Chair, Chair-Forward-Poised Position, Change-Feet-Tap, Change-of-Sway, Closed-Promenade, ContraCheck, ContraCheck-and-Switch, Corte, Criss-Cross.   Dip, DobleCruz, Drape Position, Drop, Drop-Hinge.   Fallaway, Fallaway-Promenade, Flick, Front-Hook.   Gauchos.   Heel-Strike.   KneeFlick.   LaPuerta, Leg-Stretch-on-Arm, Lift, Lunge.   Natural-Fallaway-Whisk, Natural-Twist-Turn.   Ochos, Ochos-para-Atras, Open-Promenade, Outside-Swivel-and-Tap.   Pickup, Progressive-Back-Fans, Progressive-Link, Progressive-Side-Step, Progressive-Side-Step-Reverse-Turn, Progressive-Tango-Rocks, Promenade-Ending, Promenade-Link, Promenade-Sway, Promenade-Tap, Promenade-to-Counter-Promenade, Promenade-to-Left-Outside, Promenade-Vine.   Reclining-Lady, Reclining-Lady-with-Develope, Reverse-Turn-Closed-Finish, Reverse-Turn-One-Half, Reverse-Turn-Open-Finish, Rock-Back, Rocking-Chair, Rocking-Steps, Rock-Steps, Rock-Turn.   Sentado-Line, Serpiente, Side-Corte. Tango-Close, Tango-Drag, Tango-Draw, Tango-Switch, Tango-Switches, Tango-Tap, Telemark-to-Semi-Closed, The-Break.   Whisk.

          Tango American-Style or **American Tango**(2) or **American Competition Tango:** A highly Disciplined, Rhythm Traveling-Coupledance, that has been lumped together with the American-Style of Smooth Traveling-Coupledances at Competitions. This Formal, Competitive, distinctively structured, **Tango American-Style** differs greatly from the many other Tangos, except for its similar **International Tango** cousin. [The extremely different and Soft **American Tango**(1) is a much simpler dance than is this brittle **American Tango**(2).]
          Danced at DanceSport events that include the Foxtrot, Waltz, Viennese, and sometimes the Peabody, the **Tango American-Style** is almost imperceptively the same as the **International Tango,** with identical music and Timing. The only differences being more Figures and Patterns are allowed, and there is more freedom in Couples separating, i.e., Partners are allowed to Break-Apart from their Patch while Competing.
          See **International Tango Step-Listing.** (Also see Tango, Continental Tango, and Argentine Tango. Also see Tango-Music.)

Tango-Apilado or **Tango-Rhythmic-Style** or **Tango-Club-Style:** (*ah-pe-LA-do* is Spanish for *piled up* or *heaping up*.) An **Argentine Tango** Coupledance of the **Linear-Tango** type that is predominately popular in Buenos Aires. Called "*the close embrace*," the Man's close Embrace (Abrazo) of his Lady is emphasized more than any complicated Footwork for this dance. This dance Style is simpler than the Tango-de-Salon. In this Tango, the Man really has to dance for his Lady.

Experience *el alma del tango* -- "*the soul of the tango*."

Same as **Milonguero-Tango.** [See Milonguero(2). Also see Tango-Orillero; Tango-de-Salon, which includes the Rotary-Tango and Linear-Tango; the Show-Tango; and the Continental Tango.]

[Much from http://nfo.net/dance/tprimer.]

Tango-Argentino or **Exhibition-Tango:** **Argentine Tango** was revived after thirty years of dormancy, by a particular Stage Performance made famous by an excellent group from the Argentine Tango "*old guard*". This show opened in Paris then toured in the U.S. in 1987, featuring the Dinzels. From this exciting show, **Argentine Tango** fever took off world-wide. **Tango-Argentino** grew out from the social **Tango-de-Salon** Genre of the 1950s, and from **Show-Tango**(1).

The following is from *Daniel Trenner*, *www.dancetraveler.com*:

"*Exhibition tango was first developed within the social vernacular. For the most part it was danced as a kind of loose warfare between different neighborhood schools, at the social dances, in breaks between the social dancing. In the fifties, Juan Carlos Copes led the development of tango for stage dancing, which culminated in Tango Argentino and modern show dancing. With this development, the tango style branched again, and the show dancers quickly broadened and evolved their vocabularies creating even more stylistic diversity.*"

Same as **Show-Tango**(1).

Tango-Arrabalero: (*ar-rrah-bahl-AY-ro*, Spanish for *suburb dance*.) The kind of **Tango** of the suburbs or slums (*arrabal*) of Buenos Aires; mostly dealing with song and poem in context. An **Arrabalero** is someone of low social status, with simple, direct ways of coarse language talking.

Same as **Argentine Tango.**

Tango-Close or **Touch-at-Instep:** Two partially Leadable, General Coupledance Foot Positions, Left to Right Arch or Right to Left Arch, Staggered Trailing Rearward. Feet are brought Together **without** a Change-of-Weight. Ball-of-Foot with no Weight is tucked into the Arch, i.e. Instep, of one's other, Supporting-Foot.

More explicit than **CloseTouch.** See **Tango-Draw** for Action Toward Tango-Close. (See Tango-Stepping, Backward-Tango-Close, Drag, Close, Draw, Tango-Tap, Step-and-Drag, and Touch. Also see The-Break, and Backward-Close-Finish. Also see Marque-Pied, Marque-Talon, Continenza, Paseo, and Represa.)

Tango-Close-Finish: See The-Break.

Tango-Club-Style: See Tango-Apilado.

Tango-de-Salon or **Salon-Tango** or **Social-Tango** or **Villa-Urguiza-Tango:** (*sah-LON* is Spanish for *saloon*.) A Genre in itself, the **Tango-de-Salon** is the more Elegante Style of the **Argentine Tango** Genre that, beginning in the 1980s, developed out of the **Petroleo-Tango** of the 1940s and 50s. This **Tango-de-Salon** Style is more difficult to dance than is the also popular Milonquero-Tango. This "**Salon**" Style is sometimes called **Villa-Urguiza** in reference to the Buenos Aires city quarter where it is danced.

Ed Loomis [www.batango.com/loomis] describes the **Tango-de-Salon** as follows:

"*TANGO DE SALON An elegant and very social style of tango characterized by slow, measured, and smoothly executed moves. It includes all of the basic tango steps and figures plus sacadas, giros and boleos. The emphasis is on precision, smoothness, and elegant dance lines. The dancing couples do not embrace as closely as in older styles and the embrace is flexible, opening slightly to make room for various figures and closing again for support and poise.*"

Gold Tango [www.elmundodeltango.com/asimard] describes this **Salon-Style** as follows:

"*... in a combination of Salon Style and Orillero Style. Salon Style is an elegant and smooth style of Tango based on walking whilst Orillero Style is a faster, flashier style based on rotation.*"

This melancholy **Salon-Tango** Genre is Travel-Danced in the Milongas (Dancehalls) of Argentina, Counter-Clockwise, exercising respect for the Line-of-Dance. It is considered to be the "real" Tango, and is still the contemporary Style of today. Revived, it is now again popular with a younger Argentine generation. Few presently teach **Salon-Tango** outside of Argentina, yet competence in dancing this basic **Tango-de-Salon** is the first for learning to dance Well and gain the Character-of-the-Dance, for learning more complicated versions of the **Argentine Tango** Genre. **Salon-Tango** sometimes takes extra Dancefloor space with off-the-floor Embellishments such as Boleos, Ganchos, and Sentadas in Open-Embrace.

This **Tango-de-Salon**, with Knees barely Softened, is normally danced either in an Open-Embrace-Tango, or more often with a **Tango-Lean** in the Close-Embrace-Tango Position. It is typically danced to a strongly accented 4/4 Time Tango Beat.

This **Salon-Tango** Genre includes both the **Rotary-Tango** and **Linear-Tango** types of Argentine Tango. This **Salon-Tango** breaks down into the **Tango-Orillero, Tango-Apilado, Milonguero-Tango, Club-Style Tango, Tango-Nuevo, Tango-Liso**, and the **Liquid-Tango** Styles. See all nine of these types and Styles for more details about this subject **Tango-de-Salon** Coupledance.

Besides this **Salon-Tango** and its many Styles, (and besides the Milonquero-Tango,) there is another different Tango Style presently in vogue in downtown Buenos Aires, Argentina; it is the **Show-Tango**(1). In Argentina, it is considered rude to show off one's Fantasy **Show-Tango** Routines at a Social **Salon-Tango** gathering.

(See the earlier Canyengue-Tango.) [Some data from http://www.dancetraveler.com, wwww.triangletangueros.org, and www.tejastango.com.]

Tango-Drag: See Spanish-Drag.

Tango-Draw: A Leadable General Coupledance Action. Timing is *Slow*. Free-Foot is Slipped Forward or Diagonally Forward, Rearward or Diagonally Rearward, or Sideward, Toward Arch of one's Supporting-Foot to **Tango-Close**, Feet Together **without** a Change-of-Weight.

The most common **Tango-Draw** is the one most used in the **American Tango** with the Couple in a Closed Position, (this one is also possibly useful in the other Tangos):

Man, from Diagonally Rearward, Draws his Left to his Right Foot Arch, Tango-Close Flat with his Left Foot Staggered Rearward.

Lady, from Diagonally Forward, Draws her Right to her Left Foot Arch, Tango-Close Flat with her Right Foot Staggered Rearward.

Some argue that **Tango-Draw** is a four-Count Figure, as in the following from a 1986 pamphlet titled *Round Dance Manual*:

"*Tango Draw* - *Man steps fwd on the left foot on the first count, sideward on the right foot on the second count, draws the left foot to the right foot during the third and fourth count, taking no weight on the left foot.*"

Similar to **CloseTouch**. (See Drag, Close, Draw, Step-and-Drag, Tango-Tap, Spanish-Drag, Spanish-Drag-with-Knee-Climb, Point, and Touch. Also see The-Break, and Backward-Close-Finish. Also see Paseo, Tango-Stepping, Marque-Pied, and Marque-Talon.)

Tango-Dreams: Music for an American Coupledance in vogue about 1914 to 1918. It was a tune written by a J. Rosamond Johnson, and could possibly have been the music for the **Castle-Tango**.

(See Castle, Vernon and Irene.) [Tune data from http://nfo.net/usa/dance]

Tango-Fan: See LaPuerta.

Tango-Hustle: A novelty Fad Coupledance, to the heavy Hustle Beat of the 1970s in the U.S., especially in Los Angeles. A Hustle with an American Tango flavor, the **Tango-Hustle** was probably one of the Hustles-of-Tap-Genre, all of which were Six-Count. Its 4/4 constant Timing was probably either *1 2& 3 4, 5 Tap*, or *1 2 3& 4, 5 Tap*. From the writer's memory, its Basic-Step Started in a Tango Promenade Position; there may have been a Back-Hitch then a Pickup with a Tango-Close Tap. Opening again to Promenade, perhaps the Lady did an Outside Underarm-Turn or Spin followed by the Tango-Close. The **Tango-Hustle** must have had many additional Patterns.

(See Disco-Era.)

Tango International: See International Tango.

<u>**Tango-Lean**</u> or **Close-Embrace-Tango** or **Pyramid**(2): Used in the **Argentine Tango** and **Milonga** Coupledances, a Leadable, intimate Position while dancing, in which both Partners are Leaning Inward Toward each other, Together, forming an inverse vertical "V" Body condition. This **Close-Embrace** is alternate to **Open-Embrace**. This **Close-Embrace** is a special connection carrying subtle magic that enables Partners to communicate fully within a shared axis.

Picture the following typical snapshot of an Argentine Couple with a **Tango-Lean**, dancing in the Closed Position Argentine Tango, the Milonga, or perhaps in the Rotary-Tango or Milonguero-Tango Style:

The Man's Weight is upon his Forward Crossed Right Foot, while his contorted and shorter Lady appears to Perform Ochos. Above the waists, the Man Hugs his Lady to him, while below, Feet are some twelve inches far Apart from the Partner, and legs for both are Crossed at the Knees. Their shoulders are close together and effort is made to keep them parallel, while their hips Turn with CBMP to Semi-Closed. All elbows are Lowered. ***Off-Balance**, the Lady's Left upper arm is supported by her Left wrist being wrapped around his neck. His Right arm is wrapped High and completely around her upper Torso, Squeezing that portion of her against his chest. Assuming her **Tango-Lean**, her back arches with some Posterior-Protrusion while his Stance is more vertical, although he has some **Tango-Lean**. The Lady's Head is Open with her Left forehead pressed against his Right cheek. Their Clasped Hands are Held at her Shoulder-Level.

*Off-Balance; the following is from *Milonguero-Style Tango* of *www.tejatango.com/tango_styles*:

"*Milonguero-style tango is typically danced with a slightly leaning posture that typically joins the torsos of the two dancers from the tummy through the solar plexis (in an embrace that Argentine's call apilado) while allowing a bit of distance between the couple's feet. .... Some practitioners of this style suggest that each dancer lean against their partner. Others say that the lean is more of an illusion in which each partner maintains their own balance, but leans forward just enough to complete the embrace. The couple maintains a constant upper body contact and does not loosen their embrace to accommodate turns or ochos, which can limit the couple to walking steps and simple ochos until both partners develop the skills for the woman to execute her turns without pivoting her feet much.*"

*Off-Balance; the following is from *Club-Style Tango* of *www.tejatango.com/tango_styles*:

"*.... uses the posture and embrace of close salon-style tango. Club-style tango is danced with an upright posture in an offset close embrace in a V. The couple loosens their embrace slightly on their turns to allow the woman to rotate more freely and pivot without requiring much independent movement between her hips and torso. If the woman rotates her hips through the turns independently of her upper torso, the embrace need not be loosened as much.*"

More explicit than **Leaning-Into-EachOther**. [See Lead/Follow-for-Tango. Also see Tango-Apilado, Carpa, Milonguero-Style, Quebrada Position, and Embrace(2). Also see Lean. Also see Argentine Tango Step-Listing.]

   Tango-Liso: (*LEE-so*, Spanish for *plain, even, flat*.) An **Argentine Tango** Style for the crowded Dancefloor. This Liso Style Tango has developed out of necessity in small, crowded Dancehalls.

   Tango-Liso is a way of Coupledancing with very little available space. Knees are only Slightly Softened and Partners remain offset to their Right. The Couple might cycle between Close-Embrace and the Open-Embrace. A few tiny Steps Forward then Circling with much Couple-Rotation of the Rotary-Tango type, awaiting for space to open up through the crowd.

   The Lady Performs Turns but they are kept tight and simple. Off-the-floor Embellishments such as Boleos, Ganchos, and Sentadas are understandably absent from this Style, or at least diminished. On a crowded Dancefloor in a Milonga, to avoid Kicking others, the dancer's Boleo Movements need to be shrunk and miniaturized. If any, instead of a gigantic Boleo, tiny and Soft Shakes and Wiggles are in order.

   Ed Loomis [www.batango.com/loomis] describes the **Tango-Liso** as follows:

   "*TANGO LISO Literally, tango smooth: A way of dancing tango characterized by its lack of fancy figures or patterns. Only the most `basic' tango steps and figures such as caminadas, ochos, molinetes, etc., are utilized. Boleos, ganchos, sacadas, sentadas, and other fancy moves and acrobatics are not done. A very early term for Tango de Salon.*"

Similar to **Milonguero-Tango.** (See Crowded-Floor Dancing, Tango-de-Salon, Tango-Orillero, and Liquid-Tango.) [Most from http://en2.wikipedia.org/wiki/Tango]

   Tango-Milonga: See Tango y Milonga.

Tango-Music: There are about seven different primary kinds of **Tango-Music** Rhythms and maybe more, but all have that recognizeable, certain Tango flavor. All the various Tangos are danced on the One-Beat Rhythm-Station, and are danced with often Split-Measures nominally at 32 Measures-per-Minute (MPM) Tempo. **Tango-Music** is in Syncopated 2/4 or 4/4, or sometimes in 4/8 Time. When in 2/4 Time, *Slows* take one Beat of the Music, while *Quicks* take a Half-Beat.

Both the brittle American(2) and International Tangos are rather Staccato-Style Coupledances, while the more polite and romantic American(1) and Continental Tangos are more simple Coupledances. But all of them are usually Coupledanced to "orchestral" **Tango-Music** with strong Marching Rhythms at about 28 to 34 MPM. Conversely, the more sophisticated, fiery and passionate Argentine Tango, with less-than-regular Tempi, can alternate between being sharp then fluid, and is normally Coupledanced to playful, "authentic" **Tango-Music** as played with **Bandoneon** and guitar accompaniment.

(See Dance-Music, and Danceable-Music.)

Tango-Nuevo or New-Tango(1): One Style of the **Tango-de-Salon** Coupledance, **Rotary-Tango** type and part of the **Argentine Tango** Genre.

This **Tango-Nuevo** is a more schooled approach that analyzes dance structure, seeking new Step and Figure combinations versus specific Figures, although many overturned Ochos and Changes-of-Direction after Turning are normally Performed. Consequently, for ease of accomplishment, this **Tango-Nuevo** is Coupledanced only in the **Open-Embrace-Tango** Style of Hold, in which both Partners continually maintain their own Center-of-Balance.

(See Neo-Tango.) [Much from www.tejastango.com.]

Tango-Orillero or **Orillero-Tango** or **Orillero-Style:** (*o-re-l'YAR-o*, Spanish for *to border*.) One Style of the **Tango-de-Salon** Coupledance, and was both the **Linear-Tango** and **Rotary-Tango** types of the **Argentine Tango** Genre.

Before 1950, this **Orillero-Tango** Style possibly originated out from large social Dancefloors located in Buenos Aires suburbs, or possibly it originated in its back-streets, (*Orillas*.)

The following is from *Athene School of Dancing* - *www.pleisuredance.biz*:

"Tango Orillero - It is a raw, earthy and compact style requiring little floor space. The couple weave intricate figures around each other as they step between each others feet and legs entwine to perform some of the most sensuous moves."

Ed Loomis [www.batango.com/loomis] describes this **Orillero-Style** as follows:

"The style of dance which is danced in the suburbs, characterized by the man doing many quick syncopated foot moves and even jumps. See seguidillas." (*Saltitos*, Spanish for *little jumps*.)

Before 1950, this **Tango-Orillero** was not considered acceptable inside refined salons in central Buenos Aires, but by now it resembles today's **Tango-de-Salon**, with both Styles normally Traveling somewhat. But this **Orillero-Tango** differs in that, at times, it adds playfully Syncopated Embellished Patterns that take space and are irrespectful of the Counter-Clockwise Line-of-Dance that it mostly follows.

With Knees barely Softened, this **Tango-Orillero** is normally danced either in an Open-Embrace-Tango, or more often with a **Tango-Lean** in the Close-Embrace-Tango Position. This Traveling **Tango-Orillero** usually is danced within a group that emphasizes intricate Footwork instead of Flashy Leaps and Steps. Parada Stops are sometimes made to the Travel-dancing in order to Perform various Adorno Embellishments, including Dibujos, rapid Kicks and other Foot Movements.

Gold Tango [www.elmundodeltango.com/asimard] describes this **Orillero-Style** as follows:

"... in a combination of Salon Style and Orillero Style. Salon Style is an elegant and smooth style of Tango based on walking whilst Orillero Style is a faster, flashier style based on rotation."

(See Linear-Tango, and Rotary-Tango. Also see Tango-Apilado, and Tango-Liso.)
[Some data from http://nfo.net/dance/tprimer, and www.tejastango.com.]

Tango-Phrase: See Five-Step-Basic-Tango.

Tango Position-on-Ice: See Outside Position-on-Ice.

Tango-Rhythmic-Style: See Tango-Apilado.

Tangos: A Spanish Gypsy **Flamenco** Spot-dance of unknown origin, perhaps Andalusian, but danced early in Malaga, Spain. Allied to **Cante Chico**, **Tangos** should not be confused with the Argentine Tango. **Tangos** del Piyayo are from Malaga, named after the singer, El Piyayo, who made them renouned.

(See Spanish Dance, and Spanish-Folkdance-by-Region.)

Tango-Salute: See Salute.

Tango-Stance: See Closed Position #1 for International Tango.

Tango-Stepping or **Junta:** (*hOON-tah*, Spanish for *bringing together* or *closing*.) The characteristic Walk of the **Argentine Tango** and the **Milonga**. This Walk amounts to Stepping Flat (using Whole-Foot) without Float, i.e., in Level-Progression, with Knees and ankles passing and coming together closely.

Ed Loomis [www.batango.com/loomis] describes the **Junta** as follows:

"In Tango it is essential that the ankles and knees should come together or pass closely by each other between each step to create an elegant appearance, preserve balance, and to communicate clearly the completion of the step to one's partner. This applies equally to the man and the lady."

(See Flat-of-Foot, Flat-Step, Flat-Whisk Position, Eight-Step-Basic-Tango, Resolucion, Tango-Draw, Tango-Close, and Walk.)

Tango-Switch or **Switch:** Two Leadable, General Coupledance Actions, Left or Right. To Switch Direction-of-Dance, Starting with having Stepped Forward and with Center-of-Balance Forward, **Half-Turning** with no Foot Movement and with no Change-of-Weight. As a Couple, Tango-Switch from Promenade to Reverse-Semi-Closed Positions.

(See Tango-Switches, and Promenade-to-Counter-Promenade.)

Tango-Switches: A Leadable, General Coupledance Figure, mostly suitable for all **Tango**s. Rhythm Timing is *Slow Quick Quick*. Begins and ends in Promenade Position, with no Foot Movement throughout. They reverse Direction-of-Dance twice.

Begins with both Partners (1) Moving their Center-of-Balance Forward onto Outside Feet; (2) they Left Tango-Switch, Half-Turning into each other to change to Left-Promenade Position; (3) they Right Tango-Switch back. Twice they have a Change-of-Weight to their new Outside-Feet.

(See Tango-Switch, and Promenade-to-Counter-Promenade.)

Tango-Tap: Two Leadable **Tango** Coupledance Actions or Movements. There are two means of Tango-Tap; see Brush-Tap, and Change-Feet-Tap.

Tango-Trance: One old Style of **Argentine Tango** Coupledancing the Argentines used to Perform was **with their eyes closed**, Chest-to-chest, and Cheek-to-Cheek. This is what is known as the **Tango-Trance**.

(See "**Closed**" for the listing of Contact subjects and conditions nearest Together against Partner. Also see Neo-Tango.)

Tango-Twist: A **Novelty Fad** Coupledance of 1963. This had its own Eponymous record, "*The Tango Twist*" by *Paul Wayne*.

(See Novelty-&-Fad Dances-of-the-1960s.) [From www.bluejuice.org.au]

Tango-Vals: See Argentine-Waltz.

Tango-Waltz: See Argentine-Waltz.

Tango-with-Turns: See Rotary-Tango.

Tango y Milonga or **Tango-Milonga:** (*TAHN-go e me-LAWN-gah*) A Leadable Coupledance in 2/4 Time. An early Argentine forerunner of the **Argentine Tango**, this **Tango-Milonga** was a **middle step** between the **Milonga-Candombera** and the actual **Tango**. Awhile before 1923 in the Plata region of Buenos Aires, it was derived from the original **Milonga** Coupledanced by Gypsy Flamenco dancers, immigrants from Spain.

The following is an extract from an article by *Vittorio Pujia* in the *El Tanguata* magazine (April issue, Buenos Aires):

"We know tango arose as a way of dancing, that dancers adopted milonga as their favorite rhythm to dance tango. Musicians adapted milonga to the needs of the dancers and so tango-milonga was born, from which tango and milonga portena came."

The following is an extract from *Re: [TANGO-L] tango/milonga* [http://pythia.uoregon.edu/]:

"It is my understanding that milonga (as we know it) did NOT predate tango. Rather that the music of the 1910s & 1920s had a generalized tango/milonga feeling. As tangos slowed down in the 1930s with the `de Caro sensibility', milongas sped up."

The **Tango y Milonga** was and is a Traveling dance in Fast 2/4 Time, mostly using the Hold described under **Argentine Tango**. Rhythm Timing is *1 2, 1 2, 1 2*, etc. There are no pauses, such as there are in the **Argentine Tango**.

"Tango/Milonga are the potential of one moment; the ability to explore the `now,' the awareness!" -- Ive Simard

(See Argentine Tango, Milonga, Milonga-Candombera, and Candombe.)

Tanguero: (*tahn-GAY-rro* is Spanish for a *male tango dancer*.) **Tanguero** is an **Argentine Tango** Coupledance Term for this dancer and life style. **Tanguera** is Spanish for a Lady Tango dancer.

Ed Loomis [www.batango.com/loomis] describes the **Tanguero** as follows:

"TANGUERO (feminine; Tanguera) Refers to anyone who is deeply and seriously passionate about any part of tango, such as its history, music, lyrics, etc. In Argentina most tangueros are scholars, of lunfardo, music, orchestrations, Gardel, etc. One can be a tanguero without being a milonguero and a milonguero without being a tanguero (very few milongueros would be referred to as tangueros). And of course one can be an extremely good tango dancer without being either, such as stage dancers, who are quite distained by real milongueros and tangueros, unless they go the extra distance and become milongueros by going to the milongas, and/or tangueros as well. An Afficionado."

Similar to the **Milonguero**(1).

Taut: A General Coupledance Term for a condition of the dancer's Body and/or arms. An undesired, too-**Taut** condition might be for a **strained** Body, Stretched tight with Tense Muscle-Tone, not at all loose or slack.

But desireable **Taut** conditions would be as follows: Sufficient **Tautness** is a firmness between the upper and lower Torso, ensuring Body-Tone, and preventing Slumping. Another desireable **Tautness**, in the dancer's arms, would create unity between the arms and Body, i.e., a Firm-Frame, without which, true Unity-of-Movement between Partners could exist.

Inverse of **Collapse**, and **Slumped-Torso**.

Telemark-from-Left-Outside-to-Semi-Closed or **Open-Telemark-from-Left-Outside:**
A Leadable Coupledance Figure suitable for Argentine and International **Tangos**, for Slow- and
Medium-**Foxtrots**, for the Slow-**Waltz**, and for both **Quicksteps**.

Identical to **Telemark-to-Semi-Closed** except begins in Feathered-Left Position.

(For Footwork for Mirror-Image Opposite Figure, see Natural-Telemark-Facing-Offset-
to-Reverse-Semi-Closed.)

Telemark-to-Semi-Closed or **Open-Telemark(1)** (*op tele*): A Leadable Coupledance
Figure suitable for Argentine and International **Tangos**, for the Slow-**Waltz**, the Slow- and
Medium-**Foxtrots**, both **Quicksteps**, and for other dances. Rhythm Timing is *Slow Quick
Quick* for Foxtrot and Quickstep, sometimes *Slow Slow, Slow* for Quickstep, and *Slow Slow
Slow* for Waltz.

Begins in a Closed Position, one Measure, three Steps, total Couple-Rotation is 3/4- to
7/8-Turn Counter-Clockwise. Lady is Hub-Partner; Man is Rim-Partner.

Man dances *forward* with CBM *Swivel7/8CCW* with Right Side-Stretch *diagforward*
Left-Side-Lead.

Lady, Following, dances *BackTurn1/8CCW* with CBM *heelturn3/8CCW DiagForward*
Right-Side-Lead.

Similar to **Telemark-from-Left-Outside-to-Semi-Closed.** (For Footwork for Mirror-
Image Opposite Figure, see Natural-Telemark-to-Reverse-Semi-Closed.)

Telespin or **Full-Telespin:** A Leadable Coupledance Pattern suitable for the Slow-
Foxtrot, International Tango, both **Quicksteps** and Slow-**Waltz.** Timing for Foxtrot, Tango
and Quickstep is *Slow Quick Quick, And Quick Quick Slow*; Timing for Waltz is *Slow Slow
Slow, And Slow Slow Slow.*

Begins and ends in an International Closed Position, two Measures, 1 3/8- to 1 5/8-Turns
Counter-Clockwise total. After second Step, Man is Hub-Partner, and Lady is Rim-Partner. By
third Step, Man keeps Left Side Forward Toward Lady, or he may Open Lady for a Whip
sensation created by his Spinning. Lady's Head remains Closed.

Man dances *forward* with CBM *DiagForTurn1/4CCW Swivel3/8CCW* Point Left Toe
and Open Lady, *spinonball3/8CCW continuespin1/4to1/2CCW SideTurn1/8CCW forward.*

Lady, Following, dances *BackTurn1/8CCW* with CBM *Heelturn1/4CCW
ForTurn1/4CCW* in Semi-Closed, *forturn1/4CCW* in CBM *ForTurn1/8CCW* Right-Side-Lead
closeswivel1/2CCW DiagBackward.

(See Mini-Telespin, and Telespin-to-Semi-Closed.)

Telespin-to-Semi-Closed: A Leadable Coupledance Pattern, suitable for the Slow-Foxtrot, **International Tango**, both **Quicksteps** and Slow-**Waltz**. Pattern consists of **Two Telemarks with a Pivot in the middle.** Timing for Foxtrot, Tango and Quickstep is *Slow Quick Quick, And Quick Quick Slow*; Timing for Waltz is *Slow Slow Slow, And Slow Slow Slow.*

Begins in an International Closed Position, two Measures, 1 5/8- to 1 7/8-Turns Counter-Clockwise total. After second Step, Man is Hub-Partner, and Lady is Rim-Partner. By third Step, Man keeps Left Side Forward Toward Lady, or he may Open Lady for a Whip sensation created by his Spinning. Lady's Head remains Closed to the last two Steps.

Man dances *forward* with CBM *DiagForTurn1/4CCW Swivel3/8CCW* Point Left Toe and Open Lady, *spinonball3/8CCW continuespin1/4to1/2CCW SideTurn1/8CCWRecover forward* in Semi-Closed.

Lady, Following, dances *BackTurn1/8CCW* with CBM *Heelturn1/4CCW ForTurn1/4CCW* in Semi-Closed, *forturn1/4CCW* in CBM *ForTurn1/8CCW forturn1/8CCW Forward* in Semi-Closed.

(See Telespin and Mini-Telespin.)

Tension or **Tense:** An undesirable General Coupledance Action or condition; a Mental Strain or uneasy suspense, with **Tense** muscle effort, Singularly or between Partners.

Take note of this advisement:

"*TENSION in the neck, shoulders, arms, feet, knees, etc. which gives a stiff, hackneyed bearing, is usually caused by over-concentration on other co-ordinations. Some dancers never have this problem but when it exists then the best cure for it is... if your arms and shoulders are tense, take five basic variations of a dance you know very well and dance these repeatedly, but concentrate only on relaxing the arms and shoulders. The moment you start tensing up, stop and start again, relaxing the arms and shoulders.*

"*Another successful method is, before the start of any dance, first relax the arms and shoulders. Don't worry about how long, or for how many steps they'll stay relaxed, just start off in a state of relaxation. You will soon find that where your arms and shoulders were relaxed for 3 steps, they stay relaxed for 5 steps, until the tension disappears completely. If tension is your problem, then the only cure for this affectation is to make a conscious effort to relax - a tense dancer is an awkward dancer.*" -- [From www.geocities.com/danceinfosa.]

(See Taut, Strain, Agonized-Expression, and Raised-Shoulders.)

Tenuto: A General Latin Musical Term, meaning dancing that is **sustained** or **held.**

(See SlowHold, Slow-Motion, Rallentando, Calando, and Con-Dolore. Also see Slow, Saunter, and Lagged-Timing.)

The-Break or **Tango-Close-Finish:** A Leadable Coupledance Ending Figure that is common to all **Tangos**, and is especially suitable for the American and Continental Tangos. One 4/4 Measure long, Rhythm Timing is *Quick Quick Slow.* **The-Break** is danced entirely in Closed Position for a Tango.

The-Break is normally preceded by one other 4/4 Measure in Closed Position, where the Man takes *slow Slow* Steps Forward in a very Slight Counter-Clockwise Curving arc.

The most common **Basic Step** for the American and Continental Tangos, consists of these two Forward Steps, followed by **The-Break**. **The-Break** itself, consisting of a Forward half of a Box-Step, encompasses a **Tango-Draw** to a **Tango-Close**, (similar to a CloseTouch,) to an **Arch**, (with possibly a Brush-Tap.) (See Tango-Tap.)

Man dances *forward BrushSideward drawtoucharch.*

Lady, Following, dances *Backward brushsideward DrawTouchArch.*

Opposite of **Backward-Close-Finish.** (See Step-and-Drag, and Natural-Resolution.)

The-Foot-Tap: See Puntada-del-Pie.

The Mark: See LaMarka.

The Promenade: See Promenade-Ending.

The Trip: See AnkleTrip.

Through: See Step-Thru.

Throwaway (*thrwy*): A partially Leadable, Coupledance Ending Picture-Figure, suitable for **International Tango**, both **Quicksteps**, Slow-**Foxtrot**, Slow-**Waltz**, and for other dances. Timing varies.

Begins from the **Oversway Position**, from Promenade-Sway or from Side-Lunge-Left. Man assumes then holds their Patch by Turning his Right side into his Lady, Contrabody Counter-Clockwise, and looking at her face.

This causes Lady to **Throwaway** her Left leg. Their Knee-contact is lost as she Quarter-Turns Counter-Clockwise to Slide her Left Toe straight Backward, under her Body and past her Right Foot, to directly Behind her, but keeping her Left side and hips Up, toward her Man to hold their Patch. She Turns to look Well to her Left and Up.

(See Throwaway Position, and Oversway-Change-of-Sway.)

Throwaway-Oversway or **Oversway-Throwaway:** A partially Leadable, Coupledance Ending Picture-Figure, suitable for **International Tango**, both **Quicksteps**, Slow-**Foxtrot**, Slow-**Waltz**, and for other dances. Timing varies. Misnamed, since the Oversway Movement precedes the Throwaway Movement in this Figure.

From beginning in Promenade Position, the Couple first Performs the **Oversway** Movement, ending in the Oversway Position. The Couple next Performs the **Throwaway** Movement, ending in the Throwaway Position.

(See Oversway-Change-of-Sway, and Side-Lunge-Change-of-Sway.)

Throwaway Position (*thrwy*): A Coupledance Picture-Figure Position, suitable for **International Tango**, both **Quicksteps**, Slow-**Foxtrot**, Slow-**Waltz**, and for other dances.

Man's Left Supporting-Leg has a Flexed Knee, and his Right Free-Leg has a Pointed Toe and is Extended Sideward. He holds their Patch by keeping his Right side Turned into his Lady, Contrabody Counter-Clockwise, and he looks at her face.

Lady's Right Supporting-Leg has a Flexed Knee. As the **Throwaway**, her Left Free-Leg is Extended and Stretched straight, directly Behind her; her Left Toe is floored and is Pointed Slightly Outward. She is keeping her Left side and hips Up, Toward her Man to hold their Patch. She looks Well to her Left and Up.

(See Throwaway, Hinge-Line, Oversway Position, and Oversway-with-Extension.)

Tic: See Tick.

Tick or **Tic**: A possibly Leadable, General Coupledance Action, suitable for most all Closed Position dances, but mainly **International Tango**. A characteristic Tango look, an Accent.

A Tick is a brusque, suddenly Jerking Action in Opposition to the Direction of the Step subsequently danced, and to which the Lady responds. A Tick is initiated mainly by the Man Lurching his arms and Upper-Body Sideways, to his Right, for an *And* Count.

Caution: A Tick at times can send the wrong message to an unfamiliar Lady Partner.

Similar to **Head-Flick, Head-Fan**, and **Abrupt**. (See Salute, Staccato, Knee-Lead, Flourish, Gesture, and Head-Flick-Link.)

Tijera: (*te-HAY-rah*, Spanish for *scissor*.) A Coupledance Genre of Movements and Figures danced in the various **Argentine Tangos** and in the **Milonga**.

Ed Loomis [www.batango.com/loomis] describes the **Tijera** as follows:

"TIJERA Scissor: A movement, usually danced by the man, in which an extended leg is withdrawn and crossed in front of the supporting leg without weight so that it remains free for the next step or movement. May also refer to a figure in which the man steps forward in outside position (left or Right) caressing the outside of the lady's leg with his leg (as in 3 of basico)[Eight-Step-Basic-tango]*, then crosses behind himself which pushes the lady's leg to cross in front. May also refer to a jumping step from stage tango where the lady swings her legs up and over with the second leg going up as the first leg is coming down (frequently seen as an aerial entry to sentadas)."*

(See Sentada.)

Titubeo: (*te-too-bay-O*, Spanish for *vacillate*.) In some Argentine or Latin Coupledance, a **Titubeo** is a possibly Leadable, Spanish in-Action, within a Movement, Figure, or Pattern. A **Titubeo** is a momentary wait, Hold or Pause in Progression; a Checked Balance, temporarily Suspended in a Hovering in-Action. Weight is (probably purposely) Suspended upon one's Supporting-Foot for one or more Counts in a Measure.

Same as a **Hesitation**. Similar to **Vacillate**. [See **Pausa**. Also see Collect, Check, Suspension, Lull, Freeze-and-Melt, Pause-Step, and Balance(1).]

To-Dance-Inside: One of three Coupledance Basic Feet Positions for the **Argentine Tango**; Feet of both Partners are intermingled as described in Closed Position Argentine Tango. Leadable.

(See To-Dance-On-The-Side and To-Dance-Outside.)

To-Dance-On-The-Side: One of three Coupledance Basic Feet Positions for the **Argentine Tango**; the Lady is perpendicular to her Man's Facing-Direction, i.e., at right-angles to each other. Here, the Man's Feet are normally Standing Closed, and are literally on the side of his Partner's Feet, as when she dances Ochos. Leadable.

(See To-Dance-Inside, and To-Dance-Outside. Also see "L" Position.) (Not the same as On-The-Side.)

To-Dance-Outside: One of three Coupledance Basic Feet Positions for the **Argentine Tango**; the Feet of both Partners Face each other as described in **Facing-Offset Position**, i.e., Outside of Partner to one's **Right**. The Lady normally ends this with a FrontLock, Left over Right Foot. Leadable.

More explicit than **Pocket**. (See To-Dance-Inside, and To-Dance-On-The-Side. Also see similar Offset-Facing-Opposed Position, Feathered Position, and Right-Foot-Outside Position.)

Toe-Tap: Many Unleadable, General Coupledance Actions, Left or Right Foot.
Striking lighter than a Stamp but harder than a Pat, one's Free-Foot **Toe-Taps** the
Dancefloor, at various locations relative to one's Supporting Foot, **without Weight** thereby
applied:

(1) **Toe-Tap-at-Instep** is to **Toe-Tap** next to Instep, with no twisting of the Free-Knee.
(2) (See **Toe-In**, which is to **Toe-Tap** next to Instep, with Free Knee twisted Inward.)
(3) **Toe-Tap-In-Front** is to **Toe-Tap** ahead of one's Supporting Toe.
(4) **Toe-Tap-Crossed-In-Front** is to **Toe-Tap** Crossed loosely or tight.
(5) **Toe-Tap-Behind:** (See **Dot**, which is to **Toe-Tap** Trailing Toe Behind one's Heel.)
(6) **Toe-Tap-Crossed-Behind** is to **Toe-Tap** Trailing Toe Across and Behind Heel.
(7) **Toe-Tap-Sideways** is to **Toe-Tap** one's Free-Foot Sideward.

Toe-Tap is more explicit than **Tap**, and **ToeTouch**. (See Toe-Movements, Footwork,
and Foot-Placement. Also see Dot, LaCunita, Toe-Lead, Heels-Out, Toe-Out, Toes-Out, Toe-
Fan, Toe-Splits, and AnkleTrip.)

Toe-Twister: A General Coupledance slang Term used by dancers to try to describe a
dance Figure or Pattern too tricky for words. **Toe-Twister** is also a buzzword for a complicated,
tangling Footwork.

To-the-Side or **Al-Costado:** (*ahl kos-TAH-do*, Spanish for *to the side*.) A common
Term often used in **Tango** Practice.

Trabada: See Cruzada, and Trabada-Step.

Trabada-Step: (*trah-BAH-dah* is Spanish for *fastened*.) **Trabada** is an **Argentine
Tango** Genre and **Milonga** Coupledance Term for a partially Leadable *crossinfront* Movement
Executed by the Lady, as described in **Salida**.
Tango York [www.bakers64.freeserve.co.uk/] describes **Trabada** as follows:
*"Trabada Fastened, a lock step. The step that the woman takes when the man
steps outside his partner with his right foot and then straight forward left, together right. At this
point the woman crosses and this cross is referred to as a trabada."*
Ed Loomis [www.batango.com/loomis] describes **Count 4. of Eight-Step-Basic-Tango**
as follows:
*"4. The man closes his right foot to his left with weight and rotates his upper
body to face forward, leading the lady to cross her left foot in front of her right with weight
(cruzada) as she finishes moving back in front of the man. Many variations for the lady begin
from this position."*
Same as **LaCruz**. Similar to **Cruzada**. (See Ochos-Largos.)

Traditional: A General Term for the time-honored passing down of certain talents of a
Coupledance culture from generation to generation; taught especially visually, orally, and with
Traditional sound. Or, Coupledances so long continued in certain ways, that their mode of
Performance has almost the force of a law. Verbal clashes often occur between Traditionalists
and innovators.
(See Vintage-Dances, Purist, and Structured.)

Trap: An Unleadable Coupledance Movement or Figure, suitable for the **Argentine Tango.** One "Traps" Partner's Extended Foot, which prevents that Foot's Sideward Movement.

With Facing Footwork upon the Dancefloor, "Trap" refers to where his Lady "Traps" the Man's one Forward-protruding Foot by straddling, i.e., by placing each of her Feet against a side of that Foot. Or it may be the Man who "Traps" his Lady's Forward-Extended Foot.

Traspie: (*trahs-pe-AY*, Spanish for *trip*, *slip*, or *stumble*, or a *sudden slide*.) This word usually refers to several different **Syncopated** Movements or Figures, Executed while dancing the **Argentine Tango** or **Milonga.**

Some say that a **Traspie** can be deliberately Led upon any Step where the Man chooses. Ed Loomis [www.batango.com/loomis] describes the **Traspie** as follows, (although perhaps too specifically):

That the **Traspie** is a "*cross foot; triple step: a walking step with a syncopated cross. Using two beats of music the dancer does step-cross-step beginning with either foot and moving in any direction.*"

These **Traspie** Series are especially fun for dancing in Close-Embrace.

Similar to **Tumble-Turn**(1)&(2), and **Rabona.** (See Trip, Slip, and Stumble.)

[Mostly from www.tangocanberra.asn.au]

Traveling-Swivel: A Leadable 1 1/2-Measure, Coupledance Pattern, suitable for the **International Tango.** Rhythm with 2/4 Timing is *Quick Quick Quick Quick, Slow.*

Begins in Closed Position International Tango, Turns to Feathered then ends in Promenade Position. Couple-Rotation is a 7/8-Turn Counter-Clockwise total; four Steps then a Touch.

Man dances *forturn1/4CCW SideSwivel1/2CCW diagbackturn1/8CCW* leaving Right leg Forward Feathered *StepThru* with CBM, *touchdiagforward.*

Lady, Following, dances *BackTurn1/8CCW Heelturn1/2CCW ForwardFeathered mulekickstepthru* with CBM, *TouchDiagForward.*

Similar to Traveling-Swivel for Slow-Foxtrot.

Tres-Ochos (*trayss-O-CHOss*) or **Three-Eights:** Mainly suitable for Coupledancing the **Argentine Tango,** and possibly other Tangos and also PasoDobles.

A continuation of the **Doble-Ochos, Tres-Ochos** is three Measures long in 2/4 Cut-Time, and is only partially Leadable. For three times, the Lady dances her **Ochos**(1) throughout this Pattern with no change, while her Man joins in and dances Ochos with his Lady as described below. Total Couple-Rotation is a Three-Quarter-Turn Counter-Clockwise.

With Partners dancing in a very Loose-Closed condition, except at each Pickup, and with both Swiveling on Ball, the Man joins her as he feels his Lady begin to Turn at each **Ochos** beginning. Rhythm Timing is *And Slow And Quick And, And Slow And Quick And, And Slow And Quick And.* Each *Weight* is a Delayed-Weight-Shift.

Man, beginning with his Feet Closed, dances *Swivel1/4CCW* Shoulders-Parallel *backpoint weightback Close PickuptoFace, Swivel1/4CCW* Shoulders-Parallel *backpoint weightback Close PickuptoFace, Swivel1/4CCW* Shoulders-Parallel *backpoint weightback Close PickuptoFace.* Man eyes his Lady throughout the Pattern, or else he looks in the directions his Lady is about to Turn.

The Man Leads to keep his Lady always dancing her **Ochos** in front of him. The Lady adjusts her **Ochos** in order to be Facing her Man at each **Ocho** Ending.

[See Ochos(2), Ocho-Abierto, Ochos-Largos, and Ochos-para-Atras. Also see Salida-Modified.]

Trip: See AnkleTrip.

Tripping: See AnkleTrip.

Turning-Mutual-Boleos: (*bo-LAY-o*, Spanish for *bowling-green.*) One of the different Cadena Patterns Coupledanced in the Argentine Tango of the Rotary-Tango and Show-Tango(1) Styles. Partially Leadable and Performed in the Open-Embrace-Tango Style. As with all other Cadenas, this Pattern Travels, Curling Counter-Clockwise, while continuously Couple-Rotating Counter-Clockwise. But with this Cadena, each Partner alternately Performs a Boleo:

1. To-Dance-Inside, the Man Steps *forward* Left, Lady Follows.
2. Couple-Rotating with the Man the Rim-Partner, the Man Steps a wide *Sideward*, Spiraling the Lady upon her Right Foot as she Performs her Boleo with her Left leg.
3. The Man Spirals a Half-Turn upon his Left Foot and Steps *Forward* into To-Dance-Outside (Banjo) Position.
4. Becoming the Hub-Partner, the Man Steps *backward* and Leads his Lady around To-Dance-Inside as he Swivels upon his Left Foot and Performs his Boleo with his Right leg.
5. All is repeated except roles are reversed; i.e., the Lady Steps *forward* Left, Man Follows, etc. [Most from www.dancetutor.com]

Uneven-Rhythm: A musical and Coupledance General Term for the uneven Tempo of a melody, as compared to its Underlying-Beat. At times, one may successfully Coupledance to the melody's Uneven-Rhythm, rather than normally dancing to the Underlying-Beat of the song, if the Couple is Skilled and knows the melody Well.
(See Rhythm, Body-Rhythm, Rhythm-Pattern, Sensation-of-Rhythm, Timing, Lagged-Timing, Beat, Count, and Cadence.)

Unstructured: A General Coupledance Term for no Fixed-Pattern, i.e., **not being formed into an organized structure**, such as a Choreographed dance Routine. Instead, extemporaneously dancing Free-Form with Free-Expression.
(See Winging-It, Improvise, and Interpretative-Dancing.)

Unwind or Uncross or Half-Twist-Turn: Two Unleadable, General, one-Measure, Singular or Coupledance Figures, either Left or Right, Mirror-Image Opposite. Suitable for many different dances. Danced Apart by either or both Partners. Can be danced to any *Slow Slow Slow* or *Slow Slow* or *Slow Quick Quick* or *Quick Quick Slow* Rhythm. Rhythm Timing is usually *Slow slow.*
Beginning with legs either Crossed or Hooked, in CBMP and with Weight on both Feet, one's Body is Rotated a Half-Turn maximum, either Clockwise or Counter-Clockwise in one Spot, to a Position with legs Uncrossed.
Unwind is a more General version of Cross-Unwind, Cross-Wind, Hook-Unwind, and Hook-Wind, but has less Rotation. Similar to the General Corkscrew Figure, which Rotates a Half-Turn minimum to a Full-Turn maximum. Similar to Hook-Overspin-Left, Hook-Overspin-Right, Cross-Overspin-Left, Cross-Overspin-Right, Toe-Spin-Clockwise, and Toe-Spin-Counter-Clockwise, which Rotate a Full-Turn minimum. Generally similar to the About-Face! military command. (See Military-Team, Cross, Hook, FrontLock, and LockBehind. Also see Unfold.)

Valentino Tango: An American Tango Style of Coupledance, ideally suited for beginners. The dreamy **Valentino Tango** is danced to a Slower Tempo, 30 MPM or less, in Syncopated 2/4 Cut-Time.

The **Valentino Tango** is danced with Rocks, Swivels, and Fan Movements. Its Basic-Step is common with that for the American Tango, and it is Patterned upon the Man taking the Five-Step-Basic-Tango, (three Forward Walking Steps, a Right Sideward-Step, a Tango-Draw then a Tango-Close.) Basic-Step Rhythm Timing is *slow Slow, slow Quick Hold, slow Hold.* The Tango-Close finish without Weight can have several Foot Stylings, (see Brush-Tap.) This subject Basic-Step is danced Starting in Closed, Banjo, or in Promenade Positions; the Lady is Picked-Up from being in these last two Positions.

A simple version of the **American Tango**. [See Basic-Step(4), and Contest Tango.]

Vals: A Leadable, Argentine Tango style **Waltz** in 3/4 Time, with **Tango** style music, mostly using the Hold described under **Argentine Tango**. **Vals** is popular and currently Coupledanced in Argentina.

Same as **Argentine-Waltz**. (See Milonga, and Tango.)

Vals-Criolo: See Argentine-Waltz, and Vals-Crillo.

Vals-Criollo or **Creole-Waltz** or **Vals-Peruano** or **Peruvian-Waltz:** A Coupledance and type of music in 3/4 Time from coastal Peru, possibly dating from as early as the late 1700s. This **Vals-Criollo** is known outside of Peru as the **Vals-Peruano**.

The **Vals-Criollo** was derived from but feels quite different from the Viennese-Waltz, in that its lush character is absent. The music has a dry, restrained sound. Still, the **Vals-Criollo** carries themes of love.

(See Argentine-Waltz for further data.)

Vals-Cruzado: See Argentine-Waltz.

Vals-Peruano: See Vals-Criollo.

Vals-Porteno: An **Argentine-Waltz** of the 1800s, danced by the inhabitants of the port of Buenos Aires.

(See Argentine-Waltz for further data.)

Ven-y-Va: (*come and go* in Spanish) See Coming-and-Going, and To-and-Fro.

Vibes: Short for "*vibration*", a General Coupledance slang Term for an emotional sense felt between two dancers, good or bad. **Vibes** can be either pleasant or otherwise.

Viborita: (*vee-bo-REE-tah*, Spanish for *viper* or *the little snake*.) A Coupledance Figure of the **Lady's Feet Displacements** by the Man, danced in the various **Argentine Tangos** and in the **Milonga**.

Ed Loomis [www.batango.com/loomis] describes the **Viborita** as follows:

"*VIBORITA Viper; the little snake: A figure in which the man places his right leg between his partners legs and takes a sacada to first her left and then her right legs in succession using a back and forth slithering motion of the right leg and foot.*"

(See Sacada, Desplazamiento, LaLlevada, and Arrastre.)

Viennese-Turn (*vien trn*) or **Basic-Left-Turn** or **He-Locks-Then-She-Locks** or **Viennese-Reverse-Turn** or **Reverse-Turn** or **Viennese-Left-Turn** or **Left-Cross-Turn** or **Basic-Reverse-Turn**: A Leadable, two- or one-Measure Coupledance Pattern, suitable for Hesitation, Slow- and Medium-, and both Viennese **Waltzes**; both **Foxtrots**, both **Quicksteps**, and for International **Tango**, among other dances.

Timing varies; Timing for Viennese and the other Waltzes is *1 2 3, 4 5 6*; or, *Slow Slow Slow, Slow Slow Slow*; for the Foxtrots and Quicksteps is *Slow Quick Quick, Slow Quick Quick*; for International Tango (one-Measure) is *Quick Quick And Quick Quick And*.

Viennese-Turn Footwork is Performed the same way in any dance. **Lock** when Turning **Counter-Clockwise** only; no **Viennese-Locks** are made during Clockwise Turns. Danced in a Closed Position. Total Couple-Rotation is a Full-Turn Counter-Clockwise in six Steps, with **He-Locks-Then-She-Locks**.

Man dances *forturn1/4CCW DiagBackSwivel1/4CCW* Right Side-Stretch *risecrossinfrontturn1/8CCW* Right Side-Stretch, *BackTurn1/4CCW diagforturn1/8CCW* Left Side-Stretch *RiseClose* Left Side-Stretch.

Lady, Following with Head-Closed, dances *BackTurn1/4CCW diagforturn1/8CCW* Left Side-Stretch *RiseClose* Left Side-Stretch, *forturn1/4CCW DiagBackSwivel1/4CCW* Right Side-Stretch *risecrossinfrontturn1/8CCW* Right Side-Stretch.

(See Samba-Viennese-Turn, Left-Face-Waltz-Turn, Viennese-Lock, Progressive-Rotation, Cross-Turn, Tight-Turn, and Canter-Rocks-Left.)

Notes: 1) Partners dance in Closed-Position International Standard throughout for **International Viennese Waltz**, while they dance in Closed-Position Informal for **American Viennese Waltz**.

2) May be preceded by a **Forward-Change-Natural-to-Reverse** or a **Reverse-Fleckerl**.

3) For International Viennese, repeat either eight or sixteen Measures of **Viennese-Turning**, while Traveling Line-of-Dance around the Dancefloor.

4) May be followed by a **Forward-Change-Reverse-to-Natural** or a **Reverse-Fleckerl**.

5) This **Viennese-Left-Turn** is the most used Viennese Waltz Pattern in the United States, while the **Natural-Right-Turn** is the most used Viennese Waltz Pattern in Europe.

Villa-Urguiza-Tango: See Tango-de-Salon.

Vine or **Grapevine**: A Leadable, General Coupledance Sideward Movement, Figure, or Pattern. A Sequence of Steps, consisting of *Side-Step, Cross, Side-Step, Cross*, etc., alternating the Crossing Steps to Cross Behind then In-Front or visa-versa. This Sequence can Start with any Step and continue for any number of Crosses.

(See Open-Vine, Side-Behind-Side-Front, Weave, Chekessia, Giro, Molinete, Enrosque, and Twisty-Vine.)

Vis-a-Vis: A General Coupledance Term for one of two dancers that Face each other from Opposite sides, Face-to-Face. Also means "compared with", "in relation to", and "opposite".

(See Eye-Contact.)

Voleo: See Boleo.

Vuelta: (*voo'ELL-tah*, Spanish for *turn, turn around*, or *revolve*.) See Turn, Volta, and Media-Vuelta.

Walking-Tango: See Linear-Tango.

WallFlower or **Planchadora:** General Coupledance slang Terms, referring to a single Lady who is never asked by a Man to Coupledance. She may be shy. She is without a Partner and may feel she is "Just a wall decoration". She may hopefully sit to the side or stand all evening along the Dancehall wall.

The following is from the *Encyclopedia of Word and Phrase Origins* by *Robert Hendrickson*:

"..... *But the romantic story is nicer. This holds that such girls are named after the common wallflower of Europe (Cheiranthus Cheiri), a sweet-scented, yellow spring flower that grows wild on walls and cliffs. Indeed, the English poet Robert Herrick (1591-1674) claimed that the flower itself is named after such a girl, his delightful derivation telling of a fair damsel who was long kept from her lover and finally tried to escape to him:*

" `Up she got upon a wall
'Tempting down to slide withal;
But the silken twist untied,
So she fell, and, bruised, she died.
Love in pity of the deed,
And her loving luckless speed
Turned her to this plant we call
Now the `Flower of the wall.'"

Ed Loomis [www.batango.com/loomis] describes the **Planchadoras** as follows: (Argentine Ladies and the Argentine Tango.)

"*The women who sit all night at the milongas without being asked to dance. The main reason for that, is because they don't know how to dance well enough. Yes, it may seem cruel but one of the many tango lyrics actually says something like, `let them learn as a consequence of sitting all night.*"

(See Delicado, Mignon, and Dolce.)

Weight-Connection: A Leadable, General Coupledance Movement. **Weight-Connection** is that condition resulting from Partners' Body Weights either **Leaning-Into-EachOther** or **Leaning-Away-from-EachOther**.

Similar to **Giving-Weight**, and **Support**. (See Push, Pull, and Change-of-Weight. Also see Counter-Balance, Counter-Movement, Counter-Sway, Hanging-On, Clinging-Vine, Stable, and Steady.)

Whisk (*wsk*): A Leadable one-Measure, three-Step, Checked-Coupledance Figure, suitable for the International, American, and Argentine **Tangos**. Rhythm with 2/4 Timing is *Quick Quick Slow*, with both Partners Crossing Behind and Flat, with no Rises.

Begins in Feathered or in Closed Position International Tango. First Step Moves to or is in Closed Position, then ends in Promenade Position except with Inside-Feet Touching-Thru. Only Lady is Opened, while the Man may Turn Slightly into Lady.

Man dances *forcheck Sideflat* in Closed *crossbehind* take Weight Flat.

Lady, Following, dances *BackCheck* Head-Opens *sideturn1/8CWflat CrossBehind* take Weight Flat.

See **Flat-Whisk Position**. (Also see Progressive-Link. Also see Back-Whisk, Fallaway-Whisk, Ecart, and Whisk Position.)

Winging-It: A General Coupledancing Term, slang for no routine or cues, where the Lady follows the Man's extemperaneous Lead.

(See Improvise, Free-Expression, Free-Style, Unstructured, Ad-Libitum, Freewheeling.)

<u>**With-Abandon**</u>: A General Coupledance and Classical-Dance Term meaning to dance **without restraint**; yielding in utter surrender to one's feelings, emotions, natural impulses. Or, the appearance in a dancer's dancing of careless or impulsive, unrestained spontaneity.

   "... *Approach love with reckless abandon. Share your knowledge, it's a way to achieve immortality. Be gentle with the earth. Dance like nobody's watching.*" -- Dalai Lama

   Similar to **Expand**. (See Apassionado. Also see CareFree-Way, Emote, Facials, Verve, Flashy, Flash-and-Pzazz, Flaunting-It, Comedy, Agitato, Energico, Animado, Con-Anima, and Con-Expressione.)

<u>**X-Line Position**</u>: A partially Leadable Coupledance Picture-Figure, suitable for ending **International Tango**, **Quickstep** and **Viennese**, Slow-**Waltz** and Slow-**Foxtrot**, among other dances. With Lady on Man's Right, both Turning Head and Body Away from Partner to Side-by-Side, and both Pointing Free-Leg Away from Partner. Optionally, Clasped-Hands may be released and Pointed Up and Away, to form an `X'.

   (See Spread-Eagle.)

<u>**Yumba**</u>: (*YOOM-bah*, Spanish.) A General Argentine word for the Music's *tempo accent.* "*A phonetic expression that describes the powerful, dramatic, and driving musical accent of a moderate or even slow tempo which is characteristic of the music of Osvaldo Pugliese.*"

   (See Ritmo, and Compas.) [Mostly from *Tango Terminology*, *www.tangoafficionado.com.*]

<u>**Zapatazo**</u>: (*thah-pah-TAH-so*, Spanish for *shoe taps*.) A Flourishing Movement or Figure; a **Dibujo Adorno**; an Embellishment used in the **Argentine Tango** and **Milonga** Coupledances.

   Ed Loomis [www.batango.com/loomis] describes **Zapatazo** as follows:
      "*A dancer taps their own shoes together.*"

   Same as **Flicker**(1), and **Heel-Splits**. (See Lapiz, ShoeShine, Puntada-del-Pie, Caricias, Lustrada, Golpecitos, Levantada, Chiche, Fanfarron, and Enganche; all Performed during a Parada.) (Also see Flourish, and Gesture.)

<u>**Zarandeo**</u>: (*thah-RAHN-day-o*, Spanish for *to sift* or *to shake*.) A Coupledance Genre of Movements or Figures, Executed mostly by the Man, in the various **Argentine Tango**s and in the **Milonga**.

   Ed Loomis [www.batango.com/loomis] describes **Zarandeo** as follows:
      "*ZARANDEO A vigorous shake to and fro; a swing; a push to and fro; to strut about; in Tango it is the swinging back and forth, pivoting in place on one foot, marked to the lady in time with the music.*"

   The **Zarandeo** is a Man's Dibujo (doodling) that he often does during a Parada (Stop). While Embracing, his **Zarandeo** in this case is Slightly **Twisting his Upper-Body** Left and Right, once or several times, Fast or Slowly, Energetically or Gently. If clear, his Lady might improvise here by attractively Raising her Free-Lower-Leg at the Knee and Pointing her Toe Back. Keeping her Knees Together, the Man's **Zarandeo**, Holding her, Sweeps her Free-Foot Side-to-Side.

   [See Shake(1), Amplitude, To-and-Fro, Shift-Weight, Sube-y-Baja, Ven-e-Va, Back-and-Forth, Rock-Back-and-Forth, Sway-Back-and-Forth, Sway-to-and-Fro, Rock-with Feet-Crossed, Sway-with Feet-Crossed, Coming-and Going, Push(2), Strut, Pivot(2), and Mark-Time.]

7.   GLOSSARY for TANGO

"a"   A character designating 1/4 of a music Beat in 4/4 time, normally the last 1/4 of the beat in which a Step or Action is completed.

About to Go On   A common Dancer's Term, meaning one is about to Perform to an audience.

Acceleration   An increase (or decrease) in the speed of the dance, i.e., a bodily velocity rate of change with regards to the magnitude of direction.

Accent   An emphasis placed on one or more Beats of music such that the beat(s) stand out more than others. The beat(s) may stand out by being louder (dynamic), higher in pitch (tonic), or held for a longer time than other beats (agonic).

Accent of Execution   The sudden application of increased Energy within the pattern of Movement forms an **Accent-of-Execution**. For instance, in the Sequence *Step Jump Step*, the *Jump* forms an **Accent-of-Execution**.

Accordion   Successive Together and Aparts.

Across   (*acrs* or *XLOD*) Either or both dancers Move **Across** their Direction-of-Dance, or **Across** their own Body. Or, one's Foot or leg **Crosses** the path of one's other. See Cross, Lock, and Cut.

Action   A Motion without a Step or Weight Change. See Movement.

Activate   An Action to set in Motion.

Active   Dancing rather Quickly and/or lively, with agile and/or nimble Movement. Or, briskly abounding in energetic Action. Not lazy, passive nor quiescent.

Adjust   To change from one Position to another. Also see Blend/Blending.

Ad-Lib   To dance at will, to suit one's own idea of Timing and the like, i.e., to Improvise as one wishes without regard to any set Pattern or Movements.

Advanced   Generally used as a qualifying term defining a specific form of a Figure or the level of the dance.

Aerial   An unleadable Action in which the foot is well off the Dancefloor by Raising one's knee.

Aerial Ronde   A form of Ronde, either rearward or forward, in which the moving foot is elevated Well off the floor, describing a high arc between the beginning and the end of the Ronde. Supporting knee is well bent until Ronde completion.

Aerials   A Cabaret-style series of Exhibition Figures, Patterns, or Routine-Sections, where the Lady-Partner is Thrown or Lifted from the Dancefloor. Opposite of Ground-Bound.

Aerobic   Flying in the air, lively and athletic with vigorous agility.

Aggressive Following   A derogatory dance term, referring to the lady dancing her own dance, thereby Leading her man instead of Following his Body-Movement.

Aida Line   To achieve the Aida Position without taking all the normal Steps of the Aida Figure.

Aida Position   An open "V" Position of the Outward-facing bodies with Inside Hands joined and the Inside Feet free and extended Forward and slightly side toward the point of the "V".

Alight   To **lightly** descend and settle Down on one or both Feet, after a Leap or flight En-L'Air. Similar to the harsher **Land**, and to the Softer **Touchdown**.

Alignment   Most often, Alignment refers to the Position of the feet (not the body) in relation to audience orientation at the end of a Step. Also, Alignment is partners' relative bodily positioning, especially shoulder Alignment; or, the positioning of one's body parts in relation to one's other parts.

Amount of Turn   The amount of rotation of one's feet occurring in one Step, or that occurring between two consecutive Steps, and often specified in total. Usually measured in fractions of a Turn. Body Turn is generally indicated only when different from that of one's feet. See Foot Rotation, Body Turns Less, and Body Completes Turn.

"&"   A character designating 1/2 Beat, normally taken as the last 1/2 of a beat, in which a Step or Action is completed; read as "and" (rather than "ampersand"). For example, 4/4 Swing Timing might be 123&4 1&2, (or Slow Slow Quick & Slow, Quick & Slow,) meaning that Steps 3 and 6 get 1 1/2 beats while 4 and 7 get a 1/2 beat. Steps 1, 2, 5, and 8 get 2 full beats each.

And Step   Inferred in many terms and cues, such as the cue, "Cross-Behind," whose full meaning would be, "Cross-Behind-**And-Step**." Weight is transferred, otherwise the foot Crossing-Behind would remain in the air.

Anticipation   Generally a derogatory Coupledance Term, in reference to premature Action by the Lady anticipating her Man's Lead prior to his Lead.

Apart   To separate from partner, with or without releasing a hand hold. See Open Work and Break.

ApartTouch   With a Change-of-Weight, one Steps to separate the feet Apart; or else one Steps Apart from Partner, Accordioning, then Touches the Dancefloor and Holds, with Free-Foot usually Touching next to Supporting-Foot.

Arabesque   A basic pose with one leg straight out to the back and one arm usually stretched out to the front. The Toe of the back leg may contact the floor, however more commonly the toe will be well free of the floor.

Arch Turn   A Turn to the right or to the left, individually or together, through an Arch formed by the joined arms.

Arm Link   Arm-in-arm, one's elbow is linked in the crook of the partner's arm.

Arm Raise   Lady's styling for Raising her free left hand in four forward Steps: 1) Hand palm-out against buttocks; 2) Index knuckle touches left armpit; 3) Fingers turned upward with back of wrist touching left ear; 4) Shoots straight arm up taut, palm outward, arm against ear.

ArmWork   The particular positioning, working, and displaying of arms, shoulders, and hands while dancing, reflecting the character of the dance or style of dancing.

Articulation   Meaning Clarity of Execution; coherent and well presented with exactness, and distinctly jointed together with space between Movements. Same as Clean.

Artist   One who excels in Performance of the dance; a craftsman whose skilled work exhibits Artistic qualities.

Attuned   A term describing the lady's Action of quality Following. She must coordinate and remain Attuned in harmony with her man, from even before their very first Step. Conversely, the man must remain Attuned to his lady as he Leads her, as feedback.

Away   Movement Apart from each other, or Stepping Free Foot Away from Supporting Foot. Opposite of Together.

Axial Movement   Movement upon a stationary base; or, one's body parts regularly Moved about a centerline; or, one's body parts Moving on or along an imaginary Axis. See Pencil-Turns, Toe-Spin, PittyPatter-Turns, and Pinwheel.

Axis   The imaginary line from the Ball or heel of the Supporting Foot through the center of the body around which the body Spins, Spirals and Turns. It is also an imaginary line between a couple about which they rotate. See Couple Rotation.

Back   The Alignment direction Opposite that which the body is Facing. Also, a Backing Away in the opposite direction one is facing.

Back Feather Position   In Banjo Position except bodies are Patched and torqued CBMP closed with partner. Right hips overlap, with man's weight back on left foot and lady's weight forward on right foot. Lady's counterpart of Feather Position.

Back Lead   An Action in which the lady partially Leads the man.

Back of Hand Lead   Man Leads lady by pressing against her back to start her circling him.

BackSwivel   Stepping backward, then Swiveling on that same foot, Outward, Away from one's other Foot.

Back To Back   A Movement or Position such that the couple is facing Away from each other, normally clasping Opposite hands. The position may be only partially Back To Back.

BackTouch   Stepping Backward with no Weight and Touching that same foot where indicated.

BackTurn   Stepping Backward then Turning on same foot.

Backward   Movement in the direction Opposite to that one is Facing.

BackwardCheck   Stepping Backward to or past the Supporting-Foot with a Rise, then Braking-Action is taken in that Line-of-Motion in preparation to take a different Line-of-Motion. Check is taken on Ball-of-Foot, not Flat-Footed.

BackwardClose   Stepping Backward toward Supporting-Foot and Closing with a Change-of-Weight.

BackwardHold   Stepping Backward to or past the Supporting-Foot, applying Weight then maintaining Position, usually for one Beat.

BackwardTouch   Stepping Backward, taking Weight, then Touching Closed with Opposite Foot.

Balance   The correct distribution of body Weight between the feet or over the Supporting Foot when dancing. Balance is determined primarily by placement of the Center Point of Balance in relationship to the feet.

Ball   Refers to the placement of the foot or Change of Weight, e.g., to the Ball of the foot only. The Ball of foot is that part of the foot between the arch and the Toes.

Ball Change   Two Changes of Weight, the first upon the Ball of one foot and the second onto the other foot.

Ball Flat   The placement of the Weight, first onto the Ball of the Free Foot and then allowed to lower so Weight is upon the whole foot.

Ball Heel   A Step Backward, Toe first then Ball then flat with floor.

Ball of Foot   The Forward, underside, rounded part of one's Foot, that includes the Inner-Ball and the Outer-Ball, between Toes and Arch; while `Toe' is the adjacent bottom-side of the Toes.

Ball Step   A Step Forward, toe-first followed by lowering one's heel.

Ball Tap   Free Foot Taps floor with Ball.

BallTouch   The Free-Foot Ball is Touched to the Dancefloor in a given direction without Weight applied. More explicit than Touch. Less explicit than Ball Tap.

Ball Turn   One Swivels In Place, perhaps to remain Facing as Partner Circles.

Band Step   Forward or In Place Stepping at the rate of about 160 steps per minute.

Banjo Position   A Closed Position except offset Outside Partner; partner's Facing feet are to one's right; shoulders are parallel with no CBMP or Feathering, and without hip touching hip. Opposite of Sidecar Position. Similar to Contra Banjo and Feather Positions.

Bar   One measure of music. Refers to the vertical lines on each end of a measure of sheet music.

Base   The body's lower half, including hips, legs and feet. Also see Torso, Top Line, Back Line and Frame.

Basic   The fundamental or primary dance Figure, Step, stance or term.

Basic Figure   A Figure that is considered to form the basis or a part of the foundation of a particular dance.

Basic Step   The Basic, fundamental Move(s), Step(s), Figure(s), or Pattern(s); the foundation for many or even all other Moves, Steps, Figures or Patterns of a certain dance, identifiable to its particular Rhythm.

Basketball Turn   Both fore and aft feet Switch a half turn to the Opposite direction.

Beat   The underlying single pulse of the music that continues with equal duration and force, within which the Rhythms are produced.

Behind   Used to describe the relationship of one person to the other, such as Crossing or standing Behind the partner. Also used to describe foot Movement or Position such as Cross left Behind right (XLIB).

BehindCrossCheck   A Step directly Behind one's Supporting-Foot or even beyond, and then Braking-Action is taken in that Line-of-Motion, with a Change-of-Weight, in preparation to take a different Line-of-Motion. Opposite of ForCrossCheck. Similar to DiagBackCheck.

Biomechanics   The study of mechanical forces, i.e. Drag, Torque and Inertia, at work in the bodily Movements. See Body-Rotation.

Blend/Blending   A transition or adjustment, or combining of Movements, from one position to another in a smooth and natural manner.

Body Completes Turn   With Foot Rotation having preceded Body Turn, then upon beginning the next Step, one's Body Completes Turn. See Body Turns Less.

Body Flight   The smooth, uninterrupted and unrestrained, and natural release of body weight from a swinging Action, that carries one's body into its next Step or Movement. Also used to describe the rate of speed or intensity with which the body is driven to move.

Body Lead   The area between partner's bodies in contact, Body-Contact is a very successful means of Leading for many Movements. The Man's entire torso Leads his lady in most Coupledances.

Body Mechanics   The technical aspects needed to achieve the desired or proper execution of bodily Actions, Movements, Figures and Patterns. See Mechanics Memory and Muscle Memory.

Body Ripple   A Movement normally taking more than one Count. Ripples up from bottom to top. See Body Wave.

Body Tone   Each Upper Body requires a precise amount of Toning for Lead and Follow relationship of partners. Also, their overall muscles need moderate Tension for great dancing.

Body Turn   The Amount of Turn of one's Twisted Torso or body extremity, when different from one's Foot Rotation amount. See Body Turns Less and Body Completes Turn.

Body Turns Less   Foot Rotation normally precedes Body Turn. Upon beginning one's next Step, Body Turns Less is always followed by Body Completes Turn.

Body Wave   A Movement normally taking more than one Count. Waves down from top to bottom. See Body Ripple.

Body Weight   Weight of the complete Body in Neutral Position in relation to one's Feet, that is often affected by repositioning of one's various Body parts. See Center, and Center-of-Balance.

Braced Arm   Stiffened Tension applied to a bent arm.

Break   To separate by release of Position or hand hold. To Step Apart from partner and release at least one hand hold. Also, the Downbeat upon which the couple initially Steps.

Break Apart   To Change from a Closed Position to a more Open Position. Or, to release a Position.

Break Away   From some Open Position, partners Step further Apart in Opposition.

Brush   To Follow Through the inside edge of the Free Foot against the inside edge of the Supporting Foot, in one or more motions between Changes of Weight. When the moving foot is being taken from one open position to another open position, the word *Brush* indicates that this moving foot must first Close up to the Supporting Foot without a Change of Weight. A Brush is normally followed by a Side Step change in direction.

Brush Flare   Moving foot Forward-swipes the floor, lightly Brushing along and past the Inside Edge of the Supporting-Foot. One's free Leg then raises and Flares by Swinging with a whip-like Movement in a small arc until lowering and Locking Behind the Supporting-Foot, taking weight.

Butterfly Banjo Position   In Banjo Position but with hands as in Butterfly Position.

Butterfly Position   Facing partners clasp and spread all Opposite hands at shoulder level or chest level; man normally clasps with thumbs up.

Butterfly Sidecar Position   In Sidecar Position but with hands as in Butterfly Position.

Canter   A *Step Draw Close Step* in one Measure; two Steps danced possibly in 2/4 Time, normally in a Closed Position, Forward, Backward, Sideward, Crossward or Diagonally.

Caress   With a Crossed Hands Hold or a Double Crossing Hands, man raises all arms then slips HER head between them, as a Caress. Similar to Wolf Glide.

Catch   Man's means of Checking lady's motion Apart to initiate her next Movement.

CBM   Contra Body Movement - used in commencing Turns and to create a Line. The good looking Action of turning the Opposite shoulder in the direction of one's moving leg, i.e., torquing one's Upper Body to Face one direction while actual Movement is in a direction angled to that Faced.

CBMP   Contra Body Movement Position - the cross-shoulder body Position when either foot is placed across the front or back of one's body, onto or across the line of one's other foot without the body Turning.

CCW   See Counter Clockwise.
Center   Refers to the neutral Position for one's body, or to the Center point between partners.

Center of Balance   Balancing of one's Body Center from which Movement projects.

Center of Hall   COH - A Direction to Face or a Direction of Movement in relation to the Center of the Hall.

Center Person   See Hub Partner.

Center Point of Balance   Normally, in Closed Position for Standard Dances, the area behind the rib cage for man and the area behind the navel for the lady.

Chair Position   From Semi-Closed Position, partners have danced a Forward Thru Lunge, Stepped with Inside Feet, with strong lowering and Checking Action. All feet are in Third Position Extended. Lady has placed her left knee cap barely inside of her Man's bent right knee, in preparation for his Knee Lead if a Slip is to follow. Both are looking Inside and Behind. See Forward Poised Chair Position.

Challenge Line   Partners have Stepped to the man's left, on Balls of their Lead feet, into a tight Semi-Closed Position with a slight right face Turn through their bodies. Their Supporting knees have Softened and their Lead sides are stretched upward toward joined and raised Lead hands. In a high upright Poise, both look over their joined hands in a High Line Position. Their Free legs are behind, straight.

Change   The shifting of one's weight, or the altering of Position or Direction of Dance.

Change Feet   Changing the Position of one's feet, or feet Change Places during the Movement or Figure. Similar to Transition.

Change Hands   Partners Change from one hand Position to another.

Change of Direction   A Turn to another heading.

Change of Hold   A couple's Transition from one dance Position to another.

Change of Location   A Change in the place where one's Body is located, or the act of occupying a different space.

Change of Position   A Blending from one to a different Position.

Change of Weight   The transfer of body Weight from one foot to the other, either completely or partially.

Change Places   Lady's Underarm Turn, right-to-left or left-to-right, with a Change Sides.

Change Point   Changing Touching foot from one to the other. One's Free Foot is Closed to the Supporting Foot and as a part of the same motion, the new Free Foot is Pointed to the side and Touching the floor, all in one quick Movement.

Change Sides   Partners switch sides with each other in relation to their Direction of Dance.

Change Step   A multi-directional Movement or Figure consisting of three or more Steps, where one's feet Close on the third or last Step with a Change of Weight. Used to Change between left and right Turning Figures. See Closed Finish.

Chase   A series of dance Steps where one partner pursues the other. Also, the name of a Figure in International Tango.

Chasse Turn   A Turn normally consisting of 3 Steps, where the feet are Closed upon the second Step.

Check/Checking   The Action of stopping one Line of Motion in preparation to take a different Line of Motion.

Choreograph   To create or arrange a dance or its parts, by defining Figures, Timing, etc., necessary to fit a given music.

Choreographer   One who arranges dance Routines.

Choreography   The art of the planning and arrangment of Steps, Figures and Patterns into a dance Routine; matching Phrasing with the musical arrangement.

Chug   Back on heels with feet Together and all hands clasped for leverage. All knees abruptly straighten, pulling against each other.

Circle   Forward Movement in a circular pattern.

Clap Hands   Can be used to mark Time with the music in place of Steps; also used in Syncopation.

Classical Walk   The Slow and dignified Walk from Ballet. The Pointed toe stretches Forward to reach the floor first, then one's heel is lowered so that the foot turns slightly outward. As the heel Touches, one's weight is transferred Forward, then the rearward knee bends and with a small Develope, one's rearward foot Steps Forward to perform the next Step on alternate foot.

Clatter   Fast Tapping of the floor motion by heel(s) and/or toe(s).

Clean   To dance with one's Steps, body and manner clearly and sharply defined. Opposite of sloppy.

Clinic   An in-depth instructional Workshop or Teach on the Styling and Technique of a Rhythm and/or Figures, Positions, etc., in that Rhythm.

Clockwise   CW - Movement in a Right Face Turning direction, the same as the normal movement of the hands of a clock, (clock on floor, not ceiling.)

Close   A Movement in which one foot is brought to the other and takes the Weight. Or partners' Movement Together.

Closed Finish   When the last Step of a Movement or Figure Closes to the Supporting Foot and ends in a Closed Position.

Closed Position   Basically, partners Face with Lead Hands joined and there is some type of Closed contact by their Trailing Hands. Any of several Holds are in use in Closed Position, depending upon the Styling and the Rhythm being danced.

Closed Position Informal   Partners Face close and fairly straight legged, slightly offset to their right, with right feet Pointing between feet. With shoulders parallel, joined Lead Hands are at her shoulder- to eye-Level. Man's right fingertips are at her backbone. Elbows may be low and heads look where they may.

Closed Turn   Turning with feet Closing, rather than with Passing Feet. Consists of at least three Steps, Closing Together upon the second or third Step. Opposite of Open Turn and similar to Closed Finish and Chasse Turn.

Close Touch   Feet brought Together without a Change of Weight; touching with Ball, toe, heel or Flat of foot.

Collect   The Action of drawing the Free Foot beneath the body at the completion of a Step.

Compression   The Action of relaxing or bending the supporting knee to lower the Center Point of Balance at the commencement of Movement. Also used to describe the lowering of the body when in a static position.

Connection   A means of communication between the partners, either visually, or as an actual physical point of contact. Also, the Tension applied to a physical point of contact through the manipulation of body Weight toward or away from the point of Connection.

Continuity   A Blend from one Step to another, or one Figure to another, in order that a continuous flow of Movement is achieved.

Contra   Meaning Opposite of a direction, Position, Action or Movement, Not Shoulder Lead.

Contra Banjo   Same as Feather Position.

Control   Maintaining one's entire body in a stable balance throughout the dance.

Count   One unit of time in a measure of music in relation to body Movement.

Counter Clockwise   CCW - Movement in a Left Face Turning direction, contrary to the normal movement of the hands of a clock, (clock on floor, not ceiling.)

Counter Movement   Where the Center Point of Balance of each partner is moving in opposition.

Counterpart   Opposite Footwork, etc., correspondingly danced by one's partner.

Counter Promenade Position   Same as Reverse Semi-Closed Position.

Coupe   With a slight Springing Action, Close the Free Foot to the other foot and extend the new Free Foot without Weight. See Cut.

Couple Rotation   Amount is often specified in total. Partners rotate CW or CCW together in unison, while either retaining or changing various Positions.

Crescendo   An Action or Movement with a gradual increase in stride or dynamics.

Cross Body   One passes Across in front of partner, or one's body part passes across one's other part.

Cross Body Position   Lady stands extremely close to man's right side, 90 degrees from facing him and facing across his front. Lady's right hand is joined with man's either hand at Waist-Level. Weight is on man's left and on lady's right feet. See Fan Position.

Crossed Feet   One foot is Crossed in front or behind other foot, with no Weight applied.

Crossed Hands Hold   Facing with all hands clasped right to right and left to left, with right hands usually on top. See Double Crossing Hands.

Cross Stretch   An Action where both partners' clasped arms are stretched while stepping across and apart.

Cross Touch   An Action where the Free Foot is Crossed close to one's Supporting Foot, either ahead of or behind, with the toe touching the floor with no Weight applied.

Cross Walk   A Forward Contra Body walk where each foot is Stepped toe-heel, in front of the other and beyond.

Crossward Diagonal   A Step across and Diagonally in front of or Diagonally behind Supporting Foot and Well beyond, with a Change of Weight. An inversion of Outbound Diagonal.

Crush in Closed Position   A Picture Figure. From a Closed Position, the man's weight is upon his left foot and his right foot is slightly extended Sideways. To Crush, Man has brought the lady tightly closed to him with his left hand on her back. Lady has her left hand on his right upper arm, and has placed her right cheek upon his right shoulder.

Cuddle Position   A Position where the lady is facing the man, slightly apart, with her hands caressing the man's neck or face, the man's hands loosely on the sides of the lady's back.

Cup and Pin Hold   A standard Hold by which the lady is led through Changes of Positions and Turns, where the man forms the "**Cup**" with his left hand, and the lady forms the "**Pin**" with her right hand. Subject joined hands are held at about Waist-Level. The man's outstretched left hand is held with palm facing Inward. With his thumb over his lady's right fingertips, the lady curls her fingertips over her man's left fingers.

Cup and Pin Holds   For finger Turns, the man forms the "**Pin**" with his left hand, and the lady forms the "**Cup**" with her right hand. There are two different standard Holds by which the **lady is stabilized by the man's fingers as she Spins**; (1) for Inside-Spinning his Lady and (2) for Outside-Spinning his Lady. For the "**Pin**" for either Hold, man Leads with his hand over lady's head, with two fingers pointed down. He uses the index and middle fingers, or else the middle and ring fingers, and he Leads by his first knuckles and not by his fingertips. For the "**Cup**" for Inside-Spins, (CCW,) lady's heel-of-hand is **up**, over her Head. For the "**Cup**" for Outside-Spins, (CW,) lady's heel-of-hand is **down**, over her Head. In both cases, she forms a cup with her fingers without protruding her thumb up or down and without squeezing her man's fingers.

Curving Torso   Various Movements, but commonly a full body inclination, undulating sideward with hip leading, immediately followed by the shoulder.

Cut   One foot closely Crosses the other above the ankle and applies Weight, which forces the other foot to swipe either Backward or Forward. See Lock.

Cut Time   Music having two Beats per Measure, i.e., time signature of 2/4.

Dance Count   Counting out foot Movement and Change of Weight Rhythms, (not music Beats.)

Dance Glide   Omni-directional locomotion unlike the natural walk, i.e., (1) in the **Forward Glide**, with Softened knees and with Weight upon skimming Ball-to-heel, one's stride is no choppy Step. Legs are kept close together with feet passing closely. (2) in the **Backward Glide**, with Softened knees and with Weight remaining Forward, one's swinging Free Foot skims with a stride. The legs and feet pass closely.

Dance Step Description   A detailed narrative description of a term, Position, Action, Movement, Figure, Pattern or routine, etc., to ease learning and to settle arguments.

Dance to the Music   To be adept at interpreting Music Phrase by blending it into the physical motion of a particular dance.

Deep Into Knees   Positioned low enough to be uncomfortably Bent Kneed.

Delayed Weight Shift   A delayed Action in the Weight transfer, causing one's knees to bend and straighten alternately. One's foot is placed flat to the floor Bent Kneed, delaying Weight transfer from the straight supporting knee until the next Step.

Demi Pointe Position   The Weighted trailing foot toe almost touches one's front foot outside, near its heel, as in the Latin Cross.

Demonstration   To show by example the execution of a Step, Pattern, Figure, or dance Routine.

Diagonal(ly)   Any direction that is 45 degrees from the Line of Dance or Reverse Line of Dance. See Direction.

Different   As a dance term, it generally indicates that the lady's dance part is completely different than that for her partner's, not just mirror-image opposite.

Dig Step   Normally replaces Triples. The Ball of the Free Foot is strongly pressed to the floor near to one's Supporting Foot, then Step In Place transferring Weight.

Direction   The line along which the next Figure will begin, relative to the Line of Dance (LOD). It is designated in degrees of 1/8 Turn as (going Clockwise from LOD) Diagonal Line & Wall (DLW), WALL, Diagonal Reverse & Wall (DRW), Reverse Line of Dance (RLOD), Diagonal Reverse & Center (DRC), Center of Hall (COH), and Diagonal Line & Center (DLC).

Dishrag   Performed in two Steps from Butterfly Position. Hands are retained throughout while rotating in opposition; Facing to Back To Back to Facing.

Displace Hop   A traveling Hop, not In Place, that begins and ends Balanced upon one foot. To push off aerially from the floor, driven by the Ball of one Supporting Foot, i.e., spring up then land upon the same one foot, in some predetermined direction. Simpler than Scoot.

Dot   To Tap free toe behind one's Supporting Foot without a Change of Weight.

Double Spin   Either or both partners Spinning singularly on one Ball of foot two full Turns before transferring Weight.

Double Step   Any "one-two-three" Step in which the same foot leads twice, as in a polka-step or rant-step. The second Step usually tends to Close.

Double Timing   A series of stepping twice to a Beat normally one-stepped.

Downbeat   Commonly Termed the first Count of a Measure, but the story is more complex. The various **Downbeats** are usually accented differently. For example, take the first two Measures of a song in 4/4 Time, Stepped *1&2&3&4&,5&6&7&8&*: All eight numerals are DownBeats, (while all eight ampersands are UpBeats.) Numeral *1* is the **One Beat**, the **Major Primary Downbeat**. Numeral *5* is also a **One Beat**, but it is the **Minor Primary Downbeat**. Numerals *2* and *6* are both **Two Beat** and **Secondary Downbeats**; of these, *2* is the **Major Secondary Downbeat**, while *6* is the **Minor Secondary Downbeat**. Numerals *3*, *4*, *7*, and *8* are **Tertiary Downbeats**.

Drift Apart   An Adjustment from a position close to the partner to one where partners still have contact but are Apart at arm's length.

Drive   The smooth, horizontal Movement of one's Center of Balance from off the Supporting Foot.

Duck   From a Hand in Hand Position, one Ducks by dipping low and passing under one's own arm that is retaining partner's hand.

Dynamics   Intensity variations in body motion, and characterized by energy, Timing and mood changes.

Eight Beat Segments   That to which most music is written and to which most routines are Choreographed.

Elbow Sweep   A flattering Movement for either or both arms. From against one's side then raised to Chest-Level, the elbow slowly Sweeps Forward and outward in a circular, horizontal arc. The elbow protrudes, then forearm, wrist, and back-of-hand Sweep.

Elegance of Movement   Tastefully opulent and ornate Movement, fastidiously danced with richness in Styling, refinement and grace.

Ending   The pattern of Steps, Figures, or Actions which ends a dance Routine.

Ending Position   The stance assumed, having executed an Action, Movement, Step, Figure, pattern or dance.

Engagement of Knees   Satisfactorily acquired from the lowering by both partners close in a Closed Position.

English Style   The style of Ballroom Dancing which evolved in England, the first country to standardize dance Figures and execution technique. Currently known as "International Style."

Equilibrium   When one is in a Balanced condition in which all reacting influences are stabilized.

Eros Line   A line created (normally) by the lady in which she extends her right Free Leg out to the side and slightly back, with leg bent, calf of the leg nearly level to the floor and toe pointed away from the knee, body arched well back, head to the right.

Escort Position   A Side By Side Position where both partners Face the same direction. The lady's left arm is passed through the man's curved right arm, with her left hand resting on his right forearm.

Even Rhythm   Each Step or Count with an identical Timing value.

Exercise   A type of lesson designed to increase the dancers' skill.

Exhibition   Dancing that is formally Performed before an audience as a stylized theatrical presentation.

Exit   A Pattern danced to the last bars of music ending a routine.

Explode   A quick Movement Away from the partner, usually with the Free Arm thrust up and out, away from the partner.

Expression   To display the feeling, character, and emotion felt by the dancer in the course of Performing a dance Routine.

Extension   The Action of Stretching or extending parts of the body.

Face   To Face the partner or to Face in a particular direction.

Facing Position   Partners Face toe-to-toe about an arm's length Apart and with no hands joined. See Open Facing and Left Open Facing Position.

Fake   Changing from the usual foot, by adding or eliminating a Step to or from the normal step pattern. See Transition and Change Feet.

Fallaway Position   The Position after the man and lady have taken one Step Backward with Outside Feet from a Semi-Closed or Reverse Semi-Closed Position. Compare with Step Thru.

Fan Kick   After first Kicking Forward, the extended high and straight leg is Flared circularly outward and rearward. See Develope and Ronde.

Feather Left Position   In Sidecar Position except bodies are Patched and Torqued CBMP Closed with partner. Left hips overlap with man's Weight Forward on left foot and lady's Weight Back on right foot.

Feather Position   In Banjo Position except bodies are Patched and Torqued CBMP Closed with partner. Right hips overlap, with man's Weight Forward on right foot and lady's Weight Back on left foot.

Feet Between Feet   Closed, opposing feet are offset, allowing knees to interlace. Tips of toes may not quite overlap past partner's toe tips.

Fencing Line   A dancing line in which the couple emulates the stance of a fencing competitor as he/she thrusts the foil forward toward the opponent.

Fifth Position   Heel at toe, one foot in front of the other with heels and big toes aligned. Outside of front heel touches inside of back toe, with Weight upon one foot only.

Fifth Position Extended   Identical to Fifth Position except feet are definitely apart, with one's feet aligned as if walking a wire.

Figure   A defined (named) Pattern of dance Steps and/or steps combined with Actions that are Performed in one or more music measures. See related terms: Basic, Pattern, and Variation.

Finger Clasp   A series of light hand attachments between partners that clasp without gripping. See Cup and Pin Hold, Fingertips to Fingertips, Pistol Grip and Wrist Hold.

Finger Flourishes   Various dramatic gestures by one's fingers for visual effect. These include Fingers Flick, Finger Snaps, Finger Styling, Flaring Fingers, Flinging Fingers, Shaking Fingers, Spirit-Fingers and Circle Hands.

Fingers Flick   A dramatic gesture. Both hands begin either tightly fisted or else with all fingertips touching. All fingers are then spread straight with a very quick burst, instead of just Flaring Fingers.

Finger Snaps   An accompaniment Flourish. To produce sound, snap third finger to second finger by rolling thumb. Alternate hands. Sound should be sharp.

Finger Styling   For an attractive display of the lady's free fingers, second and ring fingers are curved and remain together, while the first and little fingers are held straight.

Fingertips to Fingertips   With either Single Hands or All Hands in Hand, lady's hand(s) palm down as man's fingers lightly hook her fingertips. No thumbs are pressed. See Pistol Grip and Catch.

First Position   Feet together with heels touching and toes a thumb-width apart.

Fixed Pattern   A grouping of Figures in a unified design for dancing to a Choreographed routine.

Flare   Sweeping a foot, either rearward or forward, in a circular arc a few inches off the floor, then bringing it to the Supporting Foot without Weight.

Flaring Fingers   The dramatic gesture of tensely spreading out one's fingers very straight and flat.

Flash Break   A sudden and dramatic pause during the dance.

Flat   Normally used to indicate the flat foot, i.e., the whole foot Flat on the floor. Also used to indicate no rise.

Flat Turns   After a Forward preparatory Step, singular Turns on the Ball with no rise. Turning with Spotting, often in multiples, with feet together and with a minimum of travel. Spinning on one foot with no Change-of-Weight at half-turns, leaving the Free-Foot barely off the floor. Alternately with each total Turn, arms are often spread fore and aft then fingertips are brought together.

Flat Whisk Position   Tight and Semi-Closed, with Inside Feet Thru and supporting 1/4 of one's Weight, with all feet flat, with both upper bodies in CBMP, man's right elbow is slightly raised for lady's head open. Inside hips are in contact and inside toes point down line and toward partner.

Flick   The Action of moving the Free Foot quickly Backward without taking Weight, normally in a sharp or staccato manner. Or a minute Kick Forward from the knee.

Flicker   Quick and light Movements of body-parts, such as clicking heels in quick succession; on Balls, heels out then in, normally twice.

Flinging Fingers   A dramatic Flourish. With fingers together and hand held flat with wrist bent Inward, one then can fling one's fingers Outward.

Flirtation Position   Man Shadows very closely with lady to his'right. Right hands are joined and held at lady's right hip. Looking at him and blinking, lady touches man's left cheek with her left fingertips. See Varsouvienne Position.

Floor Craft   Describing a couple's ability to maneuver fluidly in a skillfully uninterrupted and courteous manner, in crowded circumstances.

Floored   Where some body-part of a dancer is in intimate contact with the floor.

Floor Pattern   An imaginary delineation of the path in space, a Choreographed description for each dancer's prescribed route, traveling along and over the dancefloor from place to place. Floor Pattern is separate from its Step Sequence.

Floorspace   Couples can only Spot Dance upon insufficient Floorspace; requiring increased Couple Rotation, Turning more to keep their momentum.

Florid Style   Derogatory; describing dancing that is ornate and flowery to an excessive degree.

Flow   The term used to describe the smooth continuation of natural Movement.

Fluidity   The couple's capability of flowing smooth and effortless upon the floor, easily changing direction. See Flow.

Fold   Where from Apart, one rotates (Folds) to Face partner. See Pickup.

Follow Thru   The passing of the moving foot underneath the body between Steps. Or, the continuation of one's foot and body Movement in anticipation of the next Step. Or, the Free-Foot's passing by of one's Supporting Foot before a Change of Direction.

Foot Action   Movements without a Change-of-Weight include **Touch**, **Draw**, **Stamp**, **Point**, **Dot**, **Swing**, **Brush**, **HeelBrush**, **Flick**, **Kick**, **Mulekick**, **Dig**, and **Lift** Movements, among others.

Football Kick   A long Forward swipe into the air after an extreme Backward extension.

Foot Placement   The Position(s) or Pattern(s) in which dancer's feet are placed on the floor.

Foot Pressure   Pressure applied to the floor by one's Free Foot, whereby partial Weight is applied by that foot.

Foot Rotation   Without or prior to any Body Turn, one executes a Foot Rotation, normally for initiating a Turn. See Body Turns Less, and Body Completes Turn.

Footwork   A term for the particular Steps each partner takes. Or, that foot part in contact with the floor at a point in time, such as Toe, Heel or Ball. With relation to her man's, lady's Footwork can be labeled "Same," "Opposite" or "Different."

Forearm Grasp   Partners Grasp each other by their forearms, normally just below the elbow.

Fore Hand   One's hand moves Forward palm-front with its Heel-of-Hand leading, i.e., as a policeman signalling to stop.

Form   The shape, structure or contour a dancer takes for a preconceived look or characteristic. Or, the orderly arrangement of body Movement.

Formation   A specified arrangement of couples in an ordered array on the floor.

Forward Check   Stepping Forward to or past the Supporting Foot with a rise for braking action, taken in that Line of Motion, in preparation to take a different Line of Motion.

Forward Close   Stepping Forward toward one's Supporting Foot and Closing with a Change of Weight.

Forward Cross Check   Either or both partners Step, in unison, directly In Front of their Supporting Foot or even beyond, then braking action is taken in that Line of Motion, with a Change of Weight, in Preparation to take a different Line of Motion.

Forward Hitch   Three Steps, Forward Close Backward. Opposite of Coaster Step.

Forward Hold   Stepping Forward to or past one's Supporting Foot, applying Weight, then maintaining Position, usually for one Beat.

Forward Limp   Consists of two Beats, half a Limp Step. First a Step, then the other foot Steps Forward on its Ball, with a Change of Weight to that Limping Foot. This Limp is usually Crossed in front of one's other foot.

Forward Poised Chair Position   Same as Chair Position but with weight of both partners Forward upon Inside Feet.

Forward Rise   Free Foot is Stepped Forward, then a Rise is made on same Foot.

Forward Roll   One's hip and shoulder are first swept Forward, then sideward, rearward then Inward.

Forward Swivel   Swiveling on one foot, Outward, Away from one's other foot, a quarter- to half-turn. Usually half-turning one's body causes rotation on the Ball of Foot.

Forward Touch   Stepping Forward, taking Weight, then Touching where indicated (usually Closed) with opposite foot.

Forward Turn   Stepping Forward then Turning on same foot.

Forward Walk   The natural Walk for most dances, except for certain Latins and Tangos. Weight is carried more Forward, over the moving foot. One's moving Ball skims, rolls to the heel then rolls to the Ball. Knee Bend increases with increased stride length, while Spot Dancing is more Straight Kneed.

Four/Four Time   With four Beats to each Bar, a slow Count equals two music Beats while a quick Count equals one Beat. With an "&" Count, two Steps may be taken to one Beat.

Fourth Position   Walking Step, where Weight transfers from foot to foot, one ahead of the other by about ten inches, with some foot-part always touching floor. Moving Forward or Backward, one's Weight is carried more Forward.

Free Expression   Unconstrained by propriety or dignity; not adhering to strict form or rule, and not bound, controlled, restricted or hampered in one's dance.

Free Spin   Detached from partner and from some Facing Position, one Spins CW or CCW on one Ball, normally for a Full Turn.

Free Style   Improvisation; extemporaneous with partner to no Fixed Pattern and according to individual desire. The art of dancing in partnership which allows free expression and unique interpretation.

Free Turn   A Turn made while unattached to one's partner.

Freeze   A stop with no Movement; a momentary Hold where one's body is fixed in time.

Front Cut   Moving foot closely Cuts over the toe and across the ankle of the Supporting Foot and Weight is applied, forcing the former Supporting Foot to be swiped rearward. See Front Lock.

Front Lock   Moving foot Crosses in front and beyond the Supporting Foot and Weight is applied.

Front Vine   A general three Step Figure, Timing varies. Each partner dances Sideward Cross In Front Sideward. See Vine Behind.

Full Spin   Rotation of 360 degrees in one Step on one foot, in a direction Outward from that foot. See Full Spiral.

Full Spiral   Rotation of 360 degrees in one Step on one foot, in a direction Inward from that foot, whereby one's Figure Four may form.

Gait   A general dance term for moving one's feet that includes walking, running, cantering and trotting.

Gesture   Aside from the support of one's Weight, a purposeful motion of one's head, limbs or body, made to emphasize, express or impress some dance emotion. Similar to Flourish.

Glide   The slick, striding Movement that smoothly skims the floor as one travels.

Grip the Floor   An Action to avoid. Gripping the Floor by tightening the toes, lowers the heel and moves one's Center of Balance rearward, causing stiffness and late spinning problems. Instead, one should Press into the floor by spreading your toes up and off the floor.

Guapa   (Pronounced Wah-pah) A Rhythmic Variation used in certain basic Actions, Movements or Figures. The variation calls for a delayed first Step by a 1/2 Beat, followed by normal Timing for the remaining steps; i.e., if normally counting 1,2,3&,4 then Guapacha would be danced 1&,2,3&,4 with the first step delayed until the second half of the first Count.

Half Close   The Free Foot is Stepped near but not Closed to one's Supporting Foot, followed by a Change of Weight to the Stepping Foot. The Half Close Step occurs on the *And* Step in Swing or Jive, (*Quick And Slow.*)

Half Moon Position   Partners face same direction with the man slightly to her right and behind the lady, clasping right hands and with Weight upon Outside Feet. Man extends his left arm behind lady or may touch her back with his left palm. Lady's left arm is extended.

Half Natural   See Natural Turn One Half.

Half Open Position   Almost Facing same direction with lady on man's right, similar to Semi-Closed Position except still more opened. Partners' Weights are upon Outside Feet, with Outside Hands free and extended Outside. Inside Arms hold bodies together in a wide vee. The man's arm is around lady's waist while her hand rests on his shoulder. Partners are ready to Step Thru with Inside Feet.   See Left Half Open Position.

Half Swivel   With one foot Forward in Fifth Position except Weight is on both, Swiveling a Half-Turn on both Balls of feet.

Half Timing   Dancing at half-speed to fast music, i.e., Stepping to every other Beat, or perhaps only one Step to several music Beats.

Half Toe   The Action of raising the heel so that one's Weight is Supported by the Ball.

Half Turn   A Change of Direction, 180 degrees total, CW or CCW, singular or Couple Rotating, either Forward or Back, and either traveling or spot.

Halo   A Halo signal as with a ring surrounding the lady's head; a Turn, Alemana or Spin is led by the man's (normally) left hand high and directly over her head. The overhead circular pattern may be tiny or large but never forcefully cranked.

Hammerlock Position   Facing Side By Side with Matched Hands joined at Waist-Level. One hand of one partner is behind his/her back. Similar to Pretzel Position.

Hand in Hand   A generalized Action, where partners lightly clasp only one set of Opposite or Matched Hands.

Hand Shake   Right hands joined, normally at Waist-Level.

Head Closed   A term related to Standard Dances in a Closed Position. Lady's Head Closed stance is to view high and over her own left wrist, with at least one Head Space Apart. Man's is to view slightly high and looking in a range centered over his lady's right shoulder.

Head Loop   Raising and retaining his lady's hand, the man slips his own arm over his head, as if combing his hair, before releasing.

Head Open   For Standard Dances, a term referring to the lady only. Her Head Opens almost always only momentarily and for only as long as her man signals. In some Closed Position, the man stretches his right side and bends his right wrist fingers-down, which slightly raises his right elbow, which in turn Opens Her Head.

Heel Bounce   With Weight Flat on both feet, both heels are raised simultaneously In Place and lowered to Flat again.

Heel Brush   Smartly Brush rearward one's heel and toe against the floor.

Heel Fan   With feet together then pivoting on Ball, the heel of one foot is rotated Outward then returned to Close.

Heel Pivot   After Stepping Backward, a Turn on the heel of the stepping foot with the Free Foot being brought to the Supporting Foot without another Change of Weight. See Heel Turn.

Heel Splits   With feet together and Weight on both Balls, both heels are rotated Outwards, pigeon toed, then returned to close. See Flicker, and Heel Fan.

Heels Stomp   No change in one's Center of Balance. With feet apart and Weight on both, and with Knees Back, both heels are lifted then lowered with a Stomp. Similar to Heel Bounce and Knees Pop.

Heel Strike   With feet together, one might Heel Strike one heel once to the floor while standing, then immediately Step Out with the same foot. Similar to Stamp.

Heel Tap   Free Foot Taps floor with heel.

Heel Touch   A series of Actions In Place. The Free Foot Heel Touches the floor in a given direction without Weight applied.

Heel Turn   The Heel Turning Hub Partner rotates without travel, remaining Facing as the Rim Partner Circles. The Rim Partner begins by rising, in order to put partner on Heels, then dances past the Heel Turned one. After Stepping Back Toe Heel, one's Heel Turn begins with Weight over that Supporting Heel, toward one's Free Foot with the Free Foot Closing against the Supporting Foot. One's toes and knees remain parallel together throughout. One Turns on one heel with Weight gradually transferred to the other heel by Turn ending. See Ball Turn and Heel Pivot.

Hesitation   Movement is temporarily suspended while the Weight is retained upon the Supporting Foot for one or more Counts.

High Kick   With a Softened Supporting knee, one flexibly Kicks the Free Leg as high as possible, while keeping a straight Free Knee and a pointed toe. Followed by a Softened Touchdown.

High Line   A position of the body caused by a high upright Poise.

Hinge Position   Lady is on man's left, with man partially supporting her with his left knee. His hips are eased contrabody into his lady and he views her face. His unbent right leg is stretched sideward. Lady's right toe points with no Weight at his right instep. Her Closed Head has chin up and her hips are well up.

Hip Bump   In Open or Left Open Position and slightly Back To Back, partners Hip Bump Together.

Hip Lead   The Man Leads his lady while facing same direction or 90 degrees to her. To contact his lady, the Man's hip is projected sideways from the same side as his Supporting Foot, then he Recovers. With care, he aims for her pelvis, not into her stomach. He has only soft items in his pants pocket for this.

Hip Shift   With Weight Balanced over one leg, one's Weight is Hip Shifted to over the Free Leg.

Hip to Hip Position   Offset Outside Partner; partner's Facing feet are to one's right; shoulders are parallel with no CBMP or Feathering. Right hips are touching and right arms are around partner's waists. Left arms are overhead or spread horizontal.

Hip Turn Position   Offset Outside Partner; partner's Facing feet are to one's right; shoulders are parallel with CBMP. Right hips are touching. All hands remain held Double Hold as in Butterfly Position. Man's clasped right hand has been placed at lady's left hip, and his clasped right hand is at his own left hip.

Hip Twist   An Action, often following a foot Swivel, in which the hips Turn more than the foot and Upper Body, one's hips turning in the same direction as the Swivel.

Hip Waves   Left and right, side to side hip sweeps, usually performed by the lady. Hip Waves, either Forward Roll or Rearward Roll, forming Figure Eights and rising at the outer extremes. A Circular Movement, starting in the pelvic region then moves through the diaphragm, chest and shoulders.

Hitch   A Closing Action in which the Movement direction is reversed, as in *back close forward*.

Hold(1)   A momentary pause. A Beat of music in which no Step or Action is taken. A Position maintained for one Beat or longer.

Hold(2)   The Position of the hands, arms, and body in relation to one's partner, when in a dance Position with contact. A Hold could be moving so as to include many Positions, i.e., partners beginning with a Butterfly Hold may have their torsos twisting and feet flying, but they retain their Hold by all four hands, while a Butterfly Position would be static.

Home   The original starting place or area, or when Spot Dancing In Place, the location of one's feet when in Balance, directly under the body. See Neutral Position.

Hook   To Lock one's Free Foot close to and behind the Supporting Foot without taking Weight.

Hop   Springing up on one foot then landing upon the same one foot without travel. More than Bobbing. Begins and ends Balanced on one foot, with Weight upon one Ball and with the other foot raised. The springing toe only barely clears the floor. Similar to Displace Hop and Scoot.

Horizontal Rhythm   Dancing in Timing with the Beat of the music through flat travel Movement. See Vertical Rhythm.

Horse and Cart   The rotating Hub Partner Fans or Flares as the Rim Partner propels the other by Running in an arc.

Hover   A part of a Figure in which the moving or Turning of the body is slowed or checked, while a rise in the body, leg and foot is performed for the purpose of changing direction or rotation.

Hub Partner   As a Couple, the Hub Partner is momentarily the center person of a wheel-like Movement or Figure; the one who must take tiny Steps while rotating, and usually is the one who momentarily Follows. Opposite of Rim Partner.

Impetus   An impelling force that drives the lady into a Movement or rotation.

Improvise   Extemperaneous dance Step execution, spontaneous impromptu composition, or to add variations to a set Choreography.

Impulse   The Action of inducing a sudden impelling force that produces Movement.

In / Inward   A term, Action or Movement, meaning toward the inside or center, or moving inbound or Inward. Opposite of Out.

Inbound   Inward bound, heading toward one's partner or one's own body. Opposite of Outbound.

Indian Position   With one partner in front as in Tandem Hold. In Trail Indian Style with Matching Hands joined, each clasped hand of the person behind has been placed on each shoulder of the one in front.

Initiate Strongly   Initiating a Movement with much energy, i.e., the man's energetic driving to execute a Figure.

In Lock Step   Dancers precisely complying with dictated dogma without individual expression.

In Place   Without changing one's general Position on the floor, returning Weight to the foot previously activated. Or, a Weight shift from one foot to the other, with no directional or rotational Movement. Or, dancing in one spot.

Inside   A person's side nearest one's partner.

Inside Arm/Foot/Hand/Knee/Leg   A body-part nearest one's partner when not facing directly toward or away.

Inside Edge   The instep side of the foot, the inner edge along its entire length, including heel and toe.

Inside Line of Dance   Inside of an imaginary line around the room perimeter which dancers follow.

Inside Spin   A Spin that initially Turns toward one's partner, normally from a Facing Position and normally for a Full Turn.

Inside Turn   A Turn that initially moves in or toward the partner. See Turn In.

In Step   Being in the correct Step with relation to one's partner.

Interlude   A short piece of connecting or fill-in Choreography between two major sequences or musical passages, at least two measures long and normally less than eight measures. Also see Bridge.

Into   To Turn or Step toward partner. See Away.

Inward   Positioned, directed or moving toward one's Supporting Leg; or, toward another part of one's own body; or, toward partner or Pattern Center. Opposite of Outward.

Isolation   Movement of one body-part independently and apart from the rest of one's body.

Jazz Hands   A position of the hands in which the hands are opened as far as possible, fingers widely spread, with palms out.

Jete   A spring from one foot to the other. A sharp rising on one Step, followed by a sharp lowering and pointing of the Free Foot, usually to the side. See Change Point.

Jog   To quickly veer, swerve, dog-leg sideways in the dance.

Jump   Springing so that both feet leave the floor, beginning and/or ending on both feet.

Kick   The Free Foot exerts a sudden Forward Action, followed by a slower Recovery without a Change of Weight. A Kick is a knee lift and Spring Action in a selected direction with the toe pointed down, where the knee does not completely straighten, then the foot is retracted to against the Supporting Foot or is returned Home.

Kick Away   To Kick Outward, Apart from Partner.

Kick Ball Change   In Syncopated Rhythm Timing, a Forward Flick then a Ball Change. The Flick then a Ball Step on same foot, followed by a flat Step by the other foot.

Kick Hop   The Free Foot is Kicked then the Hop is made upon the Supporting Foot.

Kick Step   A minute Flick of the foot from the knee, grazing the floor, followed by a Change of Weight onto that same foot.

Knee Back   The ending Action of certain Steps. Stepping, the supporting Knee straightens then Flexes Backwards.

Knee Bend   A term for defining amount, from Straight Kneed, to Softened Knees, to Deep Into Knees.

Knee Cap Room   To avoid bumping knee caps with the Engagement of Knees, Knees interlace by Opposing Feet being Offset.

Knee Drape   With Softened Knees together, one Knee is protruded Forward then rolled Outwards at least a Quarter Turn, with its foot rolling to its Outside Edge, Swiveling and applying Weight.

Knee Lead   Various Actions where the man partially Leads his lady by use of his Knee.

Knees Back   No Center of Balance change. Begins standing with Feet Apart, Straight Kneed and with Weight upon both feet. Both Knees are then Flexed Backward and held. See Knee Back.

Knees Pop   With Knees Back, quickly Soften Knees then recover Knees Back, with no Center of Balance change.

Knee Up   Performed all with the same foot in Butterfly Position with Leaning Into Each Other. A Knee is brought up across the waist, then kicked sideward aerially to a straight knee, retracted then returned In Place.

Knee Up Position   With one Knee Up and Free Foot against inner Knee, toe pointing down. Usually the Free arm is straight up. Normally for the lady.

Lady's Inside Spin   Two Movements or Figures. Turning from partner from a Facing Position, the lady is spun Counter Clockwise on her left Ball, usually for a Full Turn. Rarely is the lady spun Clockwise, (on her right Ball.) The lady is either Free Spun off by the Man, or she is led overhead. The man Leads her hand diagonally up across her face. For a lady's Underarm Inside Spin, the lady rotates Counter Clockwise under her man's left or right hand holding her right hand; or rarely done, Clockwise under her man's hand holding her left hand. Counterpart of Lady's Outside Spin.

Lady's Inside Turn   Turning towards man from a Facing Position, Turning the Lady Counter Clockwise, to her Left, usually for a Full Turn. The partner's joined hands, her right hand and either his left or right Hand, pass IN-between them. There is initial CBM for the lady, i.e., her shoulder Opposite the Turning direction starts Forward. A roughly oval, closed, or nearly closed Turn is made. Counterpart of Lady's Outside Turn.

Lady's Outside Spin   Two Movements or Figures. Turning Away from partner from a Facing Position, the lady is spun Clockwise on her right Ball, usually for a Full Turn. Rarely is the lady spun Counter Clockwise, (on her left Ball.) The lady is either Pushed Off by the man and Free Spun, or she is led Away from him overhead. For a lady's Underarm Outside Spin, the lady rotates Clockwise under her man's left or right hand holding her right hand; or, rarely done, Counter Clockwise under her man's hand holding her left hand. Counterpart of Lady's Inside Spin.

Lady's Outside Turn   Turning Away from man from a Facing Position, Turning the lady Clockwise, to her right, usually for a Full Turn. The man Turns the lady's right hand Away from himself, OUTSIDE, using a Halo Lead and using either of his hands. Counterpart of Lady's Inside Turn.

Lady Under   An Arch Turn under man's and lady's arching hands, which remain joined while lady takes three Steps under. Lady begins with either foot but on Opposing Footwork.

Lagged Timing   To purposely retard and Step Behind the Beat. Lagged Timing is the Action of Stepping between Beats, or at the 'back-of-the-beat'. Commonly, one's Step is quickened to On the Beat after leisurely Lagging the Beat first played.

Lateral Movement   A sideways bodily Movement, or a Movement both side and Forward or side and back. See Diagonal.

Lead Foot/Hand   Normally refers to the man's left and the lady's right foot/hand.

Lean   Out of Balance, tilting. Partners Lean Away from each other, clasping for support, dancing Spin Turns, Swivel Walks and such. Partners Lean into each other in certain Patterns.

Left Cradled Position   Same as Cradled Position except man Shadows with lady to his LEFT. Lady's LEFT arm remains on top. Similar to Left Wrapped Position.

Left Dancing Skaters Position   Partners Face same direction with man Shadowing lady on his left. They clasp and spread right hands. Man's left arm is wrapped around behind her. Lady's left hand is turned palm Outward at her left hip, clasping man's left hand palm to palm. Partners are less overlapped than in left Shadow Position, more Side by Side. Opposite of Skaters Position.

Left Face   To Reverse Turn or Face or move to the left, in a Counter Clockwise direction.

Left Flirt Position   A modified Left Varsouvienne Position. Lady looks at her man and touches man's right cheek with her right fingertips. Partners Face same direction, clasping left hands, with the man beside lady on her right.

Left Half Open Position   A Side By Side Position with the man and lady facing the same direction, with bodies together in a vee shape with their Weights upon Outside Feet. Lady is on man's left with his left arm behind, at or near the lady's waist. The lady's right hand is on or near the man's left shoulder and their Free Arms might extend to the side.

Left Hammerlock Position   In Sidecar Position except for Hand Hold. Right to right and left to left hands are joined, usually for Tunnels. All hands are at Waist Level. One partner has their right arm behind their back while their left arm is to their side. The other partner has both hands Forward with arms to their side. Opposite of Hammerlock Position. Similar to Left Pretzel and Left Tamara Positions.

Left Hand Shake   Left hands joined, normally at Waist Level.

Left Open Position   Both partners Face the same direction with lady to the man's left side, man's left and lady's right hands joined. Inside Hands are held Forward, either with man's Palm Up or clasping back of lady's hand. Outside Hands are free and Extended level toward Outside. Similar to Left Side By Side Position.

Left Open Facing Position   Partners are facing with the man's left and the lady's right hands joined at Waist Level, similar to Butterfly Position. Either the Free Hands are spread or held close to one's body. Same as Open Facing Position except for hand hold.

Left Open Facing Offset Position   Partners are facing and Apart with facing feet sideways to their left, and with the man's left and the lady's right hands joined in front of the lady. Same as Left Open Facing Position except for Offset. Opposite to Open Facing Offset Position.

Left Pretzel Position   Right to left and left to right hands are joined and all hands are at Waist Level. Partner's facing feet are to one's left. Both partners' right arm is behind their own back, while the left arm is stretched across their (side by side) partner's front. Opposite to Pretzel Position.

Left Promenade Position   Lady is on man's left, side by side and both are Facing same direction. With right hands on top of left hands, all hands are joined in front with wrists crossed, and with man's hands Palm Up.

Left Shadow Position   Partners Face same direction, one to the right and behind the other, overlapping, either clasping right hands or not touching. Opposite to Shadow Position.

Left Shake Hands Position   Partners face and clasp left hands at Waist Level. Free Hands are either spread or held close to one's body. Opposite to Shake Hands Position.

Left Shoulder to Shoulder Position   Partners are in a left shoulder to left shoulder Position. Shoulders touch. Partner's facing feet are Offset to their left. Positioning of arms and hands are various. Opposite to Shoulder to Shoulder Position.

Left Star Position   Same as Sidecar Position except left hips are touching, left hands are Palm to Palm with elbows touching, and Free Arms are behind backs. Opposite to Star Position.

Left Tamara Position   Same as Sidecar Position except for Hand Hold. Right to left and left to right hands are joined. One set of hands are at Waist Level while the other set is raised with curved arms forming a Window, through which partners view each other. One partner's right arm is behind their back with their left arm held high. Opposite to Tamara Position.

Left Turkish Towel Position   Man is Positioned in the lady's Left Varsouvienne Position. Partners Face the same direction, with the lady Shadowing the man on her left. They clasp and spread Matching Hands behind the man at Shoulder Level or at Waist Level, or at a mixture of the two. Opposite to Turkish Towel Position.

Left Varsouvienne Position   Partners Face same direction, with the man Shadowing the lady on his left. They clasp and spread Matching Hands behind the lady at Shoulder Level or at Waist Level, or at a mixture of the two. If at Shoulder Level, each set of Matched Hands are clasped slightly in front of lady's shoulder, and each has both elbows at equal height. Opposite to Varsouvienne Position.

Left Whisk Position   With all feet flat, with Inside Feet Thru and supporting about one quarter of one's Weight, trailing toes are turned slightly Inward. Opened slightly in a vee shape with each Upper Body in CBMP, the lady's right and the man's left Inside Hips are in contact. Clasped man's left and lady's right hands usually are raised in a soft curve just over their heads. Man's right wrist is loosely around lady's waist, or man has taken a Paso Doble Hold if lady is short or buxom.

Left Wrap Around Position   Partners Face same direction, side by side, with lady on man's left. Both of his arms extend in front of lady; man's left arm crosses over her right arm with Matched Hands. Similar to Left Open Position.

Left Wrapped Position   Same as Wrapped Position except man Shadows with lady to his LEFT. Lady's RIGHT arm remains on top. Similar to Left Cradled Position.

Leg Wrap Position   With partners facing, man is lowered and is supporting lady with both his arms around lady's lower back. Lady's right arm is around man's neck. Lady wraps her leg outside and around partner's leg. Usually her Left leg is wrapped around the man's Extended right leg, with his left Side Stretched and with his Head Open. Her toe is pointed down.

Level   Dancing heights; Eye-Level, Shoulder-Level, Chest-Level, Waist-Level, Hip-Level, and Knee-Level; normally referring to the lady.

Leverage   A term for the man's body Lead, for either slowing or quickening their dance Movements.

Lift(1)   With the assistance of the partner, any Action or Movement that simultaneously raises both feet of a person slightly off the floor.

Lift(2)   To raise one's own body, i.e., to rise upon one's Supporting Foot(s), or to raise a leg and/or foot.

Lift Bent/Straight   To Lift a fully relaxed human body Bent at the waist, dead-weight, is much more difficult than to Lift a body that is stiff and Straight, live-weight.

Lightly   Moving quickly and easily, or having less force and/or intensity than normal.

Limbering   Dancers often execute a variety of Stretching Exercises to loosen and Extend their muscles prior to their actual dance.

Limp   Consists of two Beats or Steps, half a Limp Step. First a Step, then either the left or right foot steps on Ball of foot, with a Change of Weight to that Limping foot. The Limp usually is either Locked behind or Crossed in front of one's other foot.

Limp Arms   Derogatory when referring to a lady's poor Following ability; due to her lack of applying sufficient Tone to her arms, by which her man may Lead her.

Limp Behind   Consists of two Steps, half a Limp Step. First a Step sideward, then the other foot Locks behind on Ball of foot, with a Change of Weight to that Limping foot.

Line   A defined position of the body(s). Also, the Action of moving to a specified position without taking an additional Step, e.g., a SWAY LINE or LUNGE LINE.

Linear   Movements that follow straight directions, rather than Curved or Rotational directions.

Line of Dance   Pertinent only to dances that travel. Refers to Forward flow of traffic, traditionally CCW about the floor. An imaginary line around the room perimeter by which dancers follow, with rounded corners and at a given distance from the wall.

Line of Direction   Same as Line of Dance.

Line of Motion   The horizontal direction that one's Center Point of Balance is moving.

Link   Steps connecting or inserted between two Figures or Patterns, forming a Phrase.

Lock   A position of the feet where one foot has been Crossed closely behind or in front of the other, feet nearly parallel. See Lock Step and Latin Cross.

Lock Step   The Movement in which the Free Foot is moved to a Lock Position with the Supporting Foot and then Weight is transferred to it.

Lock Twice   Figures where the second Lock is upon the same foot. Compare with Forward Lock Forward Lock, which changes feet.

Locomotor   Movement of one's body to a Change of Location.

Look Away   Turning one's head Away from partner.

Looking Circle   An expanded circle, all couples looking toward the demonstrating couple in the center of the floor. Man stands behind and slightly to one side of his partner, to enable all couples to observe the instruction or performance being conducted on the floor without an obstructed view.

Loop Turn   An American Style term used to describe any one of a number of underarm Figures or Movements, in which one of the partners "loops" the arm (using joined hands) over his or her head while Turning. An example of a loop action would be the Head Loop. See Right Skin and Left Skin.

Loose Closed   A versatile Closed Position with separation between partners, normally about a hand's width. Man's right hand holds lady at her side.

Loosen the Lightbulb   Arm high wrist rotation; right hand Outward, left hand Inward. Opposite of Tighten the Lightbulb.

"L" Position   A Latin stance, where the lady stands perpendicular to man's Facing direction, at right angles to each other.
At Waist Level, lady's right is joined, Hand in Hand, with either of the man's hands. Lady stands extremely close to man's right side, 90 degrees from facing him, and Facing Across front of man. Weight is upon man's left and on lady's right feet. Opposite of Fan Position.

LRL   An acronym for Left-Right-Left. Refers to Triple Movements or Steps such as Shuffles, Subtle Triples, Chasses, Double Steps, Coaster Steps, Anchor Steps, etc. See RLR.

Man's Free Spin   From some Facing Position, normally Pushing Off his Lady's right Palm of hand, the man Spins himself, detached, usually for a Full Turn Counter Clockwise on his Left Ball of foot.

Man's Skaters Position   A Skaters Position with the man's and lady's positions switched. See Skaters Position.

Man's Tamara Position   A Tamara Position with the man's and lady's positions switched. See Tamara Position.

Man Under   An Arch Turn under man's and lady's arching hands, which remain joined while man takes three Steps Under. Man begins with either foot but on Opposing Footwork.

Mark Time   To continuously shift Weight In Place from one foot to the other and back, in time with the music.

Matched Hands   Hands are joined right-to-right and/or left-to-left.

Maxixe Hold   Pronounced `*mah she she*.' Normally from a tilted Butterfly Position, partners switch to Matched Hands clasped overhead while the other two arms grasp around the other's waist.

Measure   A division of music. A group of Beats marked off by the regularly recurring Accent of the music. See Bar.

Mechanics Memory   The converse of Muscle Memory. Memorizing intellectually some bodily Action, Movement, Figure or Pattern, rather than memorizing through bodily repetitive practice. Muscle Memory is retained longer than retention by Mechanics Memory.

Medium Height   With Softened Knees, the median between Standing Height and deep flexing of one's knees.

Medley   A succession of dances, danced to a succession of melodies, all to a constant Rhythm.

Melt   Gradually settling onto the floor.

Meter   The division of Time or Rhythmical structure indicating the number of Beats in one Measure.

Metronome   A device with a pendulum adjustment for ticking at constant speeds of from 40 to 200 ticks per minute. Cadence for Largo = 40-60, Larghetto = 60-66, Adagio = 66-76, Andante = 76-108, Moderato = 108-120, Allegro = 120-168, and Presto = 168-208.
     Example: For 4/4 Time, Bars (or Measures) per minute for Largo = 10-15, Larghetto = 15-16.5, Adagio = 16.5-19, Andante = 19-27, Moderato = 27-30, Allegro = 30-42, and Presto = 42-52.

Metronomic Motion   Movements of a tic-toc nature involving easy, natural Movements of one's Upper Body or its parts, accelerating then reversing in larger Movements than those of one's Lower Body. Opposite of Pendulum Motion.

Mid-Height   Approximately Chest Level for arm motion; or, one's height at normal standing stance when not dancing.

Mirror Image   The natural diametrically Opposite stance, Action, Movement, Figure, or Pattern, etc., of one's Partner. Synonymous with Opposite.

Mixed Meter   A Rhythmical structure composed of an irregular division of underlying Beats into Measures of different Meters.

Moderate Timing   Between slow and fast Timing, from about 100 to 130 Beats per minute. See Metronome.

Modified   Meaning somewhat of a change to a dance stance, Action, Movement, Figure or Pattern.

Momentum   The force or Impetus driving body Movement at a certain velocity across the floor.

Mood   The compelling Tempo, state of emotion or feeling, or tone of Movement in a dance.

Movement   Movement is motion with a resulting Change of Weight. Conversely, Action is motion without a Change of Weight.

Movement Count   Numerically counting every foot Step plus every non-Change of Weight Action.

Moves   A very general term that encompasses Actions, Movements, Motions, Steps, Breaks, Figures, Patterns, Sequences, and Routine Sections. See Dance Step Description.

MPM   Or Measures per Minute, in relation to Tempo. Dancers think in Terms of MPM, while musicians think in Terms of Beats per Measure. See Timing.

Mulekick   Followed by a Leg Position, a sudden straight Backward Movement of the Free Foot from its Bent Knee, till one's shin is parallel with floor, followed by a slower Recovery. There may or may not also be some throwing of the thigh included; Mulekick-Major includes the thigh. More Kick than a Flick. See Heel Brush.

Multiple Hand Changes   Left or right, rapid singular or multiple Toe Spins, suitable for use normally by the lady. On Balls with feet Closed or close together, a Change of Weight with each Half Turn. She may Toe Spin In Place or she may slightly travel. Her hands are held close together over her head. The lady is led by her partner's body moving toward her. Every two Beats, he changes Opposing Hands with her, beginning with his Left to her right hand for either direction. See Illusion, Halo Lead, Pencil Turns, PittyPatter Turns, and Pinwheel.

Muscle Memory   The converse of Mechanics Memory, the ability to subconsciously Perform without thinking. Memorizing Movements, Figures and/or Patterns by bodily repetitive Practice. Muscle Memory is retained longer than retaining by Mechanics Memory. See Body Mechanics and Subconscious Dancing.

Muscle Tone   The degree of firmness, vigor and/or Tension in resting muscles. See Tension.

Muscular Control   The power to exercise a regulating influence over one's own muscles.

Musical Eccentricities   A Routine most times fits, or fits best, only a certain rendition of a particular song. Most dances are Choreographed in Eight Beat Segments, due to music usually being written thusly, but the music often varies. In only one of the verses or choruses, or in a Break Sequence, there may be a different organization or an additional Measure or two; or, there may be an additional Intro Segment and/or Coda Segment. Additionl Steps may be added as a Tag, or Steps may be truncated.

Musicality   A term for one's skillful ability to discern music in the way that is correctly interpreted, with regards to both mechanical and artistic expression.

Music Bridge   A passage connecting two sections of a composition.

Music Chorus   The repeated or main section of the music, a refrain. Normally a Chorus means going through the entire number one time, whether that means as few as 12 Bars (Measures) or as many as 32 Bars. Usually the Chorus is divided into Phrases of eight Bars each.

Music Ending   A short musical Phrase at the end of the entire piece of music, usually two to eight Bars long.

Music Interlude   A piece of "fill music" between the sections in a musical composition.

Music Intro   Music that is played before, and leading up to the Music Chorus. Usually the Intro is four Measures long, but may be anywhere from two to eight Measures of music. In dancing, the Intro will normally set the mood, Rhythm, and Tempo in preparation for performing the body of the dance Routine.

Music Phrase   A segment of musical structure. Phrases are unified by Rhythms, melodies and harmonics, and will come to closure with a cadence or resolve. Musical Phrases are normally composed in two-to-four Bar segments. A Mini-Phrase in 4/4 time is eight Beats of music, and in 3/4 time is six Beats of music. A Minor Phrase in 4/4 time is 16 or 24 Beats of music. A Major Phrase is a series of Mini or Minor Phrases which expresses a complete musical thought. See Music Chorus.

Music Tag   Any music that is added to, but not part of the Chorus is referred to as the Tag. A Tag may be added between Choruses or to end a music composition and is usually two to eight Measures long. In Round Dance Choreography, the Tag (if used) defines the ending of the dance Routine. See Music Ending and Tag.

Narrow Base   Usually refers to one's unsteady Center of Balance, due to feet being Closed, close together, or In Line with the other.

Natural Turn   A Clockwise Turn to the right. Opposite of Reverse Turn.

Neck Wrap   From an Open Position, beginning with Inside Foot and looking toward direction of Turn, the partner to be Neck Wrapped rotates toward one's own joined hand, raising that hand onto one's own shoulder then retaining that hand joined for to brake one's Roll In.

No Contact   Dancing together as one, but without touching each other. See Open Step.

Nod   To bow one's head briefly as in a gesture of Acknowledgement.

No Float   Dancing Flat with absolutely no up-down Movement.

No Foot Rise   An Action of rise which is taken through the knees and body only (not through the feet). No Foot Rise occurs when Stepping Backwards on the inside of most Turns, when the heel of the Supporting Foot will remain in contact with the floor until full Weight is taken onto the next Step. The Rise is felt in the body and legs only.

Notation   Abbreviated instructions to assist Routine remembrance. Many systems of dance Notation have been devised.

Oblique   A slight Position, Turn or Movement that is neither parallel nor perpendicular. Oblique is most commonly a Forward Change of Direction, one-eighth Clockwise or Counter Clockwise. See Diagonal.

Offbeat   An unaccented Beat in a Measure.

Offset   Partners Positioned Diagonally from each other, on the Oblique. See Alignment.

Offset Facing Opposed Position   A less-explicit description of Banjo, Sidecar and Outside Positions. Partners Face each other and to the side of each other, Left or Right, Offset diagonally with Facing Feet. Hand Holds are various or none.

Offset Facing Same Position   A less-explicit description of Skaters, Skirt-Skaters, Shadow, Varsouvienne, Turkish Towel and Flirt Positions. Partners Face the same direction but are Offset diagonally, Left or Right, and the man is either behind or in front of Lady. Hand Holds are various or none. See Open Position, Side by Side Position, and Spaghettis.

Omni-Directional   Direction Forward, Backward, Sideward, Crossward or Diagonal.

One Beat Timing   Dancing on the first Beat, sometimes called "the Downbeat". One Beat is the first Beat of a 2/4 or 4/4 music Measure, or of a 3/4 Waltz Measure. See Downbeat and Two Beat Timing.

One Piece   An unleadable Movement. One's Stiff Body, mechanically Moving without Forward, Backward, or Sideward Sway.

On Point   Meaning Pointing with one's toe.

On Stage   Dancing for effect on one's audience, as if On Stage. See Perform.

On the Beat   Center of Balance begins Forward Movement at the instant of drumbeat, followed by Stepping Forward with one's heel to the floor, as with servicemen Marching. See Beat, Lagging the Beat and Step.

Open Break   A Step taken in Open Facing Position in which the partners move in Opposite directions.

Open Choreography   A general term for where partners dance a Routine Apart, without touching each other; limited to visual Lead and Follow.

Open Dancing   A category where at times the only Lead is through their one set of Joined Hands, his left and her right. Unable to definitively Lead her with such minimum contact, the man can still signal, indicate and invite Movements for her body by means of his hand Actions.

Open Facing Offset Position   Partners are Facing and Apart, with Facing feet sideways to their right, and with the man's right and the lady's left hands joined in front of the lady. Same as Open Facing Position except for Offset. Opposite to Left Open Facing Offset Position.

Open Facing Position   Partners are Facing toe-to-toe, arm's-length distance Apart, with the man's right and the lady's left hands joined at Waist Level, similar to Butterfly Position. Same as Left Open Facing Position except for hand hold.

Open Figure   Usually traveling, any Figure or Pattern involving continuous Passing of Feet or Continuity of Movement, without any feet Closing together. Dancing a Chasse or a Box is NOT an Open Figure. See Open Reverse Turn, Open Natural Turn, and Open Finish.

Open Finish   The last part of a dance Movement, Figure or Pattern, ending with the Passing of Feet, without feet Closing together. See Continuity.

Opening Out   A Swivel and Turning of the body, normally by the lady, of at least 1/4 Turn in the Opposite direction of the Supporting Foot.

Open Position   With lady on man's right, side-by-side and both Facing same direction. hand-in-hand, Inside Hands are held Forward, either with man's Palm Up or clasping back of lady's hand. Outside Hands are free and extended level toward Outside. Same as Side By Side Position except hands are joined. Opposite to Left Open Position.

Open Step   Steps taken without touching partner.

Open Turn   A Turn in which the feet pass continuously throughout all Steps without Closing Together.

Open Work   Any Movement or Figure in which the couple is not in one of the closed dance positions. The couple may or may not have physical contact.

Opposite   The natural Counterpart. In Footwork as well as hands, the man's left and the lady's right or the man's right and the lady's left. In any of the facing or closed dance positions, refers to the man's Step Forward and the lady's Step Backward, or visa-versa. See Counterpart.

Opposite Rotations   Partners Turning or Spinning in Opposite directions, as when Turning their backs to each other from Facing. See Chopper.

Opposition Line   A Picture Figure created by both partners in a Closed Position, lowering on the Supporting Leg and Pointing the Free Leg Sideward, Opposite and Away from the partner.

Orbit   A Circular Movement, Figure, or Pattern. Turning Forward, partners Orbit Clockwise in Butterfly Facing Offset or Banjo Positions, around a central point between them. Amount of Steps varies. Opposite direction of Windmill. More general than Wheel.

Ordinary Steps   A class of Steps that are simple and easy to Execute.

Outbound   Outward bound, Steps heading Outward, Away from one's partner or from one's body. Opposite of Inbound.

Outbound Diagonal   A combination of both lateral and progressive or regressive Action or Movement, Outbound and Away from one's Supporting Foot, slanted and oblique in direction, usually at about a 45 degrees angle, diagonally Forward or Backward, left or right. An inversion of Crossward Diagonal.

Out of Balance   A loss of Equilibrium. Refers to one's Center of Balance being off-centered; or to have one's body Weight distribution going askew.

Outside   Away from a person's side farthest from one's partner. Or to Step into an Outside Position.

Outside Arm/Foot/Hand/Knee/Leg   A body-part farthest from one's partner when not facing directly toward or away.

Outside Partner   A Forward Step taken to the right or left of both of partner's feet.

Outside Turn   From a Facing Position, a Turn made by either partner CW or CCW under raised arms, initially Turning out and Away from the partner, usually for a Full Turn. Only one set of hands are joined, which form an Arch Extended up and to the side, over the head of the turner. For the Partner Turning, one's Forward shoulder rotates in the same direction as the initial Step, (not Crossed.) Counterpart of Inside Turn.

Outstretch   An Action where partners face same direction with Opposite hands clasped and with arms straight and wide Apart.

Outwards and Upwards Style   Here the essence of one's Movement is extrovert and outgoing, lightly lifting one's Weight upwards, and covering a wide space. One's arm Movements are Open. Opposite of Inwards and Downwards Style.

Overspin   Identical to the Spin Turn except Couple Rotation is a 7/8-Turn, (rather than 5/8-Turn.) Added rotation is taken on the second Step. See Closed Impetus.

Oversway Position   Bodies are Closed square with Shoulders Parallel. Their Lead hands are joined and raised; both are looking over these Lead Hands in a High Line Position. The man's left and the lady's right Supporting Legs each have a Softened Knee, and both his right and her left sides are Stretched upward. There is a slight turning of the man's Upper Body to his left, in order to turn his lady's head Strongly to her left. Both Free Legs are Extended sidewards and parallel with toes Pointed. This Position is normally followed by a Change of Sway.

Overturn   To Couple Rotate a Turning Figure in excess of its normal amount of Turn. Since Overturning takes extra time, the Couple begins a `nano-second' early. The lady should not resist the early Lead here. She must not Plant the Foot before her man does, thereby stopping the Turn. The man decides the amount of Turn.

Pace   The rate of speed or length of Step; or the Pace of repeated identical Steps. Similar to Cadence.

Palm   The inner surface of the hand between the wrist and the base of the fingers.

Palmas   Hand clapping to accentuate Rhythm for dancing.

Palm Down   Wrist Twist until Palm is facing down. Converse of Palm Up.

Palm Front   The Hand Hold Adjudicated in International Standard Coupledance Competitions. Useful in describing the man's left hand prescribed position while holding his lady's right hand in a Closed Position. Similar to Fore Hand.

Palm Inward   Arm high Wrist Twist until Palm is Facing Inward, toward one's head. Converse of Palm Outward.

Palm Outward   Arm high Wrist Twist until Palm is Facing Outward, away from one's body. Converse of Palm Inward.

Palm to Palm   Hand interaction between partners, such as a way of holding hands or patty-caking.

Palm Up   Hand Wrist Twist until Palm is facing up. Converse of Palm Down.

Partner   A term for one of a Couple, man or lady, who are dancing together.

Partner Combination   A term for dancing while connected with and touching one's Partner. Converse of Open Step.

Partner Heights   Extreme differences, whether the lady is taller than man or visa-versa, may create problems with their Turns and Spins; problems that usually can be adjusted for, to an extent.

Partner Outside on Left   Same as Sidecar Position.

Pas de Basque   A three step Movement or Figure, consisting of a side step followed by a quick and light Crossing Step, high on the Ball of the foot and return to the first foot. The Crossing Step may be taken in front or in back. Normally associated with the Waltz Rhythm.

Paso Doble Hold   Same as Loose Closed Position except, instead of holding lady at her side, man grasps lady's left upper arm with his right hand and Leads her in the crook of his right elbow at the lady's left elbow point.

Pass   With one set of hands joined, lady is led past the man, straight, without Turning.

Passing Feet   Feet passing each other without Closing Together.

Passing Pattern   With the man remaining near one spot, the lady dances about him in a Pattern.

Pat   Lighter than a Tap but harder than a Touch, the toe, Ball, heel, or Flat of foot contacts the floor without a Change of Weight.

Patch   Partners retain body contact at their waists.

Pattern   A routine-section, a sequence of Figures grouped into a unified design.

Pattern Dancing   Various types of Choreographed dancing.

Pause   An in-action, a momentary Hold, a break where one ceases to dance for a time.

Peekaboo   The playful Action of glancing quickly or of peering furtively at one's partner.

Pencil Turns   Rapid Toe Spins, normally by the Lady, In Place or slightly traveling, led by a Cup and Pin Hold. On Balls with feet close together, a Change of Weight with each Half Turn.

Pendulum Motion   Pendulous Swinging Movements of one's Lower Body, accelerating then reversing. Converse of Metronomic Motion.

Performing Surface   The surface area Performed upon, such as the dancefloor, rug, mat, grass, ground, etc.

Phrase   As used in dance Choreography, Phrase refers to recognition of the individual segments of musical structure. Dance Choreography will normally recognize and respond to the musical Phrases by structuring the Figures to be executed into segments of two, four or eight Bars. See Music Phrase.

Pickup Notes   A term counting the notes of music prior to the first Step of the dance.

Picture Figure   A dance Figure in which an attractive Line or pose is created by the bodies, often held for one or more Counts.

Pitch Point   Upon the Lead in a Closed Position, like a seesaw in Balance, one's (usually the Man's) Center of Balance is readied to Move instantly Forward at the Beat, before his foot Movement.

Pittypatter Turns   Forward Running, tightly Circling with quick, tiny Steps on Balls of feet. Could be Partner-led by Halo Lead or by Illusion.

Pivot   Couple Rotation is one Full Turn in two slow Steps, danced Clockwise, and is normally danced Traveling, rarely in one Spot. May regress or progress, in line or curved, or be danced stationary, in place. Executed in a tightly Closed Contrabody Position with CBM; right foot remains in front of left foot for both while Pivoting, as in Fifth Position Extended. Forward right Steps between Partner's feet. Heights are lowered so that knees interlock. Thighs remain locked. Free Legs alternate from either Forward or Backward. Partners Swivel Half Turns alternately on the Ball-Heel then Heel-Ball of the feet, or visa-versa. Heads remain strongly Closed. Lead is traded, the Partner with back to their Line of Dance Leads (powers) that Impetus, i.e., the Partner that Steps Backward Leans Backward.

Pivot Half   Swiveling one Step, Couple Rotation is a Half Turn Clockwise, and is always danced traveling, never in one Spot. In a Closed Contrabody Position, right foot remains in front of left foot for both during Pivot Half. Heights are lowered so that knees interlock. Free Legs are Moved from either Forward or Backward, danced either Ball-Heel or Heel-Ball of the Foot. See Pivot, Singular-Pivot and Reverse Pivot Half.

Pivoting Action   A Turn upon the Ball of the foot, with the Free Leg NOT held in CBMP, e.g., the lady's Action on step two of a Spin Turn.

Pivot Turn   A Swiveling or Spiraling Movement in one Step, right or left, on the Ball of one's Supporting Foot. A Pivot Right Turns one's body Clockwise, while a Pivot Left Turns one's body Counter-Clockwise. A Pivot Turn is either a Swiveling Outward Away from one's other foot, or a Spiraling Inward toward one's other foot, with one's Turn taken after a Forward or Backward Movement, respectively. One's Weight is held upon one foot during the Swivel or Spiral portion, i.e., most of one's rotation occurs as one's Weight leaves the Supporting Foot. See Spiral Hook, Figure Four Position, Singular Pivot, and Chaine.

Place   The Action of Placing one's feet; the Stepping, rather than Sliding, by raising one's foot or feet from the dancefloor, as when Walking. Or, the correct Placing of the dancer's legs, arms, Torso, and head, in any of the dance Positions.

Plant the Foot   Usually refers to the lady's error of early Changing her Weight to her Opposite foot during a Couple Rotation, before her Leader Weight Changes, thereby braking his intended amount of Turn.

Pointing   Refers to the Alignment of the feet when different from the direction the body is Facing or moving.

Poise   A dance stance with stable Balance; or, the Pitch Point and/or Placement of one's body Weight in relation to one's feet and arms; or, correct Posture, composure and/or dignity of manner.

Popcorn   Two Beats long, Timing is *Slow Slow*. Executed Bent-Kneed, with Weight on both Balls of feet, and with feet some 12 inches apart. Only one knee is rolled at a time, and both Balls are kept In Place. Either knee is rolled Forward then Outward in a half circle then returned Home to center, to Neutral Position. See Knee Pop.

Port de Bras   The graceful carriage of one's arms from one Position to another.

Pose   A bodily Position, posture or attitude assumed and/or held for a length of time.

Position   Refers to the placement of a couple relative to each other.

Posterior Protrusion   A dance term pertaining to both Man and Lady. Buttocks-in is the required Posture for the majority of dances. Posterior Protrusion is a derogatory appearance, but is probably acceptable in other's eyes for certain dances.

Power Lead   A Movement where the man Leads the lady with much energy, possibly from a Backward Step or a Press Line. The Man Strides Out and initially Leads the lady with Strong Forward energy.

Prance   A Forward Walking Step, to proudly swagger on the Balls of the feet with knees being lifted very high.

Preparation   An introductory Action or Movement, such as an Open Out, or a Tuck, or presenting a hand. Or an initial Step, preparing for a Turn or Change of Position. Or in Preparation for a specific Step, a sudden Change of Direction, or carriage of the body, one's bearing. See Push Off and Compression.

Press   The Opposite of being elevated upon one's toes, pushing with steady Force, Pressing one Ball of foot "into the floor". Used for faster Spinning in various Swings. Pressure exerted into the floor raises one's body up and/or Outward. By Spreading Your Toes so that they point up and off the floor, one can feel the Ball Pressing into the floor. Conversely, the Action of Gripping the Floor by Tightening the Toes is generally unwanted, since this Lowers the heel and relocates one's Center of Balance Backward. Synonymous with Compression.

Press Line   A body (and foot) Position, attained by Forward Pressing the Ball of the Free Foot into the floor with light pressure (heel off the floor). The Supporting Foot is flat on the floor in an Open Position behind the Pressing foot. The body and Supporting Foot are normally turned out 1/8 relative to the knee of the pressing leg with a slight forward Poise of the body. Arm positions vary dramatically depending upon the dancer and/or Choreographer.

Pretzel Position   In Banjo Position except for Hand Hold. Right to left and left to right hands are joined, and all hands are at Waist Level. Partner's facing feet are to one's right. Both partner's left arm is behind their own back, while the right arm is stretched across their (side by side) partner's front. Similar to Hammerlock and Tamara Positions.

Primary Downbeat   A certain complexity in dancing to musical Timing. There could be two Primary Downbeats in dancing certain songs, a **Major Primary Downbeat** and a **Minor Primary Downbeat**. Both are also the **One Beat**. For example, take the first two Measures of a song in 4/4 Time, Stepped *1&2&3&4&, 5&6&7&8&*:   All eight numerals are Downbeats, (while all eight ampersands are Upbeats.) Numeral *1* is the **One Beat**, the **Major Primary Downbeat**. Numeral *5* is also a **One Beat**, but it is the **Minor Primary Downbeat**. Most all American dances, and some International dances, are danced Breaking on the One Beat.

Progressive   The continuation of Forward Movement in a general direction.

Progressive Rotation   A Movement or Figure that both Progresses and Rotates, such as with Pivots, Chaines and Viennese Turns.

Projection   An Extension of one's body and/or personality to a higher level of Performance, with regards to one's Posture, Position, and/or Movement. See Elegance of Movement, Free Hand, Style and Technique.

Promenade Position   Same as Semi-Closed Position, except Weight is upon Inside Feet.

Pronate   A momentary Flat-Footed Position; or, Outer to Inner foot rotation. The foot is rolled Inwards so that only the inner edge is momentarily Pressed to the floor, and one's instep is tilted lower than the outer edge. Over-Pronating is useful for certain Movements in Latin and Rhythm types of dancing. Opposite of Supinate.

Proud Chin   Raising the head just enough for good appearance, but one needn't be viewing the ceiling. Conversely, one should almost never be viewing downward, because such a look is rarely appealing.

Proud Stance   Pertaining to a Taut appearance, where the body carriage is high. One holds the hips Well Forward with the chest high and Proud, at times arching the back.

Pull Back   An Action of the hip and Knee, causing Backward Movement.

Purist   One who studiously avoids deviating from precisely described dancing instructions. Term may either be derogatory or a compliment. See Traditional Dance Doctrine.

Quality   A dancer's term for the inherent and essential characteristic or distinctive property of a Figure or Pattern; its distinguishing flavor or color.

Quarter Turn   A ninety degrees total Change of Direction, either Right or Left, Forward or Backward, and either singular or Couple Rotating.

Quiver   A Quick Swiveling Action of the hips, left to right Contrabody and back. Normally with heel at toe, Foot Position #5. See Twist.

Rag Doll   A Quick head Movement Performed by the lady during an Outside Turn. The lady whips her head circularly Clockwise as the man's wrist passes over her face. With movement from her neck only, she begins by tipping her head to her right then quickly tips her head way back, then up. In tipping her head to her right, she attempts to put her ear to her shoulder, not to just turn her head.

Raised Turn   A Turn on the forward part of the Ball of foot, more toward the big toe. A less common method than Flat Turning.

Range   The relative extent of dance Movement; the distance between two extremes of the Movement.

Reclining Lady   A Picture-Figure of at least one Measure long. May begin in Skaters Position. Partners remain Side-by-Side throughout. **Man** Head Loops then releases clasped left hands, laying lady's left arm about his own neck. Man Leads lady to him with his right hand at her lower waist. Man widely spreads his legs and deeply Knee-Bends his left knee, with his right leg straight and with Left Side Stretch. Man views lady's face and Extends his Left arm. Caution: Avoid pressing lady's rib-cage; lightly press below bottom rib, at her hip. **Lady**, with her left foot remaining parallel against man's right foot, **Reclines** thusly: Lady lays sideward to her left, along and against man's right leg and side, holding man's right hand safely low. With extensive Left Side Stretch, lady views ceiling and raises and spreads her right knee, placing sole of her right foot against her inner left calf.

Recover   The Movement of returning Weight to the Free Foot, without moving it from its last position of contact with the floor.

Rejuvenate   A **cutie flick of the lady's head**: With the Couple in a Loose Closed Position, except with the lady relaxed in Neutral Position, the lady awaits Rejuvenation with her own left hand held against the back and neck of her own head. The man gently and momentarily Pulses against or below her left wing with his right hand. **His pressing automatically flicks her head** Backwards, with her left hand catching it. Action is repeated in Sequence, usually twice.

Repertoire   The stock of Steps and/or Figures of a certain dance that the Man knows and is well prepared to Lead and/or Perform.

Resistance   Negative, tending to oppose, retard or work against Movement or Lead; or positive **Cooperative-Resistance** through Single-Hands contact or All-Hands-in-Hand, to provide the necessary **Spring Action** for coordinated Leading and Following.

Reverse Indian Position   In Trail, with either lady or man in front, with Matching Hands joined. Each hand of the one behind has been placed **behind the hips** of the one in front.

Reverse Left Position   Partners Face same direction, Side-by-Side with lady on man's left, with their arms crossed behind their backs, and with man's crossed arm underneath. Partner's right to right and left to left hands are joined. Both right hands are held at man's right hip, and both left hands are at lady's left hip.

Reverse Line of Dance   Refers to the dance area Clockwise about the dancefloor, in reverse to flow of traffic. An imaginary line around the room perimeter in reverse to that which dancers follow; or, the direction in Reverse to that which the man usually is dancing, i.e., the direction Opposite to that which the dance normally flows. See Line of Dance.

Reverse Right Position   Partners Face same direction, Side-by-Side with lady on man's right, with their arms crossed behind their backs, and with man's crossed arm on top. Partner's right to right and left to left hands are joined. Both right hands are held at lady's right hip, and both left hands are at man's left hip.

Reverse Turn   A Counter Clockwise Turn to the left. Opposite of Natural Turn.

Rhythm   This term usually refers to the Accented Beats of the music which occur regularly and give character to the music. Although the Timing of several pieces of music may be identical, it is the Rhythm that gives the music an entirely different character, which the dancer will attempt to express in his/her dancing.

Rhythm Break   Normally a contrasting variation in Rhythm between dance Patterns, possibly with Choreographed Steps to match. See Link.

Rhythm Dance   This term may refer to a dance that does not adhere strictly to a single Rhythm, thus requiring the dancers to more carefully listen and dance to the changing Beat and/or to the melody.

Right Angles   Refers to straight arm positions while in a Facing Position, when one arm is pointed Forward while the other arm points Backward and high overhead.

Right Arm Lead   The Man's right arm is his primary means for Leading the lady in most dances. When dancing in a Closed Position, his lady lightly rests her left elbow upon his right elbow in order to better sense his Lead. No Lead is supposed to come from his left hand when in a Closed Position.

Right Banderillas Hold   In Banjo Position except right hips touch, the man's right elbow is slightly lowered and his left arm is slightly raised.

Right Face   To Natural Turn or Face or move to the Right, in a Clockwise direction.

Right Shadow Position   Partners Face the same direction with the man slightly to her right side and behind the lady.

Rim Partner   As a Couple, the Rim Partner is momentarily the outer person of a wheel-like Movement or Figure; the one who must take Stride Out Steps, and the one that momentarily Leads, usually Forward. Opposite of Hub Partner.

Ripple   A dance Figure without foot Movement. Chin down then out then tummy out then back; "Down then up, punched in the stomach then kicked in the butt." Or, with legs straight and apart, lead with chest. See Side Body Waves and Shimmy.

RLR   An acronym for Right-Left-Right. Refers to Triple Movements or Steps such as Shuffles, Subtle Triples, Chasses, Double Steps, Coaster Steps, Anchor Steps, etc. See LRL.

Rocking Chair   Partners are in Chair Position with an added Rocking back and forth by the Couple.

Rocking Maneuver   Usually danced to two music Beats. One's Feet are Spread and kept In-Place. On the first Beat, full Weight is upon either Foot in any Direction, and is shifted to the Opposite Foot upon the second Beat. Similar to Rocking Steps.

Roll   A series of two or more Half-Turning Steps, Spirals and Swivels, which progress along the same line.

Roll Across   A Roll in three or four Steps, Man or Lady Changes Sides. From Side-by-Side in Half Open or Left Half Open Position, dancing Forward and looking in Turn direction, one Rolls Across with Inside Foot in front of partner a Full Turn, to the Opposite Left Half Open or Half Open Position, changing arms, as partner Chasses sideward in Opposite direction.

Roll In   Man or Lady Rolls In in three Steps. Begins in an Open or Left Open Position. Beginning with Inside Foot, the partner Rolling In rotates toward the hand joined, raising that joined hand onto one's shoulder before releasing. See Roll Out.

Rolling Cradle   From either Cradled or Left Cradled Position, the man transfers his lady Across his front to either Left Cradled or Cradled Position, right to left or left to right. There may be Couple Rotation but he does not individually rotate her. See Rolling Wrap.

Rolling Wrap   From either Wrapped or Left Wrapped Position, the man transfers his lady Across his front to either Left Wrapped or Wrapped Position, right to left or left to right. There may be Couple Rotation but he does not individually rotate her. See Rolling Cradle.

Roll Out   Beginning from a Wrapped, Cradled or a Neck Wrap Position, Man or Lady Rolls Out in three Steps. Beginning with Outside Foot and looking in Turn direction, the partner Rolls Away to a Hand-in-Hand Open Position. See Roll In.

Rolls   Circular motion of hips and head, left or right. Deep Into Knees, Movement begins Forward then Circles completely.

Rotate Under   Several Actions of Rotating Under either direction while retaining all four Hands or retaining a single pair of Hands, such as Dishrag, Duck, Alemande and Underarm. Usually only one partner Rotates Under the joined hands.

Routine   A series of dance Patterns, usually entailing an opening, high lights, a climax and a Tag.

Rules of Dance   There are "Official Rules" in order to dance "By-The-Book", such as principals, maxims, orders and decrees. See Purist.

Running   Any Figure which includes an extra Step, usually with Syncopation or all-Quick Timing and Passing Steps. In Round Dancing, *Running* often refers to a Figure or Pattern that rotates Clockwise, such as Running Finish, Running Hover to Semi Closed, Running Open Natural, Running Right Turn, and Running Spin. Conversely, "Quick" refers to a Figure or Pattern that Rotates Counter Clockwise.

Same Feet   Opposite of "Opposite", where both partners dance In Step using identical Footwork.

School Figure   A Basic Figure that is commonly taught in dance schools.

Scoop   A long Step, normally to the side, with the feeling of lowering and rising in the body, followed by the Trailing Foot Closing. Similar to Swoop, where feet do not Close.

Scoot   The Action of Sliding the Supporting Foot along the floor, normally Forward, followed by a Closing Step.

Scuff   A minute Forward Kick with one's heel swiping the floor, followed by a slight lift of the Free Foot.

Second Position   Astride, with feet a foot-length to shoulder-width apart. Weight upon one foot only, with the Free Foot sideward and completely Touching the floor.

Seguey   A succession of dances to a succession of Rhythm changes with varied melodies. See Medley.

Semi-Closed Position Informal   Weight is upon their Outside Feet, usually for readying to Step Thru with Inside Feet. May be Opened in a Vee as much as is Half Open Position. Man's left and lady's right hands remain clasped, and Inside hips are in contact. Lady's hip is normally behind man's.

Seminar   A dance meeting involving audience activity, presenting knowledge and developing talent. See Clinic.

Sequence   Delineating the order in which dance Figures, Actions or Movements are to be Performed.

Shadow-Enfold Position   With man in a Shadow Position, man clasps the back of both hands of the lady, at her wrists. The crook of his right arm rests at his lady's right shoulder, and their left arms are about her waist. All palms nearly overlap and face her solar-plexis. Man is prepared to spread her arms, her left then her right.

Shadow Position   The Position where partners are Facing the same direction, with the man slightly to her left side and behind the lady. Either clasping left hands or not touching.

Shake Hands Position   Partners Face and clasp right hands at Waist-Level. Their free hand positioning is variable. See Crossed Hands Hold.

Shake Left Hands   Same as Shake Hands Position except for hands.

Shape to Partner   With CBM, retaining shoulders parallel while Lower Body and/or feet are turned away from partner.

Sharp Step   A Stomping Movement. With a Change of Weight, one Steps Smartly, i.e., abruptly with noise.

Shimmy   Alternate flat rotation of one's left and right shoulders Forward and Backward, either rapidly or slowly. With knees together and Softened and with one's Lower Body isolated for no Movement, the Shimmy is Performed above the waist.

Shoulders Parallel   Both shoulders are spaced the same distance Apart from partner's opposite shoulders.

Shoulders Rolled Back   The desired Posture for the majority of dances, not hunched up or drooping. (1) Lower shoulders downward; (2) Roll shoulders Forward then up; (3) Continue rolling shoulders rearward then downward; (4) Retain result with shoulders positioned thus, rearward and relaxed.

Shoulders Square   Both shoulders are spaced the same distance Apart from partner's opposite shoulders, and also aligned perpendicular, not canted.

Shoulder to Shoulder Position   Partners are in a right shoulder to right shoulder Position. Shoulders touch. Partner's facing feet are Offset to their right. Positioning of arms and hands are various. Opposite to Left Shoulder to Shoulder Position.

Showcase   A formal Tango Dance Performance, usually lasting more than one day. See Demonstration.

Shrug   At least six Actions, left or right, rolling one or both shoulders in a circular motion Forwards or Backwards.

Shuffle   A foot is slid across the floor creating a dragging sound.

Side   To a partner's left or right; or toward a Free Foot; or an area to the dancer's Side.

Side Body Waves   The quivering one's body sidewards from head to toe, especially at the hips. Begins with torso in Neutral Position, then Center of Balance transfers from side to side, and whatever is to one side, all else is to the opposite side.

Sidecar Position   One's facing feet are Closed and to the right and Outside of partner's feet. Hand Holds are various or none. Shoulders may be either Parallel or Feathered, and hips either Hip to Hip or not. More explicit than Offset Facing Opposed Position, but less explicit than Facing Offset and Feathered Positions. Opposite of Banjo Position.

Side Jog   While dancing Forward or rearward, a Side Jog is a Step sideward, a veer, a swerve, a dog-leg sideways.

Side Rise   A Side Stretch accompanied by a slight Body Rise in the direction of dance. Possibly starting with a Side Step, a Rise is made upon same foot.

Side Step   A Step in line with the hips and Away from the Supporting Foot.

Side To Side   A Sideward motion in both directions, usually with the hips. Normally, it is the lady who Sweeps her hips from Side To Side in time with the music.

Side Turn   Stepping Sideward, left or right, then Turning upon the same foot, Clockwise or Counter Clockwise.

Side Walks   Left or right Movements Sideward, without Crossing feet or rotating body. *Side close side* Steps are taken onto Ball, then heel is lowered to take Weight.

Sideward   Free Foot is moved to either Side, Away from Supporting Foot, with or without Change of Weight. Or, referring to the direction to the side of the dancer.

Sideward Check   A Step to either Side, applying a braking action taken in that Line of Motion in Preparation to take a different Line of Motion.

Sideward Close   A Step to either Side, applying Weight, then another Step is made to bring feet together with a Change of Weight.

Sideward Hold   One Step to either Side, applying Weight, then a freeze is maintained, usually for one Beat.

Silhouette   Referring to the outlined illusion presented by the dancers, as viewed by the audience.

Single Hands   One hand from each partner clasped together. See Shake Hands Position and All Hands in Hand.

Single Spin   Spinning singularly a Full- or 3/4-Turn Clockwise or Counter Clockwise on one Ball of foot, usually in one Beat of music, then transferring Weight.

Sit Break   Normally begun from Left Open Facing Position and one Measure long, Sit Break is usually Performed by the Lady. One Sits with Weight centered over a single Bent Kneed Supporting Foot. The Free Leg is Stretched Forward, Pointing toe along the floor, as the Free Arm is raised overhead.

Skate   Progressive dance Movements, left and right, where body motion is as if on Skates. Rhythm Timing is *And Slow*. One drives Forward by use of the Trailing Foot, in order to Slide Forward on the Lead Foot. Corresponding Movements are usually danced in sequence. A Fast Floor is helpful.

Skid   After being driven Forward by powering the Trailing Foot, and with the lead toe-in and its heel-out, one Skids to a stop upon the Lead Foot outer edge and Ball, especially with a Slow Floor.

Skim   To progress while lightly Sliding one's foot along the floor, or to move lightly over the dancefloor. Similar to Sweep.

Skip   A Step followed by a progressive Hop on the same foot, leaving the floor. This can be repeated using alternate Footwork.

Slide   An Action of moving a foot, in which the foot maintains contact with the floor.

Slow   Relative to how long one's Weight is upon the foot, a **Slow Step** is often approximately the time of an average Walking Step, some 90 to 120 even Steps per Minute. A notation **Slow Step** takes twice the time of a *Quick* Step. *Slow* can be the length of time in Movement of a very Slow funeral March. *Slow* can be a Dirge, as *Slow* as 50 Steps per Minute. One *Slow* Step danced usually equals two music Beats in 4/4 Time, or one Beat in 2/4 Time. *Slow* Rhythm is danced to a Tempo Slower than about 40 MPM.

Slow Floor   Referring to a Dancefloor too sticky for easy Coupledancing. See Fast Floor.

Smartly   An abrupt, brisk, Quick and/or emphatic Action or Movement. See Sharply, Well and Clean.

Smile   For certain Tango dances, one may continually Smile when just wanting to look good while dancing. For other Tangos, (International,) Smiling is forbidden.

Smooth Dances   Refers to Rhythm Dancing that progresses around Line of Dance, such as the International Tango. See Travel Dancing.

Smoothness   The term used to describe the ease of Movement and Control with which the dancer Performs.

Snap Turn   Refers to that certain head Movement while Spotting, where one's head is Snap Turned at the last possible moment as the body Turns.

Social Dancing   The term used to loosely describe recreational, non-competitive Social Dancing. Almost always danced Free Style.

Soften   A lessened degree of muscle tautness.

Sombrero Position   Partners Facing Opposite directions, with the arms on the same side as adjacent hips held around the partner's waist, Free Arms extended upward and curving with hands above the head. Similar to Hip to Hip Position.

Spacing Between Couples   Spacing for the look and/or for necessity when dancing. It is the man's responsibility, with his lady's cooperation, to space themselves Well clear of other dancing couples during their dance. Also, if dancing on a very crowded floor, both need to aid each other to avoid touching other couples.

Spaghettis   Complex armwork that accomplish various poses while Swing Dancing, such as Wrapped, Cradled, Pretzel, Tamara, Hammerlock, and Double Face Loop.

Spanish Line   Any pose which utilizes the arm positions of Paso Doble or Flamenco dancing. A Proud Stance with Toned arms.

Spin   A fast Turning Action, Single Spinning Solo on Ball of foot, or partners Couple Rotating together. See Swivel, Spiral and Double Spin.

Spiral   Performed Solo, one's Spiral occurs after an initial Forward Step, then the Free Leg wraps around the Supporting Leg. One Turns, on the Ball of one foot, in the Opposite direction of the Forward Foot, i.e., Turning toward one's other foot. Dancer Spirals a Half- to a Full-Turn, until thighs cross or until the Free Foot crosses over and forms a Spiral around this Supporting Foot. One's Free Toe may remain In Place Touching the floor, in front of and crossing against the Supporting Leg. Initially Stepping Forward to Spiral, it is helpful to first Point that toe slightly in the Opposite direction of intended Turning. See Figure Four.

Split Measures   Incorporating half-Measures in the Swing Dance Pattern.

Split Ronde   Performed either in Loose Closed or Banjo Position with Same Feet. Man Pauses as the lady Changes Feet. Simultaneously, each partner begins their Ronde with Feet Together. Both lower then Backward Ronde Counter Clockwise, each with their Left leg, while Couple Rotating approximately a Half Turn Counter Clockwise.

Spot Dancing   Where a limited floor area is utilized throughout the dance; i.e., dancing without Progressing around the floor. Opposite of Travel Dancing.

Spotting   An Action while Quickly Turning, where one's head is the last to leave the "Spot" and the first to arrive toward the "Spot" as one's body completes the Turn. Begins Facing front with eyes focused on one particular "Spot" with a Fixed Stare. One's eyes remain fixed on that "Spot", looking over one's shoulder as the body begins to Turn Away from the "Spot". The Head is Snap Turned at the last possible moment in the Turn of the Body, with chin laid from shoulder-to-shoulder, so as to quickly refocus upon that same "Spot". Spotting should provide at least 60 degrees of view.

Spot Turn   A Turn without progression. Normally taken as a Solo Turn.

Spring Action   Through Single Hands contact for Leading and Following, Equal and Opposite cooperative resistance of both partners is required to provide the necessary Spring for coordinated dancing. Similar to Pulse and Accordion.

Staccato Action   An Action that is rapid, faster than the normal rhythmic *Quick*, involving head, body or foot Movement.

Stamp   An Action of noisily driving the Free Foot flat at the floor without a Change of Weight, followed by a rebounding leg retraction. The Stamp is normally next to one's Supporting Foot, and strikes harder than a Tap or a Pat. Similar to a Heel Strike. Also similar to a Stomp, which has a Change of Weight.

Stance   The prescribed, characteristic leg and/or body Position, look or image, that one assumes or moves to or strives for, while dancing a particular Style of dance. Often there is a different Stance characteristic for that dance.

Standard Dances   This term refers to the International Style Rhythms of Waltz, Tango, Viennese Waltz, Foxtrot, and Quickstep. These dances are danced almost exclusively in a Closed Position.

Star Position   Partners Face Opposite directions and to the side of the other, with Inside Hands joined palm-to-palm at the lady's Eye-Level, with elbows nearly touching. Right hips are touching and Free Arms are behind backs.

Starting Position   The Stance required to begin a dance, Pattern, Figure, Movement, or Action. Opposite of Ending Position.

Stationary   Dancing without traveling or not even moving.

Statue of Liberty Position   The lady's hand Position, in Preparation for Outside Spin Figures such as her Pencil Turns, Toe Spins, and PittyPatter Turns. She Prepares for her Halo Lead by cupping her fingers of one hand overhead, with its heel down, for the man to lightly Lead her with a Cup and Pin Hold. Hense, the Statue of Liberty holding her torch.

Steeple Position   Usually achieved beginning in Butterfly Position then rotating in opposition. All hands normally remain clasped. Partners face Away from each other, close, forming a narrow vee, not quite Back To Back. For a Right-Steeple, man's left and lady's right hands are clasped and held over their heads, either straight up or formed in an arch. Their other hands are clasped and held straight down, or else man's right and lady's left elbows are hooked together.

Step   A compound Movement involving a Change of Weight from the Supporting Foot to the Free or Moving Foot. A Step has a time value and is not completed until ready to commence another Step. A Step is also the distance covered by one motion of the leg.

Step and Close   Consists of two Steps; Rhythm Timing varies. First a Step, then Movement of one's Free Foot next to and against the Supporting Foot, with a Change of Weight.

Step and Drag   Consists of a Step then an Action; Rhythm Timing is *Slow Slow*. First a Step, then the Free-Foot is Drawn Slowly to Closing with one's Supporting Foot, without a Change of Weight.

Step Close Turn   Various Movements left or right, Forward or Backward or Sideward, Turning Clockwise or Counter Clockwise. Three Steps, Closing on the second and Changing Direction on the third.

Step Kick   A Single Step followed by a minute Forward Flick from the knee by the Opposite foot, grazing the floor. See Kick Step.

Step Length   The faster the Rhythm the shorter the Step; the slower the Rhythm the more Striding and Gliding the Step.

Step Pattern   An arrangement of dance Locomotor Movements into a Choreographed Pattern.

Step Sequence   A series of dance Steps and/or Rhythm Timings, usually repetitious.

Step Swing   A person Steps (usually) Forward, then Performs a Swing Foot (usually) Crossward.

Stomp   An Action of noisily Driving the Free Foot flat at the floor, followed by a transfer of Weight. One's Weight ends either evenly distributed upon both feet or all upon the Stomped foot. The Stomp is normally next to one's Supporting Foot. Similar to Stamp, which has no Weight Change.

Stoop   The Action of Bending Forward from the waist or middle of the back; or to carry head and shoulders Bent Forward.

Stork Position   Standing upon one foot with the Free Foot raised beside the knee of the Supporting Foot, with the Toe pointed toward the floor. Same as Knee Up Position.

Straight Arm   With elbow locked straight. See Braced Arm.

Straight Hands   Any Hold with all hands clasped left-to-right and right-to-left, and with all arms uncrossed. Converse of Crossed Hands Hold.

Straight Kneed   Knees straight as when walking.

Straight Line   Dancing with no Turning of the Line of Dance, or with no Couple Rotation.

Street Dancer   One who dances with individualized Styling and who has learned their dancing through their own and their peer's experience, but not by formal training. One who successfully executes emotionally the dance without precisely knowing how it was accomplished, i.e., one who feels the feeling of each particular dance but is mainly ignorant of its exact Footwork. Primarily by Muscle Memory, one who memorizes bodily Movements, Figures, or Patterns by repetitive practice, instead of learning by Mechanics Memory. The Lady Street Dancer Follows Well by Subconscious Dancing the Movement, Figure, or Pattern, as long as she does not try to Think It Thru. Converse of Schooled Dancer.

Stretch   The Action of lengthening, widening, elongating, or distending one's Step or bodily parts; such as, to Extend a limb or muscle to its full length; or, to cause to Extend one's legs Across a given space; or, to reach out, Extend oneself with elasticity; or, to make Taut or tighten one's muscles; or, to strain with a Step or Movement. A Stretch example is the elongating one side of the body in order to create body shaping (Sway) in the Opposite direction.

Strict Tempo   The term applied to dance music which consistently adheres to a Tempo that is within the range that is specified for the Rhythm being danced.

Stride   Dancing with Stretched Steps, Using the Floor. A Stride is taking a lengthy Step to a Slow Beat at a low height without pause. Strode Forward, Backward, Sideward, Crossward or Diagonally with learned bodily Control, a Stride handles nicely any extensively Slow Time.

Structured   The disciplined Positioning and arrangement of one's whole body in a specified manner. A dancer who studiously avoids deviating from precisely described dancing instructions. As a purist, the insistance upon Traditional Dance Doctrines, perhaps stiffly but precisely Stepping as taught. Term may be either derogatory or a compliment.

Styling   The appearance and Technique of a couple in motion, i.e, that certain look that adds character to the dancers. By projecting one's own individual interpretations, Styling is a distinctive manner of expressing the dance, with regards to Positions and Movements accompanying the actual Step placement. Styling is a personal mode, a fashion or way of Performing which endows dance Movements with a particular character or mood.

Subconscious Dancing   Dancing with one's mind busy elsewhere, other than on one's exact Footwork; i.e., being not wholly conscious of one's own bodily Movements and/or Lead. Compare against Think It Thru. See Street Dancer and Muscle Memory.

Supinate   A momentary high-arched foot position or an Inner to Outer foot rotation. To Supinate is to roll one's foot onto its Outer Edge, momentarily pressed against the floor, with one's Instep tilted higher than this Outer Edge. Over-Supination is almost always considered poor Floorcraft Technique. Opposite of Pronate.

Support   Usually refers to the man's stabilizing his lady and visa-versa. Without hanging-on, partners Balance each other.

Supporting Foot/Leg   The appendage bearing the majority of one's Weight, bearing one's Center of Balance. The weighted or standing foot/leg/knee. Opposite of Free Foot.

Sway   There are two types of Sway: (1) Same as a Side Stretch, which is a Sideward Upper Body inclination toward the side of the moving foot; this Sway is normally used in Turning or Curving Figures, or for starting or stopping, or while executing CBM. A Side Stretch is also used in non-moving Picture Figures such as a Sway Line, in which the Sway inclines the body toward the Free Foot. (2) A Sideward full body inclination; Undulating Sideward with a hip leading, immediately followed by the shoulder.

Sway Position   Supporting Leg has a Flexed or Softened Knee, and one side of the body is Stretched; the other leg is extended Sideward and Pointed. Otherwise, positions of partners is various. See Side Stretch.

Sway To and Fro   A fore and aft Movement, a Forward and Backward body inclination; undulating with one's Upper Body, inclining Away from the Movement direction of one's Lower Body.

Swing   The pendulum-like Swinging Action of one's leg from the hip, resulting from the continuation of body Movement.

Swing Time   Describes the amount of time one's foot spends off the dancefloor while simply Forward Walking. While Walking, (not dancing, where one Skims with their feet,) one Shuffles less to increase their Swing Time.

Swipe   A dance Movement as in Brushing. Long, heavy, Cross Body sweeping or stroking the foot along or across the floor. See Scuff.

Switch   A quick change in Facing Position, accomplished by a Swivel on the Supporting Foot and transferring Weight to the Free Foot. The amount of Turn in a Switch will vary, and may encompass from 1/4 to 1/2 Facing change, depending upon the preceding Figure or relative positions of the couple.

Swivel Step   Turning Outward, Away from one's Free Foot, the dancer Swivels In Place a Quarter to Half-Turn on Ball, then Steps In Place with the Free Foot, changing Weight.

Swivet   With Weight upon both feet and one foot apart, a 45 degree Swivet is Turned on the Ball of one foot and on the heel of the other, ending with Weight on the Forward heel and Trailing toe.

Swoop   With a strong lowering Action, a long Step to the side or to a diagonal. Feet do not Close after Swooping. Similar to Scoop, where Trailing Foot Closes.

Syllabus   A grouping of pertinent educational information, about the teachers and material being taught at a weekend/festival/convention/etc.

Synchronization   Partners dancing together in Unison, in time with each other. Primarily, the lady Synchronizes to her leader's Rhythm.

Syncopation   An accenting of unexpected Beats. A Variation from the standard Timing of a particular Rhythm, such as by dividing particular Beats into several parts, possibly with differing lengths. Rearranging of the metered Beat, such as by first Stepping on the `And' Count, then Kick-Ball-Changing or the like, to come into Step with the regular Count.

Tacking   Dancing a Zig-Zag course. Dancing where Tacking occurs is usually International Standard or Modern and Smooth. For instance in the Slow Foxtrot, the Three Step is supposed to be danced heading toward Line of Dance and Wall, while the next Figure danced should be Tacking, i.e., heading Line of Dance and Center.

Tamara Position   In Banjo Position except for hand hold. Right to left and left to right hands are joined. One set of joined hands are at Waist-Level, while the other set is raised with curved arms forming a Window through which partners view each other. One partner's left arm is behind their back while their right arm is held high. Similar to Pretzel and Hammerlock Positions.

Tandem Position   One partner is directly in front of the other and Facing the same Direction. Each of follower's Matched Hands is held upon each of the leader's shoulders. Danced upon either Opposing or Same Feet.

Tap   The Action of Touching the floor with the Free Foot, Tapping one's toe, Ball, heel, or Flat-of-foot. Striking the floor without a Change of Weight; Striking lighter than a Stamp but harder than a Pat. Tap may be Forward, Rearward, Sideward, Diagonal, or Crossward. Less explicit than Dot.

Tempo   A measure of the rate of speed of the music, at which body Movement occurs and at which music is played, normally in terms of Measures per Minute (MPM). May also be measured in the number of Beats per minute (BPM - Metronome beat). In Round Dancing, although an incorrect use of the term, Tempo often refers to the RPM (revolutions per minute) at which a dance's Choreographer recommends that the record should be played. Tempo expresses the mood of the music and dance. See Strict Tempo, Time of Music and Time Signature.

Tether   Restrained by various hand holds, a runaround Pattern that confines the lady as she Circles around the man. Man is the Hub while the lady is the Rim.

The Moves   A general, overall way of referring to specific Figures, Patterns or Steps.

Think It Thru   Dancing by mental exercise, the thoughtful and rational plotting out of dance Steps, Movements, Figures, and Patterns. One means of learning the dance. Compare against Subconscious Dancing.

Third Position   Toes are slightly turned Outward, with heel to instep or Ball, perhaps not quite touching, and with Weight upon one foot only.

Third Position Extended   Identical to Third Position except feet are definitely apart, with heel pointing to instep.

Thru   A Step with the Inside Foot between the partners.

Thumb Against Thumb   A Closed Position Stance where the man clasps his lady's right hand in his left, with Thumbs in contact vertically and retained at her Eye-Level. Neither Thumb protrudes above the other, resulting in a void inside palm-to-palm. Argumentive and bothersome to many dancers, this practice has been dropped.

Tighten the Lightbulb   Arm high wrist rotation; right hand Inward, left hand Outward. Opposite of Loosen the Lightbulb.

Tilt   To lean or slant the body Out of Balance.

Time of Music   Determined by the number of Beats occurring in each musical Measure. Closely related to Timing.

Time or Time Signature   The number and kind of Beats in each Measure of music. Designated by the musical signature, e.g. the Time Signature of Waltz is 3/4, meaning that there are three quarter notes in each Measure, and the Time Signature for Foxtrot, Swing and Cha Cha is 4/4 Time.

Timing   Adherence of the Movement to the Beat of the music. Dealing with the element of Time, the Beats and Steps taken per Measure of music, with possible Beat Accents. The Synchronized Weight transference in Stepping together in Unison to the Metered Beat. See Cadence and Tempo.

Tips   Forward, Diagonal, Sideward and/or Backward Off-Balance head Actions. Tips are from the neck, with only the head displaced without displacing the torso. Similar to Tilt.

Tip-Toe   Walking stealthily or quietly upon Tip-Toe, with one's Weight on Balls of foot.

Toe   Refers to the tips, the inner-toe, outer-toe, or to the bottom-side of one's Toes. "Toe" does not refer to the Ball of foot. See Tip of Shoe.

Toe Multiple Spins   A rotating Figure usually Performed by the lady. Skillfully and speedily rotating with feet together, transferring Weight from one Ball of foot to the other and back again. Her Balance is supported by the man's hand directing with skill over her head. There is either minimum or quite a bit of travel, set according to the man's Halo Lead. See Toe Spin.

Toe-Out   The Action of Turning one heel Inward. An example is where the Free Toe is Turned Outward as in a Swivel Walk Figure.

Toe Spin   A Turn upon the Ball of one foot, in which the body Weight is kept slightly more Forward than on a normal Spin. This technique is used for example by the lady on Steps five and six of a telespin. See Pencil Turns.

Toe to Toe Position   A Facing Feet Position. Distance Apart varies and hand holds are various or none. Less explicit than Facing Position.

Toe Touch   The Free Foot Toe Touches the floor in a given direction without Weight applied. More explicit than Touch. Less explicit than Toe Tap.

Together   Movement toward partner, or Stepping to Close with Supporting Foot. Opposite of Away.

Tone   Usually in reference to the lady's arms having sufficient Tone, just enough stiffness applied by which her man is allowed to Lead her. Another meaning is to soften the man's Lead.

Top Line   The Line created by the head, neck, shoulders, arms, hands and back, usually in dance position. Also see Back Line and Frame.

Torque   The effort to Twist the Torso or a body extremity.

Torso   The trunk of the body. Also see Base, Top Line and Back Line.

Touch   An Action in which the Toe, Ball, heel, or Flat of the Free Foot is lightly Touched to the floor, where specified in relation to one's Supporting Foot, and with no Weight applied.

Touch Hold   An Action In Place, Touching where indicated with no Weight applied, then maintaining Position usually for one Beat. Same as Touch except Held. See Hesitation.

Touch Thru　From Semi-Closed or Promenade Positions, one or both partners Cross In Front Touch Thru with their Inside Foot without Weight applied. Similar to Step Thru.

Tracking　The placement of a foot on a line directly in front of or directly behind the preceding Step.

Traditional Dance Doctrine　In order to observe, a dancer must studiously avoid deviating from precisely described dancing instructions. This insures conformity to a strict Standard. See Structured.

Trail　Tagging separately in Tandem Behind one's partner. See Indian Position and Open Step.

Trail/Trailing Foot/Hand　Usually refers to the man's right and the lady's left. Opposite of the Lead Foot/Hand.

Transition　An adjustment in dancing, to Change from Opposing to Same Footwork or visa-versa. Normally accomplished by a Count on which either the man or the lady will not take a Step while the other person does take a Step. Similar to Change Feet.

Traveling　Any Figure or Pattern that continues to progress, normally with the addition of one or more Steps.

Triple Rhythm Unit　Not normally considered Syncopation, the three Beats in two Counts of music.

Triples　Three Changes of Weight to two Beats of music, Forward, Backward or Diagonal, with feet usually in Third Position. See Chasse.

Tumble Action　The Movement of quickly lowering from an elevated position on to a small left-turning Forward Step, Checking the Forward Movement.

Turkish Towel Position　Man is Positioned in the lady's Varsouvienne Position. Partners Face same direction, with the lady Shadowing the man on her right. They clasp and spread Matching Hands behind the man at Shoulder-Level or at Waist-Level, or at a mixture of the two.

Turn　A circular Change in Direction the dancer is Facing, measured by the Direction of one's feet in 1/8 increments. The amount of Body Turn is specified only when different from feet. All Turns originate from the Solar Plexus, the Center of Balance. One's Center of Balance, not one's Foot, Moves instantly On the Beat, which at first rotates slightly in the Opposite direction of the Turn. This Twist in the Torso, this Torque, gathers the necessary momentum to initiate the Turn. For one's Center of Balance to reverse and begin rotating in the direction of the Turn, the head Twists first and then one's shoulders follow. Always look in the direction of your Turn. The outer, rim shoulder rotates Forward, as the inner, hub shoulder moves rearward. Upon Turning, there may be a slight dip in the hub shoulder with a slight lift in the rim shoulder. See Direction, Amount of Turn, Couple Rotation, Foot Rotation, Body Turns Less and Body Completes Turn.

Turn Around   To reverse Direction of Dance by rotating the body(s) CW or CCW between 90 and 270 degrees, singular or Couple Rotating, either Forward or Back, and either traveling or spot. Similar to Half Turn.

Turn Close   A singular Upper Body rotation that causes one's Free Foot to Close against the Supporting Foot, then with a Change of Weight.

Turn Face Close   In three Steps, Turn Inward to face partner, Step In Place and Close.

Turn In/Out   A Solo circular Movement to face toward partner or to face Away from partner.

Turn Under   From a Facing Position, the man Turns the lady to her left for a Half Turn. By first raising her right hand, he Leads her hand towards him. He invites lady to Turn by Leading her raised hand diagonally up across her face. Partner's joined hands pass IN-between them. Lady Turns under her own arm. Partners usually Change Places. Similar to Reverse Turn. Opposite of Outside Turn.

Twirl   A progressive Full Turn by the lady under joined hands, or to Spin or rotate the body briskly.

Twist   To Turn the Upper Body to a new Facing Direction without turning the feet or taking a Step. Also a Swivel upon the Supporting Foot or feet without Turning the Upper Body.

Twisted Feet   A Quick Swiveling Action of Torquing the Lower Body, for a Change of Direction for one's feet without changing the direction the Upper Body is facing. With feet Closed and kept parallel together, and with Weight Forward onto Balls, **Swivel both Balls.**

Twisted Waist   Only the trunk portion of one's body is Torqued either Left or Right, while one's shoulders and feet remain unchanged in position.

Twist Turn Action   Turning with the Weight between the two feet, using the heel of one foot and the Toe of the other foot.

Underarm   The basic Movement of passing one's body under one's own arm under joined raised hands. See Arch Turn.

Underarm Single Turns   Hand-in-hand from some facing Position, partners normally Change Places, since the turning partner usually Turns only 180 degrees, and the non-turning partner usually rotates in the Opposite direction 180 degrees to face. The eight
Underarm Single Turns are: 1) Lady's Inside Turn, Left Hand Lead; 2) Lady's Inside Turn, Right Hand Lead; 3) Lady's Outside Turn, Left Hand Lead; 4) Lady's Outside Turn, Right Hand Lead; 5) Man's Inside Turn, Left Hand Lead; 6) Man's Inside Turn, Right Hand Lead; 7) Man's Outside Turn, Left Hand Lead; and 8) Man's Outside Turn, Right Hand Lead.

Underlying Beat   A musical term for a song's regulated Rhythm, i.e., the steady, continuous, even pulse that underlies a Movement or a Rhythmic pattern; or, the number of Beats in the music Measure. Of Fast, Slow or moderate Tempo, this time measuring device is the Underlying Beat, which is the constant pulse that continues with unchanging duration and force. A melody may well have an uneven Rhythm that is synchronized with the Underlying Beat of its song.

Underturn   Less than the standard amount of Turn in a turning Figure.

Unison   Refers to partners being attuned in harmonious accord when dancing together. See Timing and Synchronization.

Unleadable   A Movement, Figure or Pattern not followable by a skilled lady unacquainted with same.

Unphased   Music with no apparent Rhythm pattern or Timing.

Up and Over the Top   Either the hips or one's chin is Slowly rotated vertically, starting upward, either Forward, Backward or Sideward.

Upper Body   One's Torso between waist and neck. See Lower Body and Metronomic Motion.

Variation   Variation means a modified form of a defined Figure; or, modification of a section of a dance routine; or, a more advanced version of a Step, Figure or Pattern; or, Footwork different from the original; or, a non-syllabus; or, a dance Figure not accepted as a Basic Figure; or, a grouping or mixture of ways of dancing. See Wedging.

Varsouvienne Position   Partners Face same direction with the man Shadowing the lady on his right. Lady's Inside Foot is slightly forward of man's Inside Foot. They clasp and spread Matching Hands behind lady at Shoulder-Level or at Waist-Level, or at a mixture of the two. If at Shoulder-Level, each set of Matched Hands are clasped slightly in front of lady's shoulder, and each has both elbows at equal height.

Vee-Line Position   Positioned almost Back To Back, forming a "V", with one set of Opposing hands joined; all arms are extended in-line, slightly less than horizontal.

Verve   To dance with vitality and liveliness, but perhaps without precision.

Visual Lead   A Lead given by the man and recognized visually by the lady, in order to execute certain Open Work Figures when the normal Lead is not desirable or not possible.

Waddle   A Charlie Chaplin-like Traveling Movement or Figure. With no hands touching and usually Trailing in Tandem, one Waddles Forward with *Quick* tilting Steps, usually four, (Waddle-Four.) Steps are very short and flat with Toes pointed Outward. Swaying, the hip Opposite the stepped foot protrudes (Side-Stretch) as the Lower-Body Torques with CBM.

Waist-Wrap Position   Eight total positions, four for her and four for him. The person that is Waist-Wrapped may have their left or right Wrapped arm tightly Wrapped around, either in front of or behind their own Waist. The partner clasps the fingertips of the Wrapped arm. Rarely is the man Waist-Wrapped.

Walking Step   A series of even-Rhythm Forward or Backward Steps. Feet are Stepped alternately at a Slow to moderate gait, about 120 Steps-per-minute Cadence, transferring Weight from one Foot to the other with one foot-part always Pressing the floor. If Walk is in a straight line, there is no Crossing of feet or rotation of body. For Forward Walk, the moving Ball-of-foot Skims, rolls to the heel then rolls to the Ball. For Backward Walk, the Ball-of-foot Skims rearward and rolls onto its heel, where the second foot, after its Toe release, begins its Backward Travel with pressure on its heel. See Fourth Position.

Walk Thru   A general dance term for practicing; for Stepping through a dance Figure, Pattern, or Routine without its accompanying music playing. See Structured.

Wall   A general term referring to dance area. To the right as one Faces Line of Dance; visualized as Circular or oval when Round Dancing. See Center of Hall.

Weave   A leadable Traveling Pattern. A **Weave** is a **Grapevine** with eight or more Steps, although some say with four or five or more Steps. Some others say a **Weave** is a Movement or Figure, to the right or left, having two or more Sideward Steps plus two or more Crossing Steps, in front and behind alternating, or visa-versa.

Wedging   A general dance term for the insertion or placing of a particular Movement or Figure within the Steps of a Standard Figure or Pattern. See Interlude, Bridge and Variation.

Weight   A General dance Term. The Supporting Foot bears the majority of one's Weight and Center of Balance. The Center of Balance is located at the Solar Plexus, a fist-size volume above the navel. One needs to support one's own Weight at all times by centering the Balance correctly over one's own foot or feet. A Change of Weight is shifting or transferring one's body Weight from one foot to the other, either completely or partially.

Wheel   Various leadable Couple Rotating Movements or Figures, with the center point between the couple being the Axis of rotation.

Whip   A Turning Movement with a Whipping Action, where the man smartly Leads the lady to Change Sides, as he executes a Backward and/or Cross behind Action with his right foot. The man's Turn is usually 180 degrees.

Whisk Line   To Cross the Free Foot closely behind the Supporting Foot, ending in a Whisk Position, without taking all the normal Steps of the Whisk Figure.

Whisk Position   Positioned with Inside Feet Touching Thru, with both Upper Bodies in CBMP, and with man's right elbow raised slightly for lady's Head Open. The man's right and the lady's left Inside hips are in contact. Both partners' Weights are on Outside Feet. Inside Toes Point Down Line and toward partner. See Left Whisk Position.

Wiggle   An Action Performed on Softened Knees, in which the hips are quickly moved side to side while maintaining an immobile Upper Body.

Wing   From a Semi-Closed Position, the Lady is Led a Half-Turn total CCW to Cross man's right foot, ending in a tight Feathered-Left Position. Partners end this Figure looking into each other's eyes with Shoulders Square.

Wing Catch   With lady at his right side, 90 degrees from Facing, man catches her at her left wing with his right fingers, in Preparation for Leading her Cross Body. He catches lady early, before she has time to Face him.

Woodpecker Taps   Any number of tiny Hops or rises on one foot, simultaneously Tapping Toe of Opposite foot behind one's Supporting Foot and beyond. Timing is *And Quick* for each Woodpecker Tap.

Workshop   A special review class. A dance lesson in which emphasis is placed upon selected Figures or Patterns and their Execution in a particular Routine and/or Rhythm. See Teach and Clinic.

Wrap   Man Wraps or Left Wraps to Position her so that the **lady's right arm becomes crossed on top.** Partners end Facing same direction side by side with all Opposite Hands in Hand. See Left Wrapped Position.

Wrap Around Position   Partners Face same direction, side by side, with lady on man's right. Both of his arms extend in front of lady; man's right arm crosses over her left arm with Matched Hands. See Left Wrap Around Position.

Wrapped Position   Lady's arms are crossed in front with RIGHT on top. Man Shadows with lady to his RIGHT. Lady's right and man's left hands are clasped in front; man's right hand around lady clasps her left hand. Similar to Cradled Position where lady's LEFT arm is on top. Position is variable, can be Side by Side or Tandem; see Left Wrapped Position.

Wrist Dip   A leadable Spinning Movement. Spinning in Reverse directions, man CCW and lady CW, he catches her when instantly Back To Back. With his quick Right **Wrist Dip** into her left elbow crook, he reverses her Spin with his body-Lead, by his continuing to Spin Counter-Clockwise.

Wrist Hold   With a Finger Clasp, the man encircles his lady's wrist with his finger tips, without gripping, thumb-tip to middle finger-tip and optionally his ring finger-tip. This ring-of-fingers barely contacts her wrist until it slides to the widening heel of her hand. She may be Led either along her wrist or at this heel-of-hand.

Wrist Position   The prescribed Position of the man's right wrist at his lady's back in Closed Position International Tango. Man's wrist is under and past lady's armpit, fingers together. Man's right fingers may be pointing slightly down, which raises his right elbow. Or his fingers may, by having a straight wrist, point parallel with the floor. The way his fingers point depends upon the lady's relative height to his, to Position his elbow, since she needs to lightly rest her arm on his arm as an aid in Following him.

Wrist Twist   Man's Single Hands Lead in order to **Swivel** his Partner. Led while in Shake Hands Position or in extended Left Open Facing Position. **Wrist to Wrist** is the most efficient method. Man's Lead is to rather extensively **Wrist Twist** his lady's right arm either CCW or CW. His CCW **Wrist Twist** causes lady to Swivel right on her right foot, and visa-versa.

X-Line   A Picture Figure resembling an "X", created by both partners in a very open Semi-Closed Position. With Trailing Feet Weighted, partners lower on their Supporting Leg and Point their Free Leg and Upper Body Away from the partner.

Zig Zag   To travel diagonally of Line of Dance, left and right, in and out. See Tacking.

8.   BIBLIOGRAPHY

Blair, Skippy. *Disco to Tango and Back*. GSDTA, 1978.

Bottomer, Paul. *Tango Argentino*. Lorenz Books, NY, 1996.

Bottomer, Paul. *Let's Dance!* Black Dog & Leventhal, NY, 1998.

Castle, Mr & Mrs Vernon. *Modern Dancing*. 1914.

Cohen, Selma Jeanne. *International Ency. of Dance*. Oxford Univ. Press, NY, 1998.

Collier, Simon. *Tango!* Thames & Hudson, NY, 1997.

Dance Action. *Magazines*. 1990.

Dance Drill. *Magazines*. 1997.

Dancers' Guide. *Magazines*. 1987.

Dance Teacher Now. *Magazines*. 1997.

Dancing USA. *Magazines*. 1999.

Gault, Lon A. *Ballroom Echoes*. Andrew Corbet Press, Wheaton, IL, 1989.

Goldman, Albert. *Disco*. Hawthorn Books, NY, 1978.

Green, Benny. *Fred Astaire*. Bookthrift, NY, 1979.

Haile, Laure'. *Dance Notebook*. (Typewritten.) 1986.

Hamilton, Frank. *Roundance Manual*. Sets-in-Order, L.A., CA, 1975.

Hamilton, Frank. *American Round Dancing*. Sets-in-Order, L.A., CA, 1978.

Harris & Keys. *Teaching Social Dancing*. Prentice-Hall, NY, 1940.

Harris, Pittman & Waller. *Dance A While*. Burgess, Minneapolis, MN, 1963.

Hayes, Elizabeth. *Intro to Teaching of Dance*. Ronald Press, 1964.

Hering, Doris. *25 Years of American Dance*. Dance Magazine, NY, 1954.

Hoctor, Danny. *Dance Caravan; Teacher's Notes*. (Typewritten.)

Howard, Guy. *Technique of Ballroom Dancing*. 1995.

Humphrey, Doris. *The Art of Making Dances*. Grove Press, NY, 1959.

Imperial Society of Teachers of Dancing. *The Ballroom Technique*. London, 1994.

Jonas, Gerald. *Dancing*. Harry N. Abrams, NY, 1992.

Kennedy, Douglas. *Community Dances Manual, Books 1-7*. PBC, Princeton, NJ, 1986.

Laird, Walter. *The Ballroom Dance Pack*. Dorling Kindersley, NY, 1994.

Loren, Teri. *The Dancer's Companion*. Dial Press, NY, 1978.

Marks, Joseph. *America Learns to Dance*. Exposition Press, NY, 1957.

Martin, John. *The Dance*. Tudor Publishing, NY, 1946.

Nagrin, Daniel. *How to Dance Forever*. Quill-Wm Morrow, NY, 1988.

National Teachers Ass'n. *Newsletters*. 1999.

RDTA, Int'l. Ass'n. *Round-A-Lab Syllabus*. 1992.

RDTA, So. CA. *Syllabus*. (Typewritten.) 1994.

Rother, Mary Ann. *Reference Manual*. (Typewritten.) 1990.

Schreiner, Claus. *Flamenco*. Amadeus Press, Portland, OR, 1996.

Shaw, Lloyd. *The Round Dance Book*. Caxton Printers, Caldwell, ID, 1948.

Silvester, Victor. *Modern Ballroom Dancing*. Trafalgar Sq. Publ., N. Pomfret, VT.

Spencer, Peggy. *Teach Yourself Ballroom Dancing*. Contemp. Publish., Chicago, IL.

Stephenson, Richard. *Complete Book of Ballroom Dancing*. Doubleday, NY, 1980.

Thompson, Betty. *Fundamentals of Rhythm & Dance*. A.S.Barnes, NY, 1937.

Thornhill-Geiger, Rickey. *Thirteen Ballroom Dances*. NCDTO, 1981.

Universal Round Dance Council. *Technical Dance Manual*. 1998.

USA DanceSport. *Rulebook*. USABDA, 1999.

Wallace, Carol. *Dance: A Very Social History*. Rizzoli Int. Publ., NY, 1986.

Wright, Anita. *How To Dance*. Blakiston Co., Philadelphia, PA, 1945.

Wright, Judy. *Social Dance - Steps to Success*. Human Kinetics, Champaign, IL, 1992.